You Got Maled!

"Volume 2"

The SURVIVAL GUIDE
To Laughing Your Way Through The Crazy
World of ONLINE DATING AND BEYOND...

Unfortunately, "still" based on a true story.

STORY & PHOTOS BY:

By: Robin Roth

Illustrations By: Aimee Goren
Additional images from: Pixabay.com

ISBN: 979-8-9854012-8-8 (hardback)
    979-8-9854012-9-5 (paperback)
    979-8-9900604-2-5 (ebook)

IMPORTANT DISCLAIMER, WAIVER AND RELEASE OF RIGHTS

Disclaimer: Robin Roth is **not** responsible for **any** advice or information working out, or not working out for you from reading, "You Got Maled! Volume 2" **Hence… Proceed at Your Own Risk!**

The Expressed views, opinions, suggestions, and advice written in "You Got Maled! Volume 2" were generated purely and solely for entertainment value and should not be relied upon at all. NEITHER Robin Roth, the Author, Publisher, Distributor(s), Retailer(s), nor anyone else involved with the writing, preparation, dissemination, sale or otherwise of this Book is responsible for any negative consequences of any kind whatsoever in the event anyone relies on any opinions or advice set out in the Book. ABSOLUTELY NONE of the advice or opinions has been subject to any kind of scientific, professional, federal, state, or local governmental or agency review, of any kind whatsoever and has not been approved by any person or entity. It is not even known whether any professional, medical, financial, or even competent person has read the Book.

Waiver: Anyone who takes any action based on any opinion, suggestion, thought or any statement of any kind in this Book does so entirely "AT YOUR OWN RISK".

This Book is first and foremost written for entertainment, not to provide any actual advice whether medical, financial, health or otherwise. The Book is simply the experience of the Author written for entertainment purposes and NOT to be taken as a serious, proven basis for any action by the Reader.

Neither Robin Roth (the Author), Publisher, Distributor(s), Retailer(s), nor anyone else involved with the writing, preparation, dissemination, or sale or otherwise of this Book (collectively, the "Book Originators") will be held liable or responsible for any actual or perceived loss or damage of any kind whatsoever caused or alleged to have been caused Directly or Indirectly by anything in this Book, including, without limitation, actual, compensatory, incidental, consequential, nominal. punitive or any other kind of damage whatsoever. THE READER AND ON BEHALF OF ITS HEIRS, SUCCESSORS AND ASSIGNS SPECIFICALLY WAIVES ANY AND ALL RIGHTS OF EVERY NATURE AND SORT WHATSOEVER TO ASSERT ANY CLAIM AGAINST ANY OF THE FOREGOING PERSONS OR ENTITIES IN ALL RESPECTS WHETHER SUCH CLAIM ARISES NOW OR HEREAFTER OR IS NOW KNOWN OR IS UNKNOWN.

Release In Full of Rights: In consideration of the writing, preparation costs arising from the Publishing. Disseminating and other related costs of the Book and other good and valuable consideration, the Reader and any heirs, successors and assigns irrevocably and

Dedication

Thank you, my beloved extraordinary parents, for being the greatest mom and dad who ever lived. You have exceeded the parental bar of excellence. Your goodness, kindness, intelligence, virtue, and integrity live within me. You will always remain a constant source of love, support, my rock, and forever north. You are missed, loved, and cradled in my heart, eternally. I was so fortunate and blessed to have you as my role models and parents!

To my amazing children, Jennifer and Chloe… I thank you for your endless love, encouragement, inspiration, and, above all, your humor. I am also grateful for your friendship, support, and your astonishing wisdom and spirituality. My precious daughters, I love you more than love and you are the light of my life! Thank you both for putting up with me and letting me be your mommy.

I also dedicate this book to your incredible children: Hadley & Jacob, Devorah, Chaya, & Levi, as well as all their children and children's children, to follow.

To my treasured, lifelong, best friend, Shara… I extend to you all the love and appreciation in my heart. You've always been my touchstone of sagacity, advice, balance, insight, and reality. Thank you for always being there for me with your never-ending love, immeasurable support, and our incredible memories. Throughout our many years of friendship and the endless trials and tribulations of life, you've brought to my world unimaginable balance, laughter, and fun. I am grateful for the gift of your friendship today, tomorrow, and evermore! You are the family I chose!

Table of Contents

Introduction

Let's Review, Shall We?

And just like that, (again) I, Mollie Sloan, a successful, well-known news reporter, was at last ready to fall in love. I'm speaking of the deep, passionate, sappy, all-consuming, unconditional, gag me with a stick, forever type of love. I mean, the way over the top, love. And proud of it!

On a beautiful, sunny spring morning, I decided that it was finally time to settle down and find *"The One."* You know, "The One!" "The One," who has you at, *"Where have you been all my life?"* Also known as the ultra-trite phrase... *"You had me at hello!"* You know? "The One" you dreamed about and searched for your entire life. Frequently known by the other trite phrase, *"You complete me!"* The love of your life you are supposed to be with as in, *"And they lived happily ever after."* The one you love so deeply, but understandably feel petrified introducing him to your crazy family! The one who will lovingly tell you when your mascara is dripping down your face, when your hair extensions are showing, when you have something stuck in your teeth, or when you're being a bitch! The one who remains calm, even when the Internet goes down! This easy, uncomplicated, stress-free pursuit of finding "The One," would no doubt be easy-peasy! Like, you know… a piece of cake. Positively, a piece of *wedding cake*, that is!

I confidently and optimistically predicted I would unequivocally be married by the end of the year. No problemo!

You see now, that's the funny thing about predictions. Unless you are an authentic soothsayer, with mystical powers for predicting future prophesies like Nostradamus, they will typically be *wrong*. However, I carelessly didn't predict *which year* I'd marry. Hate when that happens.

Fast forward to the end of that year and my mistakenly predicted wedding date. Shit, buggers, drats, and foiled again. I staggered to think, how was it even possible that I was still single? What a disappointing, horrible realization. This was supposed to be, "A piece of cake!" Wasn't it? Hello? There's no cake! No cake at all! I don't even have a cupcake! Not even a measly cookie!

So, there I was searching and dating online, which felt like forever and a day! All I accomplished was arduously rummaging through a countless number of, *"Totally wrong men!"* No, no, really, please try to *feel* my painful despair. I went out with men who were the bottom feeders and pond scum of the male species. I went out with the "gross, mucous, and pus that grow on the slimy Candida Fungus" class of men. They were all, *"Beyond the Totally Wrong Men!"*

I am thoroughly positive that all of you out there reading this right now are shaking your heads from your own disastrous personal understanding and dating experiences. I also sense your validation of my unreliable soothsaying abilities that shockingly failed me so miserably.

To no avail or lack of intense motivation and outrageous efforts on my part, there was still *NO*, enormous diamond ring on my finger! There was still *NO*, "Say yes to the spectacular dress!" There were still *NO*, debates or decisions to be made about the gorgeous wedding ceremony and its heavenly beachfront destination. I could not begin to fathom how there were still *NO*, expensive save-the-dates and stunning wedding invitations. How was it feasible that there was *NO*, picking out exquisite, costly flowers? Why wasn't I tasting and selecting that outrageously overpriced eight-tier wedding cake, with fresh exotic flowers and Irish lace between each layer? Last, but not least, there was still *NO*, planning or discussions over the extravagant honeymoon around the world, for which I hoped to lose 10 pounds to go on! I was trapped in the universe of "No, No, and No!" What a major conundrum! There wasn't even that *"knot"* I was supposed to tie. My universe and belief system were turned upside down. I never would have believed this could realistically happen. Holy shit and more shit!

To be honest, there wasn't a glimmer of anyone realistically completing me. Sadly, there wasn't even a hint of "You had me at hello." For that matter, there also wasn't the hope of saying, "Where have you been all my life?" I was miffed. I was flabbergasted. No correction. I was absolutely, clearly shocked, understandably pissed, and traumatized. This was an unexpected, desultory, disappointing predicament to find myself in. Especially after eight months. Ha, little did I know then!

Seriously, what was going on here? How could this be my reality? In what dimension was this conceivably happening to me? I ask, confused. Where the hell are my damn wedding bells? Even more horrifying, I don't see or hear those damn bells, even from a far-off distance! Where are my ding-dong wedding bells? Dammit, surely, they should be ringing by now!

So then, why is it, when I *was not* ready to meet "The One" and settle down, I met the greatest, in every possible way, ideal men? You know, the perfect marriage material, guys. The ultimate winners from head to toe! The men I'd want my family and friends to meet! Although fearful that they might run off leaving skid marks because my clan is a tad *insane* and a little dysfunctional. Come on, there used to be a gaggle of these guys. For the life of me, I couldn't wrap my head around the gloomy, discouraging realization of "How on earth is this possible?" I begged the question, "Where did all the good ones go?" Perhaps begged is a little too harsh. I might have only implored the question. No, wait, hold on a minute. No, I did essentially beg! Out loud, in fact.

I cannot accept nor assume that "The good ones," all quietly disappeared to another galaxy or planet far, far away. I couldn't imagine all the wonderful, eligible men gathering in the middle of the night and then, suddenly, they all jumped into a menacing black hole. As in, "OK now guys, one, two, three, jump!" Oh, come on now...

I also can't consider that "All the great guys" simply got married? With this ring, I thee wed, ding-dong *wedding bells*, and all? (MY Bells!) Did I miss the memo reporting there was an outbreak of pregnant women and the nice guys had to do the right thing and marry them? Did I miss the breaking news headline that a major war had broken out? And ironically, all the single men who were drafted wanted to go off to war as married men? Hell, this can't be right, I *proposed* with a red, white, and blue patriotic sigh.

BTW, where was the man who was supposed to do just that?

"Propose!"

After enduring online dating past my failed projected wedding date, I wondered with a sense of urgency. "Am I the only one going through all of this insanity?" Really, am I alone here? Or dare I dread to imagine, *"Is this just a 'Me' thing?"* Must I find a gypsy to conjure up a forbidden love elixir, a magic spell, or a romance potion? Like, Voilà & Poof!

As a journalist, I interviewed a myriad of women and men on the dating topic. Most were normal, others, after dating, leaned towards not so much. Thus, here are the 7 continuously asked questions that unite us all.

1. "Is all of this 'Batshit crazy' just happening to me?"
2. "Am I the only one experiencing all of these crazy, dramatic, and *way-out-there* people?"
3. "Are other women and men going through these ludicrous, outrageous incidents, too?"
4. "Is there actually someone even out there for me, or am I just wasting my time?"
5. "Will I ever find my soulmate, or will I simply be alone forever?"
6. "It's all too weird to deal with. Should I flat out and out, give up?"
7. "I wonder if I should just accept and settle for the *wrong one*?

Ultimately, after gathering all my scientific research, I wish to provide some answers to the entire community of frustrated and bewildered single women, men, and others everywhere. To the above questions, I answer for you profoundly and firmly...

1. No!
2. No!
3. Yes!
4. Most Likely and No!
5. Most Likely and No!!
6. No!
7. No!

Those 7 captivating questions were the impetus and the driving force, which motivated and inspired me to write this book. I wanted to bring reassurance, truth, and, most importantly, comic relief to each one of those questions and more. I felt it was my journalistic civic duty and moral imperative to do so.

For all the single people tirelessly searching for "The One," well then, I broadcast emphatically with total certainty...

"You Are Not Alone!"

It was astounding to discover there was radically more than a scintilla of truth and clear evidence proving this fact! So, wipe away the puzzled, pained, perplexed expressions that woefully linger upon your faces. I will not obfuscate the truth in any way. Hence, know this fact... "We Are All Going Through It!" Therefore, I send my utmost compassion to all of you confused daters, and I assuredly state once again, and once and for all... *No, nope, nada...*

"You Are Not Alone!"

Gosh, can't you just hear that song in your ear right now? You will undoubtedly find yourself hearing many of Michael's iconic songs while dating. Like: "Thriller," "Beat It," "Bad," "Leave Me

Alone," "Scream," "Dangerous," and "Smile," way more than you would ever want, need, or care to.

Clearly, we've all endured and suffered ridiculous dating dramas, both off and online. AKA: PTSDD. *("Post-Traumatic Stress Dating Disorder!")* Yes, I made this syndrome up. I had to for the sake of medical advancement. Let me tell ya, I did the legwork and earned the right to do so.

One of the most important pieces of guidance I can offer anyone that cares to know… "It's OK to be extremely selective!" Please hear me when I state, *"Don't Settle!"* Because if you do, and take my word, there is no mistaking the statistic, you will be back online, combing the dreaded dating sites once again in no time at all. That is… for sure, for sure!

I'm not a gambler. You see, if I put down my hard-earned dollars, the least I expect to get is a designer outfit, a pair of couture shoes with a lovely matching bag, and all of it on sale! Regrettably, all dating, in a sense, is gambling. Only without the tables, slot machines, angry faces because you didn't anti-up quickly, the grandiose screams of winning and losing, or the fabulous fashion and great shoes. You'll no doubt be screaming, though! Like a lot! The debate is still out on whether dating or gambling has the greater odds of winning. Honestly, for me, it's a toss-up.

Nowadays, we are all enormously busy. In our fast-paced world, sadly, this avenue of dating is one of our best and yet worst options. No matter what, don't give up on your search for love with that special person you'll cherish, as they will hopefully cherish you. *"The One,"* is there waiting and most assuredly buried unpretentiously at the bottom of all the codswallop. I reiterate, the very bottom of the huge mountain of garbage.

Keep in mind, "Cynicism chases away optimism!"

OK, for real, that quote is such rubbish. Go right ahead. Be cynical. Enjoy yourself and bask in it. Complain, bitch, and moan all you want to your friends. It could essentially help to vent, and you have nothing to lose. Surprisingly, it might add a whimsical touch to your agonizing dating torment.

By the way, *be yourself completely!* Your true love should know the real you from the very beginning. "The One" needs to find out all your good, your bad, your ugly, and everything in between. It's a friendlier way of saying, to discover your weird, strange, and eccentric qualities. You're special and your future mate should know it. As a matter of fact, he should sincerely love and adore all those things about you.

Because I know that you will absolutely wonder...
It's now necessary for me to Make This Important Disclosure.

"You Got Maled!" is not merely *based* on a true story. *It is* a true story. Most of this book is *non-fiction,* with true-life stories that happened in real-time. All the good stuff, and by that, I mean the *"Oh My God, crazy, outrageous, shocking, messed up, and are you fucking kidding me," stuff,* all transpired! Seventy-five percent (maybe more) of the events literally occurred and the rest, by my calculations, twenty-five percent, are pure fiction. That quick calculation came as a result of 9-years of college (counting grad school), endless student loans, and some occasional weed. But like Bill Clinton, "I never inhaled!" *Wink-wink.* There was lots of flowing alcohol, mostly tequila and cheap wine from a box, which for 3 years was bought with a fake ID. And let's not forget the billions of study hours (groan) and too numerous to count innocent frat parties. Whoo-Hoo! Whatever, they could have been innocent, you know? Hey, don't judge me!

As you continue to read, naturally they'll be many times you will understandably doubt that I am writing any probability or semblance of the truth. I imagine you will surely be thinking... "Yeah, right." "No Waaaaaay." And "Oh, of course. That must be the 25 percent fiction part!" Most definitively, those are positively the parts that for sure transpired. I, being a compassionate girl, changed all the characters' real names. I did so to protect, to be kind, in rare cases, to shield the innocent, plus my lawyer insisted.

It's a given you will go out with many of the same types of people I have written about. Hopefully, this will bring you much-needed comfort, while proving again that you are not alone. You'll unquestionably identify with and relate to my stories. I fear my demeanor towards several of these online men might be pejorative at times. To that, I say with an unashamed, sneering smirk, "Oh, frickin' well!" You must trust me when I justify in my defense, *"They totally, completely, and entirely had it coming!"*

Above all, and in a positive therapeutic way, the primary purpose of this book is to *"Make You Laugh!"* I felt it was vital to help you see the irony and with any luck, add some humor and comedy to the dramedy of it all. Trust me, you'll experience more drama than in any Broadway play!

My objective is to educate and bring you crucial knowledge, insight, and direction. I strived to share some informative, relevant, optimistic awareness and wisdom, which you can apply to your own dating experiences. All the while, I implore you to always keep your eyes wide open. I aspired to caution you about the probable and endless pitfalls hiding beneath the surface of online dating. Primarily, I was determined to focus on guiding all of you, seekers of love, in an amusing 'LMFAO' fashion. I can assure you that if you don't laugh your way across this journey,

I guarantee you will go completely berserk, if not entirely mad.

Understand because I am a *reporter*, I will pretty much tell it like it is. I will not attempt to sugarcoat it for you in any way. If I don't shoot from the hip, how could I honestly guide you? If the sound of this worries, scares, or hurts your feelings in the least, then for sure, don't even attempt to go online. I am the "*SuperCaliFragilistic*" Mary Poppins, and the Good Witch reincarnated, compared to what you'll witness and endure out there amidst the forest of wolves, in the insane world of dating. This isn't a place for the innocent "Little Red Riding Hood" types. Accordingly, fill your basket of goodies with balls of courage, and I'm talking big ones!

I hope to inspire, motivate, encourage, cheer you on, hold your hand, help you troubleshoot, and keep an optimistic energy while offering fun, healthy laughter throughout. My educational tutorial about everything concerning on-and-offline dating, love, life, and my shoulder to cry on is well worth reading this book. For you men, it will provide an enlightening, instructional experience. You will benefit greatly by sticking with it until the last page. Fair warning though guys, you might find it offensive at times. You might even rip the pages out and throw them on the floor as you read, saying out loud, "Fuck this stupid book! This is total bullshit!" That's cool with me. But keep reading because you can learn a thing, or two, or more. Try to be open. After all, love is the prize, isn't it? But dude, if you really hate the book, don't throw it away! Go ahead and repurpose it. It is the perfect size to put under any table to keep it from wobbling!

I fancy and consider this novel to be my version of an "Oprah Winfrey, Master Class." I trust my stories will provide men, women, green and purple aliens alike, with comfort, giggles, and a sense of camaraderie during your dating adventures. "Adventures?" Huh, such a darling way of saying "Hell!" Gee, who knows, you might theoretically find online dating entertaining and fun. Or perchance, even like it. Wow, that idea scares me!

Sometimes, we must climb over an intimidating wall, or a Twilight Zone Tower of Terror to find love on the other side. We might have to travel to the ends of the earth in pursuit of love. I must emphasize, throughout your search, *Never Stop Being, "You!"* You're the only person in the world *like you*. Appreciate that you are unique and deserve all your romantic dreams to come true. Search for what you want and need, and for all the things that will make you happy. This is about you! So don't let go of your desires. Stick to your guns. In the immortal words of the great Scott Stabile… "Don't worry if you're making waves simply by being yourself. The moon does it all the time!"

I hope my personal stories foster gobs of fortitude and enthusiastic, courageous boo yah! Dating is a constant whirlwind and a tornado of tumultuous sagas. After one of these storms, remain cool, smile, wipe yourself off, brush your wind-blown hair, and ease on down the road!

Also, be aware when searching for love, you will enter a world of total uncertainty. Nevertheless, do go on and take that leap of uncertain faith! Ergo, strap on your sanity belt, for you should know that you're in for a daring climb and a wild and crazy ride. But after all, how bad could it be? Okay, sorry, that was indeed a daring, stupid, and foolish comment…

As I stated in "You Got Maled!" Volume 1… To those who have already ventured into this chilling and menacing world of online dating (or any form of dating, for that matter), hang in there. For I promise you, it gets so much worse!

Yes, indeed, you just heard me giggling. Hopefully, you shall too. However, don't give up.

Remember, you need to fight your way through the battles to reach the joys of victory. And you will!

To all the seekers of love out there who haven't yet begun the online dating circus and home of the courting clowns, I want you to jump into the crazy game with zeal and courage, pushing all boundaries fully armed and guns loaded. Hmm, the NRA would totally love that concept.

To those of you beginners out there who say, *"Ha-ha-Ha-ha-ha! Whatever?" To you clueless fools,* I fiercely respond, giggling again with, *"All righty then… I wish you Godspeed and stacks of it!"*

Here is the part where I tell you, if it doesn't work out, you can freak the hell out, all you want if it helps. Afterward, go throw on a tiara, and have a margarita, with a big bucket of popcorn, and oodles of chocolate. For real, that pretty much fixes just about everything. Temporarily, anyway.

One final thought. In the world of dating, you will undoubtedly come across many lovely people. It's perfectly fine to go have fun with them, even if they are not your someone special. On the contrary, I've also included in this book, many types of people who will, for sure, not be your forever person. The purpose of this is not only to make you laugh (I hope), but for you to learn why, who, how, and what to avoid in your search for "The One."

In conclusion, my main objective is to save you time, disappointment, and heartache. Embrace the fact your excitement and fervor will not go unnoticed. Hey, what are you waiting for?

In the illustrious, famous words of Obi-Wan Kenobi…

"Remember, the Force will be with you, always!"

Fiddle-dee-dee. *One can always hope! Right?*

NOW… READ ON!

P.S: Well, to be precise, it's more of a fair warning…

IF BAD LANGUAGE OFFENDS YOU, PUT THE
BOOK DOWN!

NOW! Right Now. Seriously, you will NOT be OK
continuing on.

CHAPTER 1

The Pain and Recovery of Drew...
BREAKUPS ARE DIFFICULT NO MATTER
HOW YOU LOOK AT IT!

Yes, it's true. It didn't work out with: "Aubry, without-an-E. Yale, the egomaniac. Valerio, the Italian Bam-Bam. Devin the Short-Guy. Fabrizio, like-a-Boom-on-the-plane. Stone, and his legendary Jewel. (Wink-Wink.) Jeremy, the Tattooed guy *HWwwwwhannnn and his famous tang-gasms. The endless perverted playas. The Geek-Nerd,"* and all the rest. *Nevertheless, I proudly survived them all!*

Well, I did, Until Bobble-Drew!

Wouldn't it be awesome if we were born with a built-in "Love, delete button?" Then we could erase the excruciating wake of pain and the agonizing memories caused by some of the people who enter our lives. People who promise forever, break our hearts, and devastate our world! I know all you romantics hoping to find "The One" understand exactly what I'm referring to, from your own earth-shattering, love-lost experiences.

Ladies, don't you just wish men came with flashing caution signs? *"Warning, Beware of This Man!"* (Or Woman.) Biochemical plants must put up warning signs, and they are far less hazardous than relationships are! It's only a suggestion, but why not? While I'm on this male topic (substitute men instead of women throughout, when needed) after serious consideration, I believe men should be made to wear a device that displays a forewarning signal. As unavoidable as the police, when they flash their lights to pull you over to give you a ticket, or worse. Wouldn't it make life ultimately easier for us all? It would also be outrageously cool if we could put on specially designed glasses, which revealed the demons lurking within these guys. Even cooler yet, in 3D! I would call them "*Demon Busters.*" Gosh, that sounds dark, even for me. But guess what? I would buy them. Who wouldn't? They would sell like hotcakes.

This brings up another topic. I don't see hotcakes selling all that much. Do you? Who even eats them anymore? They're so fattening with all that syrup and whipped cream. Consequently, I ask, what's up with the hotcakes analogy? Edit... Demon Busters would sell like Apple products!

Wouldn't it be great if guys came with a lie-o-meter chip implant that went off with every lie they told? Just like Pinocchio's nose grew bigger by the lie. I know lying alarms would certainly be going off all day long around the world. An interesting sidebar to this thought. Congress and the Senate would at least have an excuse for never getting any work done, from the constant lying alarms going off all day in their chambers.

With some of these men, I hardly know which fallacy to start with. Why do we ignorantly believe everything they say and tell us when we first fall in love with them? Why do we girls turn into jelly-mush with a new love? Is it trust, hope, blind faith, or sheer stupidity? I imagine it comes from longing prisms of desire. BTW, I've discovered women lie as much as men. Even more. Although we lie for *entirely different reasons!*

It would be great if there were a foolproof recipe for men to follow on relationships and love. Being a genuine, smart-ass, I cooked one up.

Mollie's Foolproof Love Recipe

Combine Daily:
Mix in tenderly 8 cups of passion…
Simmer 7 pints of cuddles…
Steam 20 cups of hugs and kisses lovingly under a covered pot…
Deep-fry 6 pounds of compassion and tenderness on a full flame…
Stew, 12 pounds of understanding…
Dust and roast 15 pounds of heartfelt patience…
Whisk 10 gallons of truthfulness and honesty or *More If Needed*…
Sauté gently 1 pound of back rubs…
Marinate one large pinch of frisky fun, and tushie smacking…
Fold in 25 morsels of adoring looks, and then lick to taste…
Drizzle in immeasurable amounts of compliments…
Grind, passionately & lovingly 7 cups of weekly sex, *or more if needed*…
Knead 100 pounds of No Fighting, kindness, and caring…
Merrily, stir in many nights of naughty lovemaking, until blended well…

Bake forever with love at a warm, cozy temperature.
Serve affectionately and thoughtfully with all your heart!

I also made up a recipe, which includes only a measly dash of disappointment, instead of infinite tons of it. Guys, yes, "You shake a tree to get the fruit. But after you gather the fruit, you'll have to make the jam. In other words, you must be devoted and continually work at a relationship to keep it happy and exciting."

Sadly professing, as my teardrops fall onto my keypad, picking up the shattered pieces, and getting over a broken heart is brutal! There is no technique to dress it up or disguise the slow torture. It is the sleeping giant of pain that awakens when love is lost. Readers, I hate to disappoint you further. However, there's truly no easy way to turn the page. No tiara, girlfriends, bottles of wine, shopping, overeating, or jewelry that will banish or erase the hurt. Although, they might alleviate the unbearable struggle and heartbreak, helping to get you through it. The process is entirely fierce. Your only recourse is to pull yourself together, dry your tears (*Note: they will return for sure!*), and fearlessly move on. Since I was about to fall off the edge of the dating precipice, I boldly decided to pull myself up by my bootstraps. I got tough and put one unbalanced foot in front of another until, one day, I felt myself firmly walking again. Though they were only baby steps, I was walking again, darn it! Taking those baby steps wearing fabulous, glittery shoes and a sparkling tiara was the only thing making this process appear triumphant.

Like a toddler, I fell several times a day on the hard ground of heartache and misery. As a valiant soldier would, I courageously got right back up again. Luckily, most of the time, no one was there to witness my pathetic degrading tumbles. There is that, I suppose.

When we girls go through a breakup, it's utterly precious how we try to make some sense of it all. Our reactions are just so darn cute and entirely adorable!

Here Is How The Progression Generally Develops:

1. The first thing we do, of course, is to demonize and put down the deranged bastard and total dickwad of a man to our friends. We are angry, bitter, and indescribably hurt. We might even

temporarily become a rageaholic! A little reminder regarding *'talking smack'* about the troll. This tremendous release and helpful comfort will only last about a week.

2. The next plan of attack. We stupidly retreat and begin to defend the guy to our friends. I call this, **The Brain Dead,** *"Maybe I,"* **Period…**

Maybe he wasn't all that bad?
Maybe I should not have gained those 3-extra unsightly pounds?
Maybe *I* did something wrong?
Maybe it was entirely all my fault?
Maybe I should've tried to cook more and hone my cleaning skills?
Maybe I should have done more for him, like errands and his laundry?
Maybe I am the one who is totally to blame?
Maybe I should've paid for more things? 75% of the rent and electric isn't too outlandish, is it? Even if he earns 10 times what I do! And maybe I was being too critical or demanding, asking for a date night once a month.
And, maybe I overreacted, So, what, if he hit me? It healed up quickly. Anyway, he doesn't do it all the time!
(Ladies, Please Understand, that all ABUSE is a *BIG NO!)*
Maybe I was too quick to react? He only cheated on me 3 times. That I know of. So why did I even bring it up at all? Me and my big mouth!
Maybe he'll change? He could! I still love him. Pout… sulk… frown!

Now, here's a stern warning to *the friends* of this now

"hopeless, and severely screwed-up, senseless, once rational, girlfriend of yours." The next few months (or more) will be sticky and difficult for all friends and caring supporters. This is where your miserable, foolish, lovesick friend will observe a lot of uncontrollable eye-rolling from you. Though you might want to, "*try not to do this.*" Pinch your thigh instead. Your black and blue pinch mark will disappear much quicker than her bitterness toward you will. I realize it will be hard, but don't bash the scoundrel! Because if they ever (*God, Forbid*) get back together, you'll be the bad guy! In turn, you will lose your friend forever. Instead, nod your head *a lot,* and say several, *"Ah-Ha's," "I know,"* and a few *"I see," responses.* Give her words of validation. Insinuate none of it was her fault. Show her love and empathy, but don't give her any hopes or encouragement they will one day reunite. Most importantly, here's my strong advice. Bring her homemade fudgy caramel brownies, gourmet cupcakes & cookies, sinful candy, and some chocolate martinis.

3. Next, the natural progression for us lovesick women. We secretly read numerous books from the self-help aisle of the bookstore. I guarantee this is nothing more than a waste of your hard-earned money. On the other hand, an evening of supportive intervention with margaritas, chips, salsa, extra cheese, guacamole, and a few good friends (who have always hated the little shit) is more effective in the real world. Let me warn you, though. There are physical problems and major side effects of being a great friend to your jilted gal pal. We gain more weight by getting them through the pain storm than they do. Naturally, this does suck. But you know what? Friendship is everything. Besides, you know she would totally do it for you.

4. The next thing that ensues following a horrible breakup is try-
    ing to get the best viewpoint and the most accurate perspec-
    tive we can. This is when we call in the big guns. We meet for
    Cosmopolitans and small plates with our wonderful gay friends.
    These champions have the gift to cut to the chase and right
    through the heart of any given situation in the entire world.
    These true-blue friends have no problem whatsoever telling you
    about their all-knowing assessment without any sugarcoating.
    You'll find their direct, honest approach refreshing and better
    than a psychic. Best of all, they do it with humor. You will be
    laughing *gayly* and crying at the same time. This is, in fact, how
    they earn their halos. These good buds will provide answers
    to all the who, what, when, where, why, and how questions.
    Ultimately, they understand both sides of the 'he-she' coin, con-
    cerning any problem. Our gay friends always insightfully nail
    it! Regrettably, we are still drowning in our love-pain for their
    'treasures of gay wisdom' to be helpful while we are wallowing
    in mid-crisis. It essentially takes the gay barometer to grasp
    precisely how desperately we are grieving! Their warm and ten-
    der pity, at least momentarily, is remarkably beneficial. *There's
    nothing, and I mean nothing, like your fabulous, gay friend's super-
    hero shoulders to cry on!* Not to mention, they feel so bad for you,
    they will customarily pick up the entire restaurant and bar tabs.

5. After their 100% foolproof effort doesn't help as expected, we
    are wounded so critically we might, (I only said might. Don't
    go crazy on me) stoop so low as to watch (and Lord save us), the
    various daytime talk shows, cooking shows, Dateline, and the
    many Doctor programs. We may also resort to watching, "The
    View, The Talk, or the Soaps." If your pain lingers, you will then

find yourself tuning to TV shows like, "America's Got Talent, The Bachelor, Big Brother, or The Voice." You watch reruns of television shows you never even watched in Prime Time like, "Modern Family, or Two and a Half Men." You start viewing the History and Science Channels, which are essentially pretty good. All these crazy attempts are to keep our minds from thinking about **him**, the bastard! Sorry to reveal these shows, and especially the Hallmark Channel, only lead you back to ground zero of pain and worthless hours of watching some lousy television. Instead, maybe try Netflix, Prime, or others like it.

Beware, ladies, this is the vulnerable period. We trust in and turn to things like (big breath) religion, meditation, Kabbalah, astrology, yoga, reincarnation, Feng Shui, numerology, Reiki healing, reading tea leaves, (*you might need to take another breath here!*) Scientology, eating herbs, mediums, burning sage, Hinduism, cleansing, veganism, and psychics. Or, reading spiritual esoteric books like "Many Lives, Many Masters." Good book though and I recommend it highly. We might even watch mass quantities of Fox News, CNN, and MSNBC. Lord, help us! *Low Point! Low Point! Damn!*

Here's the thing about going the psychic route. I went out with a proclaimed psychic once. If he were truly a psychic, he would've known I wouldn't like him. We would never have worked out, and I'd never sleep with him in this life or any other. Now go on and psychic, that Damien!

6. After a breakup, when all is said and done, a girl's true blue best friends are carbs. Sugar is a good pal too. They provide sustenance, comfort, and temporary well-being. Sure, you might put on a few pounds, but no worries. You're so despondent, you won't

care or likely notice. That is, until later when you date again. Gee, that's a rather troubling thought?

7. To help us move on and ease our aching hearts, we might be desperate enough to read books by iconic ancient philosophers like Madonna, Elton John, Trevor Noah, Steven Colbert, Tina Fey, Britney Spears, and Howard Stern. If it helps you, well then who am I to discourage you? Go, read!

Though numbers 1-7 are not the worst ideas, to be honest, none of them helped or worked well for me. Granted, maybe some of them helped for about 12 minutes or so. Girls seriously, the carbs & sugar thing worked far better and longer than all the others. What the Hell, *have a chocolate chip cookie.* It can't hurt, and you'll have everything to gain. Literally!

I think Carrie from "Sex and the City" might've been right all along! "Did I ever really love him, or was I just addicted to the agony, the stunning pain of wanting a man so unattainable?" She was dead on. But what about her other quote? "It's a common belief that a relationship without any pain is a relationship not worth having." Hell no! This is a depressing quote. Who thinks like this? There should be no pain in any relationship. Perhaps Jeffrey Dahmer, Charles Manson, or the Zodiac Killer? Understand, this type of behavior is how abuse starts. Not love!

Yeah, as for me, I'll stick with Mrs. Graham's quote. "May all your pain be Champagne!"

What about the brilliant Jim Carrey quote... "Behind every great man is a woman rolling her eyes." Profound and true, Jim!

I also trust in the divine Audrey Hepburn's words of wisdom. "I believe that tomorrow is another day and I believe in miracles."

Taking into consideration all this encouraging insight, I decided to return to life. I uncorked a bottle of red and jumped back online. I needed the distraction. Besides, I was proud of myself because this was a daring and brave, healthy decision. The one thing you can count on concerning online dating is that it's a total distraction, and I didn't want to fall deeper into the bottomless, disappointing pit of no return. It's ugly down in there, I tell you! It's an ugly, deep, dark, miserable, scary abyss, and I wasn't about to hide in limbo any longer!

So, I boldly climbed my way up and out of the Drew ditch all the way towards, next! *"I mean, how much worse could it get, anyway?"* Combining all the dating experiences I have lived through, and my adorable, naïve, piece-of-cake attitude, I have learned to never ask a question like that again. Especially out loud. Ever, for the rest of my life, and the next one even. Mother Nature and that evil Murphy guy's law just love a foolish, tempting fate question like that.

Back online, I found the latest responses on the 'online-merry-go-round' notably humorous and entertaining. These emails were so preposterous they had the opposite effect on me. Oddly enough, each one provided me with mild, laughable pain relief. I have concluded that someone should be appointed to watch over and monitor these online sites. Maybe even government appointed. I'd nominate a person like Ralph Nader or Pete Brownell, the President of the NRA! And instead of TSA, Transportation Security Administration, it would be DSA… *"Dating Security Administration!"* Here is a sample of a few random, outrageous emails sent to me in the exact way I received them. I cut and pasted them, and I present them to you with their poor grammar, misspelled words, bad punctuation, and all! The only upside was the laughter they provided, which helped me through the horrific days of sadness from Bobble Drew-In-the-Box.

Hold tight for an offensive bumpy ride. Warning: they are not for the squeamish.

All the emails below are authentic and real. To be clear, I never went out with any of these men! These guys weren't just flying red flags. They were flying flamboyant banners, considered pageantry worthy. Naturally, I didn't write them back. But if I had, here is what I would have loved to say to each of them. Note, don't even think of replying!

1. Your pertty faze is like a rainybow on a sunnyday! Wood bee so excited I'd fall off a cliff to mete you. I'm optoemisstic my tue love is you. Albert

"This guy is the poster child for why one should show up every day to English class! Did you mean to say my pretty face? I do declare, I've never seen a rainybow! "Dear, amiable, innocent Albert, I feel it my civic duty to tell you, it's just fine to be optimistic about online dating, as long as you cautiously realize there are plenty of explosive mines lurking on the field! Stay optimistic and don't fall off a cliff. From, pertty faze."

2. You are sexy as hell! I'm Ryan. So you know, I'm actually 18. This site has a lame Rule that won't allow you to sext or massage someone outside your age range. I had to Change my age so I'd be able to massage the older women, who I tend to attract! Even tho you due knot luk a day over 24. ;)

"You charmer. You sure know how to flatter a girl, don't 'cha? Dude, this is so wrong and sketchy. Ryan, I'm not your mommy. You should discuss attachment issues with a therapist! I don't want a text, massage, message, or a sext either. Stop luking at my profile! Due Knot luk anymore!" Lord, caring about others can be such a burden. Delete!

3. *How could we live so close to each other and have never met. This is a tragedy. I am sadd. We can cure this. We do have quiet a few things in common. I hope you had a good day, Tim. PS their are some great converts coming up we could go to. It's an awful tragedy we haven't met.*

"Hey, Tim, I assure you there are far more horrific tragedies in the world than never meeting each other. Such as catastrophic world events and disasters. Still, I'm seldom quiet. Maybe you meant, quite? I'd much rather go to a concert than convert to anything. Bye, Tim. From Tragedy"

4. *Love your profile and would love to get to know you better! I love to travel. Love similar things like you and i do love to help others! I am like your other haf. let's at leest chat. I would love that. I come from a different culture than you. You said you love other cultures! Love to Chat? Mike*

"Wow, lots of loves, Love! You used 8 loves in one paragraph. Loving Mike, congrats. Your email could be Guinness worthy? Love, me."

5. *U R Cutie. When you're 80, you'll finally look around 40. I'm with you on the fun thing. I like to be and make mary. Most folks I meet are dour and serious for my taste. Are you a TV jurnalest? Or something likes that? I tour in a rock band - I'd go bonkers without a creative outlet cutie. Eric*

"Eric, here's the latest scoop just in. You're already bonkers and quite dour yourself. As for myself, I prefer to be Dior! And yes, I am a journalist but more, 'something like that.' Also, I don't and will never do, make,

or be with Mary! I wish you a merry day." A Cutie, Next.

6. Hi, I say. I have a Penis the size of a thumtack.Which is virtually an innie. It bend to the left to. Wanna se it and touch it? It looks weird but it works. No problim I can cock your tub 4 sure. wat du u say? Fred

"Gee Fred, you've swept me off my feet! You're a real people pleaser. Not! Why, pray tell, would you disclose this info to a total stranger? Guys never confess to a small penis. I give you credit for that at least. But Fred, it's not the best thing to brag about." A thumbtack, Delete!

7. Well, well, well. I love what I see and like what I've read. We have a lot in commin and need to speak to realize it. I can fill all your wet desires and fuk you good. I make you scream to god. I know what you want, I kow what you kneed. I can give it too you good. Please text me at… You my litle slut, hav what Im looking four. Let's speak thoughts. Jerome

"Well, well, Are you high, Jerome? That was fiendishly distasteful. BTW, I checked you out and we have nothing in common. Surely, you don't know what I need or want. I don't even want to be in the friend-zone with you. The only time I'd scream with you is running away from you. And please, leave poor God out of this. FYI, I'm not your little slut!" Next!

8. hi i hope you ok are. you are nice for me. Wanna getting married.if you want try me if you like to talk and going out. I spend lots a tons good money for you. I am rich, rich rich. I am richly. Roberto

"Dear moneybags, yippee-ki-yay to your generosity? Rob, though you are not the guy for me, you're unquestionably the guy to teach proper ('Gooder,' so you understand) English & grammar too." A rich, rich next!

9. You're absolutely amazing! I'm Walter – I really unbelievably want to be with you. I know I could make you happy. I know I can please you. I spend many hours staring at your photos. You like younger guys? I am 13.

"OK, Walt, this was unbelievably unbelievable! Seriously? Walter, my way too, 2, two, X 100, young-for-me compadre, I mark my dating age limit to at least a college grad, plus ten years! Walt, if there is one thing, I know for sure about myself, it's that I wouldn't survive a single night in prison. For starters, have you seen those disgusting prison out-fits? Walter, your idea is not just half-baked, it's burnt! Find someone your own age, kid! I say to you a demanding, stop looking at my photos! And right now!"

Would anyone not understand why this is a big problem and ask, "Huh, gee, what should I do?" Totally Freaked Out, Delete, Blocked, and Next!

10. Laughter chases away pridde the enemy of all relationships. Being shot out of a canon with out wearing a belt could be awkward especially when there is no net and 30 out of work dumpster clowns eating cotton candy waiting to catch you. Its no myth a clowns staple food is cotton candy. They especially like to lick there fingers consuming vats of the stuff. They also like to wipe there hands on each others clown costumes. this brings great joy. so wuld licking yor cottoncandy Happy landing.Tim

"Holy Moly, are you tripping or day drinking? Did you fly off to find Neverland to see a fairy or Johnny Depp? It must be fascinating living in your personal Matrix! Wow, you must love Bozo the Clown, or The Joker, even! You're kidding me, right? OMG, is Ashton Kutcher here? Am I being Punk'd? Tiny Tim, thanks for eternally ruining cotton candy for me!" A clown-less, Next! Ashton, where are you? I know you're here!

11. I don't think there is anyone in the world that would ever tire of seeing your lovely smile! Whoever you choose, is a lucky man. Best wishes, Sam

Short, sweet, grammatically correct, no flags, and to the point. Kudos

to Sam! I probably should have 'absafuckinglutely' answered and gone out with him. Whoops! My bad. Can I please take my delete back?

12. I like you profile. I need to know do you have a secret bucket list? Is one of the top 3 things on that list to meet Mr. Right?! :-) :-) How about telling me 2 other bucket items? telling me what gives you the most :-) fulfillments in life? How you like me to fuck you in bed? Tell me the one thing would you need if trapped on a desert island. tell me what pain, hurt, emotions, or feelings you think you'll experience when you achieve your most far-reaching sex! Tell me everything you want to do withme. -:-) :-) I'd lick that very much. So you know, we'll meet weather you want to or not!!! Be afraid. Have a great evening! Need to kow, Lance

"I just need to know. Lance, really, WTF? ':-) Is there a book that suggests fifty insane questions in the first email you send? :- :- Way too much gross talk. Dude, you are a total ask-hole. All I can say is, I don't have a buckct list, but I do have a Fuck-it list And you are now on it! ':-) Lance, we will never meet and I'm not afraid." A question-less Next! :-

13. Thanksgiving on the way, Everything in Halowen seems so passe, Out with the candie, HORRAY!!! No more cavaties to Moms dismay. So soon is Turkie Day what do ya say Goble Goble he is now a filllet. Black Friday is one big array,Of people will in dollar and cents pay Santa is on his way. Ho Ho Ho!!!!! Don't Forget It Is Better To Give Than Receive, Jeffers

"Wow, holiday clusterfuck, what the hell? Talk about coming a little too late to the party! What can I say, Jeffers? Are you monkeyshining me? Ok, I need to ask. Are you 10 or 11 years old? Are you old enough to drive? Jeffers, do try to improve your spelling and writing. It would really be a good idea if you showed up at school now and again! Lastly, are you British? With a name like Jeffers, you're destined to be a butler or the Prime Minister." *A bloody good, happy, merry holiday. Next!*

14. Good morning, I prefer to with a healthy, sparkling, someone, like u. I'm ready and able to travel. Get your passport ready! I am an old fashion gentleman who believes in romance. My 60-year-old son says I'm too old, period. Have been told I'm better looking than my photos. Will prove to you chivalry is not dead if you let me. Wud you go on a trip with me, I am invittting you. Let me no. I wont slep till you are mine. Steve

"Gosh *Steve, you're going to be awfully tired. And as much fun as that doesn't sound, thanks, but for real, no! Tell your son, Hi for me."*
Here's to an old-fashioned, healthy, sparkling, Next!

15. Hello Ms, I realize this is a little unordinary, but I'm honestly searching for someone who'd like to accompany mee on a Greek Isles cruise this Spring, at my expense. Would you have any interest? I'll take care of you and you will learn to love me when we meet. Larry

Yes, indeed, this one is a nutty-buddy favorite! What can I say compassionately to Mr. Lonely? "Lar, *your whole email was Greek to me! Are you looking for an escort service? Larry, if you aren't, you are cruising up the wrong Greek-Isle girl. Leaving that docked for now, 'The lonely-hearts club travel historians,' will sing your praises for this invite, alone!"* *I often wonder if lonely Larry found someone to go with. An uninterested Greek Isle Next! Wow? Just wow!*

16. Good Morning beautiful angle! I awoke this morning with thoughts of you on my brain. Aparently you've left quite an impact upon me. Hmm, purr haps prayers are answered. Grandma used to say...ya never know? Call me anytime.love to hear your voice. P.S. Icopied your profile photo and your now my screensaver. I look at you constantlie all day. Lonny

"Lon, Lon, Lon, *we've never even spoken! Why would you have* *thoughts of me this morning or any other morning? I clearly should **not be your screensaver.** Your text is creepy! Take Me Down, Lon! Take me down, right now! Put up Superwoman, a Porn star, or a Supermodel, even. Regards to Grandma!" A beautiful angle screensaver Delete and ICK!*

17. Wowza, LOL, when I first saw your pictures. LOL, I didn't realize you were 30. LOL you look amazing for someone 30. LOL. I don't mean to sound like most guys that email on here. LOL, but just thought I say it anyways. LOL. Funny. LOL, about the long walks on the beach, LOL. Were you a model in the past? You look like a model! LOL. Would love to ear from you. I'm the most desirable sex machine alive...Pablo

"Hey sex machine, Pablo... LOL!" A funny, Ha-Ha, LOL, Delete!

18. Hi, I am busy with managing my investments portfolio. I'm rich, worth over 19 mill. I think you are cute. I'm a Former competitive body-builder with 30 years of fitness, nutrition experience, health conscious, speak many languages, former mortgage banker of 25 years. Semi Retired. I'm super rich, smart, and cultured. Well traveled, will make you laugh daily, I like all types of music but personally enjoy classical, jazz and island music. Born in Casablanca. People say I look like a young Alice Cooper. I am 51 but feel 25. I've often been told I look like I'm in my early 30s. Great genetics. Desire to retire on Private Island. I am goofy and love to play. I am a very special person. Passionate, romantic, but not a push over. BEWARE: Lying, cheating, or betrayal are not OK. I am super amazing at everything I do. I am a royal catch. The won who ends up with me, gets the gold. I embarrassed, I can't belieeve I told you my net worth! What got over me? I'm incredible, and the most fantastic man u'll ever meat. Dean

OMG, I dropped my cup of java! "Dean, it will take Herculean resistance, but, No! Let the record show, no, again. The one who winds up with you, you, over-zealous, self-serving, narcissist, might get the gold, but rather a deserved gold medal! It would be a Looney-Tunes, Bugs Bunny, 24-Carrot, gold. And leave Alice Cooper out of this. He is talented, cool, and humble. Learn to use your delete button if you're ashamed of writing your net worth. Amazing rich, Dean, your letter made me uncomfortable. I felt like a Quarter Pounder burger at a vegan party!"

From time to time, a girl needs to fight Bow & Arrow, Viking style. P.S. Sorry Alice for being dragged into this bullshit! A fake and gold, delete!

19. Your luminous smile has burnt through my screen! Warmly, Josh.

"Hi Josh, you should get that monogrammed on a pillow and sell it on Amazon!" *Damn, Josh was cute, romantic, and sweet. I probably should've given him a chance! Sometimes, a fed-up weary girl can be too fricking quick on the delete button. A luminous & regretful next!*

20. Howz you? I'm Eric. I'm lonely. Cunt wait for tonight to dress up. Happy Halloween. I got a really neet pumpkin candee korn for my candee collecyion. I want to met yu so we can play some scarey Halloween gameys and tell strange stories. You can kiss tuch and play with me. Yes? I will hold you down till I gets whut I want.

"Gee kid, aren't you just the 'toy surprise' in a Cracker Jack Box? Eric, rather than meeting me, go spend the summer at Space Camp! You can get your rocket off there too!"

This is exactly why they invented parental protection software for your children's computers, people! FYI, I discovered Eric is 21 years younger than me. He's like 10 years old, or so. This was categorically a scary Halloween proposition. I didn't know whether to burp him or blow him! I chose the Snickers Candy Bar instead of Eric. It's legal. Shit, that was disturbing, and far too spooky, even for a Halloween text. I'm now afraid to give out candy this year. Deleted and blocked, quickly, before

Child Protective Services sees it! Whew!

21. You are too adorable like Baby Spice. And you should really really really respond back to me! I joined this sight to meet you or someone like you. I am desperate to fuck you, any way, any how! I really, really, really, want you and like you. I need to be inside you, or someone like you. I wanna color you. I'm drunk, stop the room from spinning. horny Simon

"Xwf*7fA#@!?... ... ...? Fill in the dots Simon, when you're sober again, if ever!" Someone needs to invent an automatic Breathalyzer App, to lock and unlock one's phones and computers like they have in cars. This way, one is protected and unable to contact anyone while drunk. They will be powerless to do all kinds of reckless nonsense that will piss people off and get them into all sorts of social media trouble. "Simon, 'I really, really, really, wanna zig-a-zig ah,' far away from you and some- one like you! It's apparent you grew up coloring with the single box of Crayola Crayons and longed for the 120-count big box, with the built-in sharpener. So, 3 sheets to the wind bud! From, Not Your Baby Spice!"

Moms don't cheat your kids with the crayons. They could turn out to be a Simon guy! And so goes another weird alien spicy delete!

22. Well I guess one way of knowing whether you truly want to meet someone is if you are willing to re-write an email after you tried to send it and it erased. Here it is the best that I can remember it. You seem to have so many virtues and so many special qualities. I can't believe that someone doesn't take you away before you can even complete your pro- file! I am an attorney who has turned investor and entrepreneur. I love to create things that didn't exist before. It is as much art as it is busi- ness. You seem to love life and to live it to the fullest. You are passionate about it. That is great. To enjoy life is really the greatest gift. I too am passionate about life. I am very active, love to explore/travel, hike, bike, play tennis, ski, attend all sorts of events. I spend my time in several places throughout the country. While I am not wholly sure of what you do, I thought I might add one of my businesses included a record label. I started with a business partner. We are on tour now. What a great experience. I met some terrific people. Are you a reporter? We have a lot of common hopes and dreams. You have one side that loves to play and the other side that wants a deep committed companionship. I am the same. I want a caring loving special person in my life for the rest of my life. Since you are fun, exciting, and lovely... let's see how far we can go. If you want, we can meet in Florence or Rome. Really, I don't think it will matter where we meet. It will be a blast!! I hope to hear from you soon! Warmly, Payton.

Warmly, Payton, what a guy! This was the nicest, most normal, well-rounded, highly educated guy in the bunch. (Do keep in mind online dating has a very low bar.) Sadly, apart from that, after speaking with Payton, chemistry is chemistry, and it simply was not there. A big sigh, and yet another disappointing next!

23. *You are gorgeous. You've probably been on more hotel pillows than a chocolate-mint! Why haven't you been snatched up by your snatch? I'd like to snatch your snatch! Here's what I is looking for. She'll be manicured, pedicured, and emotionally cured. Unpretentious, down to earth, very facetious, and filled with mirth. Not too short, not too tall, somewhat athletic, able to catch a ball. Has a career and made a buck, not an "ice princess" and she knows how to cook and fuck. Also, she/you should know how to Pole Dance, and I don't mean the Polka with Stanislav. Lastly, and most importantly, she/you MUST wear thongs and not the type that separate your first and second toes. I love them. And very importantly, your funny bone ziz not impaired by a calcium deficiency. You, have ta be my beckon-call-fuck-girl, anywhere anytime anyplace I say! You must*

also, always be naked around the house. Any chance your snatch is horny tonight??????? Dan… Ps, "Will you be my bitch?"

And there it is! Those 5 little words, every girl dreams of hearing! "Dan, prince of malice, what an impressive charmer. Ah, so sentimental! Stop, you'll have me in tears. Are you Lucifer's best friend? You are a strange misogynist who despises women? AKA a woman-hater! Dan, slap, slap. You're a despicable, vile slimeball! Where is your moral compass? You know that pole you like and the agonizing string from the thong you love so much? Well, stick them and a mint forcefully up your funny bone. Ethics advocate your behavior is wildly unacceptable. So, after mulling it over? No creepy creep. I Won't Be Your Bitch, and that's a hard NO!"

People, I have now come to understand the reasoning behind waterboarding. Oh, just kidding! Maybe? Sorta? Delete & Reported!

24. My name is Mases and like to have sum conversation with you sit possible. Would you give me me a chance? Hope your dooing well; I reed and liked your sharp inovative suite profile. I am looking four a women like you with who will develop in a nice and beautiful relationship. I would like to emailing, talking by phone and prepare for a mutual meeting if I have the chance. Would you give me that honor? I wouold ask again but that would be a mute point .

Risking being politically incorrect, AKA a bitch, have any online guys graduated high school? Or dare I ask, college? I'm no Einstein, but ignorance shuts me down. "Mases? Who names a kid Mases? Was your mom high and meant for your name to be Michael, Mitch, Mason, Matt, or Mark? Moses is good too." For you men out there still reading, (and a Sis Boom Bha, thank you) this email brings home the point I was making when I said spelling & grammar count! "Yes Mases, I reed and read your email, and yes it would be a mute and moot point!" A case in point, Next!

25. G'day... Really enjoyed reading your profile, all the way down-under in Australia! I know I am taking somewhat of a risk making contact from so far away, but I liked your profile and thought we had enough things in common to at least have a chat. Cannot find anyone suitable locally, and I will not settle for someone just because they live nearby! There is much to say, that the right chemistry might be with someone halfway across the world! I am genuinely looking for that special person and have no problems about travelling and moving if things worked out down the track. I love travel and adventure, am well educated, believe family is most important, spiritual, financially stable, with minimal baggage. Life is about taking chances :). I would love to hear from you. Otherwise, good luck in your search! An Aussie arvo! Cheers, Hamilton

Ok, why did I let this sweet little Aussie, koala-bear, get away and delete him? I must have kangaroos loose in the top paddock? He writes and spells beautifully. He is impressively diplomatic, handsome, and beguiling. Bollocks! I'm such an arse! "#HamiltonComeBack! Please, Ham, come back, you fair dinkum, mate! I'll be your Sheila!! Hooroo!"

27. Hi, Im John. I'm 30-wordy! Do you have a band-aid? Cause I just scraped my knees falling for you :-)Was that an earthquake? No? then it must've been you, cause you just rocked my world! :-) Is your name Google? I ask, because you have everything I'm searching for! :-)Are you a parking ticket? Because you've got FINE written all over you! :) Did you read Dr. Seuss as a kid? Because green eggs and damn! :-) Dwindle, dwarf, and dwell, the three words in the English language that start with DW! oh hell! Do you care about me? Do you? Please tell me if you care!

And The Winner and Reigning Champion, Of the Craziest of the

Crazies, John! What in the world was that? You are a zany avatar. Your text was the definition of a 'word salad.' Do I care? Sorry, John. No, not really. A linguistics salad, Google stalker, green eggs, *and* damn, *Next!*

28. If you would meet me in Toscanova at 6:00 pm in the back end of the bar. The reservation will be under Featherston. If you like the Richard Gere look, and it makes your loins stir and makes you want to stick your tongue out, allowing me to suck deeper into you, while holding your head and mouth, in my hands, to suck your tongue up and down. My tongue will get you sopping wet like a vixen, moaning. You're the lucky one

You had me at your photo. You wil reach really high frequencies with me. I dont want to seem forward, but I fuck you 4 hours. You can blow me while I eatyou. Am planning a 3 day cruise. Hour stateroom will hav a large enough balcony to bring you out and throw you down. or if u wanted you cann crawl out and we proceed to ravishingly explore each other all day in the sun and wonder why not before. After dinner I'll hav you workd up and anticipate you for desert. Back on the mattress out side, your grabbing the railing and arching your back offering up your bum and your desire filled with a passion that has you blushing. How far My hard big dick fucks your core, aching in lust, moaning for more. Hangover sex is the best! Fuck me hard. We are in the cards! Night and morning. Riley

Epic! I reason Hell Just Froze Over! And London Bridge fell down, too! Now, there's a Genie way the hell out of his bottle! Repulsive Riley is a missile ready to explode! This is a gross, perfect example of why there should be an Online Prison for Riley to be locked up in!

"Mr. Cray-Cray, with unbridled fury, I declare you are sick and demented. Like What the Fuckity, Fuck, Fuck? Someone certainly needs a very long time out! I'm just wondering, did your mother drop

you on your head when you were a baby? Did you abuse hard drugs? Did you have a bad childhood? Understand, we're so not in the cards. I must find an FU meme to respond to your vile email. Hey, Riley, I'd rather walk barefoot over blazing hot, fiery coals!" Deleted, Blocked, And Seriously Reported!

29. Hi, I want to take you out fancy. I called 'IHOP' to see about brunch. Did you know 'IHOP' doesn't have a corkage charge? Amazing, I called 3 different ones inquiring about their champagne breakfast and they all said, no charge. They seemed a bit confused when I mentioned Dom Pérignon, and I might want to propose marriage someday over breakfast. Guess they don't have the great last romantic attitude? I warn you. I have a bad habit of always knocking over my wine glass. I'll bring 2 bottles knowing I will spill a lot! Will you go to 'IHOP' with me? I promise, I won't grab your tits or pussy the whole time on the 1st date. Love, Wedding Bells, for you!

"Ahhhh, Mr. Wedding Bells, I'm so thrilled I could sing and dance in a musical! Do you really consider bringing your own Champagne to IHOP for free to be romantic? I don't mean to come off like an Alpha-Girl, but I decline both you and IHOP! I found your letter vulgar, and it irritated me over my entire body, like a bad rash. Therefore, Mr. Wedding Bells, I reject you. But, hey, science won't reject you if you left them your body, for discovery. BTW, the way I see it, always spilling wine is a sinful, offensive waste!" A Wedding Bells, I-HOPPIN, Runaway Bride Next.

30. Email 1: Ready for love? I'm SAM

Email 2: Like to say hi

Email 3: will you say hello to me?

Email 4: happy fryday too you

Email 5: where do you live?

Email 6: I don't want to give up

Email 7: i am as fun and caring guy you will ever meet?

Email 8: what shall we do together lets not waste our life?

Email 9: can i bid for a key to your heart?

Email 10: what time shall i pick you up?

Email 11: be good to yourself and let me into your life

Email 12: What's your life like? Why you waiting. there is allot to do

I threw Sam in, just for shits and giggles! He had a better chance of learning grammar in school than getting a date with me. Guys, if she doesn't answer you the second time, then she doesn't like you! What part of her not answering your 12 emails don't you get? "Sam, bugger off!"

Lord, one can't be craven or lack the courage enough to go online. Trending down, for sure. Next, Next, Next, times 12!

31. Hello Miss Love to hear from YOU!I hope YOU don't mind me saying...That YOU are Very Gorgeous and Striking Beautiful! YOU are "the Perfect Storm" Do YOU like to dance?What kind of music, food, movies, excersize, concurts, wine, cofee, clothes, nail polish, television, deserts, shoes do You like?Please tell me your FAVES!I I sing and dance, And know how to show a girl a good time.I'm not a player!Been a hopeful Romantic my entire life.Just want a lady to Love and Adore fourever!Maybe it's You. Give me a clue. Give this pirate a whirl! GOD Bless,Love to Love YOU baby!Mark,YOUR Pirate!

"Ahoy, matey, and shiver me timbers. Mark, you give me the heebie-jeebies. That was a wealth of mumbo-jumbo there, buccaneer. I won't *hesitate to tell you this is way over the top, and too many questions for a first greeting. So, do batten down the hatches! Avast ye, pirate, you need to read my book! That's a clue! 'Yo, Ho, Swashbuckler,' blimey, I'm not your treasure chest, but I'm treasuring a whole big chest of... Next!"*

32. My name is Georgia. I'm in the middle of my transgender process to become George. Like in case you're wondering, I'll be getting a penis and breast surgery removal to fully cross over. I can learn so much from you. You're beautiful and I like you a lot. You're hot, and like, my type. I'd like to know, do you think being my lover will be a problem for you? G

"*Like, yeah, being your lover would present a big problem. Like, sorry, Georgia-George. But I wish you good luck, man!" Like, Blocked...*

It's a good thing these sites don't put a limit on the total number of deletes & blocks you can use. And the search for civilization continues.

After rummaging through these mind-blowing emails, I needed to wash my brain out with anti-bacterial, extra-strength soap! The only thing left to say is, Let's play Jeopardy! I'll take: "Reasons why so many people are out of their filthy, revolting minds. For $500 please, game-show host!"

Readers, I am exhausted from all this cascading nonsense. And I just got back on. I've received and endured hundreds of these types of emails. Fair warning, you will too! Seriously, if I worked 18-hour days in the coal mines, I'd be less drained than being in this dating charade.

"Dear, sweet, 'Love of My Life,' where are you already, and how long must I dance with these devils?"

To ask why dating is so bizarre is like asking the oceans why they wave, asking the sun why it shines, and asking birds why they sing? Crazy, like asking why the slowest driving time of the day is called rush hour, and bizarre as asking the crying baby on board to fly the plane.

Dating is basically an ecosystem of oddities, eccentricities, and peculiarities. There is just no explaining the wackiness that exists. Yet, it does. Therefore, you'll have to deal with it like the rest of us.

Honestly, don't bother writing these men back. It just infuriates them further, and consequently, they'll take it out on other online women. Just delete and block them. Report them if they cross over the *'Holy Crap'* line. Don't feel bad for not responding to any man you are not interested in. It would be a full-time job. No response can sometimes be better than a written rejection, no matter how thoughtful you are. Going out with any of these types of men above would be as ludicrous as walking into a carwash without having a car. Or taking your little old grandma to an XXX-rated male strip club! Nevertheless, think about that. It would be super hilarious.

There are days, and many of them, when a girl needs her, *"Shield Me from The Outrageous Men Fairy"* to protect her. Where the hell has, she been, anyway? "Hey, Men Fairy, I feel like I've been shaken to my core by a violent 7-point, Dick-quake. Help Me!"

Speaking of a Dick-quake, "Bobble Drew, look what you've done to me, making me return to the *'drama-dating-fiasco.'* Damn you, Drew! Was all the love you showed me just a placebo of love? Was it just a cruel ruse to entertain you for the moment? You wounded me with false hopes, turned my world upside down, deceived me, hurt me, and yet, I still love you. Sadly, I probably always will." Enormous sigh.

I'm certain, all you, seekers of love, have experienced and been hurt by a Drew or 2 of your own. Again, *"You Are Not Alone!"* We've all been there and done that. Don't be too hard on yourself for loving with all your heart, for it is wonderful to have known this kind of love. Life can suck when it comes to love equations and chemistry. It was hard enough trying to understand math and chemistry in school. How the hell are we supposed to figure it out with a life partner? Advice to all teachers. these are *tools we could've used and benefitted from way more than geometry!*

I believe what consoled me the most was listening to Miley Cyrus's liberating song, "Flowers." An independence, wake-up call for women.

In the immortal words of Maya Angelou...
"Remember, every storm runs out of rain."

Regardless, magnificent Maya, I'll continue to keep a raincoat and umbrella handy, all the same.

CHAPTER 2

Moving On and Staying Positive

BETTER KNOWN AS... LYING TO ONESELF AND DENIAL

Where is he already? "The One?" Where is my beloved, who is supposed to come gallivanting into my life on a white horse, wearing a suit of shining Armor? You know what? Scratch that. I don't particularly care if he gallivants in on a white horse. It could be a black horse or even a brown horse. Guess what? It's not important. I don't even care if he comes clippety-cloppety in on a horse at all. For all I care, he could come walking in with a dog, or a cow, a turtle, or a frickin' duck. I just want him to come, already! Seriously, let's keep it real. We live in modern times, right? So then, he might come into my life wearing a suit of shining Armani, driving in on a BMW, or whatever! Just come, already!

After careful consideration and too many first dates to count, I've ultimately concluded, *"I am the man I want to marry!"* Talk about circumventing "The One" topic? To deflect the issue further, it is said...

"All Men Are Created Equal."

Are you kidding me? Let me go on record stating, *No. No, they are not!* Not in any way, shape, or form. Thomas Jefferson was out of his mind or smoking some primo, exotic weed when he penned this quote. Quite frankly, this is the most incorrect, preposterous statement ever written in the history books. Let's review and assess this notion. "Created equal?" What about intelligence, looks, height, weight, personality, kindheartedness, compassion, ethics, caring, education, health, body type, looks, thoughtfulness, integrity, and the all-important sexual stamina, for heaven's sake? Wait, there's more! Talent, athletic ability, musical and artistic skills, political views, spirituality, morals, penis size, (this one alone proves my point) sensitivity, creativity, position, family, financial status, sexual preference, hair, *race*, fun-loving, and religion. Must I go on? We are all unique but indeed, *"Not Equal."*

Men are **not** created equal. (And BTW, why doesn't it say, 'A*ll Men and* **Women***?*') I don't care what our forefathers declared in the Declaration of Independence. I believe we should all be equal when it comes to *being treated fairly. Such as civil liberties, civil and human rights, all freedoms, (for men, women, black, white, gay, straight, etc.) all matters of justice,* and the right to hate the Kardashians, Justin Bieber, rich and greedy hoity-toity people, girls who are perfect in every way, people who can eat anything they want and never gain weight, tarantulas, dictators, and the IRS! It is not self-evident. The fact we are different and not equal is what makes us all fundamentally special and distinct individuals.

I heard the phrase "All men are created equal" recently at a lecture. I bring it up as it relates to many expectations and views about dating.

Everything in life is unique and probably not equal. Hence, one woman's frog is another women's hero. With that said, I'm going to tell you about some random men I met online who weren't created equal. Like at all! And remember, all the stories I write about are *preposterously and sadly entirely true.*

Some Random Online Men

THE ISRAELI GUY

That would be Eli, the chef and karate instructor with a very fashionable man bun. This online guy was deliciously sexy, impressively hot, and totally yummy. I *Almost* went out with him, too! I *Came this ~~~~ close.* We spoke a few times, and I admit he was mysteriously cool. At first. When we emailed each other, I ignored most of his obnoxious, cocky comments. Eli first struck out with me after I wrote "LOL" just one time in an email to him. He wrote back, *"Are you for real? Stop with the LOL!!!!!!!!!!!!!!! You're not a teenager!!!!!!!!!!!!!!!"*

Maybe it's me, but I think 15 exclamation marks are a bit much. Don't cha think? Ten would be plenty! How else could I respond to him with other than, ":~ (((((((((((((((((((((((((!!!!!!!!!!!!!!!!!!!!!"

Anyway, I couldn't look the other way with what he did next. We were texting the following night. After a while, he wrote, *"Well, good night, I'm going to take a shower."* Following my sweet goodnight reply, I went about my business, editing a few articles. An hour later, he wrote, *"All clean!"* Then he sent me *completely naked photos of himself.* Totally naked, people! A stranger sent me photos of himself fully naked! Yeah, like that's normal!!!!!!!!!!!!!!!!!!!? Eli effectively *upped the crazy.* The Karate-chef should keep his very

(very) impressive genie in the bedroom.

Sipping wine while scratching my head, I thought, "What is wrong with you men out there? Why do you need to show it off like a monkey?" I hadn't even met this guy yet and already I had seen him naked. Regardless, I might add, with a stunning erection. This brought further support to the phrase, "Too much too soon!" Nicely taken selfies, though. God, I hope they were selfies! Although I'm not stupid. I kept the hot pictures for a rainy day! I do wish I could share them with you.

I never took his calls again. Too bad he was sexy, sexy, hot. LOL!!!!!!!!!!!!!!!!!!!!!!!!!!!!! I also loved his man bun!!!!!!!!!!!!!!!!!!!!!!!!!!!!

Phew, I didn't get "Maled" this time!
A karate chop, and a wax-on-wax-off naked truth. And, Next!
"All men are 'Not' created equal!"

THEN CAME DEMETRIUS DELAINE
THE DOG TRAINER AND DIRECTOR GUY

Demetrius Delaine. I swear on perfect hair days that I didn't change his name. Demetrius Delaine... it's a typical pompous name in any Nicholas Sparks romance novel.

He explained that he trains medical service dogs for the blind and people with other medical conditions. At first, I thought, how enormously sweet, how cool, and philanthropic is that? But then, he went on to clarify how he must be with the dog 24/7. Appreciate what I am saying here. He never, ever (Like Ever) leaves the dog. The dog is present while he is at work directing films, at restaurants, movies, concerts, shows, dentist and doctor appointments, sports events, bars, church, airplanes, buses, strip clubs, and houses of prostitution (Just seeing if you're paying attention, but probably there, too!), boats, trains, and in bed. In bed! During sex and sleeping. He divulged the service animal is always there, front and center.

This humanitarian director/dog trainer keeps the pooch for a year and a half before the animal is matched with an owner in need. Demetrius is now on his 12th dog! He was a good guy with the best of intentions (I alleged) but no, all the same. Logically, after the "Aubry without an E" episode, I was very cautious with the "I love my dog more than life itself" men. I suppose that is why I didn't give the Hollywood Director a real chance. Moreover, it's not easy introducing a man with the name Demetrius Delaine to people, with a straight face. It ended before we met. A barking, disobedient, Take-5! Delaine is still single, directing movies, and training dogs. I really should hook him up with "Aubry without an E!"

"All men are 'Not' created equal!"

AND HOW COULD I EVER FORGET?
THE BRUNO MARS CONCERT CHEAPSKATE GUY

Gage appeared quite normal, as they so often do. This illusion pulls you in falsely and catches you off-guard. I should start a business, inventing a gizmo to detect these trickster guys. I'd be a zillionaire and save people a lot of stress. Note to self: Must contact Shark Tank, CEO.

Anyway, Gage was not very attractive and not at all my type. However, he seemed nice enough. More to the point, he invited me to come to Los Angeles to see Bruno Mars in concert. In all fairness to myself, he could be "The One." You never know? Besides, I really love Bruno! So, come on, what's a romantic music-lover girl to do, decline the invite? That would have been rash and rude. Instead, I thought awesome, dope, yes, yes, and yes! Gage told me graciously,

"Go ahead and buy an airline ticket to L.A. No worries, I will reimburse you when we meet."

Since my dear friend Barbara lived in *the Valley,* I was excited and happy as well for the opportunity to visit and stay with her. I hadn't seen Barb for ages, and I would also get to meet Gage and attend a Bruno concert! That would be considered a perfect trifecta. A total win, win, win!

The night of the concert and 3-hours before Gage was due to pick me up, he called reasoning, "Hey, I was thinking. It would be much faster for you to jump on the LA Metro Rail and meet me at the Staples Center."

"Um, Gage, I don't know how to do that."

"Oh, girl, you're smart. You'll figure it out, for sure!"

I had never been on the Metro Rail and another note to self… *"Never take the Metro Rail again!"* As it turned out, it wasn't at all faster, but it was a lot scarier. Faster was simply code for, "Gage gets to save on gas money rather than going out of his way to pick me up and take me back home, like a gentleman!" He also saved $45 on parking. Once off the train, I had to walk over a mile in my very high, adorable heels from Rio. You know, the shoes that are only designed for looks, and positively *not for walking in!* Gage conveniently neglected to tell me of the long walk alone part to get to the concert arena. And in these shoes, that's Dating-Abuse!

Even Bruno Mars could not put a smile on my face at this point. I reconsidered my previous opinion, declining his invite might be rash and rude. Funny, as it turned out, I now had a major rash on both of my ankles from my new shoes and this selfish guy making me take a metro rail. In the end, his ask was infuriatingly rude!

Wait, it gets better.

Gage had bragged repeatedly about how he bought super

fantastic seats for the concert. Shucks, again, and yet another eye-opening revelation. Our seats were in the 300 level, nosebleed balcony seats, all the way to the left, behind a big column. We were sitting next to a large group of rowdy non-Bruno-Esque Hoosiers, who were loud and disruptive. When an unknown band opened the concert, I was starving, my feet were killing me, and I was not at all a happy Mars fan. I told Gage I was hungry. He replied, (Like I was 4 years old) "Wait till later. Snacking will spoil your dinner."

"Dude, are you kidding me?" I questioned, brutally annoyed!

He gestured offensively, holding his hand up, "Shh-Shhh, quiet, I'm listening!" Oh, no, he didn't? With that, bobbing my head from side to side, I ran out to buy regular-sized M&M's for $12. When I returned, this selfish guy grubbed most of the candy. My inner fury heated up past what is considered healthy for one's heart. Aha, I understood now! If Gage paid $12 for a small, 89¢ bag of M&M's, it would indeed spoil his dinner.

Regrettably, sitting in the worst seats, I didn't see or hear much. But I was sure the concert was spectacular. The following day, a friend boasted, "Bruno Mars was brilliant! Best show ever!" Yeah, sure, she sat in the VIP seats, way up front! This event turned out to be a "Nosferatu," a symphony of horror. After the concert, we walked (Ouch!) to my "unspoiled dinner." And oops, another predictable bombshell. Surprise! He forgot his wallet.

Now entirely disgusted with Gage, I wished I could've waved a magic wand, returning to Barbara's house to have fun and go out to dinner with her. This story about the not-engaging Gage would have kept her laughing for hours. I contemplated making a run for it, but my shoes and curiosity got the better of me. Being a trooper, continuing with this date took every bit of effort I could muster up. As it was a beautiful California night, we sat outside, and people watched. After dinner, he ordered dessert and coffee with Baileys and whipped cream, which Gage was only too thrilled to order since I was obviously now footing the bill.

As I sat there, *dessertless* (thinking it would end the date faster), he began putting down homeless people walking by on the busy street. This date was blossoming like a weed. His comments progressed to him saying awful things about LGBTQIA, overweight, Asian, and Mexican people. To be honest, he was insulting all minorities equally. Unable to tolerate another racial slur and far too many politically incorrect comments, I clobbered him with my, "You go, girl, bitchy defiance." Listening to the voices behind my anger, "Gage, your crass, prejudiced, ignorant remarks are not only false but disgusting and insensitive!"

He yelled back, "You open-minded, liberal chicks are all alike!"

I countered angrily. "Well, Gage, I'd rather be an open-minded, liberal chick than a hating, narrow-minded, stupid, racist fool!"

In an open-minded, liberal chick way, I threw down a $100 bill, left deep Brazilian high-heeled skid marks, and took an Uber "wee, wee, wee" all the way home to Barb's house in the Valley. We stayed up all night eating, drinking, having fun, laughing about Gage, and listening to Bruno Mars' music!

I didn't gage the night with Gage very well. Every nuance of his spectacular bigotry infuriated me. It was not at all shocking that he never paid me back for the airline ticket or the dinner. I say with great humility, "I had it coming!" With my mind and logic working in concert, "*I Got Maled!*" But happily, he never got to sing to me, "*When I was your man!*"

Coincidently, and as fate would have it, 6 months later, I was assigned to interview Mars. He is cool, humble, talented, and an amazing performer. He giggled hysterically when I told him the

Gage tale. And, yes, Bruno, I still believe in love, and just like your Grammy Award for song of the year, "That's What I Like!"

"All men are 'Not' created equal!"

THE MOTION PICTURE PRODUCER GUY

I didn't trust him from the start...

Sawyer, the ostentatious guy, spewed nonstop rhetoric and wrote telling me all about what a Hollywood "Big-Wig" he is. The big clue, from the get-go, was he did 'Not' post a photo. I never open any profiles without photos, but I accidentally pressed the wrong key, and it opened. Foolishly intrigued, I wrote back to him.

"Why no photo?"

To which he defended, "I'm flying under the radar."

Obviously, that sent up a universe of *flags!* Flapping and waving red, neon, flaggiddy flags! I'm flying under the radar? Really? You wouldn't dare make an actor say such a dumb line! Nonetheless, in my world, that is code for *'married!'*

I told Sawyer I must see a photo of him to continue. I explained I didn't like the "You get to see me, but I don't get to see you" game. He agreed, obnoxiously calling me a little minx, and sent me to his Facebook page. Scrolling through his profile confirmed he certainly was a huge, successful Hollywood Producer. His accomplishments in the industry included countless blockbuster movies, starring hugely famous A-list actors. Admittedly, I was justifiably impressed. Still, I was concerned about his *'under-the-radar comment'* or his need for it. And this just in, "I am *not a minx!*" Moreover, there were no photos of him on his FB page.

A day or two later, he wrote, "Let's chat." As I didn't want to share my number with him, I asked for his and blocked my number when I called. He arrogantly filled me in about himself.

"I am single, 6 feet, great looking, thin, fit, with wonderful hair and skin. I'm 42, outgoing, fun, and very successful in the film biz. Not to brag, but realize, doll, I'm a catch!"

I thought, doll? Eek, Mr. Catch. And just so you know, that was indeed bragging. Laughing, "Well, Mr. Producer, before we continue any further, you must send me photos of yourself or upload them to the dating site." Then I quickly hung up. Taking control of the situation, I decided to Google-stalk him. I discovered countless hideous photos of this self-proclaimed fancy-schmancy producer. I also learned he was nothing more than your unethical, fancy-pants liar. Kind of like, most unethical fancy-pants, liar politicians today. Uh-Oh! You didn't know that? Sorry, spoil alert!

The truth is, Sawyer was 5'5", 62 years old, very married, heavy, bald, and for sure, "*not* great looking!" Another exquisite example of *"The Smithsonian Guy."* I might be typecasting, but this is the quintessential tale of many powerhouse Hollywood producers and celebrities who believe because of their prestigious, elitist status, they can have whatever or whomever they want. Regardless of morals or ethics, and absurdly classic. Am I right, Harvey Weinstein, Hugh Hefner, Jeffrey Epstein, and many others?

Hey, Sawyer, in terms even you can understand…

"Camera, action, cut, print, and that's a wrap!

Too bad though, it could have been quite advantageous for me! *I was so totally ready for my close-up!*

Yep, "I Got Maled!" again! Blackout, Cut, in the Can, and 'Fin'…
"All men are 'Not' created equal!"

AHHH! THEN CAME BRIAN, THE CEO CONTROL GUY

Although Brian was a looker, totally, "Bada, Bing," and all that, he was the essence of everything I loathe in a man. I went out with him three times and the alarming thing is, I have no idea why I did that. I think Brian only hung in there to see if the third time would be the charm that he conceitedly expected would get me into his bed. Deplorably, Brian was too oblivious and delusional to realize getting me into bed with him was never going to happen. There was not even a remote possibility. Not even if hell froze over. Not even when donkeys, or pigs for that matter, fly. Not even drunk out of my mind. Not even at gunpoint. Not Even!

He believed he could have his way with me. He not only implied it but also boasted underlying hints about it. Brian insinuated to my face remarks such as, "I am going to eat you up and then lick my fingers later tonight!" I thought silently, Du-hu-hu-ude! If that wasn't *gross* enough to make me disgusted (and trust me it was), with a sick-o glare in his eyes he barked, "After dinner, I'm going to peel your clothes off like an onion."

I held my tongue from lashing out. I'm not an onion, a banana, or a potato and I cannot be peeled, you CEO, vile, Neanderthal Man. Any good opinions I had about Brian fell precipitously into the abyss. It was horrible how he took pleasure in bossing me around. Do this. Do that. You should be doing this or saying that. Wear this, don't wear that, stop this, start that. Brian managed in only 3 dates to make my skin crawl. Truthfully, it only took 1 date.

This also brings up another point, I'd like to question. "Does skin really crawl?" If so, how does skin crawl? I mean, does the skin on your arm just get up and crawl over to your leg or armpit? How does this concept work, exactly? Does skin virtually crawl or is it more like a slither? Whatever the answers, it sounds unimaginably revolting if one had to watch it occur. I never learned about any of this in my biology, chemistry, or physics classes. Maybe this phenomenon was discussed on the days my friends and I skipped school and went to the beach. I mean, how stupid were we going back to class the following day all sunburned? Ah, yes, wonderful memories of forged parents and Dr.'s notes, getting busted, and detentions. It was well worth it. I'm sure you can visualize just how great a tan looks with a vivid blue dress and blonde hair?

Brian was a skilled master of mind games and flamboyantly brilliant at it. To his disadvantage, I saw right through him and his flinty demeanor. He had another thing coming if he thought I was about to play any of his childish games. Except for maybe jacks! I was a Jacks legend. I was also a champion at jumping rope, performing Yo-Yo tricks, and the hula-hoop, which can likewise be fun childish games. When it came to games with Brian, I knew right away, I wasn't going to place my *man* on any board to play his game, even if it was just "Candy Land!" But sorry, Brian, "That's Life!" And know this, you have no "Monopoly" over me.

When he picked me up for the last supper, as it were, he snapped his smug little manicured fingers and demanded. "Move it. We are late for our reservations. Come on, hurry it up. Let's go, Mollie! *You look fine.*"

Ok men… Stop, look, and listen up! As I have previously mentioned, never, *not ever*, tell a woman she looks *"Fine!"* Especially if you're in a hurry. Telling a woman, she looks *"Fine"* is equivalent to telling her, "You look like shit, but we are in too much of a hurry for you to change and try to look any better." Never go there, guys. You could get seriously hurt. "You look *fine,*" is just one illustration proving Brian was romantically challenged and was, no, George Gordon Byron.

At the restaurant, Brian demanded exactly what I should order, in his icy demeanor. In his haughty manner, he insisted I was not to go to the ladies' room until I ordered dinner. At that moment, I wondered if Brian was possessed by demonic entities or walk-ins. The guy was so uptight he acted as though his shoes were two sizes too small.

Three dates and a moment of clarity later, I regained my hormones, self-respect, and the return of my, *"Who the fuck do you think you are talking to"* attitude. Right there in this snooty restaurant, I sat straight up, turned to Brian, and smiled ever so coyly uttering, "Are you talking to me?" (Note, ladies, if you ever try this, it is to be said in a New York, Robert De Niro voice, including his mole and all.) Then, I repeated in a more forceful, intimidating De Niro way. "Seriously, are you talking to me?" (Again, if you attempt this approach, you must also, at this point, add a frown on your forehead, lines, and all. Then scrunch up your eyes, pucker up your lips like a fish, and give a quick twist of the neck.) I spoke again and for the last time. "So, answer me. Are you talking to me? Dear boy, have we met?" I stared him down, pointing my perfectly manicured finger (with the very latest gel nail polish color), and continued. "CEO this, you, controlling bully! I uttered, smiling, "C'est la vie, baby," and "Bon appétit!" And, so you know, that's how you "Go to the mattresses," girls!

With that, I stood up belligerently and hoisted my vintage Cherry Blossom Louis Vuitton Handbag sporting a bow on the front over my shoulder. In a flippant Cameron Diaz, Jennifer Lawrence, Scarlett Johansson, Kate Hudson manner, I charged right out of the restaurant. Feeling sustainable contempt, I rolled my eyes and left him alone to punish himself! Touchdown, Yahtzee, Checkmate, and Game Over. "Taxi!!!!!"

I'm curious! Why do the bad guys seem to outlive us all?

Here's to always looking far better than *'fine'* and next…

It's downright unnerving, and the good Lord only knows, that "I have had far better luck with used cars than I've had with men!"

My Declaration of Independence:
"All Men and 'Women' are 'Not' Created Equal!"
And that's the long and short of it!

CHAPTER 3

Cameron...
The High School Drama Teacher

'FINANCIAL RANK' AT ANY LEVEL CAN'T BUY MORALS, CLASS, MAKE A BAD MAN GOOD OR A LIAR HONEST!

☥ ✌

Cameron is a 30-year-old bohemian, with big green eyes. He is way too thin and has long blonde straight hair that he wears down or tied back in a ponytail. He's your standard surfer type but without the board, wetsuit, the beach, or the waves. I would describe him as a modern-day hippie who is adorable and irresistibly huggable. Cam is a public high school drama teacher and loves every aspect of his job. He seemed to be a refreshing change of pace. A down-to-earth change that I desperately welcomed. He doesn't live a grandiose life, nor pretends to have financial or social status.

Cameron was not at all about the money. This was fortunate for him, as he had very little in that department. Regardless, it was invigorating and fun hanging out with him. Plus, it was cool being able to dress high school casual again. I gave my Versace, Dior,

Valentino, and other favorites some time off. While dating Cam, I lived in cozy torn jeans and well-worn sneakers. However, I didn't go as far as wearing bell bottom jeans, tie-dyed shirts, moccasins, or headbands over my forehead as he did. He was an earthy, no-labels, unpretentious, casual guy. By and large, his naivety in the areas of Wall Street, fashion, travel, sophistication, and other worldly matters was an inviting respite for me. This was a relaxing and safe relationship in which to clear my head.

Indeed, there was no fancy wining and dining or *"Puttin' on the Ritz"* with Cam. His apartment looked like a pad decorated straight out of the 60s, with a lava lamp, black lights, and vintage beaded curtains. There were neon-colored posters, including the Grateful Dead, Led Zeppelin, the Doors, and the Beatles. Ankhs, daisies, love & peace signs, were displayed everywhere. Like, cool man! I was waiting for him to pull out his obsolete collection of S&H Green Stamps and ask me to help put them in the book as we looked through the catalog to order merchandise. While long gone for over 60 years, it's been replaced by the now modern Amazon era.

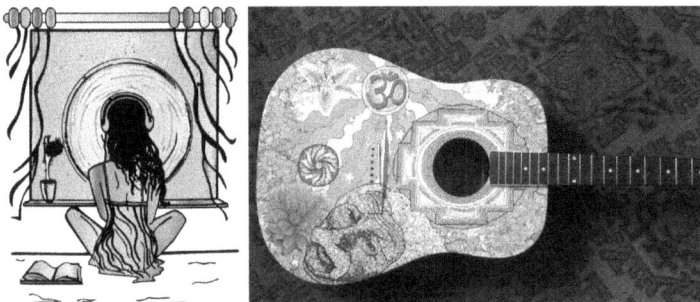

He drove a 1967 hippie van decorated with peace, love, groovy, and neon-painted flowers. Plus, 3 bean-bag chairs in the back. Strangely enough, although one would expect Cameron to be a vegan, we ate tons of greasy takeout. We picked up food to go from several gourmet food establishments such as Popeye's Chicken, Pizza Hut, Chipotle, Subway, KFC, Taco Bell, In-N-Out Burger, (animal fries included) and drank wine from a box. Yes, a BOX, people! On rare occasions, Cameron would take me out fancy to Chili's or the Olive Garden. (Hey, if I could let it go, so should you!) I never mentioned a word about how different this was from my normal way of life. For now, it was fine with me. Besides, it's all he could afford. He'd never allow me to pay for us to go out special. I respected his old-world etiquette and went with it. I was, *"livin' in the groove, daddio!"*

I never found out or understood his love for everything, 1960s. He was virtually stuck between 1960-1969, including the hippie lingo from a time decades before he was born. He used words like hip, hassle, far out, get down, in the groove, hang-ups, psychedelic, cosmic, outta sight, toke the joint; don't Bogart it, groovy, sock it to me, it's a gas, uptight, make love not war, can you dig it, flower power, peace, love, and right on man. It was imperative for me to champion my inner love child to hang in his 60s existential world.

He even wore the granny glasses John Lennon sported. Cameron spoke of Woodstock as if he were there the whole time. If he were around in 69, he surely would've attended the festival dressed in full hippie garb. For me, (at this point in my life) it was fine, and I always wore a "happy, groovy, far-out man," smile!

We didn't go out much, but he always managed to get his hands on a lot of pirated movies. Hey, there's nothing like oily, fried, fast food, and a stolen movie, to make a girl ready, willing, and able. Cam was super cool, awesome-looking, handsome, and a yummy, no-calorie dessert. Plus, the headbands he wore to keep his hair out of his face were wickedly sexy! As the 60s bumper stickers suggested, we did "Make love and not war!" What can I say? He was easygoing, fun, cozy, amusing, and great in bed! This hippie dude was a free-spirited rebel, right down to his retro, long golden locks. Our romance was truly a groovy, far-out blast from the past.

Distinguished and refined were not words I'd use to describe my little flower-power boy/man. I would depict him as playful, whimsical, goofy, simple, and childlike. Everything about him was adorable, kitsch, and curious. Cam possessed a "wow" quality. He loved making fun of everything. One night, he bit into a peanut M&M, spit out the nut, and handed it to me. When I looked at him with a perplexed expression, he announced, "Sometimes you feel like a nut, sometimes you don't!" Hence, what I meant stating that I wore, "a happy, groovy, far-out man smile." This 'WTF' grin often spent time on my face when we were together.

We laughed, played games, and watched his favorite TV shows. Of course, they were all from the 60s. Series such as "Leave It to Beaver, Bewitched, The Fugitive, Mr. Ed, Maverick, Get Smart, I Dream of Jeannie, Bonanza, Lassie, and Batman." Most of them I had never heard of. It was way out of sight. We certainly entertained each other. Dating Cameron was like being in 9th grade all over again. Well, except for actual sex and with no clothes on. He was my private Tick-Tock travel machine back in time.

As he was a drama teacher, we often joked around with various accents. Communicating with the different dialects was one of my things, as well. I loved putting people on and fooling them by speaking in different styles. I spend a great deal of time interviewing people from around the world, so I've been able to pick up on these enunciations and twangs quite easily. Cam and I would sometimes stick with one accent throughout the entire night, never breaking out of character. We had so much fun with this game. These included British, Indian, Southern, New York, Boston, German, French, Chinese, Italian, and Russian accents.

Cameron spoke much of the time using urban idioms. I assumed his high school students influenced him. Hanging out in his apartment was as close to a college dorm relationship as you can get, over the age of 22. I thought it was a tad concerning because this was Cameron's real life.

Clearly, I recognized this was not a real love connection. I was essentially playing a role in his theatrical production. In truth, I'd only be starring in a short, seasonal, "One Act Play!" Nonetheless, I was having great, childish, fun. This relationship was stress-free and exactly where I needed to be for now. I had no problem acting as the leading lady in his drama, including all the costumes consisting of old jeans, T-shirts, sandals, pigtails, love beads, ponchos, and other props needed to play my 60s role.

However, I did find one thing somewhat disturbing. We only met on Tuesday and Thursday nights. When I suggested any other evening, he would always say, "Sorry, babe. (As in, *"I Got You, Babe!"*) I have a rehearsal with my students!" Or "Regrets, babe. I've got a rehearsal for the play I'm starring in at the local theater." There were other dramatic flags as well. For instance, he'd never let me come watch him rehearse. He expressed it would make him too nervous and self-conscious. I didn't understand. *Obviously, being an actor, he* should be comfortable with this and used to being watched by people. It was suspicious and a big flag dropped.

When Valentine's Day was approaching, he was up in my face, excited, and demanded I save the date. Thank goodness it fell on a Thursday. When the morning of February 14th arrived, Cam called and insisted I get *all dolled-up* fancy to celebrate the day of lovers. Because he made such a big deal about it, I became curious and probed. "So, tell me, where are we going, *all dolled-up*?" He smiled. "It's a big surprise!" By this auspicious time, it didn't matter. I was just so happy my little flower child was taking me somewhere upscale and outside of his apartment for a rare and lovely change.

Cam picked me up in jeans (not all dolled-up) at exactly 7:00. He drove, beaming, with a smiley face. After about 20 minutes, we pulled into a parking lot. But? Umm? We were at Denny's? The guy took me for our Valentine's Day dinner to Denny's? Sitting in his car in front of the casual pancake house, I laughed, "Oh! Ha-Ha. You're just playing a joke on me. Good one." But he wasn't! I kid you not. He took me to Denny's on Valentine's Day, all dolled-up, people! Had I known this, I would've stayed in my sweats.

Lavish and ridiculously over-dressed, I gazed at him with a

blatant question mark covering my entire face. I tried to remain quiet. I tried, but suddenly, it all came pouring out of me. "Are you for real? Is this a 60s blast bomb?" I questioned him with a bewildered stare, and I was sure it was flashing on and off like the 60s, neon-colored, psychedelic strobe lights. I can only describe my demeanor as "not feelin' groovy." Not one groovy bit!

He hit his mark, stage right. "No, babe, hear me out. I spent lots of cash on your gift. I had to save some dough on dinner so I could swing it. You will see. You'll love it!"

Annoyed and disturbed, I murmured to myself, "I better!"

"Accepting the award, making history, for the most over-the-top, extravagantly dressed woman, ever to dine at Denny's, Mollie Sloan!" I won the "Best Dressed, Grand Slam, Golden Pancake Fashion Award," hands down. I can't express how thrilled I was when I dropped the greasy chicken & sticky waffles with maple syrup on my now stained Valentino red silk dress, purchased explicitly for my all-dolled-up fancy Valentine's Day dinner.

Arriving back at his 60s cave overjoyed with delight, Cam could barely contain himself. He handed me his gift with the anticipation of a child on a snowy Christmas Eve or the first exciting night of Hanukkah. People, you're going to accuse me of lying or, at the very least, assume this is the 25% made up part. I can't blame you. What I'm about to tell you now is 100% embarrassingly true.

Cameron presented to me for Valentine's Day (I kid you not) a homemade lamp he made in the high school shop department. It was a cardboard box displaying photos of us, with Scotch Tape all around it. Making it tackier, he didn't bother to use the double-sided tape. Thus, you could see the tape placed over the photos. Along the outside were empty Starbucks glass cappuccino bottles. In the center was a light bulb. I didn't know where to begin with my response. However, knowing I'm a major Starbucks Junkie, if the bottles needed to be emptied, he could've at least saved the coffee in another container for me. Moreover, the light that this whole gift was supposed to be about *"didn't work!" It didn't light up.* It was a moot gift. No way to re-gift it, either. I mean seriously, "What the Fuck?" That's all I kept thinking in my lovely, forever stained, and ruined designer red silk dress. Unable to fake my WTF response, I noticed Cam was anxiously awaiting my loving and grateful reaction. Flummoxed, I had to think quickly. Umm, do you possibly have an underdeveloped frontal lobe? Do you literally come from the 60s? Kindheartedly, though, I didn't say that to him.

This is where the *"One Act Play,* script," would have come in super handy! I mulled over a few response options. "Ahem, cool?" "Sock it to me?" "Far-out, man!" "Like really, really far-out!" "You shouldn't have, really, and I mean it!"

I ultimately blurted out, "Cam, I appreciate the work you apparently *thought* you put into my gift, but dude?" Then, while laughing, it dawned on me. *"You got me!* This is a gag gift. You're pulling my leg." I continued, giggling, "Good one! This is the best faux gift ever. Silly kidder, is the real gift hiding in your pocket? Gimmie it! You're so much fun, you little joker." He was obviously crushed. Uh-oh, it's not a gag? Oops! Adding insult to injury, he ran out of money to pay for our fancy Denny's Valentine's dinner.

I didn't know how to proceed. So, I told him I had an important early interview and thanked him. I gave Cam a 'great gift,' a quick peck, and ran abruptly, far-out. As I fled, I did manage to take his gift with me. I didn't think his trash service would take it. Besides, I needed the evidence for a visual to show my girlfriends. To this day, they still don't believe this story, even after seeing the evidence. Honestly, neither do I. We become hysterical every time we talk about Cam's moot, Starbucks VD gift, and my *all dolled-up,* fancy dinner. You can't make this absurdity up, people!

Cameron and I didn't speak for a week after that. When he finally called, he whispered, "I miss you like crazy. And Mollie, I'm sorry. I think I might have fucked up royally on your gift!" (Thinking to myself, *"No shit! Ya think?"*) "I want to make it up to you. I also want to pay you back for our Denny's dinner."

I let him off the *'light* hook,' including the one that didn't light up. "It's cool, no worries!" But worried I was and concerned too. We made a date for our usual Tuesday night. Obviously, I was still bugged, having to stick only to our designated evenings. As the proud and newly crowned Miss Denny's, I decided to dig further into Cam's secret world. After all, I am a reporter! So, I conjured up a smokescreen plan of my own. I went to his high school Monday night for the alleged rehearsal. I hoped to surprise his students with my delicious homemade cupcakes, and sinful chocolate peanut butter and red velvet brownies. Ergo, I wasn't a bit surprised or startled that the school was locked down and empty, except for the security guard on duty.

He politely informed me, "Sorry, Miss. There are never any rehearsals on Monday, Wednesday, or Friday nights."

There it was, checkmate, and the mystery was solved. Ah-Ha, the jig is up, I Gotcha, Cam! You are finally busted in Liar-Ville.

Tuesday, the next day, I arrived at his house with some hellish defiance, but I didn't show him my poker hand. "So, Cam-Cam, how was rehearsal last night?" Just like in horse races, "And… He's Off!"

"Girl, you know it went great. We ran through the entire play from the beginning to the curtain calls. It was a dress and prop rehearsal. Golly, Ms. Mollie, this production is smokin' groovy. It's coming together better than I had hoped. Since it was an open run-through, we had lots of parents in attendance. It was a huge rehearsal. Everyone showed up. It didn't end until after 11:30. It was amazing, totally epic, and the best rehearsal ever!"

"Aha, cool, wish I were there." With growling eyes, "And why wasn't I there, Cam?" Before confronting him, I handed him the red velvet brownies, and homemade cupcakes with sinful chocolate peanut butter I had made for his students. I excused myself and went to the bathroom to pull myself together. After his fraudulent performance (though expected), I was still shaken up. While trying to catch my breath in the powder room, I noticed the good teacher had left his cell phone by the sink. Naively, I never thought of snooping until hearing about 50 texts beeping in. Being lied to, I was already justifiably suspicious. Thus, I read the text messages. Yep, all of them. They came from 5 or more different women, evidently dating him as well. All of us were being strung along, playing a role in his illustrious melodramatic play. His *Off-Off-Off Broadway Production of* "The 60s, High School Drama Teacher!" Indeed, this changed everything.

Furthermore, I also noticed on his phone the endless sick and sordid porn sites he frequented. I must admit, this surprised me. What made it worse (if you can believe that), they were hippie 1960s porn sites! "My 3 Sluts!" "Bitchin Impossible!" "In and Out of Her Limits!" "Gilligan's Fuck-Island!" "The Dick Ram the Dyke Show!" Oh, and let's not overlook "Slut Trek!" How far out is that?

I froze, philosophizing. Do we ever truly know someone? Everyone has secrets. And just like that, there went my warning alarms, ringing off the hook. They were singing, *"These boots are made for walkin'!"* I never would've guessed this could happen with the 60s drama teacher. But *"I Heard It Through The (text) Grapevine."* Luckily, I was only in it for fun. I wasn't in love with Cameron. So, at least I'd escape any wounds from the breakup, which was about to transpire momentarily. Still, my real anger came from his broken promise to share a monogamous, safe sex relationship so we would be protected from the STD's situation.

In my mind, I heard the theater call bells ringing. It's Showtime! I would now face Mr. Rehearsal Liar with my 60s song list, fully loaded.

When I returned to the family room, Cam questioned very hesitantly. "So, what's up, girl? BTW, I loved the sweets. Thanks."

I walked from Stage Left Toward Center Stage. *And Action!*

"Cam, *"This Girl is a Woman Now!"* I need *"Midnight Confessions,"* or *"Runaway,"* with a *"Ticket to Ride,"* and I'm not *"Feelin' Groovy."*

He knew something was up and lashed back sternly with, "Hey, Mollie, cool it. What's your problem? What the hell? What gives?"

"The Answer My Friend Is *Blowin' in The Wind." "God Only Knows!"* And *"How Can I Be Sure?"* But *"Here Comes the Sun,"* Cam."

"Stop it, Mollie! I mean it. It's not funny. What are you saying?"

Laughing, I gathered this leading actor was getting bent out of shape. I announced boisterously, throwing my voice way up to the balcony like a pro. "Wild Thing," *"I'm a Believer!"* Cam, "If You Could Read My Mind" you would know, *"I Can't Get No Satisfaction!"* It's *"Been a Hard Day's Night."* But "Don't Think Twice, It's All Right,"

He was not picking up on my obnoxious, 60s music hints. "Mollie, what's with the malicious arcane smirk you're giving me?"

It was clear by his icy tone he wasn't happy with me. "Wow, Cam, hear that? That's *"The Sound of Silence!"* But still, *"Big Girls Don't Cry."* And *"Suspicious minds," "Like A Rolling Stone,"* are warning me to leave at once, *"The House of The Rising Sun!"* With that, standing stage right, I tore open my Pandora's box and confronted this deceitful hippie who I evidently didn't know at all.

"Guess what, Mr. Director? I went to your rehearsal last night because I made those sweets to surprise your students. And, surprise, surprise! It appeared the big surprise was on me. I discovered there was no rehearsal, and furthermore, there never is on Monday evenings. You have been lying to me our entire relationship and cheating on me with at least 5 other *leading ladies*. You are such a dishonest poser!

A heads-up Cameron. While I was in the bathroom, your phone kept texting off the hook. Now, finding out tonight that you've been lying to me, I went through each girl's text, one at a time. Though I admit, I'm still confused. I'm not quite sure who the understudies are, or the extras, or even who the supporting and leading actress is. Yet even with all the fun and games, Cam, I just can't *"Let It Be!"* Call me *Crazy*, but do I need to go on? Oh, gee, but I must!"

Accordingly, I 1960s 'Perry Mason-ed,' 'Columbo-ed,' and 'Mannix-ed' him skillfully, until he was rendered helpless!

"Camy-Cam, here are just a few of the texts I just now accidentally, on purpose, read in the bathroom...

Diane wrote: "Why are you avoiding me? This is not fair! I need to see you. I'm not right without you. Please, call me, pleaseeeeee! Cameron, I haven't seen you for the past 2 Monday nights! Why? I am desperate for you! I need you! I miss you! Please call me, baby!"

Me: *"Oh, stop, Di, you're killing me. Knock it off! You sound like a needy little whiner. If you really want to know, he was fucking another girl the past 2 Monday nights. That's probably not fair either... I'm thinking?"*

Alison wrote: "You're a dick and a little one at that. Don't call me ever again. I'm over you. And to be honest, you truly are a terrible actor! Seriously, a really, really bad actor!"

Me: *"I so totally like her! Alison's got spunk. Let's do lunch, Ali."*

Mercedes: Was begging you to come and see her! She also said she was so sorry for what happened on Friday night, Camy-baby.

Me: *"I hate when girls beg, don't you, Camy-baby? Don't be sorry, Mercedes **Bends**. He was probably lying about what you should be sorry for, anyway. Yeah, but what did happen Friday, Cam?"*

Angie wrote you: Professing her undying love for you, and she knows that you love her too. She also said you're a sex god and how great the sex was Saturday night. Angie claims she *prays nightly* for more sex with you!

Me: *"Ah sweet. Poor Ange, she's in for a rude awakening in the Next Act! Impressive, you made her religious, Cam. Good for you!"*

Sophie asked: "Babykins, when will we get all 'hot and 60s' together again? I miss you, snookums. Is Wednesday good? I want to make you a lovely home-cooked meal. Come and make love to me, snooks. Please do it again to me. Just like they did in the 60s!"

Me: *"OK, Babykins? Really Cam? How could you possibly go out with anyone who says snookums? Yes, run to her. I hope whatever she cooks for you is extra fried and unhealthy. A salmonella food poisoning scene in 'Act 2' would be theatrical and quite amusing.*

Snooks, allow me to block & choreograph this 60s drama for you:"

Actress: *wearing a tiny A-line belted, polka dot dress, a beehive hairdo, and a string of red plastic pearls from Woolworths, enters. She runs into your arms and kisses you madly and more. (You smack her on the butt.) Although she is so exhausted from her secretarial job, where she dodged advances from her boss all day, she smiles. Without complaining, she prepares an extra dry martini with 3 olives for you. All the* *while, and without a headache, she happily rubs your feet, cooks your dinner, and does your laundry. Ta-Da!"*

AND SCENE...

"Well, Cam, those were the sentiments from about 27 texts sent to you that I read during the 5 minutes I was in the bathroom. I hope for your sake, none of them are your high school students. You'll be fired, maybe even arrested. Plus, I'll go crazy ballistic if you gave me an STD. I managed to get through college unscathed, so even God won't protect you from my wrath!" *Yet, I am rather curious, Snookums. How did they fuck in the 60s, Babykins?"*

He replied, laughing in a smug, inappropriate, guilty laugh. The acting teacher, with the old lame standby spoke. "I am not sleeping with any of them. That you even suggest I am, is beyond insulting."

"Oh, Cameron, stop. We all know the best defense is a good offense." I laughed at him jesting, "Boy, I've got to hand it to that Alison. She was pretty accurate. *You evidently are a little dick!"*

Though the hippie, with his long hair was wallowing in shame, he began to lie and warily added more lies. He denied, denied, and denied some more. Disinterested, I interrupted. "Cam, *"Stop, In the Name of Love!"* Don't speak. "Silence is Golden." I won't believe anything you say, anyway. "Liar Liar," it's "Kind of a drag." "That's All!" I'm done with your drama and your whole lousy production!"

"Let me talk!" He shouted in an angry, hostile voice, I had never heard from him. I have learned the louder a person gets, the bigger the lie. This was a classically humiliating defiance on his part.

"Cam, this is the *"Nights in White Satin"* where you get busted. I'm "Swearin' to God," "Hello Goodbye," Can you dig it? Go on and talk. "Light My fire," and spare me the drama, lies, and bullshit."

After he finished miserably lying, I looked at him amused. "Surely, you jest! Is that it? Are you done? By the way, babe, I'd have to agree with Alison again about your acting. That was a dreadfully bad amateur performance on your part! I really thought you were a much better actor. That Alison was dead on." And with that, I struck a dramatic pose of my own, towards stage left.

From his fuming red eyes with rage, I could see he was about to burst into a crazed wrath. I might have gone a little too far. Too bad, he had it coming. He cheated on me with at least five girls after we agreed, for safety's sake, to remain exclusive. I was radically furious. Before I could gather my things and leave the stage, he jumped on me and kissed me viciously and abusively.

"Stop it, Cameron! I said stop! You are hurting me!"

OK, girls. Let me warn you. There's a discrete line between being frisky, snuggling, and forcibly being held down so you can't get away!

As Cameron squeezed my mouth with his hand (Ouch!), now terrified of this situation, I tried to calm him down and make him laugh. *"I call BS, that only one company sells the Monopoly game!"* He didn't laugh. He was livid and started blame-storming me. I never imagined this little hippie, love-child could be this volatile.

Although I was fearful, I gained the strength to push him off me. I thought of calling the police. But on second thought, I ran into the bathroom, locked the door, and out of an abundance of caution, I called for a pizza instead. It's bizarre, but I knew they'd get there sooner than the cops. Worst-case scenario, I would get a free pizza.

Alarmed, for he was becoming violent, "Stop, Cam! I mean it, relax! This is becoming a hot mess and you'll regret it later." Thank God the muscular Pizza Guy came in no time. I escaped Cameron's grip and ran to the door with the velocity of an Olympic Runner.

With a witness present, I felt emboldened and safer to speak my mind freely. The Pizza Guy probed, "Is there a problem here?"

"It's all good, it's cool," Cameron replied, trying to calm down.

"No, Cam, it's not at all good or cool, especially tonight. You're a cheating, violent liar and you broke it. FYI, in case you didn't realize it, you physically hurt me. I'm out! Enjoy the sweets, pal!"

He begged me to stay in his familiar sweet voice I had come to know. While Mr. Pizza Guy tried to flee, Cameron pleaded for forgiveness. *"Yeah, but no,"* was all I could manage to answer, as I unavoidably tasted the gobs of blood rapidly streaming down my mouth toward my chin.

He asked. "So that's a no, then?"

"No, Cam, that's a fuck no! BTW, you can expect *awful reviews!*"

He arrogantly retorted with every ounce of ego he could muster, "You will soon find out that you will be lost without me!"

"OH-K. Cool, dude, and far the hell out." That's when the poor Pizza Guy managed to escape without a tip. Darn, he deserved one!

Before leaving, I ad-libbed in a way only an actor could appreciate. In my perfect Arnold Schwarzenegger German accent, I spoke… "Adios, buh-bye, amigo, snookums, babykins. And I won't be back because "You've Lost That Lovin' Feeling."

With that, holding my extra cheese and pepperoni pizza, I struck another pose. (Thanks Madonna!)

After my dramatic freeze, I turned stage, 'OUT.' Cue the lights… Blackout… And… Curtain Down!" Thunderous applause, applause, applause! I took my final bows in The High School Drama Teacher's, "One Act Play!" Then I dashed out the backstage door of his house. Not to brag, but I seriously deserved a Tony Award for my theatrical performance tonight.

Cam was not rich with money or honesty. But he was rich with many women, being untruthful, cheating, and his artful deception.

At least he didn't claim to have, "Sexual Addiction Syndrome!"

I wonder if the Royal Princess Kate Middleton went through any of this man-drama, and the ridiculous mansplaining lies before her beloved Prince William came along?

Which reminds me, where the hell is my prince already?

My fellow "dudettes," we must stand in solidarity and protest the new norm of candidates in the world of online dating. This must come to an end. Where did the old normal go? Who changed the rules? How come I never got that memo? This little rendezvous was not cosmic, psychedelic, or right on, and I certainly did not dig it at all. Thank heavens I didn't contract an STD from Cameron. I suppose this was the silver lining in the very out-of-sight world I had been visiting. This surely was a true-life, "Twilight Zone." Thanks, Rod Serling. And the Twilight Zone theme song plays on.

Do, Do, Do, Do! Do, Do, DO, DO!

The worst part of the Cameron chapter? I gained 8 pounds from the shitty, greasy, fried, unhealthy food. I exuberantly returned to the gym, my healthy diet, and my everyday bling, designer clothes, Manolo Blahniks, Louboutin, and Jimmy Choo heels. I missed them all. "There's No Place Like Home!" Click! Click! I was so happy to be back home, in my shoes & my amazing world.

Girls, so you know... *"When A Man Loves a Woman"* she feels it!

I Woodstocked the hell out of the 60s and all the way Towards Next!

Peace Out...

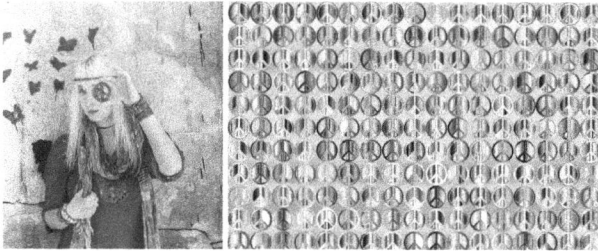

Curtain Call. Applause, Applause, and a Huge Standing Ovation!

CHAPTER 4

Four Losers in Fourteen Days

YOU SAY POTATO, I SAY TEQUILA...
WHEREFORE THE HELL ART THOU, ROMEO!!!!!?

One can find there is so much darn truth in fiction. Nevertheless, and hard to believe, pretty much all the stories in this book are sadly & entirely non-fiction. Just facts, true events, and real people.

In only 14 days, I experienced real-life stories with 4 men, which felt like an atomic explosion of absurdity. All this craziness left me with the desperate need to scream for the millionth time...

"Oh, Hell No! And Come On... Really?"

I've always taken pride in myself for being wise. Unfortunately, the foolish romantic dreamer within always blinds my sweet, innocent heart. To survive dating, it was essential that I learn to tweak my romantic dreamer attitude, for it leaves one powerless. I needed to become shrewd and tenacious. I had to stop being so gullible and trusting. It's not an easy balance being girly and soft, mixed with behaving savvy and insightful. For those of you still reading (Gosh, thank you!), you'll need to discover how to strike a balance and strive to be more diligent with your eyes wide open.

After many trips down *insanity lane,* I sat on my comfy couch in my cozy silk pajamas, listening to the blazing fireplace crackling, enjoying a glass of wine, and a bite of chocolate. Ok, a piece. (Fine, whatever, a box! Tough crowd!) I also loved listening to the calming sound of the rain drizzling outside my house as the branches slammed against the windowpane. Speaking of pain? Let me tell you about my latest, "Four, Real-Life, Short Stories."

1. THE GUY FROM ATLANTA WHO
LIED ABOUT EVERYTHING...

Asher and I spoke on the phone for a few weeks. I began our conversations knowing I had to travel to Atlanta for an interview with the Governor of Georgia. Plus, I had several appointments with the heads of CNN for future freelance work. Besides, I like multi-tasking. The guy from Atlanta and I (with trepidation on my part) arranged to meet at my favorite restaurant, Chops, in Buckhead. I was cuisine-excited since their bread assortment, crab and shrimp cocktail, and steaks are extraordinarily delectable.

Based entirely on the one photo Asher posted from the neck up, and what he wrote in his profile, he seemed somewhat promising. He described himself as toned, thin, and physically fit, with a healthy head of hair. He wrote he was quite well off, a true gentleman, intelligent, and the ideal sensitive mate. Let's be honest. How could a girl oppose any of that?

Meanwhile, there I was solo, sitting at the Chops bar with an Aperol Spritz cocktail and awaiting his arrival. As fate would have it, I was enjoying a pleasurable conversation with two handsome single men in designer suits. They generously invited me to have dinner with them, but I explained my Asher situation. They were inquisitive and asked me all about him. I explained what I knew of him and what was told to me, straight from the horse's mouth. Ironically, by this point, I was genuinely hoping Asher would be a 'no-show!' I was having such a lovely time with designer suit guys.

Ever so quickly and enough to startle me, some odd-looking man walked up to me. Who was this dangerously obese guy in my face? (**Nothing wrong** with being obese!) Anyway, this certainly wasn't Asher, for this man didn't match any of the descriptions in his profile. He sported a terrible toupee, nerdy glasses, and dressed like a used car salesman wearing a tacky yellow plaid jacket, orange tie, green pants, scuffed shoes, and all. (Reminder: True story!) The two elegant men, now roaring with laughter, pointed thumbs down when they saw the man that I had described so differently. If it weren't so darn pathetic, I would've laughed too.

Before he could speak, I announced, "Oh, sorry, Sir. I, a, I'm a, I'm waiting for someone!" He obnoxiously continued conversing.

"And aren't you the lucky girl? I'm Asher. I am *that someone!*" Disappointingly, I realized, that apparently, it was indeed Asher. I should have said, "Oh, no, sorry Sir, I am waiting for Johnny Jacobs," and then hightailed it the hell out of there. This dishonest, scam artist pulled the ever-classic bait-and-switch on me with his appearance and everything else about him. All I'm saying here is, if Asher was toned and thin as he described, it was very well hidden beneath massive layers of flab! (**Not** that there is **anything wrong** with that unless you lied about being toned and thin!) I won't bore you with all the "Are you joking with me" details of the evening.

However, he ordered the crab appetizer for two (but for him, alone), no main course, and only the bread for me to eat. Luckily the date ended abruptly when this weird fellow, while sweating, with a mouth full of the crab-cake, self-assuredly stated, "You will, of course, be following me home tonight to fool around! Hooking up? Yes? I know you like me. So then come over and show me in my bed. I'm sure you have a lot of tricks up your pussy!"

Gross! Being civil to Asher would be a heavy lift. I don't think there is a clocked time, of a person sprinting out of Chops as quickly as I did, holding a piece of raisin bread, escaping Asher that night. I literally sustained an injury in doing so. *I broke a nail!*

While dashing off, I spotted the two young, very handsome, toned men at the bar. They were still laughing as they waved for me to join them. I shrugged, implying I had to leave, pointing to Asher as he was still chomping away. Shaking their healthy heads of hair with compassion, they gestured a validating goodbye, still amused. Too bad, such a waste. They were both so good-looking. I grinned back, displaying a 2 thumbs-down smirk on my face.

Starving and upset about missing dinner at Chops, I stopped off at 'the Varsity' for a burger on my way back to the hotel.

Yep, "I Got Maled!" But this was such an acrimonious situation, even I had to laugh this time! The upside? My interview with the Governor went fabulous, as did my CNN meeting.

"All men are 'Not' created equal!"
Two handsome guys and a liar, next.

2. THE GEORGE CLOONEY LOOKING GUY...

I swear on the Prada Galleria Satin mini bag, with crystals, that Alex was the *spitting* image of George. Only younger and without the *spit.* His photo screamed suave, sexy, and insufferably dandy looking. The only problem I recognized at once (other than me saying dandy) was his excessive career boasting. I really didn't care about all that info *"on our first talk."* Yet, he went on nonstop in his braggadocious, cocky way about his big important job! I had to cut him some slack because, ya know, Clooney looking is Clooney looking! Besides, who could resist a young Clooney? Sorry, this was an enticing situation. Being all fired up and in dire need of some tinkering around, we made a date for Friday night. I was eagerly looking forward to a *TGIF* evening of fun and games.

Thursday night, sitting in a movie theater, eating popcorn, I got an unexpected call from Alex. He called to tell me he was fired. He was beside himself and explained he was too devastated to meet.

Clooney and I never spoke again!

"All men are 'Not' created equal!"
A George-less, and not so Dandy, Next!

3. THE CHIROPRACTOR BILLIONAIRE... ALLEGEDLY!

Clark never stopped gabbing about his success, his riches, and his many triumphs. Swaggering, "I own ten booming chiropractic offices and six prosperous, posh health spas. I am beyond, richer than rich. Everything I invest in turns to gold. Mollie, I want you to know, I'm astronomically and lavishly rich. As in, Elon Musk, rich!"

While I characteristically loathe showoffs, I most uncomfortably admit I was still somewhat intrigued. He lived in Florida, and I was there to write a story on "Normalizing Relations with Cuba and Boosting Commerce and Trade in Havana." So, I went out with him. Surprisingly, I had a lovely time. Aside from that, I did wonder why we met at 6:00 for dinner and why he hurriedly left promptly at 7:30. It appeared rather peculiar. Extending the benefit of the doubt, I didn't question him about it.

Still, even so... Red Flag... Flag... Fa-lag!

When I returned home, we spoke nightly for several days. That's when Clark confided in me. "Listen, I want *ya* to know that I am extremely afraid of flying. Nevertheless, I'd very much like to see you again. I believe it's important to distinguish if we have something real or not. It would be nice to find out if we were more than just a one-night dinner. Look, Mollie, if I bought you a plane ticket, would you be willing to fly back to Palm Beach to visit me?"

Why not, I thought! Now you see... I've learned and come to understand that, *"Why not,"* is such a worrisome, action-packed question, overflowing with endless, disastrous ramifications.

With my *"Why Not"* naivete, on the phone, I agreed. That's when Clark quickly informed me, *"I have to tell ya,* so you know... Breakfast is at 6:00 in the morning, lunch is at 12:00 noon, dinner is at 6:00 in the evening, and bedtime is 9:00, or the very latest 10:00. Kindly understand there is no discussion about this, set in stone, designated time schedule."

I thought, hell to the no! Was this guy in the military, prison, or what? He went on to state without any regard for my feelings or needs. *"I have to tell ya...* I have discovered the correct way to choose the right woman for myself is by her performance in bed. I am assuming that sex will be on the program. By that, I am referring to blow jobs, kinky intercourse, and, naturally, anal sex."

I wanted to ask this repulsive *Clock Keeper* what time that was scheduled for. But I forgo the question, fearing he wouldn't fully pick up on my sarcasm and likely have a clocked answer!

Justifiably offended and angry, I didn't respond to his inappropriate, vulgar sex query, which likely would've been a precisely timed answer of 2.6 seconds. Had I done so, I would have touted, *"Umm, no! That's so not on the program, you, aggressive egomaniac."* Instead, I decided to have him investigated. I learned Mr. Bragger, the mendacious carnival barker, worked as an assistant manager at Target. Nothing against Target! But I do have a thing against dishonest, vulgar, showoff, demanding storytellers.

The next day, I spoke with Clark one last time without informing him what I had learned about him. It was important for me to respond to his aggressive and disrespectful sex question. *"I have to tell ya,* Mr. astronomically and lavishly Rich, you will never experience the joy of having sex with me. Not ever. Moreover, I'm not flying back! *I also have to tell ya,* no one, and I mean no one, gets to tell me what time to eat, get up, or go to sleep!"

"Oh, and one more thing, ***Mr. Target!***" Not letting it go, I stated Target's motto: "Expect More. Pay less!" Furthermore, "Mr. Rich chiropractor, spa owner, and liar, that's the way the big giant store, the brittle bones, the hands massaging the body, and the hands on the clock, crumbles. That was 32.4 seconds. It is now 10:05 a.m. Your time is up. Ga-bye." Click!

And once again, "All men are 'Not' created equal!"
An, Aye-Yai-Yai, TARGETED, 3 seconds, Next...

4. THE CALIFORNIA MILLIONAIRE BODYBUILDER...

Ivan, the bodybuilder, appeared super-charming, as they so often do at first glance. We spoke during the same 2-week period that I was in contact with all the (*what can I say*), losers above.

Despite the fact he posted his bodybuilder photos from 20 years ago (So creepy. They ironically made me want to puke and laugh at the same time) I liked the way he sounded on the phone. After all, that was a long time ago, and egos do fade with time. He went on to claim he owned many gyms and workout centers throughout the country, which made him a millionaire. Ivan spoke about family and how he raised his daughter himself, and what a good, decent, honorable, and honest man he is.

Even though his ego clearly didn't seem to have faded with time, I thought I'd give him a chance. He was flying into Vegas from California, and we made dinner plans for that Tuesday evening.

Unexpectedly, Monday night at 9:17, he called. (Again, I remind you, it's a true story!) "So, *lookit* doll, I just thought you might want to know. I have been in prison for the last five years for armed robbery. It wasn't my idea or entirely my fault. We didn't kill anyone. But, yeah, sure, we shot a few people. I mean, like, they are all fine... Well, now. So, is that cool? Are you good with that?"

You know, sometimes I wish I could turn up the volume on the click sound when you slam down the phone on someone.

Memo to self: Good, decent, honorable, and honest people don't have to tell or convince anyone they are. That's a big clue for you. Another one bites the dust! Just shoot me now. *Oops... Maybe not?*

"All men are 'Not' created equal!" A shoot um up, Next...

It's so frustrating, how another 2 weeks flew by without those anticipated bluebirds of happiness merrily chirping away. Instead, I was blown away, as though I were hit by a gale-force wind. (Gee whiz, poor Gale. She's always being blamed for things unfairly.)

"I Got Maled," 4 times in just 14 days! That's, a new record!

My dearest Romeo, this has gone on long enough. Seriously,

where the hell are you already? I feel you. I know you're there. I've tried everything imaginable to find you. I've even gone out with guys I knew were wrong in every possible way for the, "You never know" or the "Is it you" potential. I tried all conceivable options hoping to find you, to find us.

"Romeo, Romeo, I *feeleth* as if I *hast* been waiting since the days of Shakespeare *f'r thou. F'r thou I wouldst fain waiteth f'r an et'rnity, but I feeleth it hath already been that longeth. I don't wanteth to beest impatient or pushy darlingeth, my loveith, but doth geteth thine ass ov'r hither!"*

Putting Shakespeare aside, my darling snookums, babykins (Yes, I went that low!) I don't want to start a fight because we haven't even met yet. I don't even know who you are, but I must tell you this. When we do finally meet, we are going to have our first fight at hello, for what you've put me through with all this dating craziness and torture. I can't believe I had to stoop to online dating to search for you. You are in considerable trouble with me, pal. Darling, sweetie pie, honey!

Oh, no! I just had a most distressing thought! What if something awful happened to you? What if something terrible occurred, stopping you from getting to me? Oh, my beloved soulmate, I feel guilty now.

OMG! Maybe you died? Oh no, and a resounding, Shit.

Maybe you fell into a crevice, hiking up through the Alps? Sigh! That is surely a lonely and excruciating way to go, for sure.

Perhaps your sailboat had a leak, and you were left alone floating in the middle of the ocean for days. You, poor dear. I know how hard you must've tried fighting to stay alive for me. It's so tragic that a shark may have snuck up behind you and swallowed you whole. Or worse, he took his time and ate you into tiny pieces!

Maybe you had a sex change operation? Maybe you are Caitlyn

Jenner? (AKA Bruce.) Girl, if so, be prepared to share the fashion!

Perchance you are an MGM Director who went to the wild African Jungle to shoot a movie, and you were torn apart and gobbled up by a lion. ROAR! How satirical if the MGM Lion ate you? LOL! So sorry babe, and a roaring, Ouch!

Maybe you're a famous football player and were paralyzed in a game. Oh no, too horrible and way too heartbreaking.

Maybe you are a reporter doing a story in the Ukraine and were captured by Russians. Now a prisoner of war for life! And since everyone thinks you're dead, no one's looking for you. Oh, my love, they don't have beds, mats, showers, or toilets over there. Not to mention happy hour!

Hey Romeo, I'm trying here!

Maybe you became a priest? Nah, impossible, not the way you love sex! And let us say, amen.

Maybe you got into an accident and now have amnesia? No way. Too, soap opera and dramatic for you!

Maybe you are gay? Honey, no biggie. I'd love you, anyway!

Perhaps you are a philanthropic doctor and devoted your life to helping third-world countries around the globe. Maybe you contracted malaria, cholera, Typhoid Fever, or the Bubonic Plague, and died a horrible, painful slow death! Oh, my dearest, what a humanitarian! (Or stupid!)

But then again, maybe you are an evildoer or a terrorist and sacrificed your life as a human bomb for Allah. Although, in that case, you are a brutal bastard, and I'm glad we didn't meet!

But, if nothing awful did happen, well then, you're a dead man anyway, for putting me through this cray-cray, dating insanity. You'd surely be safer and better off with the sharks or lions!

"Romeo, Romeo, wherefore art thou, Romeo? *Henceforth, just cometh to me already, and I wilt alloweth thine all wend. I wilt alloweth bygones beest bygones. Well, Kinda, sorta-ith?"*

I give up. Where are you? *Man, You Are in So Much Trouble!*

"I swear, I urgently need my Fairy Godmother!
So, where the heck are you with your magical romance wand?"

Again, "All men are 'Not' created equal!" A Romeo-less, Next...

CHAPTER 5

The Pool of Bad Men

THEY ARE HIDING EVERYWHERE
IN PLAIN SIGHT AMONGST US...
LORD, DOES IT EVER END?

Please, don't misconstrue this chapter. For the sake of clarity, there are (take a breath) many wonderful, incredible, amazing, astonishing, terrific, fabulous, great, extraordinary, ideal, magnificent men out there. Probably millions! I'm guessing? And one can *strongly* hope. I love men! Honestly, I'm a huge fan. "Go, Team-Men, Go!" Regrettably, this chapter is not about those men. Basically, the guys in these stories are 100% non-fiction. As you read, do keep in mind it's all true. It really happened. Yes, really!

You see, I have dated some... hmm, how do I diplomatically phrase this without coming off negative or bitchy? Some of the guys I've gone out with were hostile, thoughtless, insensitive, aggressive, peculiar, undesirable, nasty, and classless. And that is as diplomatic as I can get.

Then why is it when we girls go out on a first date with one of these clowns, he can easily fool us into believing he is fabulous?

Example: "Elizabeth, I just met this great guy. He's awfully nice and so amazing. Oh, Liz, I really like him! He could be 'The One.' I can tell!"

Honestly, ladies, how many times have you said this to a friend?

Realistically, I am here to tell it like it is. I call this situation… *"The so-called, great guy who acts really nice, so that he can get into your pants,"* time-period!

It's all part of his sneaking, scheming, cunning agenda. Not a mystery at all, that in a few weeks or so, "The great, nice, amazing, special guy, whom you really like, and thought could be, The One" now shows you who he truly is! The real him, instead of, and as opposed to, the guy he wanted you to believe he was. The real guy kicks in shortly after you've had sex with him. I fondly call this *"The Hit and Run"* time-period! Ergo, my guy protocol is…

Don't tempt fate and talk about him to anyone until you really know him. More to the point, don't sleep with him until you know for sure who *"Him"* is! Assume nothing is in the bag before it is. If it is real, then you don't want to jinx it. If it wasn't real, then for sure, you don't want tons of 'realization mud' trickling down your face.

Doing the math, online dating can sometimes feel like a tidal wave of maniacal misfits. These unscrupulous guys somehow manage to crawl just over the bar, reaching the bare minimum to make it possible to call themselves human beings.

What? Am I being too negative, bitchy, or not at all diplomatic?

Hello, don't shoot the messenger! I am your loyal cheerleader. I'm simply trying to caution you with honest and truthful guidance so you will potentially have something to cheer about. Trust me, I am your lifeline!

I swear to God, there were many times I felt like I was driving on a highway, in the fast lane, with bald tires, and in the wrong direction. Other times, I felt as if I was knee-deep in a bad dating dream, anxiously trying to wake up, to no avail. I warn you, escaping unscathed or getting through some of these dating adventures will seem like a monumental victory.

That said, I want to help you avoid, "The Pool of Bad Men" by teaching you some of the signs to look out for. If you heed my advice, hopefully, you'll be able to cherry-pick your way to the good guys, and perhaps find your storybook, happily ever after. Appreciate this isn't a perfect science. You must understand, in the world of dating, if you pay close attention, there are times when you know intuitively that, *"Too good to be true,"* is just that. Hence, I'd like to assist by putting you on the right road and in the right direction to, *"The Lovely Good Guys!"* I hope my descriptions of *"The Pool of Bad Men"* are painted in a kind, politically correct, non-attacking, sensitive, non-offensive, warm, and fuzzy manner. If not, then I say with a demure smile, whatever! Read on and learn.

Permit me to categorize the bastards you should absolutely avoid. What? Again, not sensitive enough? But notice that I'm still smiling demurely! That's something, isn't it? My goal is to help you identify, weed out, and confidently eliminate these pernicious, *men*acing *men*. I seek to make you aware of the obvious signs, so you won't suffer any needless, insidious harm. With any luck, I'll be able to exhibit the antithesis of the good guys!

1. THE "WEEKENDER GUY"

Predictably, he is average-looking or unattractive, older, and rich. Beware, ladies, he is most likely either married, with someone else, or has major commitment issues. And quite feasibly, all three. The plus side to the "Weekender Guy" is he usually comes bearing magnificent, generous gifts. Although, be forewarned. He is typically a liar and a cheater. He has to be, as he must keep you from his secretive weekday world. Don't fall in love with the "Weekender Guy," no matter what! *And seriously girls,* don't be a fool. For sure, keep and enjoy all the fabulous gifts! While you may have enormous fun, just realize this is only a *short-term hayride.*

2. THE "I'M STILL, IN LOVE WITH MY EX, GUY"

This guy, "bless his heart," still thinks his EX, is a saint and the most wonderful woman who ever lived. The fact she cheated on John Doe more than once, stole all his money before and during the divorce, and left him for his best friend from Jr. High School, has no relevance to him whatsoever. The likelihood of her walking out on Doe's now, "EX, Jr. High School best friend," (who has no money to speak of), is a huge probability. Since she's become rich from John Doe's money, she'll likely leave the EX-best friend too, and run off with the sexy, exquisite, (shirtless) young gardener.

It's truly a pity how the "I'm Still, In Love with My EX, Guy" will always make excuses for her actions and all her other flawed behaviors. She remains forever perfect through his blind eyes.

No doubt, he'll take you out to a lovely restaurant, but he will talk about her the whole time. I caution you, never say anything negative about his beloved EX, no matter what! If you do, he'll walk out on you and the check. So, at least wait till the bill comes, and he pays for it, silly girl.

If he is that obsessed and excessively still pining over her, then definitely take a pass on this guy. You'll wind up wasting your valuable time and energy on a lost cause. This hopeless situation and her mammoth high pedestal will never change. He will eternally carry a torch for her regardless of the atrocious things she's done or will indeed do in the future. You see, he still imagines with all his heart that she will run back into his awaiting arms, one day in the near future. The heavens will open, and they will blissfully rejoice together in their love for all eternity.

Understand, it's impossible to measure up to her or to even think of taking her place in his world. I promise you'll surely lose the battle *and* the war. Because his undying love and devotion to her are so concrete, he has no room for a committed relationship with another. He'll spend the rest of his life trying to get her back while balancing that ever-burning torch on her pedestal of gold. So as far as the "I'm Still, In Love with My EX, Guy" is concerned? I suggest you go back and look for your own guy, who is excited to place you upon his emotionally available, loving, and awaiting gold pedestal. But please, wear pretty shoes climbing up onto it!

3. THE "ME, MYSELF AND I, ME, I, ME, I, IT'S ALWAYS ABOUT ME, GUY"

Just for fun, if you go out with a "Me, I, Me I, Guy," count how many times he says, "Me and I" throughout the date. Don't bother telling him the total, for he'll surely call you a pathological liar. He is oblivious to his "I am the greatest of them all" ego. I imagine these guys haven't discovered Muhammad Ali claimed that title long ago. The thing is, Ali could back it up! Note, if you get a rare chance to speak about yourself (But, don't count on it!) he'll interrupt you with something along the lines of, "Yes, by all means. Of course, let's talk about you! What do *you* think about me? And please, do explain in elaborate detail. I've got all night."

The last one of these, "Me I, Me I, Guys" I went on a date with, shocked me while we were standing in a fancy elevator lined with elaborate gold decorative mirrors. I caught him staring adoringly at himself in the mirrors. He had the gall to state out loud, (and I'm not making this shit up), "Girl, it's unbelievable. I don't know whether to look at my reflection in the mirror or yours! That's how amazingly beautiful you are, pretty Mollie!"

It was unbelievable. I was speechless. Wait, it gets even better.

The "Me I, Me I, Guy," then went on to say, "Listen, I have no problem and would prefer, as a pet name, for you to call me Adonis. Come on, just look at me! I clearly represent the god of beauty and splendor!"

In a flash, I immediately replied, "Listen, I have no problem and would greatly prefer for you to call me *a cab!*"

My counsel regarding going out with the "Me, I, Me I" egotistical, delusional guy? A decisive, "Me, I, Me, I, Me, I, *No!*

*Next, and **TAXI!***"

4. THE "NONSTOP TEXTING GUY"

Truthfully, he isn't a bad guy at all. He's just more like a sixteen-year-old high school kid. Mr. Infomaniac, the "nonstop texting guy," is typically shy, timid, nervous, and your basic quiet type. Texting helps him get through these edgy character traits of his. However, if you really like him (*and by the way, good luck to you with that*), here is a helpful trick. If you want his attention, don't go out with him. Just text him! He'll love you for it. If you do go out with him, you're still better off texting him than talking face to face. Note, he appreciates all abbreviations. Such as OMG, BRB, LMFAO, LOL, IDK, B4N, TBH, FYI, FTW, WTF, LMK, and 143! BTW, FWIW, don't forget to use lots of emoticons and emojis!

5. THE "HYPOCHONDRIAC GUY"

I genuinely feel bad for this guy. He truly believes he is allergic to everything, including the dreaded "Callaballa Bats." No, stop! Don't think about what they are. I just made them up to freak him out. But the "Hypochondriac Guy" is afraid of them, regardless. Luckily for him, he seems to have a continuous spectacular panacea for all the diseases, infections, disorders, and illnesses that he assuredly expects to contract. His house smells like a hospital. Everything's been sanitized and rubbed down with alcohol. His bathrooms are filled to the brim with every conceivable medication. He has remedies and treatments for all medical diseases known to mankind, which he learned by endlessly exploring on Google.

Even before Covid-19, he was afraid to go out in public or use any form of public transportation. He would never dare to touch a doorknob, an elevator button, an escalator, a staircase railing, or even a pen that isn't his own. He anxiously purchases industrial-sized hand sanitizer at Costco. If someone sneezes 7 tables down at a restaurant, he'll frantically leave the establishment in the blink of an eye. In keeping with this notion, if you do blink your eyes too much, he'll assume you have pink eye, or an eye infection and skedaddle. This eccentric guy won't go to the movies, sports events, clubs, amusement parks, concerts, parties, crowded places, or malls, especially during a sale. Crazy dude, that's *the best time to go!* Don't even mention dogs, cats, or animals to him. Especially monkeys.

"Hypochondriac Guy" religiously wears an N95 mask at the airport and everywhere else. He doesn't travel unless entirely necessary for fear of being on a plane, train, boat, or bus with people who might be sick. Even when wearing 4 surgical masks and using sterilizing products.

He never shares his food or drink. No worries, for he doesn't eat anything delicious anyway, since he believes he's allergic to just about everything edible. He always thinks he is sick, getting sick, or has some rare exotic disease. I'm talking about the type of ailments that affect *one* in two million, and he imagines unequivocally that he is that *one*. Without question, "Hypochondriac Guy" swears he has had AIDS, Parkinson's disease, Cancer, Tourette's syndrome, Diabetes, Shingles, Lupus, all allergies, Crones, Epstein Bar Disease, Glaucoma, ADD, OCD, ADHD, and all the other D's, plus every other ailment written in medical journals.

Don't even get me started on his sexual death fears and random sex phobias. He is deadly terrified of "Sababa, Kawaza, Lashalla, and Kabba" diseases. Don't try to figure them out. I made those up, too, just for my own amusement and jollies. Still, he insistently claims he has had all 4 and looked them up, anyway. I admit, I'm guilty and take great pleasure in screwing with the "Hypochondriac Guy." Honestly, how could I not? It's wonderfully entertaining. He's a reality show all by himself. The last one of the "Always in distress of dying guys," I went out with went as follows.

The first week Norman and I spoke, he had a root canal procedure. He complained nonstop for 2 weeks that he was suffering in agonizing pain. Excuse me, Mr. Hypochondriac Guy, but after you have a root canal, the nerves go dead and there is no more pain! Come on, man? Then, he claimed he was coming down with the Swine flu. Next, he insisted he had Covid, though the test was negative. Three days later, he declared he had a rare African Virus that manifests into a slow, uncomfortable death. The statistics show there has never been a known case in the States. He ignored that data, demanding, "It's just because I haven't yet called the Center for Disease Control & Prevention to report it!" Norm pouted. "Don't laugh at me! This virus is worse than Ebola or SARS, with a 94% mortality rate. It's a mosquito-borne virus that kills within 4 days." With the luck of fate, he lived! Days later, he said he contracted Necrotizing Fasciitis, the flesh-eating disease. Aside from all that, his asthma, migraine headaches, and arthritis returned. He texted hysterically, "Mollie, I caught Monkeypox!"

Ewe, I hope I can't catch that from a text! After a few weeks of texting, we spoke on the phone. "I feel pretty good. How would you feel if I drove down there to meet you?" Apart from all his phobias (and that's a lot of *apart*), he seemed sweet in a peculiar way, and very good-looking, judging by his photos. Since my dating batting average was totally pitiful, I alleged I had nothing to lose. Technically, not a good way to think or to temp fate...

We went ahead and arranged to meet in Vegas for a 2-day weekend. The first night we met, he complained of a sore throat throughout the entire dinner. "Mollie, you must take me back to the hotel immediately! I need to rest and get to bed right away. I feel terribly sick!"

I felt trapped, for I committed to spending the weekend with him. The next night, we went for a divine dinner, starting with a yummy array of appetizers. Though, watching "Hypochondriac Guy" eating was making *me sick*. He was picking, plucking, rubbing, wiping, patting, dabbing, and cleaning everything that went into his "Sababa, Kawaza, Lashalla, Kabba, Monkeypox" mouth. After this bizarre food experience, we proceeded to a Vegas musical. I was thoroughly enjoying the show while trying to ignore this outlandish man sitting to my right. That is, until 20 minutes in, when Norm complained during the rest of the musical that he was nauseous and sweaty. He made me feel his forehead to check his temp. I kid you not.

After the show, he appeared panicked and insisted I take him to the hospital. Without a second thought, I drove him back to his hotel. Midway there, he announced in his distressed as usual voice, "I don't know which end it's going to come out of, but it's gonna be a huge disgusting mess!" I pondered for a sec. *It's gonna be a huge disgusting mess? Ah, yes,* I was livin' the dream.

Not a bridge I cared to cross! My dreamy romantic heart was not all aglow. I did not feel safe or cradled in a rainbow of love. But I let him think I cared and quickly dropped Norm off on his "Callaballa Bats, 98.6° temperature-less head." I was stunned, shaking my own cynical head in disbelief! I screeched away in my car, burning rubber like a cop answering a call to a shootout in progress, happily dodging his promised, huge disgusting mess.

These "Hypochondriac Guys" are forever dying. But they never do. Norman will outlive us all. Being objective, I believe they're just insecure little boys using their health to avoid reality and seeking much-needed compassion and attention!

Girls, Take a Pass Here! But hey, don't listen to me if this sounds like a good time to you or if it's your calling in life. Who am I to decide if you should or shouldn't enjoy being a nursemaid or a caregiver? Ultimately, it fulfilled and worked out nicely for Mother Teresa and Anne Sullivan!

Later, Norman surprisingly had the guts to call. His message was riddled with a nauseating fake cough. He said he had the best time and asked to go out with me again. (If you can believe that!)

I declined sweetly. "No, sorry Norm. I am so sick!" Cough-cough, sneeze-sneeze, and a runny nose filled with Monkeypox.

I never spoke to the *Grim Reaper again.*

A 98.6°, perfectly healthy, germ-free, *NEXT!*

6. THE "HYPOCRITE GUY"

I personally can't deal with and have no time or use for the "Hypocrite Guys." They say one thing and do another. They think one way and behave in another. The "Hypocrite Guy" can do whatever they want and it's perfectly fine! Subsequently, when someone else does the 'exact same thing,' he claims the individual is a horrible person. If you make a mistake about religion, politics, evil deeds, stealing, lying, cheating, work ethics, etc., you will be nailed to the cross. No matter what your religion happens to be, you will be raised high up on that cross. But don't even think of doing that to him. He religiously lives by the almighty hypocrisy standard. Here's the thing that really gets me about the irrational, unreasonably judgmental "Hypocrite Guy." He has no concerns, ramifications, consequences, boundaries, or acknowledgment of his unkind, unethical behavior. It seems he has a lifetime membership in the "Get-Out-Of-The-Double-Standard-Free Club!"

For fun, I'll share one of my encounters with the "Hypocrite Guy:"

Jerome was a horrible man, and I swiftly discovered he was also an alcoholic. But Jerome was in total denial about his disease. He blatantly made a comment with contempt and disdain on our one and only date, slurring his revolting words vehemently.

"Why the hell do I get cut off at a bar when the bartender feels I've had enough to drink? It's entirely illogical, biased, and unfair bullshit! Yet, a server never cuts off an overweight person, like *that fat-ass sitting over there*, no matter how much he wants to shovel into his obese mouth. He's telling me I can't have a drink, yet the corpulent, fatty over in the corner, breaking the chair, can stuff his 4-chinned, 500-pound pie-hole with all the grease, calories, and fat that he wants to? This is fucked-up and not okay. Yo, Bar Man, gimme another one! And make it snappy!"

As one can imagine, I wanted to duck & cover, as the lovely man overheard him and now appeared visibly hurt and offended. I replied with scorn and disgust at Jerome. "You are a drunk asshole, so I am cutting you off from me!" I jumped up and wandered over to the sweet man the alcoholic "Hypocrite Guy" viciously insulted. I looked at him graciously and said, "I deeply apologize, Sir." I asked to sit down and join him. We happily devoured three desserts. Yes, that happened! Here's to *a sober, compassionate high-calorie, Next!*

7. THE "HIGH MAINTENANCE GUY"

These "High Maintenance Guys" are basically not so bad and fundamentally harmless. Even though they put enormous pressure on themselves, they characteristically don't judge others with the same unattainable standards. Honestly, this is rather considerate of them. The bottom line? They want what they want and need what they need. At least they're candid and upfront about it. As long as they don't bother me, are courteous, not critical, and don't have a lot of demanding chutzpah (*Yiddish for Balls, big ones, pronounced with a lot of Chhaaaaas*), I can deal with them just fine.

I have a touch of this myself. I want my salad dressing on the side. I don't like sitting under a fan, or in the middle of a restaurant, by the kitchen, the bathroom, or at a table too close to the next table like in Europe (Unless I am in Europe!) If I am going to eat cake, I want a good piece. The one with the most icing on it, and not broken. I travel with my own pillow and blanket, even at a 5-star hotel. I want my hair blown out perfectly silky straight. I like my cold foods very cold, my hot foods very hot. In fact, I want my coffee burning hot. My Starbucks order is a Vente Café Latte, 190°, 5 Sweet N Low, and non-fat milk.

However, my biggest high-maintenance idiosyncrasy concerns my popcorn. I take my popcorn seriously. I get a bucket of popcorn, with no salt, no butter, and only the white pieces that come out of the popper halfway through the batch. My rationale is that it has less oil, which means fewer calories and fats. This way, I can add my Snow Caps, M&M's, or Milk Duds guilt-free. Hey, back off, I skip dinner so I can do this!

Truthfully, if you or the "High Maintenance Guys" are polite and courteous, I don't see any drawback to being fussy. Anyhow, I think you can try this guy on for size and see how he fits.

8. THE "PERFECTIONIST DEMANDING GUY"

With the "Perfectionist Demanding Guy," it's his way or the highway. This chap is frequently difficult, pejorative, critical, and highly disapproving of others. He is a clean freak from head to toe. And that goes for his car, his office, and his house. Speaking of which, his home (at all times) looks as though he expects the photographers from *"Better Homes & Gardens Magazine"* to come knocking at his door for the magazine's upcoming issue. With a photo shoot, cover photo, feature story, and all. If you decide to be considerate and clean any of his possessions, he will surely go over it again, insinuating you didn't clean it well enough. He's habitually controlling, challenging, arduous, judgmental, and a noticeably moody guy. He's your basic run-of-the-mill malcontent.

Political topics are paramount to him. So, you best agree with him on all matters, or things will get ugly fast. He can be fun, but only on his terms. Mr. Demanding is not spontaneous unless he plans everything right down to the last detail. Which is precisely why he isn't spontaneous. No matter how much you try, the "Perfectionist Demanding Guy" is hard to live with. You'll never please him or meet his unreasonable standards. It likely won't end well. BTW, this is precisely why you left home after graduation!

9. THE "SPORTS FANATIC GUY"

It's oodles of fun hanging out with the "Sports Fanatic Guy!" Predictably, he never misses any games. So, if you have the *"If you can't beat um, join um"* mentality, you could have a blast here. But if you don't *love* sports or can at least learn to enjoy them overnight, well, my dear, plan on spending lots of time with your friends on any given sports day. The real perk is the junk food and beer will always be plentiful and overflowing with this guy and his cheering pals. Unless you have a genuine passion for sports, intercept this guy, score elsewhere, and take a long Hail Mary Pass.

10. THE "SLOPPY PIG GUY"

This messy bloke is an all-around untidy man. I like to refer to him as *"The Disgusting, ick Guy!"* He is unpolished and a completely unsophisticated *sloboholic!* He rationalizes that clean clothes represent *very fancy attire.* Due to his appalling manners, he is embarrassing to go out to eat with. His atrocious table manners, lack of social graces, and poor etiquette skills make it difficult to enjoy a meal with him. He lives with very little protocol or discipline. Realistically, "The Sloppy Pig Guy" is basically a hodgepodge of unorganized chaos. There are dishes piled up in the sink (beware of a bug or 2), and ten loads of laundry lying about everywhere, waiting, and begging to be washed. There are leftover takeout containers scattered about in every room, needing to be tossed into the trash. Typically, there is no toilet paper on the roll, and you can count on a vile, nauseating, black ring around the bathtub and the toilet bowl, as well!

In his filthy world, it is perfectly fine to spit, fart, or burp aloud, anywhere, at any time. He'll find it hilarious to blame it on you, the dog, or even the bird. He might also suggest that stupid "pull my finger" thing before he farts. You will no doubt find the toilet seat continually being left up. So, when going to the bathroom in the middle of the night, girls, either be prepared to look first or fall in.

If you're his woman and you clean up after him, he won't acknowledge it and most likely won't even notice you have. He honestly imagines the Dish-Fairy flies by and places the dishes from the sink into the dishwasher, as if by fairy magic. This also applies to the Clothes-Fairy, who mysteriously picks up shirts, socks, underwear, and pants, and then puts them into the laundry bin. Doing laundry is not even a concern until he has absolutely nothing left to wear. He'll provide you with enough sloppy madness to last a lifetime and some to spare!

In an optimistic light, "The Sloppy Pig Guy" is usually loveable, sweet, easy to please, and rather harmless. If you live with him (And I interject, WHY?) cleaning will become a full-time job. If this isn't your dream job, and you still love him? Then fair warning, get a housekeeper. To spare your dignity, never go out together in public with your friends, family, or co-workers.

For giggles, I'd love to watch him hang out with "Hypochondriac germophobe, Guy." Talk about a wild "Joker VS. Batman" confrontation!

11. THE "DISGUSTING AND REPULSIVE GUY"

I have no tolerance for "The Disgusting and Repulsive Guy." For starters, he snores like a train is running through your bedroom. I mean it. The whole room shakes. He is constantly sweating, even in the winter and especially during sex. He is that guy who picks his nose at stoplights as if no one can see him, because he and his car are invisible. "The Disgusting and Repulsive Guy" bites his nails, chews with his mouth open, picks his sores, pops his zits, plays with his balls in public, and wears the same clothes over and over without washing them. Amazing, he never notices the stains.

On this topic, he is also that guy whose butt crack is fully exposed in his jeans whenever he bends down. He has chronic bad breath, rarely brushes his teeth, shaves occasionally, but still misses some spots, and wears bloody tissues on his razor cuts. (If he shaves at all.) He has wax hanging out his ears, battles with dandruff, flaky skin, and suffers (and so will you) from habitual B. O. Perhaps because he takes maybe one shower a week. I'm sick imagining it. This guy possesses many more bad traits, but I think you already get the dirt on him! So, thumbs down to TDARG. Just say no! FYI, here's a random thought about body odor? I think they should change the name Deodorant, to *"B-O-Dorant!"* Just saying...

12. THE "DOWNER GUY"

I guarantee the Donny "Downer Guy" is irrefutably one to avoid. He complains nonstop about everything under the sun, including the sun! This guy persistently whines, moans, sighs, groans, and typically in that order. All this moaning and groaning would be fine and dandy if it were during sex. But that's probably the only occasion he ever shuts the hell up.

His happy place is basking in the *"state of depression"* or frolicking in the center of a bottomless black hole. However, if he were Stephen Hawking, that would be a suitable and fitting happy place. "The Downer Guy" is all about suffering from the *"poor me, why me, and woe is me"* emotions. And if you hang with him, I guarantee it will also be, Poor, You!

'Sadness and misery' are his mottos.

'I'm so depressed' is his slogan.

'Have a nice day' is a dreadful, offensive, insulting suggestion.

'Negativity' is something he wraps his arms around with pleasure!

'The weeping willow' is his favorite tree.

'Crying' is a year-round sport and his daily aerobics exercise.

'The boy who cried wolf" is his mascot.

'Happiness and joy' are the enemies to be kept away at all costs!

'Disneyland,' to him, is the tragic equivalent of Hell on Earth.

'Laughter' is a product of the Antichrist.

I once spoke with an online "Downer Guy" and won't ever repeat that adventure again. Here is how the conversation went...

"Hi Ben, how are you? It's a pleasure to speak with you!"

"Me too. I guess? We're experiencing a terrible storm. It sucks. My computer crashed, so I couldn't email you. I hate this weather!"

"No worries, I get that. So, Ben, tell me. What fantastic and exciting things are going on in your life?"

"My wife divorced me and completely destroyed me financially." ("I'm thinking, can you blame her?") My lawyer was also part of the conspiracy. My business partner is suing me for something I didn't do. I was fired last month from my job after 13 years of loyalty. Thus, I'm being evicted from my house. My kids are behaving disrespectfully and horribly toward me. ("I can't blame them!") I think I hate them and the rest of my family, too. I'm worried that I'm getting dementia. All my friends have now abandoned me. ("Again, can you blame them?") I don't know how my wife could walk off with all my money and cheat on me with my stockbroker. And, as a parting gift, she gave me an STD. My balls itch and burn all the time. I also just found out the IRS is auditing me. Our country has gone to shit. I despise our government and all our politicians. Clearly, I hate America, too. And furthermore, I really hate…"

"Bye Bye now, Ben! Good luck with your balls and all the rest of it. Oh, and by the way, God Bless America!"

Hell, No and… Click!!!!

13. THE "MOMMA'S BOY." WHO IS ALSO THE "I WILL NEVER LOVE YOU AS MUCH AS I LOVE MY KIDS, GUY"

No further explanation needed here, girls! His title describes all you need to know, now or forever. Walk Away! You're actually better off with the Downer or the Disgusting guys. And how much does that suck?

14. THE "ANGRY, VIOLENT, ABUSIVE GUY"

This right here is totally self-explanatory. The Jekyll & Hyde Guy catches and snags you up into his web with his deceptive, delightful charms. Once you are caught in his trap, the awful nightmare begins. Dr. Charming climbs his nasty web like a spider and vanishes up the waterspout. You are now left with the bastard, real guy, Hyde, who in every way is wickedly abusive. He seeks out your weaknesses and preys upon them. "The Angry, Violent, Abusive Guy" is a predator who'll continuously watch you with his 4 pairs of eyes. You'll never have a day of peace or happiness with this man once he captures you as his prey. You were not born to love him, so dash away from his web of tricky deceit. There's nothing positive, fun, or good about a relationship with this cruel Spider-Man. You'd need a fiery femme fatale to straighten up this devious Itsy-Bitsy Spider's ass. So run, and don't look back!

15. THE "HEALTHY... I.E. VEGAN GUY"

Personally, I've got a problem and a big plate of angst with these veggie men. I question, where did all the good, respectful meat and potato guys go? I need to know. Were they shipped off to the "Red meat, lamb chops, pork ribs, chicken, Bon appétit, Anti Vegan, Beef Planet?"

I could never hang with the Mr. tree-hugging, vegan guys. Yes, of course, I'm a green person concerned about our planet as much as the next guy. Still, I also appreciate humans are the highest in the food chain. So, I am eating it all, and that's all I'm saying. These vegan and vegetarian health freaks don't eat pizza, meat, fish, eggs, cheese, chicken, bread, sugar, coffee, alcohol, ice cream, milk, pasta, honey, and so forth. I find this scary. I heard those foods are believed to be "the sustenance of Satan" to vegans. How does one possibly go through life without all the many wonderful food choices? "The Healthy, I.E. Vegan Guys," are missing a lot of food fun, and to me, they are food boring. Come on vegans, I swear you all look so pale and tooth-pasty. You, colorless-looking "veganites" with your tofu, beans, nuts, bars, seeds, fruits, veggies, avocado, hummus, carrots, and fresh-squeezed juice drinks, need to cut the absurdity. Have you ever stopped to consider that it also hurts carrots and radishes when they are pulled out from the ground by their roots, and other vegetables and fruits, while you're at it?

Sorry, but I want and need my chemicals, sugars, and trans fats. I love waking up to a fresh cup of coffee and a warm muffin. I know more people who *"eat it all"* and live to 95 than I know of any vegans that live that long. And if they do, they've surely missed out on a lot of great food!

Their slogan is, "Meatless, not flavorless." That is some serious denial there. No one believes the hype that your pumpkin ravioli is considered pasta or even delicious. Your grandiose names to make your dreary foods come to life, like "vegetarian feast" are veggie nonsense. Do you really think you're kidding anyone with your fancy names? Roasted Brussels sprouts with pecans, butternut squash burger, or spicy two-bean chili. I mean, I love vegetables too. *But as a side dish, like God intended!*

Well, I say, "Where's the beef?" I want my N.Y. Sirloin Steak, lobster, rack of lamb, and fries with Russian dressing on them.

You vegans want a feast? Go have some spicy buffalo chicken wings, pasta with vodka sauce, topped with melted mozzarella cheese, fillet mignon, and shrimp scampi, paired with a nice bottle of wine. Have a happy ending with a huge ice cream delight, hot fudge, and Oreo Cookie crumbs sprinkled on top. I'm not advocating for you eat this way daily. I'm merely saying, live a little and back away from the tofu. You, so-called healthy guys, look so visibly uptight and it's obvious you are hungry for some real food. What you're eating is making you unhappy, whether you realize it or not. There's a reason why they call it *veg out*. You, vegans, are too weak and have no choice but to veg out.

FYI, all the latest studies on meat have changed.

People, if you prefer to be a vegan, that's fine. But appreciate you'll be limiting many food pleasures and enjoyable eating experiences. Particularly when traveling. Oh, for goodness' sake, I'm not saying to rush out and eat bats and rats at a wet market in China. As a carnivore, eating next to a vegan with their lettuce and bean soup is painful to watch. What can they say? "Yum, this bean sprout is delectable?" You want delectable? Have some Osso Buco!

I've decided a vegan man is a definite deal-breaker for me!

Nevertheless, without being overly hasty here, *if he's sexy, gorgeous, and spectacular in bed, then forget everything I said above.* Ignore it all! Bring your celery, carrots, beets, tofu, avocados, pull back the covers and jump right in. That's the great thing about being a *"Hypo-vegan-crite,"* girl. A *sexy, gorgeous, guy who is spectacular in bed* can break all the rules… broccoli or not!

16. THE "I KNOW EVERYTHING AND HAVE EXPERIENCED EVERYTHING ABOUT EVERYTHING GUY"

Honestly, this guy will drive you entirely mad with his *"know-it-all attitude."* You will never have a chance to know anything more than he does. Or rather, he thinks he does. He never ceases ranting and smothering you with his obnoxious know-how and his *"been there, done that"* stance. This guy will make you want to jump out of a 30-story building, regardless that it's not on fire! It's tough to be around him for any length of time. You'll need the patience of a saint to get through a date with him, let alone a lifetime.

I went out with this bombastic guy *Marcus for a year, 'One Night!'* OMG, he presented a tsunami of pugnacious attitude with me. The mere memory of the Marcus fiasco irritates me to this day.

We arranged to get together at Michael's, my favorite restaurant in Vegas. We met at the restaurant's bar. It started out nicely enough for 3 and 1/2 minutes. I couldn't help but notice as we said our hellos that Marcus had on so much cologne, it was like being at the Bloomingdale's perfume and fragrance counter during the Christmas season. As a romantic gesture (which was very nice), he brought me 2-dozen pink roses. But, alas, when he leaned in to kiss my cheek, he scratched my face from his freshly grown stubble. It all went crashing downhill from there. Crashing hard, like a computer. Girls, you know this sort of guy, I'm certain of it.

Regardless, I thanked him warmly. "Nice roses."

He brazenly announced, "I know everything there is to know about roses. You see, my mother imported them every week from Italy for our home while I was growing up!"

"Oh, how nice," I managed to fit in, wondering if the 2-dozen pink roses were from his mother. Then, smiling happily, (feeling the onset of a rash on my cheek from his peck) I ordered a glass of Sauvignon Blanc.

"Wait," he wildly intruded. "I owned wine vineyards in Napa years ago. I can tell you anything you ever wanted to know about wines. Allow me, if you will, to order you a superior white wine."

"Ah, umm," I objected. "Just a glass of the house Sauvignon Blanc, for right now, would be nice! Thank you, though."

"But Mollie, I can order you a far better, much tastier wine!"

"No thank you," and attempted to continue. "I just saw a superb Broadway musical last week, and... ..."

"You know what?" He rudely jumped in before I could complete my sentence to state which musical. "I was an investor in N.Y. producing Broadway shows. Later, I went to London to... ..."

Naturally, I had to return his interruption and change what seemed to be his 50th, bragging topic. "It's strange, I am currently on a peanut butter for breakfast kick. I just love... ...."

And yet again, Marcus impolitely interrupted. "Funny, I owned a peanut butter factory 10 years ago. We made the famous small, packaged peanut butter snacks with jelly. It's the best recipe around. It's the one my grandmother invented."

No matter what topic I brought up, Marcus was either part of it, an authority on it, or owned it. Allegedly! Shifting themes (and wondering if this man, with his obvious juggernaut ego, might only have a causal relationship with the truth), I asked. "I'm curious Marc. Who do you think will win the fight tonight at the MGM?"

"My brother's a pro-boxing coach. But I taught him everything he knows. I know for certain who will win. Nevertheless, it now bores me so much I didn't even bet the fight." I'm thinking loudly in my head, Whoop-De-Doo. If I knew who'd win for certain, I'd so take that bet! Like, duh!

Twenty endless minutes later, when we were escorted to our table, he was still talking peanuts. Trying with all my might to change the subject. "Anyway, Mr. Flower, vineyard, peanut butter, Broadway, boxer Guy, how about those Dodgers?"

He interjected with an expert tone. "Girl, I was part-owner of the Dodgers back in the day. I also... ...."

I simply couldn't take another single one of his, *"I Know Everything and Have Experienced Everything About Everything,"* confessions. I think he said about 2 thousand, 3 hundred, and 36 of them. And that was even before the main course.

I went on, hoping to stump him. "Gee, Marcus, did you ever perform at Carnegie Hall?" No surprise, this bigheaded showoff wasn't baffled, and his response was as long-winded as usual.

"No, I've never performed there personally, but I have conducted the orchestra there more than a few times!"

Chatter and more chatter. And just like that, I gave up. He went on and on, rambling and bragging so much, that I started hearing the sounds the parents used to communicate with, in the Peanuts Cartoon TV shows. *"Mwahmwahmwah, wah wah mwah!"* (BTW, it's a trombone with the rubber end of a toilet plunger over the instrument's bell.) That's the noise I heard now instead of Mr. Know-it-all. If I brought it up, he likely would've said he invented the sound and performed it on the cartoon's soundtrack.

He claimed to know all about who, what, when, where, why, and everything else in the world. Secretly, I was laughing, thinking, if I could only put duct tape over his mouth, the evening might turn out better for both of us. Well, certainly for *me!* The air was thick with frustration. With all my obnoxious heart, I suppressed my garish offensive urge to ask him questions about famous unsolved mysteries. I'd start this war off, 'Bow-and-Arrow, Viking style.'

"Marcus, tell me, who really shot Kennedy?

Where was O. J. Simpson's other glove and did it really fit?

What really happened to Jimmy Hoffa, and where is he now?

How were the Egyptian pyramids built?

Do you know The Loch Ness Monster personally? What's he like?

By whom, how, and why did Stonehenge get built?

I assume you also knew Jesus. So, was he really all that? Was Jesus Christ of Nazareth fun to hang with? Were his miracles as awesome as they say? Was it his face in the shroud? Was his mom truly a virgin?

On the Lost City of Atlantis, surely you were there. How was it?

How many extraterrestrials have you encountered? Where did you meet the E.T. aliens? What planet are they from? What did they look like?

What really happened with the SS Ourang Medan, otherwise known as the Man from Medan?"

I desperately would have loved to ask those questions and more, just to see his puzzled face! Irritated as I was, I couldn't handle how he would have claimed to know all the answers.

By the time we got to dessert, I figured out a way to shut him up, once and for all. I stood firm and went charging right through that shiny, uncouth, arrogant door of his.

Abruptly, I informed him. "Marcus, there is a new line of vibrators out on the market that makes the Lelo Smart Wand, or the Rabbit, seem like a turtle." Finally, silence! He was sorely perplexed.

And then off he went, like a runner hearing the starting pistol at the Chicago Marathon. "Interesting you mentioned that? I have a dear friend named Harley, and we used both of our huge penises for vibrator molds. I used to market toys. And not toys for tots either. Ha-ha-ha-ha-ha!"

Ewe! Just gross, and way too much-uninvited knowledge.

Next, this self-righteous, egotistical animal, out of left field, said to me, *"Hey, Sugarplum, you make my cock feel young, which is now driving me crazy and making me have to cum all over you."*

"And game over!"

Dumbfounded, I instantaneously understood it was do-or-die time. Let me tell you, this feisty girl wasn't about to die! Disgusted and sick to my stomach from this smarty-pants creep, I made an, "I Know Everything, and Have Experienced Everything About Everything," decision of my own. *Without fuss or fanfare*, I left the flowers on the table and excused myself to go to the ladies' room. But instead, I excused myself all the way to valet parking, picked up my car, and split! I ran away as fast as a puppy chases a ball with peanut butter smeared on it. And not from his bogus companies, famous, small, packaged peanut butter snacks with jelly. Seriously,

I don't care how much cologne Marcus wore, because he couldn't cover up the stench from all his scary flying bullshit. I drove home like a maniac and sprinted into the shower. I couldn't wash him off me fast enough. *And we only had dinner!*

Because I had escaped Marcus and left him sitting there alone, I wondered how long it took him to discover I had gone. If he ever did!

I have come to learn, through the process of dating, and much to my dismay… *"Planet Earth is the psycho ward for the universe!"*

Oh, just great! Dammit, I noticed a blotchy, huge pink rash on my face from his stubble. I knew it was impossible to get out unscathed. And, By the Way… No one calls me *Sugarplum* and gets away with it!!!!

"A very loud, Mwahmwahmwah, wah wah mwah,
I know everything there is to know in the whole world…" Next!

CHAPTER 6

The Rock Star

ALSO KNOWN AS A GREAT LOVE, SAVIOR, AND A DIVINE, TRUE LOVE STORY

Truthfully, after all I had been through, nothing, not an ounce of feeling, could seep through the emotional wall of protection I had built. Frankly, I was proud of this illustrious mental Berlin Wall which I masterfully created one brick at a time, all by my little ole self. I was exceedingly careful not to pile the bricks directly onto the soft, uneven ground of emotions. This wall was bitch-solid and built on an unstoppable broken-heart foundation.

Yet, miraculously, Sebastian effortlessly made me believe in love again and kicked down my rigid, huge, brick wall of security. Somehow, he astonishingly crashed it down, like *Thor*. He didn't even need or bother to use his hammer. I found him to be my most unexpected miracle. He gently put back together all the broken pieces of my heart that were still shattered from Bobble Drew-in-the-box and all the other traumatizing men. At first, I thought he was too old for me. I came to realize sometimes age doesn't matter, and I quickly fell hopelessly in love with Sebastian. This 48-year young superhero of a man was completely exquisite and altogether luscious. BTW, Sebastian is not his real name. I so enjoy dreaming up names and royal titles for him.

FAST BACKWARDS...
ALLOW ME TO REWIND AND GO BACK IN TIME...
(LIKE IT'S A BOOK, YOU HAVE NO CHOICE!)

Sebastian is a world-famous, well-loved, British, Mega Rock Star. I lovingly call him, "My Rocket-Man." Let it go! It's an Elton John thing between us. Only without all the flamboyant glitz & flash. To fill you in, Rocket-Man has attained the same level of fame and success as Elton enjoys, perhaps even more. This man is a brilliant, impressive artist, entertainer, and an extraordinary rock legend. To say the least, Sebastian is a celebrated iconic superstar.

I say with a heartfelt, protective smile that it is important and necessary to be discreet about the identity of Rocket-Man. Out of enormous respect and the virtue of safeguarding and cherishing this secret knowledge only for us, I'll forever keep his iconic identity private. Moreover, and using the Queen's English, (Gee, I miss her!) it's not my thing to kiss & tell. That is, of course, you are one of my best friends. Then it will all be divulged like an overflowing, endless open book. Nonetheless, strictly in the vault!

I met Rocket-Man online. If you can believe that? He contacted me first. He willingly explained to me why he succumbed to this bizarre dating method. In a nutshell, he didn't want women to desire him merely for his famous rock star status. He wanted to be loved and appreciated, not only for his well-known, massively cool persona, and fame, but for his heart and the person he truly is.

Sebastian has always been skeptical and distrusting of women's motives and agendas toward his stardom and wealth. I must confess, I can't disagree with his rationale. He once simplified it for me. "I am more than a rock star. That is just what I do and not who I am in my soul." This statement alone explains how genuine and unpretentious this man is.

Coincidently, a month before getting his "Ello there" email, (The "H" is silent in his British accent!) I had accepted a great gig in London for a major American Magazine. Regrettably, I'm not at liberty to reveal which magazine it is that rhymes with lime. I was assigned to write several feature stories on royalty and all that it entails. What a lucky break and a super opportunity for us to meet. How fortunate to be able to "enjoy two birds with one stone!"

I'd like to state, I don't care much for the phrase, "killing two birds with one stone." Dreadful. I don't believe anyone should kill birds, let alone two of them, and even worse, at the same time, with one stone! Hideous.

For weeks after taking this intriguing assignment, I had clandestinely been speaking to "Prince Dudley," aka Sebastian. It was lovely and effortless, communicating and getting to know and trust one another. Although it did take quite a while for him to feel safe enough to trust me with his real identity. He seemed relieved and pleased that I was more infatuated with the man he was, rather than the celebrity rocker we all revere and are in awe of. Perhaps, because I interview and meet so many famous people and celebrities, his fame didn't overwhelm me in the least. Odd, even before

I began my career, I've never been star-struck. But talent and sexy on the other hand? Now that, I find hugely impressive.

Twelve days, a shopping spree, and some major impatient anticipation later, I was on a plane headed for London, England. After a long, tedious flight, 30 minutes before landing, I downed a cup of terrible, cold, black airplane coffee. Then, I headed to the bathroom to freshen my makeup and change my comfy travel clothes into my very trendy glad rags, and Christian Louboutin heels. After ignoring oodles of impatient banging on the lavatory door, I felt happy with my appearance. I was ready, and all glammed up as if I were going to some big Hollywood soirée. Although, I was indeed, going to something far more amazing.

"Sir Arthur," AKA Sebastian (See where I am going with this? Stay with me!), sent a car to pick me up at Heathrow Airport and drive me to his (as always), sold-out concert. I was bursting with nervous, intoxicating exhilaration. Barely able to contain my excitement and enthusiasm, I could hardly believe this fantasy was happening. "Ah, spontaneity. The exquisite freedom of the unexpected!"

While walking out of customs, dragging my awesome trendy luggage, I rejoiced and grinned ecstatically. "Oh, My God, I'm in London!" Still, in total disbelief, I immediately spotted a very British-looking driver, wearing a dark suit, white gloves, cap, and all. He was holding up a card with my name, beautifully written in gold cursive letters. He gracefully reached for my bags, rescuing me from any further strain. With his proper British accent, wearing a huge, delightful grin, he spoke softly and professionally.

"I've got it, Miss!"

I whispered back, super relieved, "You are so kind. Thank you!"

Nodding warmly, "I am Redmond, Miss. Welcome to London!"

Smiling with appreciation, I happily replied, "Nice to meet you, Redmond. And please, call me Mollie."

Unfortunately, my flight was over an hour late due to the typical London Fog. By the time I arrived at the arena, those precious lost moments afforded Sebastian and me only a minuscule amount of time to meet in his dressing room. He brought me to his chest, tenderly gave me a bear-hug, gazed deep into my eyes, and affectionately kissed me on the cheek before dashing onto the stage. Self-conscious, I feared he heard the girly-girl sounds of my heartbeat pounding out of my chest.

Seconds later, I was startled when he quickly returned with an endearing grin, shouting out. "Luv, I am so bloody glad you are here! And by the way, you are even more breathtaking in person! See you from the stage, sweet angel." He blew a kiss, winked, and ran swiftly off, beaming.

Gushing, shaking, (and needless to say) that was enough, and all it took for the sparks of enchantment to transpire. I was alone with him for only a few seconds, yet when our eyes met, I felt as if I had known him all my life. Despite floating on Cloud 9, my chick behavior was super embarrassing.

Watching him as he bolted onto the stage, his long hair flowing down over his outrageous costume, I was overwhelmed with emotions of fascination and euphoria. Then it hit me, realizing this extraordinary *meet-cute* was so unfair. I was standing on unequal ground, as he had a major home-field advantage. I felt like a Red Sox fan in Yankee Stadium. Suddenly, an OMG, just pinch me now moment, came over me. Here I was, listening to this renowned rock star I have admired for... for... Forever! What's more, there I sat in London's Wembley Arena, watching my new love interest performing and singing with his incredible recognizable voice, along with his outstanding group of musicians. Right there before me, front row center, his iconic hits went on endlessly throughout the concert. I couldn't stop myself from feeling a powerful horny twinge, intensifying with each song. I was not awe-struck, but I was indeed love-struck and smitten to the max. Gush, totally shameful. Super gush! (Thinking, "Mollie, stop this right now!")

This experience landed me right in the center of a make-believe story, only I was the real-life princess in this fable. Bloody Hell, I should have brought my tiara. And I knew it, too! After all, this is London, home of the princesses! And besides, not to brag, I look entirely fierce in it! As my mind returned to reality, Rocket-Man, aka "King William," without missing a beat of his music, sent my soul soaring. Mind you, this is not a result of his fame or thousands of screaming, cheering fans. Rather, my heart beamed from the way he looked into my eyes from the stage, as if he had known me all his life. I had no other choice but to surrender to his alluring irresistible charms! I was towering high up in the fluffy London rain clouds each time he reached down from the stage to touch my shaky hands. The groupie girls shrieked and screamed each time he bent down to kiss me. Little did they know, I was getting much more than that later in the night. At least, I hoped!

This Princess, without her tiara, wanted him to perform in, around, and on my very own personal stage. This wondrous, unimaginable online story, I jubilantly admit, is nothing short of a real-life fairytale. I am well-aware this will sound absurd, but regardless, I *knew* this man. I *knew* his heart. This innate, knowing feeling was burning inside my soul.

Right before the concert ended, a member of his team frightened me when he abruptly grabbed my arm, ordering me to move speedily. I was reassured when I heard through his earpiece that the man was escorting me to be reunited with my new man. Sebastian took my hand while we were whisked away rapidly through the backstage exit before the fans began to gather. Several intimidating men rushed us to his prestigious celebrity chauffeur-driven, shimmering ultra-stretch limousine. We screeched away frantically, as the quirky driver yelled out, "Bugger off and cheerio," to the paparazzi quickly approaching and the groupies screaming out of control. As this was a common occurrence for Sebastian, he chuckled, amused. Dizzy from my head hovering up in the clouds, I realized this was the full Monty. (But without the striptease.) I was definitely unprepared for any of this. Especially since we met on a *daft, online dating site, For Queen's Sake!!!!*

Part of me felt right at home with all this ado. No doubt the part that should be wearing my diamond-faux tiara. But as for the rest of me, on my down-to-earth side, I felt pretentious and awkward. *Nevertheless*, being a chameleon, it's something I could and would wholeheartedly be willing to get used to. "Prince Valiant" and I sat in the absurdly lavish limo with our hands held tightly together as one. Throughout the drive, I didn't have a clue as to where we were heading, nor did I care. It appeared we were now affectionately glued to each other. My infatuated eyes left his only once when I noticed we were driving on the wrong side of the road. And the driver was sitting on the wrong side of the car, as well. My Rock

Prince effortlessly strolled into my heart, whispering in my ear, "Sweet Mollie, I realize this sounds ludicrous, but I know you're going to bring me out from the shadows of my soul." My dancing emotions struggled to stay calm. I remained silent, blushing coyly, but really, who was I kidding?

Meanwhile, 40 minutes later, the limo went down a cobblestone entrance and arrived directly in front of a palace. I swear to God, I thought we arrived at Buckingham Palace. I was literally looking for the entire royal family, particularly William and Kate. I was concerned, as I hadn't perfected a royal curtsy yet. Sadly, the notion made me think of HRH, Queen Elizabeth, and my beloved Princess Diana. But let's not unpack that now.

My thoughts were interrupted as my beguiling rocker gently announced, "We're home, princess."

I responded with a very girly, "Awww," with a high-pitched lilt on the tail. When the chauffeur opened the door, Sebastian gallantly swept me up into his arms like a baby. Besides Drew, I didn't think men did that Richard Gere, "An Officer and A Gentleman" debonair move anymore. I swooned with an astonishing cocktail of emotions. Yes, I Swooned! What the hell? He carried me to the entrance of his palace and his butler let us in. Bollocks, I said Butler as if it were a typical, everyday norm.

For those of you who don't speak *"Privileged"* (And who does?), this man owns a palatial palace, lives in baronial splendor, and has a butler! He's an iconic rock star. Why wouldn't he? Gee, I wasn't thinking. Nor was I thinking saying the word Swooned. And twice!

OK, so then, the butler (I simply had to repeat that for the fun of it, and its entertainment value) was wearing your traditional movie wardrobe, butler attire. He sported a black and gray pinstriped tux with tails, initialed cufflinks, a bow tie, crisp white gloves, a handkerchief in his pocket, and a red carnation in his lapel. You know, your mainstream, commonplace butler garb that we all typically see every day? Or perhaps, like never?

Truthfully, I couldn't believe what I was witnessing. Oh, how I desperately needed a friend or 2, (or 3) at that very moment! No, really, I did! I was dying to call Shara, Elizabeth, or Debbie right then and there. Still, I knew even the first tier of my very best friends wouldn't believe this story. Dammit, I frantically needed a friend to giggle with and roll my eyes at. Oh, no! Oh, no, it's happening! I could not stop myself from opening my sarcastic mouth. Whilst looking up at my lord, out came, "Oh, come on! I mean, seriously? The butler's outfit is so Charles Carson, in *"Downton Abbey."* Sir Anthony Hopkins as Mr. Stevens, in *"Remains of the Day."* Or Brimsley, the Queen's butler in "Bridgerton!" I gasped, smiling adoringly at "Duke Alexander of Englandville."

He merely roared with laughter, stating, "I know beautiful, but it's an English uniform tradition." Sebastian went on affectionately referring to his butler. "*Sir Henry* has been with me for over twenty years and proudly insists on the whole traditional British pomp-and-circumstance attire thing. I'm ashamed to admit it, but I don't even notice it anymore!" He affectionately leaned down to kiss me, still laughing. "I suppose, lovely angel, my detachment makes it all the worse, doesn't it?"

Being myself, as usual, and risking it all, I responded with, "Ya think?" He continued laughing aloud. I looked at him with wonder, reasoning what a joyously spectacular man he was! I replied, adding, "Ah-ha, yes, I surely would indeed always notice the whole British pomp-and-circumstance attire thing." I timidly proceeded to return his gentle kiss.

Making matters more pompous (take my word they couldn't be!), Sir Henry, the "*Downton Abbey*" wanna-be butler, announced, clearing his throat, "Pardon, Sir! A prepared feast awaits you both in the Dining Hall."

Thank goodness, this go around, I had my wits about me enough to close my mouth, which had now fallen open. Nevertheless, I unwittingly blurted out, in my typical American, are you kidding me, approach. "Umm, Rocket-Man, A Dining Hall? And you are good with that? For real?"

Gratefully, and for some strange reason, all my obnoxious teasing and sarcasm tickled his fancy, continuing to amuse him.

He turned and replied to the fancy butler. "Yes, Henry, we will be there shortly. I'd like to show Mollie the rest of the house first."

"*Of course. As you wish, master!*"

I'm thinking to myself, "*As you wish, master?* Henry, you're killing me!" Utterly Bowled over, *#Asyouwishmaster?* Oh, please! That needs to be monogrammed on a pillow. In gold! I can't even.

Walking about his palace, which was ginormous (far from a house) all I could think was, why would a man without children need 24 bedrooms? I giggled, considering, if he installed extensive zip-line equipment throughout the palace, it would make it easier to move around his dynasty. Meanwhile, sitting in the Dining Hall,

further bewildered as his gentleman's gentleman and three servants brought in tray after tray after tray of gourmet delicacies and
sweets. (BTW, expressing that third, 'after tray' is necessary and
warranted.) Rock Star or not, this was way excessive and far more
than privileged. (Reminding you again, this is a true story!)

Thenceforward, like a choreographed dance, they all glided
silently out of the Dining Hall. Yep, these servants glided away
and quite possibly floated, as well. Much in the same way, a hot-air
balloon glides and floats, except lower to the ground and indoors.
I explained my confusion to Sebastian with absolutely no class or
elegance whatsoever. And more to the point, undiplomatically!

"Sebastian, when you said there was food awaiting our arrival,
I anticipated fish & chips, fried chicken tenders, or biscuits and
crumpets from a pub around the corner. Please tell me you don't eat
like this every day. On second thought, don't answer that!"

He laughed exuberantly, replying, "Luv, you are so very refreshing and charmingly funny! Your whimsical personality enter-
tains me so!"

"Dude, I mean "Andrew, Dude of Edmonton." Is this your standard, everyday normal?" (Unsure I was ready for his answer.)

With his warmhearted innocence, and a nod of his head, he
humbly smiled. Beaming, he took my hand in his. "My precious
girl, I so adore you!" (And take my word for it, that sounded far
sexier with a British accent.) He gently brushed my lower lip with
his fingertip and kissed me passionately. Wow, double wow, and
mic drop! That was the sweetest kiss, the likes of which I had never
known. He's positively all that and a bag of hit records.

Even so, I couldn't understand how Sebastian, "The Duke of
Earl," managed to slip into my soul so quickly and easily. I paused for
a moment to examine what I was feeling for this unique, astonishing

man. Was I infatuated, enamored, bewitched? I don't know what overcame me, yet I was aware I affected him precisely the same way. Our hearts were working in concert with each other. We were in tune and instantaneously touched each other deeply in the theater of romance. We shared an immediate trust and a feeling of *home.* Since Drew, I haven't been able to give my heart freely, and I swore to myself I never would. Yet, in just one night, I was powerless, unable to resist his genuine goodness and tenderness. Paralyzed by our powerful chemistry and the pheromones flying between us, it was all so intense and luminous.

As the servants floated back into the hall periodically, I felt somewhat embarrassed as they could clearly see the romance dust sparkling about from our twinkling passion and emotions. I wondered if this was a frequent occurrence here in the palace. From the looks of it, my prince was not affected by their stares or grins, in the least. As much as I tried to act demure, I couldn't manage it. Instead, I returned his gentle kiss right back. And there it was, so to speak. The OOPS... "The rabbit, out of the hat trick." My kingly rocker now displayed in his trousers (pants in England) a royal gift, which brought me back to the present, causing me to flush. His enchanting, imperial stiffened bulge, now crushed between his legs, could only be equated to a very majestic happy evening! I hoped the servants hadn't noticed his rising joy. Although I couldn't have been more delighted.

At that moment, I jolly-well considered and reflected upon my choices. The whole lot of them. So, I pondered! Yes. *I'm pondering now! I am a proud, newbie pondering and Swooning person. How scary is that?*

1. To be perfectly blunt, I was excruciatingly in dire need of sex!

It was, ya know, at this point vital, essential, physically, and medically necessary!

2. Next, I contemplated. "How often does an American girl, (besides Meghan Markle, Wallis Simpson, and Princess Grace) get to see and touch the huge, brilliant, dazzling, imperial, British Crown Jewels? Like never! Still, I unequivocally didn't want to appear aggressive or forward."

3. Although, keeping in mind (and in my defense), I was essentially sent to England in search of a story on royalty and all it entails. Well, by golly, I aimed to get every inch of that royal story. Including all the ins & the outs, the whole big, long story, in stiff detail, from the top to the bottom of him. I mean, of royalty! After all, I am a serious, dedicated, in-depth reporter. I will meticulously get my hard story, even if it's from a different royal angle. To be fair, he is in the end, and the fullness of time, Rock Royalty. That must count. Doesn't it?

In the philosophical words of Philip Treacy, *"Royalty is completely different than celebrity. Royalty has a magic all its own."*

Indeed, Rocket-Man was regally magical all on his own. And let me state clearly, before you go judging me. Any girl (and many men) who saw this hunk of a man, whether they knew who he was or not, would unquestionably go all the way down on his "Big Ben," too! There was not a doubt in my mind that I quickly needed his "London Bridges" to come "falling down!" I promise I struggled with all my might to resist him. Well, at least I attempted to wait for the second night till I naughtily and mischievously let him have his entire way with me. Though possibly, it was the other way around! It's confusing? My point is... I didn't want to appear easy, like a common 'ho' or a crazed groupie. Thus, I only toyed with him for a few hours. Quite feasibly, it was only minutes. OK, not at all! I didn't toy! Whatever? So, sue me! Bollocks again, I shouldn't be hemmed in by my scruples and ethics. Come on now. You can appreciate how this was a rare, unprecedented situation brewing.

Before I knew it, Sebastian chivalrously, for the second time tonight, swooped me up into his arms and carried me into his private, royal, palatial chambers. *In the States, we call this "His bedroom!"* The stunning enchantment of this anticipated electrifying sexual experience, with this new man (who I already adored), completely disarmed me. My heart pounded rapidly as I watched him light a few scented candles and put on a romantic playlist he had made. I was just short of being naked on his bed, wearing only a sexy pink Dior satin-laced bra, with a matching thong. After all, (and being considerate) I had to leave him something to take off. I was quietly freaking out with an abundance of horny anticipation. Walking towards me with his perfectly toned, statuesque, tanned body, sporting his *very large, hard penis*, caught me off-guard. I smiled bashfully. Blinded by his captivating smirk he sighed, "Mollie, you're gorgeous! You are the sexiest woman I've ever known. I want you. I must have you now!"

I didn't care if he was being truthful. I wanted him, too. For sure, I was toast! Real toast. Not the fake, gluten-free crap, either.

And just like that, I was in heaven as we rolled around his bed, kissing passionately, naked in each other's arms. It was all I hoped it would be. My eyes shut tightly as my body trembled with desire. I felt him caress every part of me. He didn't miss an inch. When I tried to join in, he uttered. "Relax. My Luv, enjoy!"

After the longest, sexiest foreplay, he entered me… *almost* gently.

He placed his hands on my hips, thrusting in and out at his own pace. His rhythm quickened and danced, emulating a symphonic orchestra. Panting breathlessly, I desperately tried not to let my orgasm fly this quickly. Feeling out of exquisite control, he pulled me even closer, fucking me intensely. It was overwhelming. I moaned deeply, like the tuba in his orchestra. Begging him to fuck me harder, he stopped and pulled out just long enough to drive me wild. He giggled impishly. Pleading, I frantically insisted, "Technical foul! Please, come back inside me!"

Like the cheap, but ultra-classy slut I had rapidly become, I savored every move, touch, feeling, and moment of this erotic, lustful, naughty, and real-life fucking-fantasy. His sex was like nothing I had felt before. It was as if his passion and hunger were swallowing me whole. The newness of our union was innocent, beautiful, and yet lovingly licentious.

With his masculine, guitar-strumming hand, he rubbed my clit artistically, making my vagina flutter and twitch. With perfect timing, he glided back inside my yearning body. Feeling my convulsing, wet pussy around his big, plump cock caused him to glow proudly. Such wild freedom, without restraint or old-world taboos, triggered my whole body to quiver with his every touch. He thrust his shaft deeper and deeper inside me, up against my pulsating, warm, vagina. I wailed as he thoroughly ravaged me. "FUUUCCK!" I bellowed out a sultry sigh and exploded.

Quite pleased, he affirmed happily. "That's 'one,' baby!"

I jumped on him, straddling and rocking back and forth as my long blonde hair tumbled down across his chest. He laughed, insinuating, "Ah-ha, so you *want to* lead this dance, don't you? No way, princess!" Sebastian forced me off him and rolled back on top of me. I could feel the weight of his amazing body pinning me down.

Breathless beneath him, I caressed his balls slowly in my hand. His *purring, hmmmm* sounds assured me that he wanted it. "That feels so good, baby! Don't stop!" I placed my other hand behind the nape of his neck, under his beautiful long hair, keeping in sync with his musical movements. I loved looking up at his stunningly chiseled face, watching him as he watched me, and feeling his sexual talents as he made love. He forced my pelvis to move up and down with him, making my toes curl. The delicate way he touched my breasts and pinched my nipples drove me crazy. The way he expertly swayed back & forth so skillfully caused me to cling to him wildly. When he drove himself harder into me, I whined with unimaginable pleasure. Wanting him, as I did, gave him complete control over me. Though I relinquished it gladly. My vagina cried out with spasms throughout my body. Pleased, smiling playfully, *"You're exquisite, Mollie. And that's two!"*

Before I could catch my breath, he hooked his knees outside my legs, pushing himself deeper within me. Our bodies were totally drenched from our sex. He began panting and roaring as we fell onto the floor. "Oh, baby, your pussy is so tight!"

Query: Why do men always say this? Why? Is it a compliment?

As he continued masterfully shagging me, he was so well endowed that the head of his todger (penis) felt as though it touched bottom. Control was clearly out of my hands when he spanked my butt. I always thought this porn trick was stupid and cliché. Oh, but *I so get it now!* Surprisingly, I loved it. I suppose I had lost all shame as each slap made me wickedly more aroused. That's when my 'spankgasm' screams surged from my mouth and through every pore of my body. I shook with erotic desire.

Boasting, he playfully replied, *"Princess, I believe that's three!"*

I'm always appreciative when a man knows exactly how to turn a woman on. As well as knowing all the right places and ways to touch a woman. I believe it is a rare quality to be highly praised.

I was startled when he interrupted my thoughts of praise, jumping down on me and putting his head between my legs. The stunning rock star teased my hunger with the perfection of his erotic tongue. His warm sexual mouth was a welcomed surprise. This man was a certified sex god and a true Titan of romance and sexual pleasure. Where had he been all my life?

I was feeling a bit shameless, which is my supremely favorite, out-of-character part of this story. *"Shame, shame, shame on me! Shame on me, bigly."* His tongue was supernatural. What was he doing? More importantly, why had no one ever done this decadent marvel to me before! Within seconds, I screamed out, confessing enthusiastically (and a bit self-conscious), *"Yes, yes, my rocker prince. And this time, I will say it for you. Yes, again, that's four!"*

He laughed, pleased, gratified, and quite content. But warned me, "Baby, your orgasms are turning me on too intensely. I can't hold back much longer. But no worries, Luv. We have all night!"

My *"Sir Holy Grail"* continued in slow motion. With each thrust, he pulled completely out, paused, and then returned inside me. He repeated this trick over and over. Interesting, I do that move with my vibrator. How does he know this shit? He is a Bona fide erotic master. A sexual oracle.

Squealing with delight and just about to cum, he stopped. He waited provocatively and then entered me once more. But this time, he fucked me harder and more rapidly. *OH*, the way his penis rubbed against my clit as he sexpertly fucked me. Fucked me like, Olivier Martinez, in "Unfaithful." It was just the way every girl wants it. I was so wet and throbbing out of control. And, just when I was about to pre-explode, Sebastian pulled out. "Faaa-Huck, get back!"

Without pulling out this time, he rocked faster and faster until, at last, we exploded, moaning in perfect erupting, unison. It felt as though our orgasm lasted forever. Holding me tightly, Rocket-Man whispered affectionately in my ear. "That's five!"

I could hear the crescendo of his imaginary orchestra playing loudly with each climax. 'TA-DA,' and ending with Queen's (Freddie's) brassy Chinese Gong in "Bohemian Rhapsody." The pretend symphony orchestra was stuck playing each one of our finales in his bedroom all night. For that's how long we fucked and made love. His brilliant sexual opus was a masterpiece. On this titillating night of fantasy, I felt every nuance of his spectacular self and the heat of his astounding physique spiraling through my awakened throbbing body. To my delight, my naughty prince came repeatedly over and over, and yet, he never got soft or had to rest. His bejeweled, royal treasure box was overflowing with rare exotic pleasures. Suffice it to say, "Sir George," aka Rocket-Man, pleased my deepest sexual desires as no one had ever satisfied me before. He not only found my "G-SPOT," he found the whole damn alphabet! If this behavior lands me in the bottomless, burning, explosive, fiery pits of hell, it'll be more than worth it. Besides, most of the people I know will be down there, anyway!

Blimey, King Rocket-Man's libido, sexual drive, and extraordinary stamina were awe-inspiring and yet another one of his many gifts and talents. I had died and gone to carnal paradise and sexual nirvana. Long live the king, and I dare say his noble, imperial, stately, and fierce Hard-Ons! He had rocked my world, and I felt an insatiable, endless desire to have him inside me all the time. In journalism, we call this "Burying the penis." Oops, my bad. I meant the lead! You see, his influence over me was inescapable! He chuckled when I asked, "What is thou Majesty's pleasure? What do you fancy, my lord? I serve at the pleasure of my king! Please, sir, knight me some more and repeatedly."

He replied, red-faced and self-conscious with blushing laughter. "Simply being with you, Luv, makes me completely happy!" Into the wee hours of the evening, my head lying on his chest, his arms wrapped tightly around me, and our legs intertwined, we were euphoric, gratified, and exhausted. Sebastian and I were locked in a loving embrace throughout the night. The orchestra (in my mind) finally tiptoed out, entirely fatigued after we fell asleep. We slept blissfully, all warm and cozy.

I awoke before Sebastian and that's when the consummate reporter in me also awakened! *'5-4-3-2-1… And… We Are Live!'*

"Good morning, America! This is Mollie Sloan broadcasting from London with a breaking bulletin and a personal news flash. Your favorite American Reporter, always in pursuit of the truth, is finally able to boast. I have been shagged royally in Britain! I've been majestically and regally shagged. I'm proud and thrilled about it, too. In fact, I'm still 'spasming' amidst this broadcast. I am also here to report on other breaking news on the latest findings from recent research on British Rockers. The study confirms, and I'm happy to report, all the silly gossip and rumors about rock stars knowing exactly what they are doing in the sack, are the best lovers, and the truest bad boys on the planet? It is all true and accurate. Screaming girls and rocker fans have a bloody, damn good reason to be groupies! The English may be reserved, proper, and stuffy in the streets. Nevertheless, privately under the sheets, it's a whole different universe of countrymen. Moreover, that stiff upper lip way of life applies to other stiff things down south. This is Mollie Sloan, reporting live from London, about a very good, CUMfortable night. Here's wishing all my good mates a fab day. That's a wrap, and back to you in the studio, Bob!"

Characteristically, "My Fit and Sexy Prince of Piccadilly Square," awakens each morning bright and early, *rock-star-time,* around 1:00 P.M. He likes to get an early start! After only one night and feeling relaxed and comfortable with me, he affectionately smacked me on the bum.

I adoringly giggled out, "Yes, yes, and more yes, please."

Grinning cheerfully, "Luv, I'm in the studio recording all day, but you are totally welcome to come with. Or, if you'd prefer, the driver will take you anywhere you'd like to go. So, baby girl, there's no rush. And while you decide, I'm going to roll out of bed and request that the servants prepare some freshly baked scones, berries, and coffee for us. Afterward, my princess, I'm going to jump into the shower."

I mean, what could I say to that other than Okey-Dokey. Even though that sounded significantly better with his fantastical British accent, it still sounded so wrong to my ears, on so many levels. Servants? He's going to, "request the servants?" It kinda just sticks in the back of my throat! I nodded, but I was completely baffled. That can't be right. I could hardly ever see myself, no matter how rich or famous I was, speaking *"Privileged"* with my besties. For instance…

"Oh, dear friends, Mildred, and Tiffany, I'm expecting my masseuse at any moment now. Do be angels, won't you, and go rummage up the servants for a spot of tea, biscuits, crumpets, strawberry preserves, and whatnot, for us in an hour! Won't you, dears? Now, go run along!"

Or… *"Servants, my friends Elizabeth, Catherine, and Victoria will be arriving shortly. Please, do kindly prepare for us a divine lunch and some marvelous, heavenly sweets, ever so quickly. That will be all! Hop to it! Snap, snap! Thank you. Now be gone and walk away!"*

I mean, come on! And, furthermore, who de facto rolls out of bed? Who? I am always perplexed by expressions in the English language, both the Brits version and the Americans. Perhaps, if one were on fire, maybe one would drop and roll. Or, if one were still hung over from being pissed (British for drunk) the previous night and unable to get up, then they might roll off the bed and fall onto the floor because their legs didn't work.

Oh, and by the way, here is my latest update. I now speak with Nigel, my imaginary, invisible British friend. I had no other choice since I didn't have a spare BFF here in England with me to share all this immense extravagance with. Hence, I absolutely and unequivo-cally needed Nigel! I had to have someone to roll my eyes and shake my head at while listening to this grandiose way of life. Moreover, he is teaching me to speak *"Privileged"* fluently. Which, by the way, is way harder than Arabic, Mandarin, or even Gaelic.

Returning to odd English terminology, "No one, my dear invis-ible Nigel, I dare say, ever *jumps into the shower!* One simply walks into the shower. But since I hadn't yet checked out Rocket-Man's personal shower, I conceded that perchance, he could indeed have a Grecian Shower, built on a 6-foot pedestal, and hypothetically, might have to jump into it." At this juncture, I didn't doubt any-thing to be possible.

Back at our conversation and in his cozy arms, I smiled with-out opening my mouth, mostly for fear of bad breath. Rock Royalty never has morning breath, for the servants tend to their teeth during slumber. I'm guessing, "Right, Nigel?" Not troubled at all about bad breath, my rocker kissed me lustfully, then disappeared. I remained in his cozy bed for a few more luxurious moments, reflecting on the past 24 spectacular, hard-to-believe hours. This man truly was the Michael Jordan of sex and romance!

It was now time for me to "roll out of bed and jump into the shower" myself. I went to my private powder room, aka the loo, to brush my teeth at once. I had to, as I don't have all-night servants on my payroll.

Oh, My God! I was startled and humiliated by my reflection in the beveled, multi-colored Venetian glass mirror from Venice. I gasped. "Shit, fuck-a-duck! Blimey! What the hell? How did this happen?" Oh, dear lord, I looked outrageous. I was an epic, hot mess in utter shambles. My hair stood straight up in the air like in the movie "Something About Mary." Plus, my eye makeup was smudged down my face like Alice Cooper, and my red lipstick smeared up to my forehead. He may rock his fans every night, but last night he rocked my entire physical world and shagged me up. Literally! I freaked out, for I didn't know him well enough to let him see me this way. But our night together was so heavenly, it was worth waking up to this disastrous, glamourless predicament. I didn't know where or how to begin fixing my tragic appearance. Shit! I had to do something quickly, as the servants were requested to bring up scones, berries, and coffee for us. I did the best I could in 8-and-a-half minutes until I heard Sebastian, King of his domain, calling me. "My Luv, breakfast in bed is now being served!"

"Breakfast in bed is now being served?" How pretentious can he be? Hmm, this raises the bar. Still, I forgave him, as this is his normal. With no time to make that ever-famous big jump into the shower, "OK, be out in a sec." Note to self... Must hire dressing servants. Looking at the mirror, all I could do was laugh. I mean, there wasn't anything else to do but laugh about this hopeless situation. "Right, Nigel, my good-ole-chap?"

Boy, did I ever mess up! How could I allow myself to fall asleep like that? Unfortunately, after flying over 24 hours and being up for 72 (due to my astronomical excitement), I had no alternative. I was knackered. You see now, waking up looking like this is precisely why we women don't sleep, and just fake sleeping all night with a new love affair. We do this just so this sort of thing won't happen. Meaning that we might snore or drool if we slept. This would assuredly ruin everything. Thus, we stay up all night and pose, just in case he awakens during the night. We'll even sneak off to repair our makeup every few hours. That way, we are ready to look innocently natural and perfect whenever he does wake up. It's nothing short of an extravagant Copperfield illusion.

It's an all-inclusive mirage, like a Hollywood façade. Those unrealistic romantic movies have ruined everything for us girls! They make it appear normal for women to wake up in the morning looking like the glamorous vision of sexy perfection, with flawless makeup, hair, and all. It's totally Fake News and utterly ridiculous.

And yes, I am speaking to you, Angelina Jolie! The reality is, all women, including the real-life Angie, wake up looking completely messed up and entirely disarrayed in the morning. Those films are nothing more than pure lies, as fake as the "Oooohs & Aaaaaaahs," moaned by the women in porn films. Don't even get me started on their preposterous outbursts of delight and phony expressions pretending pleasure. Talk about faking it! What's more ludicrous is most men believe this load of tosh. Ugh, denial & egos will do that.

Spoiler Alert: Just so you know, Sleeping Beauty wasn't sleeping at all! She was posing, faking sleep, and waiting for her handsome prince to get there already. When the prince gallantly arrived, she, Sleeping Beauty, was ready and pretending to slumber. She was physically flawless and prepared for him to see her alleged natural storybook beauty. That's basically the real reason it is called a fairytale!!! As the fable goes, Prince Phillip comes charging in on his white horse, Samson. The moment he sees lovely Aurora, this stunning sleeping vision, the prince falls instantly in love with her.

He kisses her, Beauty awakens, an orchestra plays out of nowhere, birds sing, flowers bloom, the sun shines, a vibrant rainbow appears in the sky, and true love is born. 'Voila!' Then the prince merrily gallops away.

As if this happens all the time. Ba-ha-haa! Not in real life, it doesn't. Note, in real-life, Beauty exhales with a huge sigh of relief, stating, "Shit, thank goodness! I can finally relax now, take off my damn makeup, put on an old cozy T-shirt, grab a cookie, and fickin' go to sleep for real! Voila!"

The same story goes for Snow White. However, she happily managed to catch a few hours of shuteye. Luckily for Snow, she had the dwarfs to rely on, keeping a faithful lookout for the prince. Anticipating Charming's arrival, the dwarfs woke her up ahead of time so she could fix her hair, freshen up her makeup, brush her teeth, and pose effortlessly for HRH Prince Charming's grand entrance. Do you suppose they would have lived happily ever after if he, the charming guy, had walked in on Snow, without the dwarf's alerts? I wonder. For he would've undoubtedly found her with messy hair, no makeup, or makeup smeared all over her face, bad breath, snoring loudly, and drool running down her mouth. I'm guessing, possibly not so, 'happily,' in the 'ever after,' quote?

Men, one more thing! Don't even think of coming near us before our morning coffee, or whatever our A.M. ritual happens to be. Heed this warning, unless you come with Starbucks in hand, exactly the way we take it, with a good muffin. Or else stay away.

OK. Now that's done! So, let's get back to the Sebastian story...

I was assigned to be in London for only 5 days. Nevertheless, I ended up staying for 6 weeks, as the "Duke of Music" and I found ourselves inseparable. I was thrilled to be in this energetic country of the Beatles, Shakespeare, and the city of the authentic 'other,'

Big Ben. There were gunless bobbies carrying truncheons (Billie Clubs), the other genuine crown jewels in the Tower of London, fish & chips, Buckingham Palace, London Bridge is Falling Down, countless pubs, and children hiding in Hyde Park. Fortunately, I picked up several freelance stories with an American Cable News Network. I also scored an anchor position a few days a week, sitting in at a local news station. Being that Americans are fascinated with everything British, it was quite easy for a notable American journalist to stay busy across the pond. It was adorable when they mentioned that I was the one with the cute accent.

I also had the distinct privilege to interview and photograph a few Royals and a forgotten ex-Royal. This delightful, exiled duchess has been accused of being the greatest social climber since Cinderella. I believe this banished royal (NOT Meghan!) to be more impressive and royal than most. The younger Brits, I learned, agree with me. And don't get me started on Camilla. (The Queen?) They also feel, as I do, the beloved Diana, "The People's Princess," was mysteriously murdered. Hmm, a possible conspiracy here?

When I wasn't working, I hung out watching his majesty, "Lord Collin," in concert during those six weeks. I was very proud of him, which inspired me to do greater things in my own life. For sure, I was his greatest cheerleader, loyal subject, and unequivocally delighted to be his nightly sex slave. BTW, he revealed way more than 50 Shades! Beyond my romantic feelings, I liked him. I admired and respected everything about this fine man. Being together was easy, natural, and entertaining. It's admirable how once he left the stage, he never acted like a star. Sebastian possessed style, integrity, grace, and was extraordinarily down-to-earth. I was more than crazy about him, despite his servants and all his king's men. Further impressed, I was happy to see he treated them all like family. "A good man. Don't you agree, Nigel?"

When he wasn't performing and we weren't busy having fun or making love (highly unusual), Rocket-Man would put on different wild disguises and wigs. This provided us the rare opportunity to venture out in public and hide from the relentless rags, hounding paparazzi, and his screaming, clawing fans. When they did recognize him, even with all his efforts to be incognito, he was ferociously gracious, taking the time to be kind and appreciative. The more I knew him, the more I revered everything about him.

We cherished all the wonderful moments we spent together. No matter where we went, we were openly affectionate, and our laughter was boisterous and never-ending. I loved how Sebastian made sure we never curbed our enthusiasm, the joyful energy we created, or our crazy times together for fear that he or I might be recognized. It was obvious everyone around us couldn't help but notice our immense happiness and gave us a thumbs-up glowing smile. We fit together like a completed puzzle and recognized we were being pulled by the energies of destiny. It's difficult to describe our extraordinary, effortless relationship. It's as though we were the stars in a romantic comedy, following the script and the director's lead. Something, some force, some entity, was guiding our connection. We innocently went along with whatever powers were controlling us and influencing our dazzling romance.

Most nights, the "Lord of Liverpool" and I stayed in and hung out, all comfy and cozy. We cuddled in bed and chatted about the world, our hopes, dreams, aliens, politics, and music, giggling away the hours. I never shared so much joyous laughter with a man before. Unless, of course, they were gay or high! I experienced the most remarkable times imaginable with Sebastian. No matter what we did, "Duke of Music-ville" and I made each other happy.

I remember our conversation, drinking a pint at his local pub, about Bobble Drew-in-the-box. He questioned me about why and how the love affair ended. Looking at his adoring face, I explained.

"I never really knew why, or the reason, for our demise. Sadly, I will never have closure or a resolution in my heart. Hence, my butler and Dining Hall, Prince, I suppose I'll never have an answer to your question!"

Sebastian, appearing concerned, held me close and asked lovingly. "Would you like an answer, Luv?"

"Yes, please!"

"The answer is… It doesn't really matter."

Wow. Brilliant! For the first time, after thousands of thoughts that had run through my mind, while searching desperately for answers, Sebastian's perspective, his simple assessment made so much sense. He healed me with his serene, soft-spoken, caring voice in just four simple words. *It doesn't really matter!* He's right. Like Hocus-Pocus, I was healed. Then he added, with compassion in his heart. "Drew's loss is my enormous gain! He's a complete fool, and I can only pity him. Mollie, my lovely angel, the guy will never be able to replace a woman like you!"

Wow, can a man be more compassionate or kind than that? There was a lot of "emotional medicine" in this loving relationship!

During our days together, we shared countless bloody good, incredible memories. Understandably, due to my past record, I feared the dreaded, "Great to be in love feeling," which was now creeping its way deep into my heart. Regardless, by no means did I have any intentions of stopping it from invading! Instead, I basked in this wondrous, perfect time in my life.

Some of my greatest, cherished moments with Sir Lord Sebastian transpired when it rained the whole day. Which evidently was a typical occurrence in London. These lazy rainy days were our signal to spend the entire day in bed, loving. Obviously, that's precisely what we did. In fact, we never wanted to get out of bed. However, eventually, we would throw off the covers for sustenance and wine at a little neighborhood tavern.

On some outings, we snuck on the London Eye, shopped on Bond Street and Harrods, frolicked around Notting Hill (like the movie), and visited Downing Street, where his good mate, the Prime Minister, lives. We went to auctions at Sotheby's. FYI, my paddle was never raised, but Sebastian's was. Who could afford those prices, anyway? Yet, my Princes' paddle went straight up many times. Including winning the bid on a magnificent, preposterously expensive antique heart ring filled with large, perfect shimmering, yellow *canary* diamonds. I didn't think anything of it. Until that is, he presented it to me that evening in his Dining Hall. He spoke assuredly, "You have my heart, my beautiful, stunning bird. As you wear this ring, please know it represents my heart and my spirit!" Rather pointless to say, I was speechless by his loving sentiments and his far too generous, dazzling gift. Thrilled and taken aback, I turned to my imaginary friend. "Mamma Mia, Nigel. Gosh, this *canary* is singing my name!" I was completely stunned and surprised. Although I didn't speak "Privileged" very well yet, I was beginning to love the language!

As the days passed, we patronized the theater district and saw several musicals performed by the most brilliant British actors. After hanging out all day in Essex, we'd enjoy tea, England's version of dinner. We frequented his favorite local pubs for more than a pint and visited his buddies. Better known as his best mates. We also found time to drive out to Stratford-upon-Avon, the town where Shakespeare was born and buried. Plus, we enjoyed spending a weekend at England's exquisite 'Lake District' to picnic and tour the peaceful, picturesque countryside. However, my favorite times together were just being at the palace, making love. I treasured our privacy. When Sebastian was not rocking out on stage, it was easy to forget his fame and position, making it possible to concentrate and focus on the man he was… with me.

By the way, if you find yourself in London (And Abracadabra!), you must experience the sinfully scrumptious bangers and mash. One evening, we gobbled up a traditional Sunday Roast with Yorkshire pudding. Another night, we witnessed an interesting interlude at a pub in the trendy, artsy Soho District. There was a loud, huge fight going on. Unlike in the States, it was uniquely civilized. It concluded with a gracious handshake and a polite apology with no guns, prison, or loss of life. Gee, I almost forgot the yummy Shepherd's Pie, with bread & butter pudding we wolfed down, watching this refined brawl for entertainment. Rocket-man giggled, "Now presenting your basic dinner and a show in London, The Bar Brawl! Love this city!" Oops, he almost gave himself away.

"Very classic, quintessentially British, don't you agree, Nigel?"

Around week three, over cocktails and dinner, I was honored when my love took me to meet his adorable mum, Olivia. By the end of the first course, I had learned and understood many of the reasons why Rocket-Man was so marvelously, talented, funny, grounded, kind, and warmhearted.

Imagine my delight when, only a few days later, Olivia called and invited me to share one of my very favorite things to do in England, or anywhere, for that matter. She summoned my presence twice while Sebastian was recording in the studio. Olivia invited me to join her in the time-honored High Tea Service with its fussy fanfare, glitz, hats, gloves, pearls, and all. One afternoon, we enjoyed a formal high tea-for-two at the famous Ritz Hotel Tea Room. Another afternoon, we took tea at the Dorchester Hotel Tea Room. Both were uniquely spectacular. It was lovely having the opportunity to learn more about Olivia. As I listened to her speak, I scrutinized her exquisite appearance and was astonished at how much younger she looked than her years. I discovered she was also a singer in her day, but not a star. Indeed, Rocket-Man acquired his talents from his mum, but became famously successful the world over on his own.

As we were chitchatting, Olivia proudly bragged glowingly about her son, while spreading dollops of clotted cream, lemon curd, and fresh strawberry preserves on her scone. All the while smiling, clearly noticing, and staring at my new, expensive, antique heart ring, filled with perfect shimmering yellow diamonds. Trying to divert her eyes away, "Olivia, you should be immensely chuffed!" She gushed profusely, whilst taking a bite of her traditional crustless cucumber and watercress tea sandwich.

She gloated, "My son is a gifted musician and singer. But did you know he wrote the music and lyrics to every one of his renowned hit songs? Goodness gracious, I'm so very proud of his countless endeavors and accomplishments!"

I jumped in, validating her comments. "I couldn't agree with you more, Olivia. You should be very proud, not only of your son but of yourself for raising him alone with your loving support and guidance!"

Blushing, the elegant lady went on to say, "You see, his dad passed away from cancer when he was only 6 years old. He was traumatized and devastated, but somehow pulled through the pain and emotional scars."

I said, wanting her to know, "No doubt because of your strength, love, compassion, and spirit. Olivia, you gave him the balance required to succeed in life and to move forward." She smiled, sipping her black Earl Grey English Tea, and went on to enjoy a taste of her lemon meringue tart.

Suddenly, she chuckled shrewdly. "Tis jolly good and smashing how my lemon tart and your ring share the same lovely color. My boy always did have the finest taste. Don't you agree, Mollie?"

Flushed, turning the same color as her strawberry preserves, I could only giggle back. I revered Olivia's adorable spunk, but quickly changed topics. I learned from her that my prince founded numerous charities and stayed loyal to each of them as he climbed the ladder of fame. Olivia also mentioned one of Sebastian's greatest musical achievements was being inducted into, THE...

Oops! I can't unveil that. For it would be a significant clue as to his identity! Undeniably, he's more than deserving of all the notoriety, glory, and awards he's achieved. Bloody good job ole chap, and hip-hip-hooray!

During week four, I had the distinct pleasure of meeting and going out with his baby sister. She, too, will remain nameless. But for now, let's simply name her Sienna. Although she was married once, she never had children. Ironic that neither of these siblings desired to be parents. They would have been great at it! Sienna, I quickly discovered, was truly an amazing character. She was fun and outrageous in all the best ways. We took to each other instantaneously. She is flat-out extraordinary in her own right. One couldn't help but *fall 'in like'* with her at once. Her personality was contagious and a party to hang with. As they would say in England, "She is well-nice." Sienna is lavishly amusing, spontaneous, and a grand mischief instigator. Charm and charisma are her superpowers. Rocket-Man and his sister got in as much trouble as they could muster growing up. They were only too happy to divulge many of their wildly funny stories! Oh, poor Mum!

It was not at all unexpected to discover Sienna was socially conscious, ultra-green, and globally responsible. She was as far from a pretentious snob as one could be. It was comforting to discover she didn't speak "Privileged," either. Regardless of their close bond, Sienna also mocks Rocket-Man's palace of butlers, servants, and grandeur. Still, however, she merrily spends as much time there as allowed. To be fair, who wouldn't?

This fair maiden was more beautiful than was fair or reasonable. She also earned ten extra-bonus points for being a killer shopper. We exhausted Mayfair, the district with the most prominent, high-class, elite shops in London. Afterward, we were off to Selfridges in Central London, an astronomically exclusive and expensive department store. Prada, Dior, Armani, and more! The funny thing is, Sienna typically favored the *"And More"* part. She enjoys second-hand vintage clothes far more than current trends and pulls them off like a true new-age fashionista. Shocker alert and impossible to imagine (because I was so infatuated with Sienna), I didn't buy a thing for myself all day. Although, I did pick up a few jogging bottoms for my Luv to wear, romping around his palace of extravagance. I did so, mostly because I liked how the Brits call them jogging bottoms.

"You understand, Nige?" Oh well! He doesn't always answer.

Exhausted, we stopped mid-day for a pint of Guinness, pork scratchings, toasties, and chips. It was a hoot how she found the most inappropriate moments to shout out timeless British phrases about men she saw. Like, "Yum, well fit." "I'd smash that." "I'd tap that." "He is bloody mint fine." And "He is dead nice." I expected nothing less from her, nor did all who knew her. I respected the soulful way Sienna pushed against sensibility. She had the whole pub roaring and was well-aware everyone knew who her brother was. It only untamed, the little rebel in her more. My rocker loved every unconventional, anti-establishment thing about his sis.

While in the local corner pub (much like the bar on the TV show "Cheers") we ran into many of her friends. As they entered, she shouted boisterous greetings to them. "Bugger off" and "Do one!" Translation: A nice way of saying, "fuck off!" When a guy friend of hers walked into this treasured, local hole-in-the-wall, she hollered, "Shite this" and "shite that."

I asked her, "Do you mean *shit?*"

She insisted, "No, shite! Shite, it's a nicer way of saying shit." Man, our English is so different. She echoed that this and that was sick. Meaning this, and that was great. Later, sipping her pint and munching on a crisp, she confided openly. "You know, Mollie, the greatest sex I've ever had was with Chris Hemsworth, Jason Momoa, and Ryan Reynolds!"

"OMG, Sienna, you slept with Chris, Jason, and Ryan? For real?"

"Just joking, Mollie. They were pitiful. Absolutely rubbish!"

Stoked, on the edge of my seat, "You really had sex with them?"

"LOL, maybe? But then, maybe not?" Sienna was enormously amusing. I quickly fell in love with her. She made *'my smile,'* smile!

Later that night, we met up with my prince for a trolley filled with superb desserts. We went sugar-senseless, just short of suffering a heart attack. We shared delectable Hot Cross Buns, Egg Custard, delicious Cadbury Chocolate Cakes, McVities Shortbread, and other highly caloric sweets that Sienna talked us into. We experienced *a major 'Sugargasm,' for sure.* Laughing so vehemently, I was certain we burned off every calorie we had sinfully indulged in. It wasn't hard to fall captive to her endearing, feisty charms. One had no other option but to appreciate Sienna's free spirit. I thought it was perfect how both his mum and sis treated Sebastian like an ordinary guy, rather than the megastar he was. They tease, ridicule, and harass him with the utmost love. I suppose that's what keeps him normal and grounded, and why he remains unassumingly modest and humble. Sebastian's family is uniquely special, which explains why he is such an exceptional person. I was pleased with the way his charming mum and sister accepted and welcomed me with open arms into their lives. While observing us together, they noticed our happiness and enormous love for one another, which naturally made them delighted.

Even though I cherished my time in London with work and his family, I couldn't wait to spend every opportunity alone with Rocket-Man that we could manage. Remarkable, how I never once thought about my life back home. He filled my world with all I could need or want. My love was always fun, affectionate, and a magical, thoughtful lover. He answered all my carnal desires that were well hidden in the temples of my sexual dreams. It was evident how he constantly tried to please and make me happy. (Big girly Moan!) He more than tried! My prince succeeded like his hit songs! His love continually burned like a fire inside my heart.

Because of my past unfortunate situations with men, I kept waiting for Sebastian to display the notorious dark side that some men possess, but protectively conceal. I was waiting for him to slip up, exposing his true colors and the real guy he was trying to mask! Happily, he never did. He remained the sweet, patient, considerate man I first met at his concert all those weeks ago. The man I quickly fell in love with. Confident to be on my own, I felt safe enough to let go of Nigel, my make-believe friend and staunch supporter. "Off you go, Nige. I shall miss you. Now, walk Away!"

As time went on, I found I was defenseless and weak against all of Sebastian's, the "Prince of Buckingham's" alluring, sensually seductive magnetism. His hard body was as toned and youthful as a 21-year-old boy. His stunning, charismatic face and wild, long hair kept me in a constant state of infatuation. He was the prince of charming. I was hopelessly entranced merely watching him. He possessed that mythical *"It"* quality, which is most likely what rocketed him to superstardom. I loved being a part of him and the unaffected, unassuming, non-rock star guy. My beloved's devotion and continuous words of love and adoration left me feeling secure and at peace with us. I could easily spend forever in his arms.

Ultimately, I loved my "Earl of York," but I imagine I *liked him* even more. When he smiled at me, my world stopped. He never looked or gawked at other girls, as I would logically have expected a rock star to do. He never flirted or tried to make me jealous and was always where he said he'd be. Sebastian could have had any woman in the entire world he desired. Fortunately, he desired me!

The coolest part was I had never experienced this much pleasure or serenity with a man. It was an adventure doing exciting things, and fun doing nothing at all. Heavenly, being offline and in love with someone this extraordinary. (A celebratory, hallelujah!) There was no drama, issues, syndromes, mental illness, or baggage. Well, except for his designer ones!

Although we came from two different worlds and backgrounds, we were like-minded and fused our lives in perfect harmony. We had become a real twosome, earning me acceptance into his inner circle of friends, musicians, and fame. Though I must confess, I was not very fond, or comfortable, winding up in some of the scandalous British tabloids and rags with him. I'm used to being on the other side of the lens. So, like the saying goes, "If you lie down with dogs, you get up with fleas." Or, in my case, "You lie down with a rock star, and you get up with the paparazzi!"

Late one night, after his concert, we ordered Chinese food take-out, which I consider being the best food in London, along with Indian Food. We spread the cuisine out all over the King's designer bed like a picnic, and gobbled away, totally naked, laughing, and pigging out. I paused a moment, gazing upon his fine, flawless body. "Man, you are the best Poo-Poo platter of them all!" He chuckled. To his surprise, I spotted and licked a random piece of Lo-Mein noodle that fell onto his inner thigh. I mused seductively, "It tastes so much better eating off of your skin."

He flushed, "I love how well you 'spring-rolled' on me earlier and I bloody well suggest you 'Dim-Sum' me again later. Please!"

"Anytime, baby." I winked, crunching down on the fortune cookie floating in my mouth. I adored his serene, carefree, easygoing manner. I also loved that he never once complained about the crumbs and mess we made all over his posh royal sheets. There were fried wonton noodles, egg rolls, fried rice, fried crab, and broken fortune cookie morsels scattered everywhere.

Reading our fortunes was a moot point, for I already knew Rocket-Man was the greatest fortune of them all. It was baked into our relationship cookie. He spoke, "My love, I don't need to read fortune cookies. I know you are the greatest fortune of them all!"

"OM-Gosh, jinx! Exactly what I was just thinking! Same cookie!"

At last, partying in his bed, riddled with crumbs, my lord spoke the 3 most beautiful words every girl, longs to hear...

"I love you, Mollie. I love you!"

I shouted back. "Oh Sebastian, I love you more!" On that Chinese food delivery night, Sebastian and I continued to speak of our mutual hopes and commitment for the future. We affectionately held each other, lying in a crowded bed of Lo Mein, crispy orange beef, and crushed cookies of good fortune! Dinner in bed or anywhere else just doesn't get better than this. AH, SO!

We became a remarkable team, experiencing the most incredible moments imaginable. Every day was '*fun day.' Ergo, all this bliss* left me feeling that I never wanted to leave Rocket-Man or London until the 12th of never. Forlornly, I accepted the reality of life. My absence in America was well noticed by this time. Unbearable as the thought was, it was time to face the inevitable and return to the States. "Sir Edward of Manchester" was going on tour, and I had to get back to work myself, or I'd assuredly be fired. Clearly, we didn't want to say goodbye now or ever. Not Ever!

Sadly, as grown-ups usually do, we were realistic about our situation. Although it would have been euphoric staying together, we understood it was impossible to remain in our private paradise forever. We also realized this was a turning point in our love affair. Saying farewell was like sharp daggers piercing into our hearts. There was no happiness or cheerfulness in our *'cheerio.'* It was more of a colossal agonizing struggle. We were equally distraught; sharing one last heart-wrenching goodbye kiss, filled with overflowing tears, uniting, and cascading down our lips.

You're right, Mr. Shakespeare! "Parting is such sweet sorrow."

And that was the end of our 'Act One.'

I arrived back in the States despondent and filled with an aching emptiness in my entire being. My darling Sebastian put back the fragments of my heart, only for it to be broken once again. Although this was not a broken heart emotion at all. This was an optimistic, divine feeling of hope. We were in love and permanently secure in the firmament of my heart.

As the weeks passed, I still wore him upon my lips. I could still feel, taste, sense, and smell him. We had been inseparable for so long that it was difficult to find me again without him. We spoke constantly on the phone all month, yet it seemed an eternity since we were together. I could barely catch my breath or clear my mind from thinking about him.

As we found ourselves burdening our friends unfairly, complaining nonstop, and powerless to tolerate the separation any longer, Sebastian swiftly made plans for us to reunite. After seven lonely, unbearable weeks apart, I joined him on his sold-out Sweden, Denmark, Germany, and Amsterdam concerts, which he named after us, "The Strength of Love Tour." For two weeks, "Lord Charles" was either *on* stage or *on* me. We were obsessed and needed to be physically touching. When he wasn't on me in bed, making love, I'd watch him and his fans screaming from backstage.

Indulge me a second with a sidebar to reveal those space cookies in Amsterdam were the only things that have ever gotten me higher into the stratosphere than the Concorde or my Rocker. What the Hell, do they put in those things? I ate *one* frickin' tiny bite. *ONE!* And I'm still high today! Corny, but my "King of Liverpool" and I didn't need the cookies or anything else to get us flying high. Together, *We Were Home!'*

Sebastian's outrageous, wild, and outlandish costumes are iconic and will surely go into Rock & Roll Museums one day. Although the truth is, he didn't need any gimmicks. No matter how over-the-top his stage fashions were, what always made the biggest splash was when he was shirtless, wearing his fringed skin-tight purple satin pants, with his long hair cascading down his bare shoulders. I confess, I usually led his fans in their deafening, tumultuous screams, typically overshadowing the music.

It was depressing how quickly our romantic time together flew by. Impossible to shake off how grief-stricken we were having to separate, yet again. The night before I was to leave Sebastian (for D.C. on a political assignment) my love hired a large private boat, taking us on a dreamy candlelight dinner cruise through Amsterdam's renowned canals. After dining, enjoying the beautiful sights, we made love in privacy, creating sexual bliss. My Luv, "Baron Von Oliver" made a toast to us, and poured his heart out.

"My baby, I love you too immensely to be separated anymore. It seems I am no longer myself without you in my life. I feel diminished when you are not here by my side. I admit, and much to my surprise, even performing on stage has lost its meaning and fire without seeing your smile looking back at me from offstage or in the front row. Mollie, I am beyond lost and brokenhearted without you. I don't have any desire to write new songs when you're not with me. I am distraught and insecure about not being able to play them for you in person or run them by you for your opinion. Zoom or Messenger is not cutting it anymore. Nothing, or no one has ever interfered with my creating music before. My princess, I've learned from those seven miserable weeks we were apart just how deeply we love each other." He went on in a whisper. *"I am sure we are destined to be together. Mollie, I know we are meant to be! I have never felt this way before or been more certain of anything in my entire life."*

I was astonished. No shocked, when Rocket-Man reached into his pocket and took out what appeared to be the Hope Diamond. It might have legitimately been an authentic crown jewel. After all, he is tight with the Windsors. As he continued, all I saw were his worshiping, adoring, love-filled eyes.

"My darling, please do me the honor. Make me the happiest man on earth! Marry me, my angel. Please, Say You Will Marry Me!"

I was so overwhelmed and blown away that I needed a second to process what he had just asked me. This man, with whom I was so in love with, on bended knee, romantically proposed to me to be his wife, in "Butler & Servant, Rock Star Marriage!" Thinking to myself, Holy Moly Mollie. Dazed, *for* I didn't see this coming at all.

I'd like to point out it's not an easy feat to do what Sebastian accomplished. He proposed on one knee, balancing on a boat, while going through a canal, at night, in Amsterdam. Difficult even without being high! Noticeably shaking, he went on proposing.

"Precious angel, my muse, I love you with every fiber of my being. You make my world whole. I want to spend the rest of my life with you. You are 'The One.' The love of my life. Mollie, gift me the miracle of becoming my wife! Will you marry me, my darling princess?"

My knees went weak. (Both of them!) I became dizzy from all his lavish romance and passion. Feeling goosebumps all over my body, I was speechless and panicked. "NIGEL? NIGELLLL!!!! Nige, my old pal. Come Back! I need you! Help Meeee. Come Back!"

I had not anticipated his proposal of marriage in any way imaginable. My instant inner reaction was... *Gulp!*

I wanted to reply quickly so as not to hurt his feelings. But I had to take a much-needed moment to wrap my mind around his

THE ROCK STAR | 139

unexpected four little words. This gorgeous man, "King Rock Harry the 18th," just asked me, *"The Tired Queen of Online Dating,"* to move to London, spend the rest of his spectacular life with him, and be his Rock Star Queen and Wife.

I appreciate how my tiny pause must've seemed an eternity to my love. But, in a celestial flash, this is what ran through my mind.

Love is blind to *logic & reason.* Yet Sebastian's proposal woke me up, out of my starry-eyed fog. I knew for sure I had to both, *logic & reason.* I quickly floated the idea of marriage to my rock lover. It would be far too complicated to work, I reasoned. I loved him with all my heart, but I didn't want to lose myself in his world.

As I thought it through, I concluded I'd have no real purpose in my life if I were to give up my profession to be with him in his realm. I'd have no choice but to abandon my career, goals, and very existence to support him and his music career. Could I be happy living my life in his shadow? Would I be content traveling the world, as my own unfulfilled life became only a satellite of his?

What perplexed me further, is Sebastian was 48 years old. Because of his age and constant traveling, logically and understandably, he didn't want children. But that would be very unfair to me. Was it selfish that I desperately wanted to raise a family and continue with my own career? Those two desires were of vital importance and a significant priority for me. My only goal and objective, if I made Sebastian my entire life, would be his happiness. I adored him madly, yet I questioned if that was enough. Without my family and friends, my work, and my country, I'd become lonely, and inevitably, be left feeling empty. I'd sooner or later lose my self-esteem if I didn't follow my personal visions and future aspirations. After all, I had worked since I was 12 years old. I would no doubt be lost.

Could we live 'happily ever after' if I gave up everything for him? Was happiness realistic if I abandoned my future creative ambitions and career dreams? Would I feel complete or joyful not having the children I so desperately wanted? Might I feel accomplished just living vicariously through his success, leaving behind in the dust, the success I had achieved and hoped to build on? Ultimately, as hard as it would be and knowing I'd forever have a thousand regrets, I sadly understood I'd have to say, **No**!

With a wrenching pain in my heart and sorrow in the pit of my stomach, I had to decline his spectacular proposal, no matter how profoundly we loved each other. As much as I cherished him (*And I Did!*) I didn't think in my heart of hearts that marrying him would be the right decision for either of us. From my agonizing thoughts, I let out a deep, unbearable sigh. I had no choice but to say, **No**! Though it would break my heart to endure this excruciating torture, I clearly knew that my answer had to be… NO! Dammit!

I left my inner thoughts and returned to the impossible reality before me. I saw my beloved Sebastian, silently, still kneeling on one knee. He was holding up the spectacular diamond ring with his loving, optimistic, puppy dog eyes excitedly fixated on me. He was awaiting the answer he hoped, wanted, and needed to hear.

At this enchanting moment, my head in the clouds, completely thrilled and giddy, I jumped into his awaiting arms and shouted, "Yes, with all my heart, yes! Yes, of course! YES, I Will Marry You!

My darling Rocket-Man, Absolutely, YES!"

In our euphoric fantasy world, beneath the romantical star-filled Amsterdam moonlit night, Sebastian held me and kissed me passionately. We cried as the sounds of silent joy echoed through our loving embrace.

All right, back off you judgmental people! OK, to begin with, I know what you are thinking. Ergo, I will immediately honor and validate your thoughts by stating, "You are completely, totally, and undeniably right!" But, then again, I loved-loved-loved him! Come on, he's wonderful. He would give me the most exciting life. No one gets it all. And I'm assuming that includes children. Right? Am I not correct here? No one gets everything they want! My reply wasn't rational or sane. It was passion. It was love!

And hell, yeah, you should've seen the diamond! Let me be perfectly candid. It was an engagement ring fit for a princess. More accurately, a queen. It was a Harry Winston-designed princess cut, 8, and a half-karat diamond ring. Moreover, it was 'D' in color and a 'VVS1' perfect stone. "I'm guessing. With total certainty!" Not to mention, the band itself had a double row of diamonds.

You know what? I don't need to defend myself! How could anyone judge me or ask me to refuse the two things I deeply loved? *This man and his ring!* In that order, of course!?

That would be like asking gasoline to douse out a fire, a pedophile to run a daycare school, or a gambler to manage a casino! I hardly think I should've refused the man of my *dreams*, who loved me and asked me to marry him with all his heart. Plus, with the ring of my diamond *fantasies*. As if you wouldn't have done the same thing! Sebastian is my Romeo. It was **Him!** My "Prince Von Rock & Roll" was *The One.* ~ Wasn't He???

During the next 3 months, I planned a rock star, no-expense-spared, royal wedding. Yet all the while, giving up everything I knew and loved. No longer a journalist, I was alone. Alone, without my family, friends, the comforts of my home, *all my fabulous shoes,* and other possessions. I was miserable, adrift, and off-balance. I quickly realized *I was missing myself.* I was *"Me-sick!"* Even though I loved him madly, I missed my life. I missed Mollie Sloan, the reporter. I tried to adapt and adjust to living in his world. Though massively heartbreaking, I tried, but I simply couldn't do it.

Thinking with an intelligent head that was not foolishly hovering up in the London clouds, I didn't quit my job. I only took a temporary leave of absence. Sadly, as the days passed, it became crystal clear that I couldn't deal with the inevitable regret and huge disappointment of never having children. It would be too great a loss to rationalize away. I couldn't spend the rest of my life without my own reality, accomplishments, and a family of my own. Honestly facing my deep personal desires, I had a change of heart.

Like "A candle in the wind," it wasn't the life I could keep up with, needed, or desired. It was a greater existence than being married to a king, *minus* the splendid castles, grandiosity, golden carriages, the pageantry, bejeweled crowns, and dazzling tiaras.

Regardless that Sebastian enjoyed a lavish, elaborate, majestic reality, by accepting his life, I had lost my own reality. No real truth or happiness could ever come of this. Still, there's no denying he is a great love in my life. But woefully, I had to let him go!

Telling Prince Charming, (sobbing profusely) was the hardest thing I've ever done. My beloved insisted that I keep the dreamy royal diamond engagement ring. As much as I would've loved to, *(And believe me when I say that!)* it wasn't the right thing to do.

Dammit to Hell, I hate and despise principles and ethics! Darn, high moral standards, integrity, and scruples. Sometimes it's so hard being the moral compass for the world.

I really *loved* that ring! But you see, in this story, it came down to the fact that I loved my Sebastian and our memories far more. So that's the treasured jewel and the perfect sparkle I kept instead.

Before boarding my final plane, leaving London to head back to the States, I morphed into heartbreaking sorrow. My Cinderella Xanadu world with Sebastian was sadly over. I took off my imaginary diamond, emerald, and ruby-studded crown for the last time. "Earl-Viscount-Baron-Von-Astor the 4th" and I hugged and squeezed each other with an endless loving embrace. Letting go of Sebastian was one of the most painful things I have ever had to do in my entire life. I only pray it was the right decision for both of us.

Looking at each other one last time, all we could manage was a smile with endless tears filled with love and pain. I cupped his exquisite face in my hands as he leaned in closer and kissed me, moaning. He began to speak in a shaky, weepy voice I could scarcely hear, but would remember forever.

"My love, I understand and respect your decision. I just don't know how I will live with that decision and without you! Please, oh, please know my angel, you are, and will forever be, the love of my life. I will eternally carry you and our love cradled tenderly within my heart. Baby, I will never get over the loss of you. My sweet princess, I am yours forever. I will love you for all time! Please know that I promise I will be there for you, no matter where, no matter when, or no matter what. My darling Mollie, I will always love you!"

He then gently stroked my cheek and softly touched my lips with his fingertip. Tears were raining down like a storm upon our faces. In the immortal words sung by Whitney Houston, (and don't even get me started on her demise), I sang to my Rocket-Man in London's Heathrow Airport, without a care as to who might be watching, photographing, or listening.

"And I-E-I-E-I will always love you!" While kissing and holding on to each other for dear life, we couldn't help hearing the snapping of photos and flashes wildly going off. Whatever, we couldn't care less!

As I began to board the plane, I turned around and saw agonizing tears streaming down my luvs grieving, heartbroken, stunning face. On a whim, I ran back into his arms for a final embrace. As his gorgeous long hair flowed onto my forehead, I cried, "I love you. I will love you forever, my darling Rocket-Man!"

"I love you more, my precious angel!"

Walking onto the plane, I waved a final goodbye and blew one last kiss to my king. With my eyes blinded by tears, I realized I was only taking half of my heart back home with me.

With inconsolable, painful tears of loving affection, Rocket-Man transported me all the way back down to earth, from our private universe in an alternative outer-space dimension. He released me gently into a love parachute and a treasured bejeweled chest of forever-and-a-day memories.

All by myself, enduring the never-ending flight home to America, I was grief-stricken and lovesick. Regardless, I wouldn't trade our love affair for the world. I experienced the most memorable, loving, romantic times of my life. And oh, dear me, The Sex! Now that was more than memorable.

Smiling, crying, and grateful, with a second glass of horrible airplane wine in hand, I knew that this time I was blessed...

"I Got Maled" **in the best, most unimaginable spectacular way!**

To tell the truth, it took a long while to get over the heartache, sadness, and loss of Sebastian. This whole fairytale was bittersweet at best. Regardless, Prince Sebastian and I remain the closest of friends to this very day. We could never imagine our lives without staying in touch and sharing with one another. At his request, I continue listening to his brilliant new songs and I happily give him my opinion. Although, honestly, he never needs it.

Mr. Rock and Roll remains the consummate bachelor, enjoying extraordinary fame, making music, and eternally cherishing his faithful fans. He continues to live in the palace with his butler, servants, chauffeur, and his preposterous Dining Hall. And, yes, *as always, he still "rolls out of bed and jumps into the shower"* early morning, 1:00 p.m. rock star time. Rocket-Man is forever rocking his performances the world over! And, loving it!

The moral and lesson I learned from this romantic tale, in addition to the indescribable, beautiful love Sebastian & I shared?

I now and will always stay up all night posing and preparing with a new love interest just in case he awakes during the night.

I will never forget my beloved Rocket-Man, for he lives inside me.

Alone again, I moved forward with my fulfilling career, amazing family, friends, and my wonderful life, as I continue to search for,

"The One!"

CHAPTER 7

Missing Rocket-Man

"FEELING SAD, GLOOMY, AND BABY BLUE..."
JUST LIKE A COUNTRY SONG!

I finally came to the realization and accepted I had made the right decision for both of us. Nevertheless, I was drowning in my grief with my "Rocket-Man, diamond-less, engagement finger." Although my heartbreak was seismic, there wasn't an ounce of regret for falling in love with him. Logically, I understood why I couldn't be with Sebastian. Still, it didn't pacify how deeply I pined for him. Nor did it tame the bitter sting in my soul, still burning out of control. I longed for him something fierce. From his touch to his smell, I missed everything about him. I always knew when he was approaching, for his scent announced he was nearing from a far distance away. I can still smell a trace of his sweet aroma on me.

Alas, I was bereft, miserable by his absence, and the agonizing fall all the way back down to reality. Being with Rocket-Man was the greatest adventure of my life. He is a man to be deeply missed, and sadly, the Band-Aid was ripped off too quickly. An aching, enormous ouch, now lingers within, to no avail. Heaven help me. I missed Nigel too!

Nevertheless, seeing our private goodbye moments captured and plastered all over the tabloids didn't help matters. I was forced to hide for fear of being recognized, questioned, or gawked at.

I considered my glum disposition to be greater than the typical state of melancholy. *Melancholy? Melancholy? Well, now* there's a word that needs to be put to rest. I've never used that word before. Woe is me. I'm living in a hopeless despair, in the heart of Melancholy-Ville.

After being on hiatus for so long, I gladly took a few stress-free projects my boss, Angela, assigned to me. Working from home helped me to acclimate back down to earth and settle into the real world. Getting my life on track, I focused on work and did nothing but veg out, pig out, chill out, butt out, and all the other outs, hoping to recover, to move on from the agonizing pain of love lost.

Hoping to ease my dejected, gloomy state of mind, I decided to only listen to Rocket-Man's music. Regrettably, this didn't pan out as hoped. My strategy was by no means helpful or therapeutic in my efforts to move on. It only made me miss Sebastian more.

Ergo, I began listening to all the different genres of music. Admittedly, I'm not an authority on music, nor am I a musician. I'm not a rock star, although I interviewed the best of them. Regardless, I totally loved and almost married one. I'm also not a lyricist. But here's the thing about that. Most of the songs today are fine in one form or another. Even most rap songs are great because they are loaded with meaning and important messages. Well, except for all the "Fuck you, fuck me, fuck you in the ass, fuck me harder, and motherfucker," types of lyrics. Chill, I'm only the messenger. Seriously though, I wonder how they never seem to run out of words that rhyme with fuck.

*Moving on, with my first date after Rocket-Man, and
Crashing Right Back into The Crazy Fiasco!*

OFFLINE OR ONLINE, IT'S ALL THE SAME...

LIAM AND THE DEFINING MOMENT

Walking through the renowned CinemaCon Film Festival in Las Vegas, I bumped into Liam. Rather, he bumped into me and sent my perfect, hot Starbucks venti café latte flying into the air, and all over me. Dara, a journalist I occasionally work with, couldn't take her eyes off him. She eagerly struck up a conversation with the "Attacking, coffee-villain guy." Pretty as Dara was, he didn't seem interested in her. He turned to me (drenched in coffee), with an abundance of arrogant confidence. "I'm Liam. What's your name?"

"Hey, Liam, coffee terrorist! Um, yeah, I'm Mollie." Dara got the hint and unhappily ran away. Dammit, I really wanted her to stay!

He went on bugging me. "Are you here for the convention?"

"Yes. I'm a news reporter covering the film festival."

"I knew I recognized you. I'm in the insurance biz. I happened to be hanging here at the hotel, hoping to run into a few celebs."

His celeb-stalking attitude instantly turned me off, leaving me yearning for my celebrity, Rocket-Man. "Ok then, Liam, have fun."

"No, wait, I'd love to take you out. I'm single and I assume you are too. How do you feel about going out with me sometime?"

I must say, the guy was enormously handsome. So much so, I questioned why he was single. I replied, "And why would you assume I'm single? Anyway, I'm currently getting over a serious relationship. Therefore, Liam, I'm not ready to date just yet. Sorry."

Dara, still in earshot range, slithered over to contradict me.

"Of course, she'll go out with you! Here's her number." Just about ready to take her down, she whispered in my ear. "It's time, Mollie. You need to get back out there again."

Liam grinned. "Come on. Give me a chance. I'm lots of fun."

"Yeah, that's what I'm afraid of. FYI, so was Jeffrey Dahmer." *"Oh, hell girl,* that's a comment one should never say out loud!"

The next day, as luck wouldn't have it, Liam called. "Hey, Mollie. I'm taking you out on Friday night. Dinner and a show."

Inquisitive, I questioned, "What show?" (Thinking Lady Gaga, Jennifer Lopez, Keith Urban?)

"Well, well, well, Hon. You have to wait and see. It's a surprise."

"Yeah, whatever." Just short of killing Dara, I replied, unexcited. "Well, well, well, back at you, Liam. Where should I meet you?"

"No, I'll pick you up."

"Like I said, Liam, where should I meet you?" (Dating rule # 3!)

"Fine. Buca di Beppo on Flamingo. Be there, 6:00 sharp."

Arriving 6:00, he was already eating a *small* pizza. "Dig in girl!"

"It's ok. I think I would rather order a salad. If you don't mind?"

"Jeez, you're gonna eat all that?" I felt sharp daggers in my eyes, wanting to pierce into him. "No, Mollie, just stick with the pizza!"

And "Strike 1!" I would've left, but for shits and giggles, I was curious about what show we were going to see. The most alarming part of dinner was Liam's obsessive rambling and enormous lies. He Pinocchioed his way through the date. Eating a picked-over slice of cold pizza, I wanted to make an excuse and go home.

Darn, he called an Uber. "It's safer, in case we drink too much!"

I was stuck. "Tell me already, what show are we going to see?"

"You'll find out soon enough. It's a cool surprise."

After the Uber picked us up, the driver stopped in front of the Hooter's Hotel. I looked up at Liam. "Are you serious? Hooters?"

Wait, it gets better. The guy took me to a free comedy, *open-mic* night. I have never 'not laughed' so much in my life. I am so going to kill Dara! Girl, you need to run fast when you see me. "Strike 2!"

After the "B.S. show," he made me walk along the strip, wearing 7-inch heels. So over him, I wanted to say thanks. Good night. Until we walked by one of those frozen drink huts. "Oh, I love those."

"OK, Mollie, let's get one." There was a long line, so we chatted with an adorable young couple. They were tourists from England. Naturally, this only made me miss my sweet Sebastian even more. When the guy handed us our drinks, Liam said, "Mollie, pay the man." I laughed. He repeated sternly, "I'm not kidding! Pay him."

"Umm, Ok? I don't think so, Liam!"

"Girl, he's waiting, and there is a line. Now, pay the man!" He went on demanding for all to hear and quite angrily. "Let's go. Pay up already." Then he yelled right up in my face, ever so offensively.

"Mollie, This Is a Defining Moment."

With my bitchy resting face cocked, locked, and loaded, I aimed. "You bet it is!" I placed the drink back on the counter and walked out. I heard thunderous, validating cheers from the people in line.

When he came out and handed me the drink, I demanded, "Take me back to my car. And dude, I mean right now!"

"Why? Gee, aren't you having loads of fun?"

"Defining Moment… Really?" And that was, "Strike-3!"

"Nigel, Nige, ole chap, come back. I need you. Help Meeee!"

A week later, Liam called. Had I known it was him, I wouldn't have answered. "Hey Mollie, I'm calling to invite you over to my house. I want to make you an amazing dinner. I'm an incredible master chef. After all, we had such an awesome night last week."

My god, really? I'd rather have my period and PMS nonstop for an entire month. Instead, I foolishly uttered, "Ok. What The Hell!"

With reckless disregard, I accepted. Liam was renting a house in a 50-and-over community. As he was 29, I found it, *"WTF, strange."*

He immediately handed me a glass of *wine, from a box,* and guacamole and chips, *from a box.* Ah, yes, I was back in college! We chatted, listened to music, and sat outside, which had a gorgeous city lights view. An hour or so later, we went back inside the "50 & over" house for dinner. The self-proclaimed *master chef* presented me with a plate of burnt salmon and raw rice. (I was thinking, my car is outside, and ready to escape to my favorite sushi restaurant down the street.) After more wine, *from a box,* and Sara Lee frozen cheese*cake, from a box,* he *boasted. "I made the cake."*

I mused, "Sorry Pinocchio, I hate cheesecake!" After barely eating, (Starved, but he didn't notice.) we returned outside to sit.

After a few minutes and famished, I whispered politely. "Nite!"

"No, ya can't leave. Please stay longer. We're having great fun."

Silently brooding inwardly with a puzzled expression, *we are?*

I replied kindly, thinking of sushi! "I'll stay for a few more minutes. Liam, might I bother you for a bottle of water, please?"

"Sure, no worries. Stay here."

He seemed to be gone forever. Bored, I took care of some business calls to Italy on my cell. All the while hoping someone would call me with an emergency. After 15 minutes, Liam returned with an opened bottle of water. Although it was odd, I was thirsty and wolfed down over half of the bottle in one chug. Burnt to a crisp salmon always has that effect on me. Taken aback, the next thing I knew, I was trapped in a kiss. Unable to escape or dodge it, I submitted. It wasn't too bad, I guess. To avoid any further unwanted passes, I moved my chair over and continued speaking.

Twentyish minutes later, I felt sick. I mean, beyond really sick. I was very suspicious, since I was far more wasted than the 2 glasses of wine I drank, for this to occur. I became panicked, disoriented, confused, nauseated, and my heart was racing. I urgently needed to lie down. "Liam, I'm sick. I'm going home!"

"No! if you're sick, you shouldn't drive. Go lie down on my bed!"

Yeah, right! I surmised the son of a bitch drugged me! I ran out like a thief in the middle of a bank robbery. Had I stayed, he would have used me like a whore in a brothel. And by that, I don't mean any offense to the ladies of the night! Oh God, I'm so frickin' sick. That cunning *bastard* drugged me!

Feeling deathly ill, I could barely drive home. I decided it would be best and safer to go straight to the emergency room instead. Dara is a dead woman!!! Just short of levitating in the waiting-room chair, with my head spinning backward, I heard, "Mollie Sloan?" Atypically, the emergency room staff took me in right away. Perhaps because I was vomiting green guacamole slime and charred fish crust all over the emergency room floor. Unable to walk, just short of falling down, they immediately helped me into a wheelchair. Clammy, panicked, and about to go unconscious, I became distraught, as I could see people were now recognizing me. However, that's the one good thing about the date rape drug. You don't give a flying fuck! And then, I blacked out…

Remember readers, my warning a few chapters back about this drug, insisting that you never leave your drink unattended? Well, it turns out, you should never take bottled water if the cap has been opened, either. Even coaches can screw up!

I awoke hours later to a lecture from a doctor. The worst part was that he was extremely gorgeous. I hate it when that happens! No opportunity to flirt, especially smelling like a sewer and completely drenched in green disgusting vomit.

Obviously, I never spoke to, "*Mr. Defining Moment*" again.

He emailed me for months, harassing me, asking questions *like,* "*Where did Mollie go? What happened? We were having such fun?*"

What a bastard. Clearly, I never said, "*What the Hell,*" *to an invite again! Ignored, Blocked, and* "*Strike 4!*" *Yes, that happened!*

Dear beloved Nigel... Oh, how the mighty have fallen!

My sweet, darling Rocket-Man, I miss you so much...

And in that moment, I was doubting my decision to leave him.

CHAPTER 8

Kyle The Weird Creepy Guy The One Who Lied on His Profile

WHICH WAS REALISTICALLY THE VERY LEAST OF HIS PROBLEMS

Readers, you can expect several of these types of guys during your search for "The One." Ergo, as written in the rules: Guys, as well as Girls, don't lie in your profile about who you are or what you look like! I promise it won't end well.

This chapter explains why...

Furthermore, don't say weird things or make up scary stories when you are on a date, hoping to impress. It surely won't lead to a second date. Nevertheless, if those stories and things are true? Hmm, OK then, you may not be ready to date. Moreover, and seriously, you might be ready to seek help instead. Hey, I'm just the messenger, don't shoot me!

My date with Kyle was like being in a war zone, stationed on the front lines. It was a battle listening to every idiotic, ridiculous word he spoke as well as the aggressive, inappropriate actions that he performed. I had to struggle fiercely to filter out each unkind thought passing through my brain from accidentally blurting out. This was a great deal of pressure. Editing my sarcasm and comedy was by no means an easy task in Mollie-World and a major achievement. Especially now, still emotionally struggling, and grief-stricken over Rocket-Man.

In Kyle's profile, he described himself as having an athletic build, very toned, average height & weight, and very good-looking.

Having some free time, which is rare, I agreed to meet him for dinner. I quickly discovered the only credible athletic thing about Kyle would be the guy who could bench-press him. Not wanting to be cruel or insensitive, I gave it my best shot. Still, not great odds!

Naturally, I was more than surprised when I met Kyle. The guy looked nothing like his photos. I mean, he was fairly date-worthy, until he opened his mouth, that is. Regardless he was not in any way as he portrayed himself to be. Kyle didn't have an athletic build, he was not very toned, not an average height or weight, and wasn't very good-looking. To be accurate, he was very skinny and super tall, about 6 feet 7 inches tall. Even if I had the desire to kiss him, I would've had to stand on a ladder.

Clearly, I was out with a whole different Kyle than the one he wrote in his profile, and I envisioned. That Kyle showed up different than expected, was still fine with me. But, man, don't go lying about it! That's one of the rules. Don't lie about who you are, or the jig will be up at hello. Well, hello Kyle, and guess what? The jig is up! Not because of your appearance, but because you lied!

It appeared he lived in his own parallel universe. Which is a nicer way of saying, Kyle is a towering liar. I have threaded a few tough needles in my day, but this guy was unthreadable. *Great Scott,*

I've finally lost it. I'm talking about threading needles, and I don't even sew! Who was I now, Betsy Ross or Edith Head? Low point! Low point! Kyle takes the cake. The entire cake! In fact, the whole Boulangerie. Sorry Scott, Betsy & Edith to pull you into this.

Listen up! I'm merely suggesting that people shouldn't lie about themselves and be proud of who they are. Each of us in our own way is amazing. Thus, we should love and accept ourselves.

During our dinner date, he probed confidently. "Hey, Mollie, I am exactly like my profile described, don't you think?"

As a lifelong humanitarian, I stuck with veritable white lies. I was evasive and thoughtful. I believe in benevolence forward. Regardless, just minutes after our meeting, came my first attempt and hopes of remaining cordial and silent. Struggling to keep my mouth shut, brought my first inside-voice edit!

First Edit: "Can I have the other Kyle, please? You know, the Kyle who looks like his profile described him and the Kyle who isn't a liar?"

What, too mean? Come on, after all, let's be fair. He's the one who lied in his profile about everything! Disappointed, deceived, and totally confused, I couldn't help speaking to the guy with a mistrustful lilt in my voice.

"Gee, golly, gosh, Kyle! Well, why, a, well, hmm, umm, ah…"

Interrupting me, he rudely inquired. "Are you a stutterer?"

Second Edit: "Check please and make it snappy!"

Furthermore, it was extra difficult being with Kyle because he was a *"close talker,"* and his awful breath almost knocked me over.

Third Edit: "Hey there, Scope, Listerine, Tic-Tac, Toothbrush? Would you like a mint? No trouble, pick one, I have them all!".

The date got progressively worse, and I became frazzled as

he continued his rant. "I have many insane, evil, wicked, juvenile remembrances. I admit, I did horrible, vicious, ghastly, unspeakable things. Oddly enough, I don't regret any of it and would do it all again."

He continued speaking in vivid detail of his teenage recollections about murder, rape, robbery, and other criminal acts! This was extra bizarre because he described his alleged crimes in a baby-talk voice. I do wonder if his remembrances were genuine, scary dreams, fake, bogus, shams, or just peculiar things he made up for the shock value. Whatever, it worked!

**No matter what the truth is, ladies, this is where
you pick up your keys and run for the hills.**

I imagine, at this point, he was channeling Satan! And doing it very well, I might add! So, where the hell is the dating police when you need them?

Glaring at Kyle across the table, I gasped. I had an Ah-Ha moment, realizing how my dating life overnight had gone from a "Real-life Fairytale Prince" to "Mr. Date-Rape" to a "Demon!" I hit the trifecta of insane dating! I believe that deserves a round of applause, at the very least.

Clearly feeling anxious and nervous, I decided it was best to remain nice, say nothing, and leave as soon as humanly possible. (Frankly, I should've been in my car, speeding away long ago.) It was difficult to keep my composure and my mouth shut. I repeated to myself, "Say nothing!" I promise I tried. But I couldn't stay quiet as things became far too scary and strange to continue.

"Kyle, you're kidding me, right? I can't pretend you didn't say those things. Do you realize how horrible what you're telling me is? What you've disclosed is textbook freaky and all kinds of weird.

Kyle ignored my reply, laughing it off. A few moments later, more bizarre came from his nonstop mouth as he slobbered out, "Girl, is your name Wi-Fi, cause I'm feeling a strong connection."

Honestly, readers, as if you would've stayed silent listening to his demented, menacing, psychotic comments of horror, murder, rape, and killings? No doubt, a jury of his peers would come out with a guilty verdict in seconds! If not, the judge certainly would.

To make my point, I quote the modern-day guru, Deepak Chopra: *"Passivity is the same as defending injustice."*

Help me! Deepak! Anybody? It was evident by how loud Kyle spoke the guy lacked any measure of an inside voice. Dumbfounded, I recognized this was more than a rock-bottom date. He spoke again, as chunks of grease flowed down his skinny chin.

"Sup, woman! You're a vision. The stars will be jealous of you tonight." Then, the creepy Kyle sported a sneer, bragging, *"Look at me below. I just got a big turned-on thing going on down under!"*

"I can't even," he was so offensive. Holding back chucks from spewing out of my own mouth, he continued with his delusions of grandeur about his appearance and ominous life experiences.

As far as I could tell, this horrible guy did not notice the pained, *'poker tell' worried* expression on my face. Nor did he notice the deafening silence directed at him from across the table.

Chatting away, he knocked over the entire bottle of cheap red wine all over the table, and my now soaking, ruined white skirt.

"In your wildest dreams, did you ever think you'd have the good fortune to go out with such a hunk of a stud like me?"

Fourth Edit: *"Seriously, are you high?"*

His inability to see reality was startling. Then, in the middle of this, not in any way at all a gourmet, all-you-can-eat dinner, he began making these horrific uncivilized sounds.

"*Chhaaaaaaa, Chha-Chha-Chha chhaaa, chhaaaaaa! Chhaaaaaa, Chha-Chhaaa, Chhaaaaaa, chhaaaaaa, chhaaaaaa! Chha!*"

"*What the hell,* I barked." Yes, I really barked. *Like a pit bull!*

The bizarre Kyle complained, "Nothing is worse than that itch you get at the back of your esophagus, which can't be scratched. Chhaaaaaa, chhaaaaaa, chhaaaaaa!" Hearing those hideous noises, with his mouth open (still filled with food) made it intensely vulgar to watch. Of course, I realize many people have bad manners and eat with their hands. OK, Fine...

But soup???

Fifth Edit: *"Kyle, you're a truckload of disturbing strangeness.*

I paused, looking around the restaurant to find an exit strategy. Unfortunately, there was none to be found. The sickening noises of his were a cacophony of ghastly sounds that now had everyone in the restaurant laughing and watching us. Being noticeably stared at by strangers in a restaurant is not one of my favorite things. My only option was to wave and smile at all the people now gawking at us with a desperate, "Please, please, rescue me," *gaze upon my face. I wonder why no one ever picks up on that look. Perhaps I need to work on it further in front of a mirror.*

By this time, the Chhaaaaaa-Chhaa-Man was on his seventh, or possibly twelfth plate from the buffet. It was irrelevant to him I had long since completed my portion of the dinner program. Granted, he wasn't toned, but with how much he eats, I don't know how he stays so thin. I was astonished, unable to stop observing his grotesque lack of manners. Kyle's endless food droppings were piled high on his lap, as well as on the floor beneath him. Sauces were smeared all over his face, and butter was dripping down his chin, as he continued saying batshit crazy, worrisome statements.

I was scared and terrified like a character in a Friday the 13th or Jason movies. I swear on Gucci, I could hear the people in the theater screaming at me.

"Hurry, get out of there! Save yourself!" "He's got a sharp turkey leg in his hand!" "Don't turn around, just run!" "He's carrying a loaded potato!" "Quick, escape before it's too late!" "Rush, he is going to eat you, too!" "Watch out, he has rock candy, and he's going to candy-stone you to death!" "Dear heavens, he's carrying 'Red Vines Super Ropes' and he's going to strangle and kill you with them." "Duck, he's got atomic fireball candy, he's gonna set you on fire!" "Run, Mollie, run, and don't look back!"

That's when Kyle interrupted my chilling movie thoughts and announced. "You will be flattered to know me soon. I'm going to Hollywood. I'm going to become a famous, superstar actor!"

Sixth Edit: "Kyle, keeping in line with your death comments, what kind of a star? An actor who portrays mass murderers?"

Thank goodness for edits. I kindly replied instead, *"I'm rootin' tootin' for ya!"* An error of authenticity was going on here.

"Well, well," he asked while double-dipping his strawberry into the chocolate fudge, spilling another bottle of wine everywhere. "So, madam, it's obvious ya think I'm a great catch. You've been pathetically throwing yourself at me all night. You want the honor of dating me, or do you only wish to have a butt load of sex?"

Seventh Edit: "Not in your hideous dreams or your disgraceful, juvenile remembrances. Dude, it's never happening! Did I say never?"

Eighth Edit: All Rise! I stood up and turned to the imaginary judge.

"I object, Your Honor! I'm repulsed and I plead the First Amendment. Hell, Judge, if it helps, I'll plead all 33 Amendments. I believe it's my Constitutional American right to do so!"

Editing back to Kyle: "And another thing. You spilled a ton of wine carelessly under, on, and all over the table, and me! Why? Why!"

"Your Honor, this is alcohol abuse to the alcohol! What say you?"

Returning to reality: In the calmest voice I could muster, I replied. "The honor of dating you? Or wish to have a butt load of sex with you? Let me, um. Let me think about it!" *I stuttered!*

Kyle wouldn't accept my stutter and advised me with a nauseating mouth full of fudge brownie stuck between his teeth. "You don't need to respond. It's obvious you want both choices!"

Here's the thing, I mused silently. Why is it that the most unattractive guys always seem to have the biggest egos? Disrupting my mused thoughts, he spoke like a typical narcissist.

"I am abundantly horny, little lady. I will devour you. I'm gonna lick, suck, and eat every part of your naked body. I'll show ya what filthy, dirty, lewd sex is. Porn films don't begin to illustrate, sexy lady, what I am going to show you and do to you. Bouncy-bouncy, down on your hoo-hah! I've got more than 100 tricks to please you with. And I won't have to tie you up because you'll be begging for it! You'll be ridden hard and put away wet! Now, what are you going to say to me, after I just bought you an all-you-can-eat, mouthwatering meal? You do realize you owe me!"

"Are you seriously, serious?" I'll never be able to "unhear that!"

UH-OH, and then it happened. Kyle grabbed my arm under the table and attempted to lower his pants, just enough to forcibly put my hand on his grossness. Or whatever the hell that little thing was between his hairy legs.

I wanted to chop my hand off. The poor left one, he forced to touch him. Hell no! No, no, no, and a screaming, "*ME TOO*," alert!

I was emotionally scarred and freaked out for life. I will never be able to "*unsee*" that! After his tremendously inappropriate language, actions, obscene sexual comments, and reckless disregard for my emotions, the gloves were way off! Unfortunately for him, he shut my thoughtful editing system right down. I became emboldened and confronted him in the most flippant tone I could manage. "Mr. lying, despicable, loathsome bastard, you have had more than your fair share of horrific commentary. And...

He interrupted me while spitting out chocolate pieces everywhere. "Girl, you are in such denial about me. Where is your brain? You must be mindless to find it possible to deny me! Don't be preposterous. Ya know you want me. Ya know you want it!"

In my fragile state, feeling immensely violated, I couldn't stand another moment of being in Kyle's repulsive, nasty presence. I was done. I had to be honest, but careful, as not to offend him out of fear.

"OK Kyle, just so you know, *a relationship could never work out between us. Not only do we have nothing in common, but for many obvious* *reasons, this is not going to work. I am out of here, and please lose my number! However, knowing you, you probably already ate it! And one last thing, Kyle. Let me just say to you that...*

I, Chhaaaaa, OWE YOU, Nothing! Chhaaaaaa!"

Ladies, this is precisely the reason I tell you to take your own car and independently meet these blind dates. There is a reason we call them blind dates! Girl, you don't know them! You are going in blind. Never let them pick you up until you fully know them.

This time, I listened to the invisible people in the make-believe theater screaming at me. I left a twenty-dollar bill on the table, (which was soaked from his spilled wine and food droppings), and escaped, as fast as I could to get out of there and back to reality!

Not to be disrespectful to cows, but Holy Cow! I was profusely weirded out. So much so, I was too embarrassed to discuss this disastrous online date with my friends in the car on the way home, as usual. Or, likely even for weeks? Or ever!

My poor little hand, I couldn't even look at it! I let her down. I felt contaminated. I wanted to get home as quickly as possible to sanitize it with chemicals. I even thought of calling the *"Hypochondriac Guy"* for his hygienic help and advice!

Speeding to safety, back to my house, I had a long conversation with Siri on my iPhone. Oddly enough, for a virtual assistant programmed with all the answers, she's surely not the sharpest tool in the Apple shed. She never has the answers to anything you ask, and most of the time gets your questions wrong, anyway! Regardless, Siri, with no answers, was what I needed this night! Which, all by itself, is disturbing.

Though I tried to erase the disastrous (true-life) evening from my mind, I tossed and turned, unable to fall asleep all night. I suppose I feared a *'Kyle Night Terror.'* At 4:27 AM, I gave in to my insomnia and made a pot of fresh coffee. Extra Strong! Reminiscing on my (lovely and sweet) childhood dreams of finding *"The One,"* I recalled an illustrious quote by George Bernard Shaw.

"We don't stop playing because we grow old… We grow old because we stop playing!"

With that, I rebooted my endless determination. Kyle, awful as he was, couldn't sway me away from finding my true love.

Sipping my second cup of coffee, I turned to the Internet to clear my mind. And just for the fun of it, I researched the creepy, gross, awful man further. I typed, 'Kyle Dimitri Collins,' into Google. And in typical Google style, it responded with…

"Did You Mean: Fucked Up Crazy?"

Thank you, dear Google, for bringing comfort and laughter to the true story of Kyle: **The lying, scary, strange, narcissistic guy**!

The moral of this story?

Whether you're a woman or a man, be honest, be nice, and don't lie about who you are, what you look like, or what you do.

You are special and enough. Trust me, the right person will appreciate you for being you, and especially for telling the truth. When meeting someone new, be yourself and show up looking just as you described in your profile.

And above all, telling scary stories trying to impress your date, won't get you anywhere but alone. Particularly if true.

Warning: if you're on a date with a guy like Kyle, don't stick around. Excuse yourself and walk away. The sooner the better!

**"And that's a BIG... Chhaaaaaaaa...
Chhaaaaaaaa... Chhaaaaaaaa...**

NEXT!"

CHAPTER 9

The Deceitful Italian Liar

AKA, THE CUNNING ROMAN GIGOLO, AND GODFATHER CASANOVA

I hesitate before I dare trivialize the world of dating. But I'm sorry, for there's just no way to not. It's madness. It's the wild, wild west out there. The entire process is daunting. Sometimes it seems as if every guy (and perhaps a girl) is potentially a liar and/or a fraud. Note I said potentially. If this makes me sound like a spoilsport or a bitter tattletale, okay, then so be it. I'll peacefully run with it.

That said, Anthony Mucianettia entered my life. Can't you hear the theme song from *The Godfather playing* in the background from his name alone? His name, Tony Mucianettia couldn't be more Italian.

Every phone conversation with Anthony, my unremitting sweet thought, was always the same. "Bullshit and more bullshit!" He came off so Casanova, suave that I couldn't trust a single word he said. People, this is precisely what the red flags are there for! Even so, for a short while, I came this close (insert a one-inch gesture with your thumb and pointer finger) to believing in his fancy package of deceit, handsomely wrapped up with a lovely green, white, and red, mob style, Italian bow on top.

Granted, judging by his photos, he was a 30ish-year-old attractive hunk of a man on Planet Fraud and entirely magically delicious looking. He wrote in his profile that he was a successful millionaire from Rome, the CEO of his own international company, and a prosperous entrepreneur. He mentioned several times he was divorced, but victorious in every other way. Tony claimed to own a Lamborghini, a Ferrari, a Rolls, 2 Mercedes, and mansions in both San Francisco and N.Y. He disclosed that (at this time in his life) he was finally ready to meet the woman of his dreams. I noticed, from his style of writing, that being Italian was the one thing he was most likely telling the truth about. His manner of speech was scripted in broken English and shouted an Italian accent. When we spoke, he had a deep, sexy, velvety Italian voice, making me go soft inside. Anthony sounded intelligent and smart, but pompous and controlling, which he posed with an unyielding cockiness. Bummer, for I'm a bit of a sapiophile (fascinated by intelligence) when it comes to scholarly men, as he *appeared* to be.

On our third call, whilst reeking with his obnoxious attitude and thick accent, he stated like only a man over 50 would imply.

"You know, the way to a man's heart is through his stomach."

A statement I completely ignored, being an ardent dining reservationist. Meanwhile, a few days later, I swear on the dead horse's head, lying on the bed in The Godfather Movie, he stated…

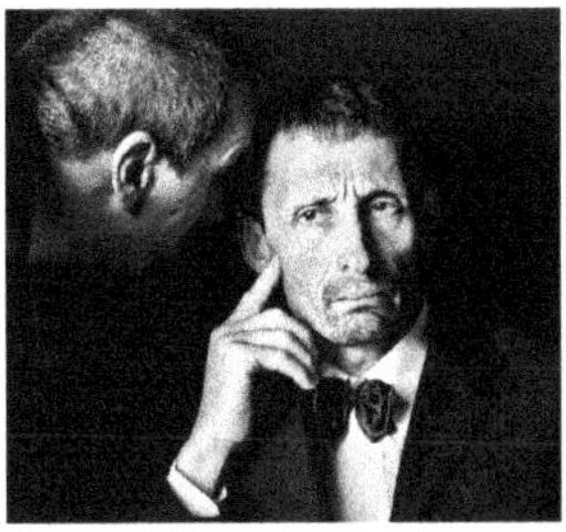

"You should know when we live together, I expect my breakfast, lunch, and dinner prepared and awaiting my arrival daily." To which I laughed wildly and should've also slammed down the phone. A loud click would have sufficed nicely here.

I couldn't believe, in today's world, a man could still boldly muse upon this ridiculous notion of what a woman should be *expected to do*! Especially for myself, being a busy working woman.

"He made me an offer I was clearly going to refuse."

Still laughing exuberantly over his comment, I inquired. "OK now, Anthony, let me get this straight. So, hypothetically, if I had to jump on Air Force One, to interview the President of the United States (Which I often do), you are seriously telling me I should cancel that to put a plate of prosciutto-e-melone and pasta on the table for you? I must tell you, that is an enormous, unrealistic ask!" I almost dropped and broke my cell when he brazenly answered.

"No! You can simply prepare the food and have it ready for me on the table before you leave for your meeting with the President."

Giggling and snickering, "Do you hear yourself? A-OK, buh-bye Anthony. I'm going now. Like, forever! Oh, BTW, I'm interviewing the President later, so remember to leave my lunch on the table."

He snapped back, "OK, fine! Never mind. OK! Let it go!"

I desperately wanted to reply with The Godfather quote…

"Never tell anybody outside the family what you're thinking again."

I didn't, but I would've loved to! Mucianettia's superiority was overstuffed, like Italian peppers, ravioli, or the cannoli he wanted, placed on the table before doing my interview with the President.

I was so intrigued and fascinated by his big, pompous Italian meatballs that I foolishly decided to continue with our peculiar conversations. It was like I was researching social behavior of culture & societies for a mid-term college project. Anthony's relentless moxie and nerve were foolishly captivating me. In between his relentless controlling style, he meticulously planted outré romantic, sweet, and considerate jargon in his emails to me. In fact, they were way over the top. I guess he thought they might bait me onto his slippery, extra-virgin olive-oiled hook. He wrote…

"I was certain about our wonderful future together from the very moment I heard you speak. Your voice warmed my heart."

Amused, I thought, I see, and a huge whatever. I was ashamed of myself for even reading it. Despite it all, it was still nice to hear the lovely sentiments even through his syrupy, bogus verbiage.

Here's another example of Anthony's lengthy emails, word for word. I cleaned it up since it would be too difficult to understand the way he wrote it in his broken Italian accent. He undoubtedly should've used an Italian/English translator app.

With Tony's full-of-himself stance, & my recent Kyle drama, for my own sanity, I was certain I needed another faux day in court.

"Your honor and members of the jury, this will be presented as Exhibit 'A.' May the record reflect that I request it to be admitted into evidence and published! May I approach the bench?"

"Your Honor here is (a long) Exhibit 'A', as written by Anthony…"

"Hello Dear,
I really want you to know more about me. I am a bright, fun, romantic, kind, caring, loyal, and affectionate man. A man that does not care about your physical appearance, but rather who you are! I am a laid-back

man and get along very well with others. I'm easy to get to know and I enjoy meeting different people. I love the intimacy between two lovers who care about one another and share such things as the rain, walks at night under a full moon, sunsets, and sunrises, roaring fires in the winter, drives along the coast, or just cooking a great meal together and enjoying many of life's simple pleasures. I want unconditional love and respect. I'm the type of person who gives his partner my whole heart. I am thoughtful, considerate, and loving. I must feel free and unrestricted in expressing and showing my love. I won't have that stifled (but naturally, I behave in public), as I must show my affection with hugs, kisses, cuddling, etc.

My partner will have no doubts that I love her. Concerning loyalty? I'm completely loyal and trustworthy in all my partnerships. I'd like someone who loves me with understanding and patience and who is honest and truthful to others. Someone who will not lie to me, even if told something that will hurt me. I am responsible, educated, worldly, and family oriented. I'm not saying I am perfect, but I am honest and sincere and will give my entire being and soul to whomever I love.

About my profession, as I told you, I am in Civil Engineering. I do it all, including the execution of projects both on and offshore. My job takes me to various countries. Therefore, I travel extensively to many locations around the world. In addition, I also work with countless contracts, presented to me by the United Nations."

I fancied hitting back nonchalantly with The Godfather quote.

"It makes no difference to me what a man does for a living, understand?" I didn't say it, but I sure was flirting with the idea.

He continued. "Mollie, as I said on the phone, I am new to online dating. I was truly lucky to find you. To be blunt, when we speak, it really makes my day. For that, I say a very big thank you, dear. I was too shy to tell you on the phone, but I am everything you need in a relationship. I am quite content to be at home working on a project, reading, or helping you cook dinner nightly. My lifestyle is peaceful and rather quiet. I'm more of an introvert than an extrovert. However, I can hold my own at any social function. You should know that at times I can be irreverent, :) acting very silly and childlike. I can be very understanding. I have a good sense of humor and I like sharing my thoughts, feelings, and ideas. :) :) :)!

I enjoy pampering and surprising my partner. But to be clear, I too must be nurtured in return. Sensuality is a must and very important to me.

All of that should give you an idea of the kind of man I am, apart from my engineering life. I also hope it was not too boring for you, reading all about me. I want to know everything about you, so please feel free to tell me anything you wish to share.

As previously, more bullshit. Plus, he used the word "I" over 45 times. Not a Guinness record for one email, but pretty darn close.

Addressing the court, "So, there you have it, Exhibit A!"
With a strike of the gavel, "Overruled! Or maybe, Sustained?"

Mr. Rome, also known as Anthony, was allegedly an engineer who owned a prestigious international company. Hence, on the next call, he explained he was in San Francisco on a big project and had to wait 6 weeks to meet. He justified he doesn't mix or split his time between work and pleasure.

With each unnerving conversation and email, he became more demanding, growing bigger meatballs by the second. He hated that I blocked my phone number, so he wouldn't have it. (For protection and one of the rules!) He let me know it, too. Too bad, for I didn't trust him, which left me with the burden of making all the calls. Anthony became outraged when he asked me to call at a specific time and I was 15 minutes late. When he displayed his disappoint-ment with my tardiness, I chuckled. This didn't go over well with him. *Oopsie,* oh well, and I laughed even harder.

Mr. Waving Red Flag demanded that I call him twice daily at an exact designated time. Of course, I didn't. "Hail, Caesar! And give me a break!" He went to sleep at 7:00 p.m. and insisted I call at 6:00 p.m. He woke up at 4:00 a.m. and since I was usually up late working, he ordered me to call him at 4:15 a.m. to wish him a good day. Lord, he was really something.

On day nine of our non-relationship, at 6:25 p.m., roughly 25 minutes late, he voiced in an annoyed tone. "You're late, Mollie. And now you are being punished. Go into your bedroom. Lie down on the bed and close your eyes. I want to know every part of you."

Annoyed, but curious, I played his little early evening game for a short while. "So, Mollie, what would you do to me if I were with you right now? I want to know about every single naked touch."

His inappropriate, offensive approach made me sneer with dis-dain. It was scary that Kyle was looking better all the time now.

Huh, Phone Sex? Really, 9 days in? Also, *Not A Record!* I was down for this game. I invented this game. So, I eagerly played.

"Anthony, I'd kiss your ears and kiss your lips with penetrat-ing passion. I'd touch your olive-colored, Italian skin ever so close to your private personal treasure, just enough to tease you. Next, I'd climb on top of you, grinding up and down with our clothes on, tormenting you with intense, insatiable desire. Just when you would beg for more and grab me, I would crawl off you extremely slow, while pushing down on your staggering manhood. Then, I would very gently open up and pull out my…" I paused.

He excitedly and breathlessly said, "Yes? Then? Then what?"

"Then, I'd open up the drawer and I would pull out a…"

"Yes, pull out what? Oh, how you turn me on! Pull out what?"

"I would pull out a deck of cards so we could play Gin Rummy."

He slammed back with infuriating scorn. "So childish. Why are you acting like a baby? You're behaving stupid and immature!"

"So, now I am a child? I'm immature because I don't engage in phone sex after just 9 days with a total stranger. Did you mean to say, why do I have morals, class, and integrity? Is that what you meant?" I hung up immediately, feeling darn good about myself.

To no surprise, he hounded me nonstop with online emails for five days. I am confident he used his translator this go-around.

"May it please the Court, your Honor, and distinguished members of the jury. I present Exhibits: B, C, and D. May the record reflect my request they be admitted into evidence and published!"

"Exhibit 'B,' as written by Anthony…"

"My sweetest, I'm presently at work, and thoughts of you won't allow me to concentrate on my job. I seem to have gotten more creative and emotional in my writing skills ever since I met you. This is something I've never been able to master with any other woman.

No words could ever express the glee and joy I'm experiencing right now. I can't begin to fathom how lucky I am to have you in this life. In any other lifetime, I'd still choose to fall in love with you. I thank God for bringing you into my life. You have given new meaning to my existence, and I could not imagine a life without you in it. I feel like you and I were born to be together forever. Meeting you is the most special thing that has ever happened to me. You possess a special place in my heart, and no one could ever replace that, be it in this lifetime, or any other. When I'm talking to you, everything seems right, leaving me feeling really blessed. I'll cherish every single day we will spend together.

I will never leave you, and I promise to be your knight in shining armor. I'm willing to go against anyone who wishes you harm. I will protect you from any danger that threatens your happiness. This will be my vow from now until eternity. Because of my deep feelings for you, I have chosen to fall in love with you, Mollie. I never imagined I would meet someone as amazing as you. I never thought I could be this happy. Allow me to spend forever with you. I have never been this sure or felt this way in my entire life with anybody. I want to celebrate my deep love by spending the rest of my life with you. I adore you and I'm willing to risk everything that life has to offer just to spend forevermore with you. You're the sunshine that lifts my dark days, and the sweet voice that makes me want to wake up every single morning of my life. I'll never need anything or anyone else for as long as I have you in my life. I guarantee to adore you till the end of my days and the life after, as well. Listen to this song I attached here. These are my words to you, for you are my heartbeat. It's by John Legend. "All Of Me." I send you kisses and hugs. Anthony"

I didn't answer his letter but contemplated. Hey, Mr. Italiano, we've never met! You don't know me well enough to feel any emotions of love towards me. I responded with 3 Godfather quotes.

1. *"When they come, they come at what you love."* (**That's not me.**)
2. *"That's like bringing a guy up from the minors to pitch the World Series."* (**I'm totally, less than minor, in your life!**)
3. *"Every man has one destiny."* (I promise, **I'm not your destiny!**)

"Overruled on the grounds of more lies and total bullshit!"
EXHIBIT 'C,' as written by Anthony…

"Morning Baby,

I just realized how happy and complete I would be with you by my side. The thought of you reassures me and gives a whole new meaning to my world. Every sound of your voice is like music to my ears, a serene lullaby that lulls me into sweet daydreams. When I think of you, I can see a brighter tomorrow. The soft whispers of your enchanting voice lift my empty spirits and calm my weary thoughts. Your beaming smile chases all my worries and uncertainties away. Your warm embrace puts me in a trance of sweet lullabies and melodies. The moment I hold your hand, I will know you are the one I want to spend the rest of my life with. I've attached pictures here. I hope you like them. Have a great day and never stop thinking of me… Ciao Bella, xoxo, Anthony."

"Your Honor, Please Let the Record Show, Overruled. On The Grounds Of, 'What is wrong with you?' Really, Seriously, and What the F$%@*&^K, Man?"

This time I indisputably had to write back. I didn't have a choice!

"Hey, Roman Guy, lend me your ears. We've never even met. Are you kidding? You don't know me or anything about me other than a few smiling photos. I mean it, Tony! You scare the hell out of me!"

Then, I recalled more words by Mario Puzo, in The Godfather.

"Why should I be afraid now? Strange men have come to kill me ever since I was 12 years old."

**"May I Present Another Letter, Your Honor?
EXHIBIT 'D,' as written by Anthony."**

"Thank you, and I understand everything you said. I am sorry if I scared you. But I am looking for forever, just like you. You're the one I want and want to be with, even in death. I have all the money in the world to take care of you, bigly! I want to hear your voice, so please call me as soon as you are awake… Much love, Anthony"

"Your Honor and esteemed members of the jury, I object to this ridiculous line of nonsensical, phony, absurd emailing!"

"Sustained!" (Plaintiff girl, I feel your pain!)

"Thank you, Judge! LOL!"

And again, reflecting upon another profound Godfather Quote.

"Many young men started down a false path to their true destiny. Time and fortune usually set them aright."

And just like that, I ignorantly and foolishly (because of his utter hotness) decided to give him a chance. All in the name of research, of course. I had to open a bottle of white and put on a pot of tea to carry on most of the conversations with this calculating, domineering poet. Tweak! A pot of tequila! He really was a titillating and most charismatic, lying sort of bloke. I must say, he had that going for him. Yet, it only alerted me further to the haunting screams of, "Buyer Girl, Beware!" But I had to find out!

I found his capricious, erratic behavior radically unnerving. When we spoke on the phone, he was an absolute, overbearing dick wad. In his letters, he was sensitive, charming, and alluring. It made me wonder if he wrote those letters himself. Or cunningly copied them from a book of love letters. Perhaps he hired his own personal Cyrano de Bergerac? Still, it angered me how he was able to get under my skin enough to occupy my thoughts. Anyway, I wasn't about to let this phony man govern my good judgment, tell me what I could, couldn't, had to do, or not to do. Now or ever.

He apologized profusely for his crass, bigheaded behavior, and surprisingly humbled himself. After 3 weeks of speaking on the phone, I caved in, agreeing to meet him on May 8th, in Fort Lauderdale. Meanwhile, we continued speaking on the phone. He revealed he had an 8-year-old son, and the mother (his 'EX') didn't want the child. Tony elucidated, "I would love nothing more than to have my son live with me. Unfortunately, I'm too busy with work and currently unable to take care of him full-time. For now, my son, Roberto, lives in Rome with my mom, his nonna."

I struggled not to interject another Godfather quote to Mr. Rome. To blurt this out would've been imprudent. Still, I should've.

> *"A man who doesn't spend time with his*
> *family can never be a real man."*

Anthony went on. "I divorced Angelina, my 'ex,' for cheating on me. Naturally, I was left feeling bitter and angry with all women, which caused me to remain completely celibate for four years."

Objection, Your Honor!

Honestly, I would've had an easier time believing Adolf Hitler and Putin were sweethearts and wonderful fun guys, than believing Anthony, with his historic good looks, had not had sex in 4 years. He added that his abstinence from sex included masturbation. *Oh, Pa-lease!* Stop it! You're killing me, Tony. I chuckled, enjoying how entertaining all his grandiose lies were!

However, this lie made every suspicious hair on my head stand straight up at attention.

And that's when I decided to call in the big guns, my loyal and dependable detective. Apprehensive and mistrusting, I was too overly concerned to meet Tony, until I had him checked out thoroughly by a professional. I explained to Private Investigator Diane Hellmer everything I knew about Anthony. Diane, 'ExperTrace Investigations' owner, realized her passion for the investigative profession during her 12-year career as a television producer. She was esteemed for identifying people in obscure videos, tracking down missing persons, locating lost footage, reuniting birth families, problem-solving, and thinking outside the box to solve each case. She's famous for being the best in her field.

I knew I could rest assured, being in safe hands with Diane's help.

Frankly, I was startled when she called me back, promptly the very next day. I answered her call with a quote from The Godfather. (I had a theme going on here and I couldn't stop.)

"Mr. Corleone is a man who insists on hearing bad news immediately!"

Diane laughed vivaciously. I anxiously questioned.

"Di, my friend, like *Corleone*, so do I. So, spill the beans, girl!"

In less than 24 hours, Diane dug up a whole lot of beans! The detective ever so quickly & professionally began to fill me in.

"Regarding the case of the Italian Stallion. In a matter of speaking, I found lots of hanky-panky and deceit here, my dear. Your gut was right. By & large, if it sounds too good to be true, then it probably is. This guy falls under the category of, *'Liar, Liar, Pants on Fire!'* I ran a background check on Mr. Perfect and discovered he is an enormous fraud. He went bankrupt 5 years ago. He is also very married. That's why he gave you the exact times to call him. I'm not done. He has 2 children. One is a 12-year-old girl, the other an 18-year-old boy, who's seeking transgender surgery."

"Shit, Diane! Tony is not liberal. If his boy gets that surgery, I know for sure, one day he'll cry out like in The Godfather!"

"Look How They Massacred My Boy!"
We both giggled.

"That's incredibly funny, and I bet he will! Anyhow, he boasts of a Lamborghini, etc. Again, big lies. He has a 10-year-old, broken-down Toyota. On his owning mansions in two separate states? Hardly! He has only one house in Ohio worth $160 grand, with a

$152,000 mortgage. Not so impressive and yet another lie. He is a worker-ant for a small building company, which he does not own. And get this. The scam artist isn't even from Rome. He was born and raised in Milan. So, no Caesar here. Plus, it came as no revelation, that Anthony is 10 years older than he said he was."

If all that didn't already blow my mind (And how could it not?), she went on. "You ready? He stole someone else's photos and looks nothing at all like the ones he sent you or posted. He used a fake identity. This swindler is not the perfect stunning vision of the man he crowed to be. He was nothing more than a scrawny, 5' 5" average-looking scammer. It was all just a ruse and a make-believe charade. Most likely, his game is focused on free phone sex with scads of women. All his letters probably came from a 'How to Romance Women' book from the library. And, Mollie, I truly doubt he was ever going to meet you in person in Florida! No way."

She went on. "I used a voice mail probe and a GPS tool to locate him through his cell to dig up the scoop on this phony, sleazy character. He uses a burner phone so he can't be traced. Too bad," she winced. "This poser is also using a virtual phone number and a new fake FB account to hide his identity. He's using someone else's identity, to boot. The crook is wise enough to know it's the perfect deception of covering all his bases!"

"Wowie, Zowie, Diane! The guy is one hell of a polished, assiduous, unabashed con man! Boy oh boy, I sure can pick umm!"

"Indeed, he is! No worries, you know I always have your back!"

"Diane, I can't thank you enough. You saved me yet again. I don't know what I'd do without you. I owe you big time. I mean it."

"Don't be silly. You don't have to thank me. But, in keeping with this theatrical Godfather theme you have going on," she paused…

"Someday, and that day may never come; I will call upon you to do a service for me. But, until that day, accept this justice as a gift on my daughter's wedding day."

"LMFAO! Diane, thank God we can laugh about this already!"

"Thank goodness! You see, Mollie, what is and what ought to be, are vastly different! Anyway, I'm very glad to help. Be careful with the guys out there you don't know. I gotta run. Love you, girl!"

Readers, let this be a warning. If a guy speaks to you on a burner phone and it sounds like he's lying, something isn't right! Be vigilant.

"Your Honor, May I Please Request Another Sidebar?"

In a room full of imaginary lawyers, I plead with the court to give this grifter the maximum jail sentence for Identity Theft. He's also guilty of being a bullshit artist and a fraud, with a bad temper! Moreover, he should get *life in prison* **for suggesting and demanding a woman must cook three meals a day, every day, for her man!**

Knowing what I had found out about the Italian Celibate Masquerader, had I continued this adventure with this guy from Milan, my life would've been headed for a complete train wreck!

I suddenly realized this fiasco wasn't over yet. I had to figure out a way to vanquish the guy without insulting or infuriating him. This would be a rather delicate dance. He most definitely needed to be swiftly abjured from my life. The last thing I needed was a violent Italian predator on my back.

When I called Anthony with the purpose of dumping his ass, I could see right through the phone that his glazed-over eyes grew bigger and more enraged as I spoke. He sensed something amiss was going down. I didn't want to get him all heated up for fear he would retaliate in some way. With that in mind, I was very complimentary and flowery in my approach. Ultimately, though, I was too nervous to tell him over the phone. I made up a pretend emergency call, explaining I couldn't talk right then because I had to take a problematic business call. (I should've told him the president was on the phone, LOL!) Then, with my heart pounding, I quickly hung up. I decided it was safer to write him an email instead. Consequently, I was a bundle of nerves, with great fear about how he'd react or threaten me after reading my email.

I cautiously and gingerly tiptoed in and wrote him a note.

"Dear Anthony,

You are a wonderful and intelligent man. Sadly, though, I don't think I am the right woman for you. In as much as I like you, and think you're terrific, I must walk away. Unfortunately, I am currently under too much pressure and stress to deal with our relationship. I am looking for an easy, serene, carefree romance right now in my life. I have feelings for you, but I can't continue. I wish you love, happiness, success, and joy in your life. I'll never forget you! Mollie."

"Your Honor, I present, EXHIBIT 'E.'
Anthony's reply by a text..."

"Yeah, right, I'm not stupid. I know you have other reasons for this, but it's fine! You really are a special kind of stupid! Be careful, Mollie, and that's more than a hint! And, without a doubt, Please Do Forget Me! :("

How cute, a frown face emoji. I didn't respond, though I wanted to write back in the worst way with another Godfather quote.

"You can act like a man!!! (Slap) What's the matter with you?"

To my dismay, he wrote to me again 2 days later:

"I miss you! You won't have to cook lunch for me. Just dinner."

Five days later: "I can't stop thinking about you. I miss you. I bought a villa set on a wine-vineyard in Italy. Please call me! :-(((((!"

Sweet, more frown faces! I don't suppose he would have found it funny if I wrote him back **with the line from The Godfather...**
"It's not personal, Anthony. It's strictly business!"

I'm guessing, not? At last, I felt calm and relieved, as that was the last communication I had with Anthony. Thank heavens, and luckily, I never gave him my telephone number.

I Rest My Case, Your Honor... Next and Blocked!

The big question with any type of dating is, how do you know for sure, '*they are,*' who they say, '*they are*?' The big answer is *you don't!* There should be total transparency, but guess what? There isn't. That's life. Remember this story and go with an abundance of caution. The Anthony Mucianettia occurrence is emblematic of the fraud and scams you might run into, now and again, in the world of dating. Regardless, do your best to stay cautiously optimistic.

Nonetheless, keep your wits and heart about you until you know who '*they*' really are! It is what it is, my friends. So, please, be your own detective. *Be Alert! Don't be gullible, trusting, and naïve, or* you will be playing with fire. I like to call this "*Romance Arson!*"

After the Anthony drama, I added another one to my already crowded "*Fuck It List!*" Which, begs the question? Is there any justice in dating? Well, is there?

"For justice, we must go to Don Corleone!"

And, The Godfather, Original Theme Song, "Speak Softly Love," Plays on. "Da-da-da-da-da-da-da-da-da-da-da-Daaaaaaaa!"

I say with a classic movie fanfare, Man, it just gets better and better!

Dear Mr. Brando, Pacino, De Niro, and
hell, even Diane Keaton…

**"If I can die saying life is so beautiful,
then nothing else is important."**
(The Godfather)
:-((((!
P.S.
"Pass the cannoli!"

CHAPTER 10

"In a World"

IN OTHER WORDS...
THE REALIZATION OF BEING SINGLE, UNACCOMPANIED, ALONE FAR TOO LONG, AND LOTS OF WHATEVER!

1. **In A World Where:** Loneliness is to be expected...

   "Guess what? Just say '*no*' to loneliness and have fun. Go on and enjoy a whole bag of double-stuffed Oreos and move on!"

2. **In A World Where:** You sometimes need to reach things in high places and lift heavy objects by yourself...

   "This one is heartless and bakes in the solo existence further. Go on, take out a ladder, and grin & bear it. You can do this!"

3. **In A World Where:** You'll have to change your own light bulbs, air filters, and fire alarm batteries...

   "A total pain. Speaking of which, don't you absolutely detest the chirping sounds those wretched fire alarms make every 15 seconds until you replace the batteries? And why do they put them in the highest, inaccessible places? Go get the ladder!"

4. **In A World Where:** You must open those tough-to-open jars, hook together those impossible-to-put-on necklaces and bracelets, and snap or zip the back of your dress by yourself...

"If you can't manage this alone, you'll have to wear some-thing else. Sorry, but the ladder won't help you here! *Whatever!*"

5. **In A World Where:** *If* robbers or murderers happen to break into your house in the middle of the night, you will have no other choice but to protect and fight them off all by yourself...

"FYI, if this happens, call for a pizza or an Uber. As I told you before, they will get there far quicker than the police! For real!"

6. **In A World Where:** Although it might not be true, it appears that everyone else is hopelessly and happily in love, but you...

"Big sigh! Just saying '*whatever*' may not help with this one."

7. **In A World Where:** You feel so alone, sad, and sorry for yourself because currently you don't have that special someone to share social events and holidays with...

"Sure, the no birthday gift & celebrating alone *thing is hard. Whatever. Go celebrate the hell out of your birthday, anyway!*"

8. **In A World Where:** You no longer need to wax, shave, pluck, or constantly be prepared for sex from head to toe...

"If you look at this in an optimistic light, it's not a bad thing and possibly a perk. It could be a wonderful consolation prize!"

9. **In A World Where:** Everyone is a potential crush, leaving you no choice but to dress nicely every day. Even going to the store...

"Surely, this situation is monotonous and exhausting. But, if you dare to go out looking dreadful, it will assuredly be the day you'll run into Mr. Right. This, regrettably, leaves you no other option but to slip away quickly without meeting. Such a loss."

10. **In A World Where:** You can blatantly see in your married friends' eyes (not your good pals), that humongous pity expression. Or their obvious, catty, jealous gaze towards you...

"Whatever, for I enjoy responding obnoxiously. 'Oh, sorry. I'm having trouble walking from all the wild sex last night. To be blunt, I don't know how I'll ever get through the long hours of crazy sex with the new, gorgeous guy tonight!' Later. Enjoy!

Giggling, I love seeing them squirm with envy and shock."

11. **In A World Where:** You need to buy an industrial-strength vibrator. After all, a girls gotta do what a girls gotta do...

"Oh, please, don't act all surprised. Like you don't have one! And girl, if you don't have a vibrator (even if you're in a solid relationship) I need to write a whole other book just for you!"

12. **In A World Where:** Me time is all the time! Ahh, yes, fabulous...

"And yet another motivating perk. Do embrace it happily!"

13. **In A World Where:** The flood of people's rude, hurtful, brainless, insensitive comments, while attending a wedding, feels equal to being at a party in the painful chambers of hell! Such as...

"Wait a minute, you're all alone? Really, you came alone?"

"Lovely girl, such a shame you don't have a man! So sorry!"

"You're here all by yourself? How very sad, but good for you!"

"What's wrong with you? Why aren't you married?"

"Why can't you find a man? You're somewhat pretty. I guess?"

"You should try looking online. It's better than nothing."

"You're here by yourself? Wow, honey, don't you have guts!"

And the forever classic,

"Oh, my goodness, poor you. Are you still single? Such a pity!"

Remarks such as these feel like you're dodging bullets. Notice next time their horrified looks. Typically accompanied by a little tilt or nod of the head, and a 'tsk-tsk' sound spewing from their mouths. To hell with their ignorant comments!

I enjoy countering with a tear in my eye. "No, I'm married! Sadly though, my husband, a volunteer doctor working with 'Doctors Without Borders,' couldn't escort me this evening. He's been in a coma for the last 4 months. My beloved Whitaker was injured rescuing over 100 children from a burning orphanage in Burkina, Faso! I pray for him every day."

I look forward to that well-earned, embarrassing, mortified regret across their faces. Come on. They have it coming! Voila!

14. **In A World Where:** You get to eat the entire bucket of popcorn (just the way you like it) at the movies, all by yourself. Even better, you can go one step further and pour your favorite candy into the bucket and no one will see, comment, or criticize you! What a delicious, lovely, nonjudgmental luxury...

"I whole-heartedly feel this is a fabulous treat! Furthermore, the way I see it, I imagine we should be given a break here. I surmise when we are in between relationships, or going through a breakup, we should get a free pass. Any, and all, calories should not count. I must talk to the big woman upstairs about this issue. And stat!"

15. **In A World Where:** It's odious that you'll have to take out your own garbage and, also, kill disgusting creepy bugs all by yourself. I hate bugs...

"What can I say? This basically sucks altogether! Whatever?"

16. **In A World Where:** There is no obligation to pretend to care...

"Saying things like, what do you think? You're right! How do you feel about it? And the always reliable, I know, me too!"

It's delightfully liberating! "I am woman, hear me roar!"

17. **In A World Where:** You grasp you're always talking to yourself...

"Warning! It does get more concerning when you start answering yourself back. Or worse, yelling back! I shamefully do this all the time. Before cell phones, this behavior would justify a person being committed to a psych ward of a mental institution, without passing go. Luckily, you can now talk freely to yourself in public all the time without looking weird, mentally ill, or strange! Thank you, Martin Cooper, for inventing the first cell phone. Your creation has freed us all."

18. **In A World Where:** You're not burdened stressing about...

"Are you upset with me?" "What's wrong?" "Are you OK?"

"Did I do something wrong?" "Are you mad at me?" "Are you angry?" "Please tell me what I did!"

Not carrying this worry around is a cathartic, no-stress, no-troubles perk. Plus, a calmer life you acquire from being single.

19. **In A World Where:** There's no one to fight or argue with you. No one to aggravate, criticize, upset, or put you down. And no one being judgmental when you eat another cookie, (or the entire box), a Kit Kat bar, (the king-size bars), or a 4th slice of pizza...

"Peace, privacy, and space. It's undeniably another wonderful positive and a marvelously alluring plus. I say, almost worth being single for." (I said, almost!)

20. **In A World Where:** You'll hear those insensitive, uninvited reactions in restaurants. "Oh, just one?" "Table for 1?" "You're alone?" "It'll just be you?" "Would you rather, order to go?"

It's the equivalent of being at a wedding alone, or a sharp, acid-dipped dagger penetrating deep into your chest...

I respond firmly. "No, are you blind? There are 2 of us! Can't you see my fiancé to my right? Table for 2 and make it snappy!" I fear I'm cynical as I relish their puzzled expressions.

21. **In A World Where:** You fabulously get to be both the king and queen of your domain. I mean, you must agree, that's so cool...

"Rather enticing, being the queen and king of my life. And I would totally wear the bejeweled tiara & crown to prove it. Whatever! It sounds amazing to me."

22. **In A World Where:** You don't have to always be concerned about

someone else's feelings. Or basically, compromising most of the time. That might be considered, Winning...

"A deep exhale of relief and another benefit of being single."

23. **In A World Where:** You can sleep on either side of the bed. Or even lie across the bed in the wrong way if you so wish...

"Ahh, super amazing and a single person's dream. Just think, you can luxuriate with the whole blanket and wear your tattered sweatshirts. Surely, another comfy incentive. You can also set the temperature any way you wish. If you look at being single through rose-colored eyes, there are lots of bonuses and advantages to being alone! I'm trying here people! *Whatever?*"

24. **In A World Where:** You won't have to suffer with those stupid, ridiculous conversations...

Him: "What do YOU want to do tonight?"

Her: "I don't know! What do YOU want to do tonight?"

Him: "I really don't care! What do YOU want to do tonight?"

Her: "Dinner and a movie?"

Him: "No, I don't want to do that!"

Her: "Then, why the hell did you ask me?"

Him: "I don't know. I just wanted to know what YOU wanted to do. OK, fine, I want to go bowling?"

Her: "I don't want to do that! I feel bloated."

Him: "Then, why the hell did you ask me?"

Or the Ever Infamous...

Him: "Do YOU want to do *it*?"

Her: "I don't know. Do YOU, want to do *it*?"

Him: "I don't know. Do YOU?"

Her: "I don't know."

Him: "Why don't YOU know?"

Her: "OMG, OK, let's just do *it* already!"

Him: "I don't want to do *it* if YOU act like that. Forget it, I'm too tired!"

Her: "Then why the hell did YOU ask me?"

Him: "I don't know! OK, let's just do *it*!"

Her: "No! Now I don't want to do *it anymore*! You gave me a headache!"

UGH, it's exhausting and unnerving. Whatever!

25. **In A World Where:** You might potentially have more sex being single than if you were married or in a relationship…

    "Can't you see how this is a pleasant and fabulous advantage? Here, being single works out nicely. Still, wear a condom!!!!"

26. **In A World Where:** You can do what you want, where you want, how you want, when you want, and with whom you want…

    "Hmm! Like, who could argue with this? It sounds fantastic and most tempting, I say happily, grabbing more M&M'S!"

27. **In A World Where:** You don't have to do his dirty laundry and see unsightly skid marks on his disgusting underwear…

    "Hey, don't judge me. And what do you mean, what? Like, as if that doesn't happen? Moreover, I must ask, why do you men have this situation happening to you, anyway? This is appallingly yuck! Hey guys, news flash. That's what toilet paper is for. Nnnnn-K? You can even try some baby wipes if this is an ongoing occurrence with you. Just so you know, this falls under the major '*Oh, gross, Ick, and fix it now*' categories."

28. **In A World Where:** Your biological clock is screaming and about to Tick-Tock out, you consider freezing your eggs or going to a sperm bank…

    "Personally, I like the sperm bank scenario. It's like, 'Build-A-Bear.' You get to create your child, including the baby's height, intelligence, hair, eyes, etc. It's wonderful and sensible if you are single and want kids. Sure, go for it!"

29. **In A World Where:** You will have to pay all the bills by yourself...

"Definitely, any way you look at it, this is indeed a negative!"

30. **In A World Where:** You contemplate and fear that no one will be around to save you if, "Help, I've fallen and I can't get up," occurs...

"Obviously a bummer, and you don't have the stupid plastic Life Alert thingy to save you that old people wear around their necks. You know, the thing you laughed at on TV. I'm affirming now, I will never wear that thingy around my neck. Unless they make jeweled ones with diamonds and emeralds. Or cool ones with colored rhinestones. Then, of course, that'll work for me. *Whatever! Just don't fall!*"

31. **In A World Where:** You pick yourself up and courageously return to desperate measures, commonly known as...

"Online Dating!"

A helpful reference: It is well known that easy times don't help to forge character. Therefore, be comforted knowing all your trying times will enhance your life and provide you with all sorts of special qualities.

And hopefully, one day you will, at last, be in a place where you are... In A World Where: You find "The One" and live happily ever after!

Whatever! Oh, no! Where is my tiara? Phew, I got it!
Now, pass me the cookies and pizza, and then, *Let's Do It!*
I don't know. Do you really want to do it?

CHAPTER 11

The Plastic Surgeon

A TRUE LOVE STORY! AND THEN, THERE WAS FATE...

His name was Justin, a prestigious, well-known, and respected 42-year-old Beverly Hills plastic surgeon. He was enormously sought-after and in great demand. His renowned popularity was notable and apparently why his calendar was continuously booked three years in advance. Women would do just about anything to get close to this multifaceted, magnificent gentleman. He was admired not only for his artistic, natural-looking surgical talents but also among Hollywood's A-list superstars and the rich and famous. Moreover, he was undeniably as sexy chic as they come.

Every move he made, every gesture, was provocative and sensual, which he performed effortlessly. Surprisingly, he was humble, unpretentious, and unaware of the wake of his charismatic aura that trails behind him. It was impossible not to notice that Justin naturally exuded sexuality. He was justifiably considered a mini-God by all, particularly among the women who knew of him and his brilliant work.

Justin's private practice was in the heart of Beverly Hills, with other offices in Miami, San Francisco, and New York. To say he was a workaholic would be a significant understatement. He never stopped, slowed down, or took time out to smell the roses. It wasn't in his DNA. Yet, it was evident that Dr. Justin didn't work this hard for the money, power, fame, notoriety, or accolades. Not even to boost his career and prosperous business. He loved his profession and excitedly looked forward going to work each day with the hopes of helping his patients. His aspirations and goals were to bring pleasure and confidence to others through his art. His thoughtful benevolence, which made a difference in the lives of countless people, brought him lasting fulfillment and happiness.

He once explained to me, "Many believe plastic surgery is only for the vein, the superficial, and those with enormous egos. Nevertheless, it's not always the case. For the darkness that may come from a person's insecurities concerning their appearance can wreak havoc upon their well-being. As a plastic surgeon, I'm grateful for the opportunity to help people with self-acceptance, self-assurance, and self-love through cosmetic alterations. I'm delighted my work provides happiness & confidence to so many!"

Justin's eloquent statements, his righteousness, compassion, modesty, and selfless ego touched my heart, echoing in my mind for days.

Let's back up a little to the beginning of the Justin story.

Crazy to imagine and purely by chance, we met online. He disclosed the process of meeting women in this approach felt more private and discreet. Communicating online allowed him to get to know someone first, before he confessed who he was, or revealed his legendary surgeries, television shows, and famous patients. His dating mindset was very similar to my greatly missed, beloved Rocket-Man. Surely, repeating his personal story to women, on or off-line, gets old quickly. However, it helped to narrow down the flood of opportunistic ladies who knew of him and attempted to come on to him with their flirtatious, cunning agendas.

From our first tête-à-tête by phone, I felt at ease and safe enough to meet him right away, unlike many of the other men.

Although no longer naïve, I still checked him out first. Ergo, his stellar reputation broke my firm, unbreakable rule. I hoped with fingers crossed we'd click and *'Just-in,'* time for some normal! After my last 2 episodes, who could blame me? 'Episodes?' Such an adorable, friendly word to describe those disastrous incidents.

Not knowing all that much about Justin before we met, I still wished to impress him. I wore an adorable Dior Sundress, with pink Gucci, strappy-summer sandals, which were too costly to justify. I had a difficult time deciding whether to swoop up my hair into a casual updo with rhinestone clips or just keep it down, simple, and silky straight.

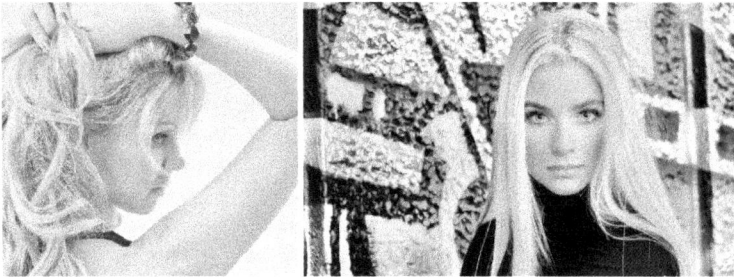

Notably nervous and excited, Justin and I met at 6:00 p.m. sharp, at Geoffrey's Malibu Restaurant, with my hair swept up for cocktails. This led to dinner, which progressed on to dessert, when I released my long blonde hair, free to cascade down over my shoulders. After dessert, came coffee, after-dinner drinks, complimentary chocolate petit fours, and truffles.

Justin and I got along famously. We shared an instant mutual attraction and a comfortable kindred-spirit connection. While holding hands, we couldn't stop sharing information, exchanging our life stories, and experiences. It was as if we were rushing, hungry to know everything about each other. It was so wonderful and easy. Regardless, I was still waiting for his other shoe to drop.

Fussing with my hair, worried it was a mistake to have taken it down, Justin read my mind. He smiled knowingly and spoke softly.

"My dear, you look stunning no matter how you wear your hair!" I couldn't distinguish if I should be embarrassed or if he just understood women so alarmingly well. This could be a little unnerving. Smiling bashfully, I continued with the conversation.

Just like that, on our very first date, I became pathetic, hooked, and hopelessly infatuated with him. Regrettably, with my history, this assured me an absolute, 100% guarantee I'd inevitably be hurt and end up devastated. Oh, hell, Que sera, sera! Justin was so strikingly magnificent that I'd happily risk it and take my chances. Being with him would be worth every bit of the pain, alcohol, tears, therapy, and chocolate I predictably knew would ensue.

Deflecting the inevitable, I eagerly jumped into this relationship with both feet. (In Dior shoes, of course!) Really, how could I not? He had such a beautiful, warmhearted presence. I honestly wanted to shake his mother's hand, congratulating her on a job well done! I mused, how charismatic and *umph-worthy* can one man be? As for Justin, *he certainly knew it, too!* He clearly worked it with an unpretentious, graceful finesse, all his own. Funny, on him, that too was charming. I was powerless and crazy about him. I hoped he didn't notice. Yeah, right, how could he not?

Justin was very "George Clooney-ish" in appearance, humor, and mannerisms. Only younger. He also had George's distinctive gestures. Such as rocking and tilting his head, paired with his sparkling puppy-dog eyes, and a mischievous pout upon his lips. Bashful and shy weren't his strong suits. I love this about him, too. I was toast! *Burnt toast.* The expensive, good, thick kind of bread you make French toast with. We said goodnight with an innocent kiss on the cheek. But I wanted more. I was in deep trouble. Deep!

OMGosh, I did it! I resisted him. "Am I good or what?" I grinned, altogether delighted with myself, feeling as though I deserved my very own personal high-five. I resisted the fierce urgency of now! "Go Me!" Driving home, I was uber-proud holding back my screaming, bad-girl impulses, and desires to jump into sex on the first date. That reckless path unequivocally would have ruined something special between us. Even so, it was challenging to resist Justin's sexual, magnetic charms, and his refined, overpowering elegance pulling me in. I knew very well my eyes betrayed me the moment I saw him. He easily detected it as my heart was unfolding before him. I sensed and felt a mortifying, red-faced teenage crush.

When I arrived home, as is so very common with us women, all the dreaded *"maybes"* and "self-doubts" came wildly crashing in. Crashing in with an abundance of girlish insecurities. It's a known force, equal to the gravitational interaction between the Earth and the moon, causing ocean tides in the wee hours of the night.

Gee, maybe I didn't resist him at all? *Maybe* he simply wasn't interested? Maybe he's not *into me* romantically? *Maybe* I was only just a dinner date to him? *Maybe* he didn't find me attractive, sexy, or sophisticated enough? *Maybe* I am not his type and I'll never see him again? *Really, Mollie, maybe* I should stop this parade of uncertainty and go to sleep. *Maybe?!*

The very next day, I awoke to an unexpected, delightful surprise. Justin sent me a text in the early morning hours, way before I had the chance to rise and greet my cup of Joe. Normally, I warn everyone against any contact with me whatsoever before my morning coffee. This made my enthusiasm for his early text deliciously unfamiliar. All my "insecure, self-doubts, and maybes" vanished when I read Justin's message. He excitedly begged for another date. Only this time, he invited me to his private residence, an exclusive estate in Malibu. I laughed, questioning silly me! Where else in California would a guy as successful as Justin live?

We shared stories about ourselves in greater detail that week on the phone. Justin conveyed. "I've been long divorced. My Ex is a very special person. She's an extraordinary, bright, beautiful woman. We share a respectful, friendly relationship, highly important to us both. Besides being the right thing to do, we felt it was crucial for the welfare and happiness of our children. We'll always share a lovely bond, only wishing each other love and joy!"

I admired their mature, impressive philosophy. It was refreshing and revealed immense class and intelligence. Justin's kind-hearted, thoughtful attitude exposed the majestic person he was. The surgeon also disclosed how pleased he was with his 16-year-old twins, Hadley, and Jacob. He boasted about what wonderful and astonishing people they had become. He confided how his teens were excelling in all their honors courses, sports, activities in the arts, community service, and many charities. They were now busy looking at colleges, which made Dr. daddy excited.

"It appears they are following in my footsteps," he giggled. "They aspire to be doctors and hope to start their own practice working together one day." He smiled radiantly with pride, which glowed right through the phone while speaking of them. "We are the 3-musketeers, sharing our irreplaceable, endless bond of love."

From our conversations, I was able to understand his heart and his dreams for the future. He explained. *"I realize this sounds more than a little silly and cheesy sentimental, but I'm looking for everlasting, hopeless, storybook, all-consuming, unreasonably romantic love, with a great desire and hope to remarry one day."*

I replied, "That's not silly at all. I find your desires honest and beautiful. For I, too, dream of that same cheesy storybook love!"

"I say humbly, due to my high profile in the medical community, it's difficult (impossible actually) to find someone who'll love me for me, my heart, the man inside my soul, and not just for who I am, or what I do."

And just like Rocket-Man, as I listened to him speak from his heart, I found his words sweet and sincere. For some reason, I believed everything he told me unconditionally. This was super unusual for me these days. No wonder every woman desired this 6'1"champion of a man. Seriously, who wouldn't have wanted to believe everything he said without any reservations?

The following night, I drove up to his humongous mansion overlooking the Pacific Ocean and waited for the grandiose intimidating iron gates to open. If I had not gone through my Rocket-Man extravagant experience, I would've been speechless and overwhelmed. Yet, no matter how successful Justin was, I doubt he speaks *"privileged."* Well, at least not fluently. Meanwhile, I was impressed there wasn't a squeaky noise coming from the gates. Everyone has those creaky noises in Malibu from the dampness and salt in the air. Proving again, he was a perfectionist.

It did concern me, Justin being a plastic surgeon. I wondered if he would look at me with critical, ornery eyes of judgment. I was very apprehensive about him seeing my flaws. I speculated on what he would do to rescue me from all my imperfections.

Thinking to myself, "Mollie, stop it! No more *maybe* talk! I'm going in with all my heart. No more negative thoughts allowed."

I arrived at the top of the long narrow driveway, adorned with spectacular multi-colored roses and gardenias. Justin greeted me at the door, with a Baccarat Glass of fine California Merlot filled to the brim, and a sweet kiss on my forehead. I hoped he hadn't detected how right there at his doorstep, I melted like a stick of butter on a stove, leaving an emotional girly mess!

As we walked into the marbled foyer, with the impressive Waterford Crystal Chandelier hanging above, he passionately over-powered me, picking me up and placing me onto his thick, warm lips. As he brushed up against me suggestively, I went momentarily weak in the knees. *All right, fine*! It was longer than a moment, and more than just my knees! Seriously, "*Let it go*," Queen Elsa. I fell completely under his spell. Goodness, this guy possessed some deeply intense, irresistible skills.

When he spoke, his voice sounded as if it came right out of a clas-sic Cary Grant film. "Hello, darling! I've looked forward to seeing you and holding you in my arms all day!" Spellbound, there was no turning back from Cary, or Justin! I was mush, gush, enraptured, smitten, a goner, enchanted, infatuated, lured, lovesick, beguiled, charmed, and all in. I was all that, and many more run-on words my college journalism professor would've strong-handedly marked, with a big F, in a bright, fat, red marker.

I was appreciative and pleased the good doctor had more discipline and discreet resolve than I had, wanting him desperately on the spot. As for me, I would've put down the Merlot and jumped on him fiercely at hello. Fortunately, I withheld my classless sexual desires. His restraint was epic. Well, maybe not so much! But at least he waited till sunset, and we had a chance to share the delicious appetizers and finger foods his household staff skillfully prepared for us before they left. I didn't have the calming patience Justin possessed. If it were up to me, the now sticky, icky, melted stick of butter, I would've attacked him after the cheese plate, and way before the duck Foie Gras. So, I reluctantly followed his lead like a lady. *A horny lady, but dammit, a lady, no less!*

I caught Justin observing me mid-bite, eating a Russian pancake with crème fraiche and caviar. Shoeless, with my legs sprawled out comfortably on his couch, I wondered if I had overstepped my welcome. Giggling, "Why are you staring? Am I making myself too much at home?"

"No, of course not!" He lifted his eyelids, and I could feel him visually taking off my clothes. "I was looking at you and thinking, I can't believe how much nicer my home looks with you in it!"

Mic-drop! *Places everyone for an old classic, Cary Grant, love scene. And… Action!*

I won't torment you further. We made love in every possible way 2 people could physically and artistically imagine. I'm talking about the *Kama Sutra positions.* The 2nd edition! It was blissful, heavenly, and hard to describe our shared sensual moments and decadent, obscene, erotic wild ecstasy. Yes, we fucked! But we also shared a warm, respectful, loving passion. Everything about our lovemaking was uniquely 'us,' and unlike any sex I had ever known. It was not at all the *"been there, done that"* sort of sex! It was intimate and sweet, but still on the edge of naughty. It was a lustful kind of movie scene with a whole different rating. A scene that old-world Cary would never have signed up for. We redefined sex! The world seemed to stop that night. Our lovemaking was the closest thing to heaven I had felt for a long time. Since Rocket-Man. At that moment, I dared to think he could be the key to moving on.

Hours later, before I could even think of dressing, Justin threw more sexual oxygen on the already burning fire between us. He gently swept me up into his toned, muscular arms. My new lover, and hopeful future, carried me down the Brazilian Mahogany wooden stairs towards the beach, and walked us straight into the ocean. Cradled in his arms, he whispered, "I am crazy about you, darling!" Terrified, because I felt the same way, I didn't reply.

Making love in the ocean was challenging, but I didn't care if I drowned. It was titillating having his hard, wet penis inside of me as the waves continued to crash down over us, ultimately enhancing our steamy passion. Later, he carried me back onto the beach, spread out a blanket, opened my legs, and we continued our sexual gymnastics on the sand. There we were, naked under the moon and stars, sharing kisses, spasms of ecstasy, impassioned embraces, and laughter. Moaning and quivering like a porn star, as he went down on me, pleasuring me with his tongue on my pussy, left me breathless and enraptured. It was a darn good thing the crashing waves silenced my screams, or the neighbors would surely have called the police, fearing a murder scene.

Thrusting his body on top of me, rocking back and forth, I moved my hips against his stiff, desperate penis. I lost track of all the intense orgasms he brought me to. I was positively hypnotized and loved it all. After hours of blissful beachfront fucking, we ran back up to the house, grabbed something to eat, and then went on making love and cuddling for hours in his Hastens Vividus Bed. Entranced and totally drunk on sex, we continued till the sun rose.

Justin and I shared the type of euphoria you can't wait to tell your closest friends about the next day over some very gooey chocolate, and other fattening creamy desserts with wine, tequila, and cappuccinos. I jubilantly squandered no time to do exactly that. Despite being in the middle of a workweek, my girls came to my house for a sex powwow and rendez*booze* session. We chatted and giggled like schoolgirls, pigging out on yummy delicacies without any guilt, as I delivered the Justin stories of rapture. I felt a tad braggadocious, sensing it made them green with sexual envy. Anyhow, they love me and excitedly wanted to hear every naughty, lust-filled detail. Thus, I continued…

"I swooned. It felt like I was thrown into a romantic paperback novel that we all would've read in high school. Well, except for you, Shara. You likely read them in elementary school. LOL!"

"Fuck you, Mollie, it was kindergarten. And what's up with the swooning? Truly, keep that to yourself." We giggled mischievously.

"And then, as the nasty romantic parts developed, I was sequestered into a badass, triple-X, trashy sex story. All sprinkled with the exceptions of loving tenderness, style, and finesse. All nonfiction. Making love with Justin was endless, slow, fast, naughty, oral, gentle, erotic, and sensually spicy. This man is a fucking, Sex Lord. He made me so wet I was ashamed. Hmm, on second thought, not at all!"

My besties listened intently, blushing with a yearning need to know every minuscule aspect of my carnal escapade. I noticed, and justifiably so, that there was a tinge of lascivious cravings to claw my eyes out! I mean, who could blame um? As they pleaded for more, I continued describing our fury and hungry sexual desires.

"What he did to my body and what we felt was far beyond ordinary sex. Our orgasms were a never-ending story. We came together over & over. The man orgasmed without assistance from pills. I don't know how hc did it, but he stayed hard all night. And the best part? I never had to fake it! I sensed his electricity running through my veins. I felt the beat of our hearts harmoniously synchronize. My head rested in the nook of his neck, our legs intertwined, exhausted from the insatiable cravings for each other. Our passion can only be described as the epitome of romance."

I concluded my story by divulging, "I'm aware that Justin has become my new happy place and sexual haven. Until that is, he breaks my heart. Ladies, in matters of love and romance, it's evident Justin was right at home in the heart of his wheelhouse! All righty, there's that! I'm through with my 'C'est un amant incroyable tale!' More wine, anyone?"

They screamed in unison, "Hell, no! You can't stop now? More!"

Naturally, Shara snapped back with her loving wit, "Yeah, all that bullshit is as gag me as it gets! I could hurl right now. Mollie, you are so overly exaggerating, no doubt, and by the way, Fuck You, again!" She giggled, her legendary high-pitched little girl, Shara laugh, as we all began chuckling for some much-needed relief. Amidst her silliness, I innately knew, Shara, my very best friend, was the happiest one of all for me. She knew all too well how I suffered from both my Drew and Rocket-Man recoveries.

After relentlessly pleading for me to go on, "OK, chill, I'll tell you! So, his ripped abs and toned, hairless, Greek god Apollo's chest, rivals a young Henry Cavill's. FYI bitches, he also waxes his huge, thick, perfectly shaped penis and balls! I swear, I was a paralyzed prisoner, captive under his mysterious savage spell. Only a select few in the entire human population are fabulous enough to live in 'Fabulosity-Land.' Justin is one of them. I think I'm in love! While dreamy-romantic, it's wildly scary, too."

Elizabeth blurted out, "Yep, ok there, Anna Karenina, Jane Austen, Juliet, or whoever the fuck you are right now. Enough of all your fairytale rubbish and let's get real here. Sexplain more about his fabulosity dick and how big it really is! Does he eat pussy like a pro? Did you swallow? Be honest, how many times did you really cum? You swear on Prada you didn't fake it? Not even once? Did he wear a condom? Did you douche? Is he (I hope) circumcised? Does he have any STD'S? Does he have smelly balls?" My girls were rolling on the floor laughing. Not with me, but at me. And I loved it.

"I'm brutally sorry guys. Trust me, I know it's all icky, girly-girl, sick! I get it. It's as cliché as a Taylor Swift song! Perhaps worse."

"Nah-Ah" Joyce argued. "Much worse. More ancient and corny than a Lionel Richie or Journey song! Wait, I forgot Michael Bolton.

Debbie asked, "Who the hell is Journey, Lionel, and Bolton?"

We laughed our asses off. "Snap, Deb, you're out of the group!"

"Whatever! Fuck all of you," I yelled out, while everyone cracked up. But I paused, thinking to myself, whatever! This is the real deal. Corny, clearly, but I loved every second being with Justin.

"Seriously, guys, I wish you all an icky, girly-girl, sick night like I had with the good (very good) doctor."

Immediately, all six of my beloved BFFs, Shara, Melinda, Barbara, Elizabeth, Debbie, and Joyce, screamed out, while laughing hysterically, "Oh, pa-lease! And Go Fuck Yourself, Bitch!"

"And there it is. The main reason I love you all! Here. Have some more chocolate cake. Oh, gosh, I almost forgot. It's tequila time, you envious bitches!"

All 7 of us collapsed into helpless laughter. My girls and I drank college-taught 'Lick, Sip & Suck' tequila shots until we ran out around midnight. We progressed to vodka, then wine, and binging for hours on our delectable, fattening get-together. Gossiping freely and catching up on each other's lives, as we carelessly mixed alcohol and got wasted. My besties and I have such crazy fun. Nothing like it. Well, that is, until the morning hangover. Ouch!

As the weeks followed, Justin and I became mutually devoted to each other. For me, it was more than Justin being smart, caring, adoring, and loving. For the first time, I could see the possibility of forever and belonging with "The One." We were happily sharing amazing times. As the months raced by, one evening, at our favorite intimate restaurant (when I least expected it), Justin took my hand, looked into my eyes, and spoke the words I so longed to hear. Well, besides, "Oh, baby, I'm cumming!"

"Mollie, my angel, I'm desperately and madly in love with you!"

I sprang back. "Darling, I'm madly in love with you, too!"

At last, our confessions of love were out in the open. Justin wasn't the impulsive type or one to rush into love or anything else. Therefore, his words professing his genuine love, commitment, and affection made me feel secure. Due to my complex dating past, I too, am no longer impulsive. Complex, how entirely adorable!?

After dinner, we went back to his house and made the sweetest, decadent love. Irrationally, as soon as my love fell asleep, I suddenly became nervous and stressed, with my usual doubts and insecurities. Even though I knew I loved this precious man, ironically, I wasn't 100% sure he was "The One." Justin was older than me and already had children of his own. We hadn't yet arrived at the point where I felt comfortable enough to question him about whether he wanted any more children. I was overcome with fear, for I had no idea if he'd want to or even consider starting all over again. Honestly, this was the existential, all-important question, and I had no clue whatsoever what his answer might be.

What's more, I knew full well, with an unwavering conviction, that I wanted to have children. I wanted to raise a family of my own. I couldn't help reflecting and remembering. This was the main issue, which primarily led to Rocket-Man and me having to say goodbye, even though we were head-over-heels in love. Indeed, making that decision took herculean resolve on my part.

The likelihood of Justin wanting more children seemed unrealistic. Yet for me, it was a deal-breaker, regardless of love. To be fair, we needed more time before making such serious commitments and promises. After all, it was only 6 months since we began dating. I couldn't sleep that night. Staying awake all evening in Justin's protective arms helped to ease my anxious, jittery emotions and troubling questions. The only thing definite, was Justin, and I were in love. And that, for now, was good enough.

Our time together was ideal. Our romance was intellectual, fun, exciting, and sexual. Being together was carefree and effortless. There were no arguments or disagreements, and no dishonesty or pretense. It was an unfamiliar love affair. Although it was a grown-up, mature love, we were foolishly silly at times. We shared many happy adventures attending the opera, the symphony, musicals, movies, business functions, galas, socials, and countless romantic dinners. It was all harmoniously serene and fantastical.

Wherever we went, I was conscious of the overt, pining glances and stares of desire most women directed toward him. And not unexpectedly, their evil daggers aimed directly at me. Likewise, Justin observed equivalent flirtations by men who gazed at me. We each, in our own way, handled it with easy aloofness, casually ignoring the situation peacefully, without any concern. As for the women, I didn't fault them in the least. Still, I could have done without all the evil eyes, contemptuous, and resentful snide looks of envy they bestowed upon me. Regardless, it was reassuring how Justin never once gave me a reason to be jealous. He never looked at other women, flirted, or exhibited any suspicious activities, strange calls, or texts of any kind. I admired this about him. He made me feel secure and safe with his endless caring devotion.

Over time, I came to appreciate Justin's philanthropic nature and his many charitable causes. He contributed much of his time performing costly, innovative surgeries for kids with physical problems and difficult disfigurations before and after birth. He did so regardless of whether the children's parents could afford it or not. This benevolent, altruistic man never charged them a dime.

As for elective cosmetic surgeries by other surgeons? Hmm, well, in my opinion, most of the women in the *Plastic World* appeared fake, and almost ghoulish looking! They are ridiculously stretched out, filled up, pulled up too tight, overdone, and unnatural. I don't mean to be cruel, but they all look like a dog with its head hanging out of a car window, going 75 mph on the freeway, while catching the breeze with its face. Most women I've seen with work performed by other dentists ('*wink-wink*,') appear peculiar looking. In contrast, when I visit Justin for lunch at his office, all his patients look beautiful and natural. I've never witnessed any of his patients with ridiculous overdone fillers, or gobs of Botox squeezed into their (fear of aging) faces. For all his lucky patients, Justin had successfully starved off the inevitable 'ravages of time.' They always emerged years younger than their actual age. I was proud of his magnificent talents and artistic skills.

Justin loved his work immensely. He discussed great concern for his patients and his desire to help them. He also believed a kind bedside manner is critical for their well-being. (I can tell you all about his kindhearted bedside manner. But in an entirely different setting!) For this reason, I never attempted to change him or make him defensive about his long hours or inability to travel. He felt (and rightfully so), he was helping people by transforming their lives and giving them a renewed sense of self-confidence. I was honored to be with such a respectable, decent man who had everything going for him. Not to mention, and I quote, Ava Gardner, referring to Sinatra, "This man was good in the feathers!"

As much as we wished, there was never the time or opportunity to travel together. He dreamed of taking me to Paris, the romantic city of lights and love. He spoke about it numerous times. Unfortunately, Justin couldn't take the time away, because of the countless surgeries booked in advance. Likewise, he never once complained about all my traveling for work, either. We had a mutual admiration of each other's professions and talents. How we shared and supported one another with encouraging appreciation for our aspirations and future dreams was extraordinary.

Time sprinted by, and after eight months, we were considered an official couple, very much in love. During these months, I grew to love his children deeply. Luckily, they felt the same way about me. Dr. Daddy was over the moon and couldn't have been happier about our beautiful and loving dynamic. His twins were his world, and we cherished all the enjoyable moments we spent together.

At last, the time had come when I felt comfortable enough to discuss the idea of having children with Justin. Late on a glorious Saturday afternoon, sitting outside in his gorgeous oceanfront garden, I mustered up the courage to address the topic. I was petrified as our relationship rested solely on his answer. While enjoying Malibu's legendary Ocean sunset, and sipping a lovely glass of Chianti from Tuscany, I felt it was the appropriate moment to bring up my all-important question. *"The big ask!"* I nervously turned to Justin, feeling butterflies in the pit of my stomach, a lump in my throat, and my heart racing wildly. I asked him, trembling.

"Baby?"

"Yes, my sweetheart? Talk to me."

"OK! Umm? So? My angel, I? Ah? I was wondering, Umm? All right. Here goes! What do you think about the notion of you and I having a? Umm? A family of our own together?"

Becoming faint and terrified, I waited for his response. Justin answered my painstaking, deal-breaking question with an instantaneous, beaming smile. My love couldn't reply fast enough.

"Sweetheart, nothing in this world would make me happier than having children with you. I'm ecstatic and all for it! My precious, Mollie, you will be the best mother in the world! Amazing, our children will be so lucky to have you as their mommy, just as the twins are. I am thrilled and ecstatic. Okey-dokey, honey! So, when can we start? How about now?"

Giggling, as tears of joy clouded my vision. I grabbed my delicious young George Clooney, "I love you! I love you! I love you! You are my forever and my happily ever, and after. I love you!"

Justin echoed my words in return, adding his brilliant smile as a bonus. "I love you more, my angel!" That was it for me. I didn't have a single *maybe*, a hesitation, *a what if,* or an insecure *doubt* left inside me. I was, at last, forever in love with *"The One!"*

Our time alone was peaceful, intimate, and bursting with endless pleasures. This idyllic joy continued throughout our relationship, never once wavering. Our future appeared bright and secure. I had never been so sure or happy with anyone in my life. The promise of our love, our future children, and our perfect life together fulfilled my every dream. It was all very surreal, like a fairytale. We enjoyed simply being us, Mollie, and Justin. It felt as though we were watching and starring in a movie about our lives.

Although everything appeared flawless on the surface, I couldn't shake the negative storm, the dark force, or the feelings of kismet I sensed were hovering over us. Despite our life being picture-perfect as a Klimt painting and harmonious as a Mozart concert, I felt an uneasy energy chasing and overshadowing us. I tried shaking it off. "Stop it, Mollie Sloan. You're being paranoid. Let it be!" But the forewarnings continuously lingered.

I convinced myself these terrible, haunting thoughts resulted from my silly fears, stemming from the joy of being so loved. It was reasonable, for my life had never been this blissful before. I suppose it worried me (as it would anyone), to feel this euphoric. Protectively, I never shared my negative thoughts with Justin. Appreciating it was critical to end these absurd feelings, I committed myself to trusting everything would be fine. I adored basking in our happiness and stopped thinking or discussing such destructive premonitions with anyone again. No more negative, for life was grand and would continue this way forever. Period!

My world was now all about Justin, our careers, our undying love, and the birth of our future children. I smiled often, thinking about it. Our lives seemed limitless. No matter what we did together, we were protected inside the bubble of our love. Nothing could touch us. At last, with immense joy and happiness, we were now discussing marriage and moving in together.

AND THEN, THERE WAS FATE...

Alas, ever so quickly, and all at once, it crumbled apart. Oh My God, out of nowhere, *we* dissolved, right before my very eyes. It all came down so swiftly that I didn't even know or have the chance to process what was happening.

One ordinary Thursday afternoon, while Justin was at work, I ran over to his house to surprise him with a sentimental gift I had made for him. I planned to leave my romantic gift displayed on his favorite chair. It was something Justin always wanted, and I knew he would love it, especially coming from me. I was giddy with excitement until I suddenly realized *I was not alone*. Afraid, I stopped in my tracks.

As one would imagine, I was shocked and taken aback when I walked into his house seeing, *Another Woman!* There she was,

212 | ROBIN ROTH

apparently feeling right at home, casually sitting on the couch with her never-ending tanned legs and her long brown, silky, flowing thick hair. Bitch! Well, they were probably extensions, no doubt!

On the spot, I was distressed and immediately jumped to conclusions. Who was she, this slut? What did she want, this whore? I scrutinized her up and down and then aimed a flinty, resting-bitch face toward her. Who is this repulsive yet gorgeous, tall, thin, toned, impeccable, exquisite seductress, homewrecker? I questioned, was Justin cheating on me? But? Why? Gawking at her, bitter, blatantly hurt, suspicious, and overwhelmed, I could not face or cope with this notion. I felt as though she kicked me right in the stomach with her eyes. I was going to be sick. Oh, bloody hell!

Once again, I had been a stupid, naïve, gullible, silly fool. Would I ever open my innocent eyes to see the truth that was always front and center, staring me in the face? Would I ever stop living in my romantic fantasy dream world? I don't know how I missed all the signs. My God, was I just a convenient casual tryst for him?

Shit! Shit, she was unbelievably perfect and gorgeous. Of course, Justin would want to sleep with her and be with her. Why would any man refuse this stunning Aphrodite, the goddess of love, desire, and beauty? Geez, I would've slept with her myself and I don't do women! I hated her instantly, with no real concrete reason for feeling this way. Also, what the hell was this tart, this tramp, this trollop even doing here, in our love-nest, our dreamy sanctuary? I wanted to take her down and cut a bitch! I was in heart-wrenching disbelief. How could Justin do this to me? How?

Moreover, this was incomprehensible and not at all like him. So then, how could he? Why would he? I felt faint, and my legs could barely sustain me. Reeling in anguish, grasping the situation, and teeming with suspicion, this unknown, whomever, low-life, floozy, man-stealing, harlot person visibly saw my look of total confusion. The expression visibly written on my face, "Aha, ya think??? Bitch!"

Then the statuesque hussy, vixen, call-girl looked straight at me and began whispering. "Hello, I am Sidney, Justin's EX-Wife." She spoke in a very solemn, sad, weak tone, and all the while, I was noticing just how impeccably elegant she was. It was unnatural to look this beautiful and not be famous. Come on, man, she stood like an airbrushed Vogue Cover Girl or a legendary haute couture supermodel. She could've been Justin's *Billboard Poster Child* or his *Plastic Surgery Masterpiece*. But shit, she was all real and natural. I despised, loathed, and detested everything about her spectacular self! Nevertheless, I was vastly relieved to hear the "X-factor."

Still, judging by her grim and gloomy expression, I ached with pain, fearing what she was about to say next. I scanned her flawless, chiseled face for an answer. Was he going back to her? My heart stopped. Devastated, I concluded. Yes, he was leaving me! They were getting back together! But wait. This vamp wouldn't barge in to tell me that. Besides, Justin was man enough to explain it to me himself. Oh My, God! Did something happen to one of the kids? Is that the reason this magnificent bitch-woman, who *I hated beyond hate*, was here to tell me? I held my breath as she spoke.

Smiling with kindness, she began. "I know all about you. Justin told me every detail of your amazing relationship. He explained he had fallen head over heels in love with you. He bragged constantly about you and told me everything you've done. Such as your extraordinary accomplishments, triumphs, talents, and achievements. Justin was so proud of you, Mollie. He went on and on, telling me what a breathtaking, gorgeous woman you are. As usual, I can see he was correct and not exaggerating at all!"

I didn't know how to respond or what she would say next. But I wanted to yell at her, "Shut up! I beg you, shut up!" Instead, I looked up at her with an expression of ill-conceived horror. I couldn't decide whether to laugh, cry, or take her down. Frustrated, irritated, and upset, I blurted out impatiently.

"Please, Sidney, go on. Please! You're freaking me out!"

She continued. "Justin and I met for lunch a few days ago."

Oh Lord, I thought. Here it comes! My eyes, like bullets, targeted directly at her. I wanted to die right there on the spot. *Wow, so they were* getting back together. I knew it! I was about to fall apart in front of her dazzling, perfect self. Or I could just shoot her! I can see the "ID Channel" vultures lurking with cameras. "Reporter, kills ex-wife, News at 11!" I had to compose myself. Defiantly standing tall with aplomb, I refused to let this *'beyotch'* see me lose it! And why is she speaking slow, like a Southern belle?

"And! And! What! Please, Sidney, for God's sake, tell me already. Why are you here, and why did you meet with Justin?"

I went from livid and annoyed to holding my breath with trepidation. She went on…

"Justin, as considerate as ever, wanted to tell me in person, to prepare me, that he was going to ask you to marry him next weekend. He wished to meet with the children as well. He sought to explain to them in a loving, non-threatening, caring approach before he jumped in and asked you. Justin hoped the twins would understand and feel included. I can't impress how totally relieved and thrilled he felt when they were both enthusiastically happy, down with it, and all for it! They love you, Mollie!" She went on…

"While eating lunch, Justin showed me the spectacular engagement ring he designed for you. He was about to surprise you. He was taking you to Paris to propose marriage at the top of the Eiffel

Tower. Romantic as ever, Justin arranged a rare, VIP, private opportunity at sunset to bring you to the tower's summit as the city lights began to twinkle. As he spoke, he was enormously excited and happier than I had ever known him to be. He behaved like an exuberant, silly teenager. I couldn't have been more delighted for him. No one deserved happiness more than Justin!"

In fear of what was coming next… "Go on, Sidney!"

"He also expressed how euphoric he was about having more children with you! I remember it well because he spoke in such a cute singsong voice. *I love her, Sidney. I am the luckiest man in the world!* Since our children were born, I've never seen him this happy or complete. Mollie, you had stolen his heart and made him supremely happy!"

My knees went weak. Shaking and distrusting, I responded in a timid declaration. *"**Made**? What do you mean by made, Sidney? You mean, make! Right? I make! I make him happy! Right, Sidney? I Make! I MAKE!"* She began to answer me, but I didn't want her to speak. I wanted her to stay silent and not say another word.

She eased in. "I truly didn't want to be the one to tell you this. Dear Molly, but Justin." She stopped short with a gasping, agonizing sigh. Her pause seemed an eternity…

"Sidney," I begged her, crying. "Please, talk! Just talk to me!"

"Mollie. Dear Mollie…"

Panicked, I cried out, *"SIDNEY, WHAT?"*

She spoke, crying uncontrollably. "Mollie, Justin had a massive heart attack today, right in the middle of performing surgery. He…" She quivered. "He… Oh, Mollie, he passed away late this morning."

I could not process her words. Even though I heard them loud and clear, I could not compute them. I couldn't make any sense of what she was telling me. She took my hand, which saved me from falling to the ground. Why was this woman lying to me? Why was she telling these dreadful, evil lies? Her words shattered me like glass, and beyond any pain I had ever known. My heart refused to beat. I couldn't begin to handle this agony.

"Nnnnn, Nnn," I tried to speak. "No! My love. He was. Justin, my angel, and I were just. We were going. And it was. It was. I was!"

I couldn't form a single sentence. Locked in severe shock, I sat there in disbelief and utter silence, trembling, and blinded by my tears. I looked up at Sidney and sobbed. "Our love was over as quickly as it began."

I still couldn't comprehend her wicked words as fact. This stunning woman, for whatever reason, was being mendacious and dishonest with me. She was lying. She had to be! I never hated anyone more in my entire life!

I went numb, screaming out loud at the top of my lungs, "NOOO! NOOO! NOOO, it cannot be true. Justin is fine! You're lying to me!" Deafening painful cries soared from my lips. From the deepest, darkest depths of my soul, the most horrific, wailing, and shrieking sounds arose. Traumatized, my saturating vale of tears brought such unparalleled heartache and inconceivable sadness.

Sidney came over and held me tight in her impeccably ripped arms. We cried together. Justin's ex-wife was too kind and compassionate. I really tried, but I couldn't hate this lovely woman.

Bewildered amidst my fog of desperation, I thought of the countless things I meant to say, do, and share with Justin. I wanted to thank him for being my best friend and gifting me the magical love that was ours. Such a rare love, I had never known and would never know again. I needed the chance to say one final goodbye. To feel one everlasting hug and eternal kiss. I wanted to tell him one last time how deeply I loved him and how much he meant to me. We were so close. I needed to share with him that my best friend, the love of my life, was gone. Fate is abusively cruel.

How could this have happened? Our life was perfect. He was too young to die! Justin was hugely generous and had infinitely more to achieve in his life. He was immensely charitable and helped so many people. So then, why God? Why? We were going to have children. We were going to be a family. Then, I remembered.

Oh, his poor children. I stopped to reflect on how tragically this would affect his beloved twins, whom Justin desperately *loves* with all his heart. *Loved. He Loved! It doesn't make sense that now everything is past tense. Why, oh why God?* Why did this happen? I was happy. We were happy. My heart was bleeding wildly in pain.

Frozen, disoriented, and refusing to believe I had lost my great love. I was trying frantically to stay in the luxurious comfort of denial. In a flash, nothing in my life made sense anymore. I was struggling to breathe. We were to be married! Until now, I wasn't even aware he was going to ask me to marry him in less than a week. I wasn't certain if this provided me with comfort or further despair. It was impossible to grasp how I'd ever get through this pain and anguish, or how I could go on living without him in my life. Alas, I was broken. My heart was forever obliterated.

The love I shared with Drew and Rocket-Man was extraordinary. But different from the love I had known with Justin. Our love was solid, unconditional, and eternal. We fit. We were complete. We are! We **were** the perfect couple. Everyone said so. During our brief time together, we shared one heart.

Oh, dear Lord, this couldn't be happening. I replayed in my mind how I should have been there, holding his hand at the end. The thought of not being there by his side, loving him, and holding him as he crossed over, would keep me weeping in misery forever. I let him down. I failed him. He left this world as he came into it, alone. Yet, in between, he was loved, admired, and respected. Without ever being a movie star, he was genuine Hollywood Royalty. He made the world a better place, just by being in it.

Sidney interrupted my private thoughts of grief when she came to sit by me. She handed me a brand-new Louis Vuitton suitcase Justin had packed for me to fly to Paris with him. It was filled with the latest couture runway fashions and designer shoes that he carefully and lovingly selected. It was typical of Justin and all a part of his surprise. She then placed a gorgeous handmade sterling silver box in my right hand. As tears drowned my vision, I slowly opened the lovely, unique box. Cradled in the center was a spectacular diamond ring Justin had personally designed for me. The diamond ring he was going to ask me to marry him with. Crying hysterically, trembling intensely, unable to see through the deluge of my tears, I felt a defiant pain from the emptiness inside my soul. I took out the ring, held it to my heart, and collapsed.

Sometime later, I came around. Oddly, it was comforting to see Sidney on the floor by my side, holding my hand. Of course, she would be caring and compassionate. Indeed, I wouldn't have expected anything less from my sweet Justin. And in that moment, I completely understood why the twins were so incredible. I had to remind myself it was a great loss for her, too.

I couldn't stop weeping as I looked at the exquisite, originally designed ring Justin made for me. This ring he created for me with all his love was so characteristic of him. Sadness and joy filled my broken soul to its core. Shaking, paralyzed with pain, I placed Justin's diamond ring on my finger, which, naturally, fit perfectly.

Crying, I looked up and vowed to Sidney. "I will never remove

this ring from my body to my dying day." She held me sympatheti-
cally. I fell apart, crumbling in her compassionate arms.

A few days passed. I was despondent, in disbelief, hopeless, and
drenched in despair. I had run out of tears, if that were medically
possible. I couldn't speak, nor did I want to. The only call I made
was to my editor Angela, to inform her I was taking a temporary
leave of absence.

Walking on eggshells, Angela spoke affectionately. "Sweetie,
we're so very sorry, and we're all here for you! I think you should
know; Justin called me last week. He requested time off for you, so
he could take you to Paris to propose marriage. He was so excited!
Mollie, he loved you with all his being. I've never seen such a love!"
When Angie started to cry, I couldn't deal with it. I hung up on her.

As word got out, everyone and their sister kept calling me,
including people I had never even met. My home phone rang nonstop off the hook, so I took it off the hook and I turned my cell
off, too. Packages of love and flowers were delivered in a constant
stream. People meant well, but it didn't help, for I was too lost in
my anguish to notice or even care. All I wanted was to be alone. I
would have slipped into a deep depression, but I knew all too well
my darling Justin would have been disappointed in me. He'd be
very upset if I fell into the bottomless web of darkness.

Crazy, I know, but I hear him talking to me forcefully with tenderness. "Be strong, my Love. You must find a way to move on."

I replied as if he hears. Oh, Justin, how could I? It's impossible!

I heard him pleading with me. "Baby, you have to pull yourself together and continue living." In my head, I heard and felt the
words he always said to me. "I crazy love you, and I will till the end
of time!" Then, I innately sensed his promise. "I am not gone. I am

always with you, right by your side! My precious, even though I have passed, I now live inside your heart." I clung to his next words, which I could spiritually and telepathically hear him saying to me. "I will forever be near you, with you, and guiding you. You will sense my comfort and love around you forevermore. You are, were, and will for all eternity be, *'The One,' and the love of my life!"*

I know I heard and felt his words unmistakably reaching out to me, but it would be unimaginable to move forward without him.

Thank God for the never-ending love of my dear friends pulling me through this tragic storm in my life. They remained by my side constantly, taking turns and not leaving me alone for a second. Accepting I had been through far too much, I was officially done with love. I can never live through this again. I was finished. Over!

Shara, my magic friend, always having my back, promised me. "In time, Mollie, you'll be back! I promise. You will see."

A few days after Justin passed, I received what I have come to learn is "A Love Tap." Justin always sent me gardenia flowers and plants, as we both loved these flowers. But, when a gardenia dies on an indoor plant, it can never bloom again. Late that night, as I gazed at his plant, I noticed something completely impossible. I saw one big, glorious gardenia in full bloom. It was a physical Love Tap from Justin, kissing me goodbye, showing me and guiding me that, although incredibly impossible, I must blossom again, too.

Four days after the crushing news of my beloved's fate, I attended his funeral. I endured profound, insufferable grief that burned through my heart like a flaming arrow. Dressed all in black, wearing no makeup, I hid behind dark sunglasses and a black-veiled hat Elizabeth found for me. I was so grateful Melinda came to do my hair, for I didn't have the strength to even run a comb through it.

She smiled at me, placing *Justin's Love Tap Gardenia* strategically in my hair. Her loving, kind empathy was relentless.

The services were jam-packed with family, friends, patients, peers, stars, celebrities, and the press. So many people were in attendance, that there wasn't enough space for the overflow of guests trying to squeeze in. I had never seen anything like this immense outpouring of love and respect. The massive amount of people gathering at Justin's funeral revealed and confirmed he was a true-life legend, admired by everyone he touched.

My heart (what was left of it) went out to his beautiful, outstanding children, Hadley and Jacob. They were visibly lost, crying, and grief-stricken. Nothing I could do or say could console them, other than holding them tightly in my arms and loving them. They were too young to face such a tragic, devastating loss.

"I love you both. You know that, right? I am here for you always and for the rest of your lives. No matter what!"

Sobbing in despair, they hung on to me for dear life, responding in unison. "Mollie, we love you, too!" They kissed me sweetly and hurried off to be with Sidney. I hoped to stay in their lives, as I knew Justin would have very much wanted that. They are extraordinary, just like their parents. I sadly couldn't help wishing I had Justin's baby inside me. Our dream child who never came to be. Feeling sick and lifeless, everything turned dark.

It appeared all in attendance were justifiably crestfallen and shaken up. Justin was young, vibrant, esteemed, revered, and his enthusiasm and love for life were contagious. He was a beaming light that shined upon all who knew him, and his death came as a shock to everyone. Somehow, I reason, this brought me a tiny bit of comfort. Many people gave a eulogy, speaking words of praise, admiration, and affection. But I felt uneasy, for it appeared all eyes were entirely fixated on me. I wished I could have disappeared. When called up to speak, I couldn't find the strength to read what I had so poorly written. I asked my bestie, Shara, to read it for me.

And so, she began. "My beloved Justin, my 'Justinator,' you were a modern-day Sir Lancelot Du Lac. You never failed to be compassionate, charitable, and heroic with your loving humanity for others. Your heart, generosity, and benevolence were infinite. All who knew you admired your majestic intelligence, humor, and moral convictions. A magnificent treasure of a man, you always jumped in immediately to help others, whether you knew them or not. You never waited to be asked. Like Lancelot, Justin, you were a knight in shining armor, willing to serve others. You, my darling, were and will eternally be a staunch champion among men!"

As I listened to Shara reading, I could no longer bear the agony of hearing my empty words, too shallow to describe my love. I fell deep inside myself, blocking out everything and everyone around me. It was all I could do not to pass out. Fortunately, I was held up by an abundance of compassion and encouragement from my caring friends. Truthfully, what helped me survive this nightmare was the support of my ever-constant hero. My Rocket-Man.

Unbeknownst to me, my besties called him to explain what had happened. He immediately canceled dates on his tour and flew in from London to console, comfort, and be there for me. I'll never forget my dear Sebastian, "Earl of Duke," for his magnificent gesture of love and support. It was so classic 'Sebastianish' to be right by my side. We hardly spoke of my great lost love with Justin, then or since. He felt my pain and sorrow, and lovingly held my hand, which kept me from falling into the dark abyss of no return. Our eternal love for one another helped to get me through!

I left Justin's funeral service, looking down at the magnificent, dazzling diamond he hoped to give me in Paris as a symbol of our undying love. I walked away with my imperfect face (*that he always told me was perfect*), my head held high with pride and appreciation for the happiness and the once-in-a-lifetime, spectacular memories my beloved and I shared.

Brokenhearted and grief-stricken, with Justin's miracle gardenia in my hair, (which I had pressed and preserved into a piece of art) I managed one smile hidden within my heart.

I achieved one brilliant smile for Justin and the amazing good fortune of having known him.

I revealed one tender smile for the gift of being loved by him. Recalling Justin's words on what he was searching for and found in us, I wore that one happy smile for our "*Everlasting, hopeless, storybook, all-consuming, unreasonable, romantic love*" that joined us together and the incredible honor of our forever bond.

Although our time together on earth was unfairly too brief, it was a blessing, a privilege, and a great joy in my life to have shared our enchanting relationship. I will hold his heartbeat deep in the center of my beating heart for eternity.

I shall remember my precious Justin with interminable love, respect in my soul, and endless thoughts of,

What Could Have Been... ... ...

CHAPTER 12

The Long Winding Road to Recovery!

"Happiness is the breath of the soul." Sorrowfully, I had run out of breath. After Justin passed away, even though I know I heard him pushing me to go on, I couldn't accept the idea of merely leaving my house. Let alone dreaming of ever going out with another man.

I missed him more than crazy. I miss being showered by his brightly colored rainbow of love, happiness, and splendor. I miss our conversations and listening to each other's opinions and beliefs. I daydream about him and everything about *us*. I miss his smile, his huge belly giggles, his sensitivity, and gentleness. I desperately miss Justin's childlike spontaneity, silliness, fun times, and passion for life. I still remember seeing him in the kitchen, looking adorable and creating a spectacular concoction for dinner. I miss the way his forehead would crinkle when he was in deep thought. I ache not being in his arms at night, safe and sleeping together with our legs intertwined. How I miss my darling Justin's smell, touch, kisses, our sex, and his calming, gentle voice. I miss the way he rubbed his bottom lip with his finger before making any decision. I miss his sparkle, his savoir-faire, advice, and how he always knew what I was thinking even before I did. I miss waking up seeing his eyes of love gazing at me with a morning kiss.

Childishly, I wish I could experience just one more day of our endless laughter and intellectual, philosophical conversations. He was so natively brilliant. I miss seeing his concern and compassion for all people and catching him performing kind deeds whilst thinking no one had seen him. I remember how he looked across the room and winked, giving me the look, which screamed, "I love you, baby!" He possessed that certain something, so endearing and intolerably irresistible. I longed for Justin, and I didn't know how to go on living without him by my side, sharing our world.

The 'two' of us became one person, one life, and one heart. Now, I had to learn to become one person on my own again. Impossible! Since Justin passed, my heart beat slower, I could no longer smile, my soul was empty and naked, and my world had become one big blur. I appreciate, of course, how gag-me and cheesy this sounds. But it's the truth. Big sigh!

At this stage, (regardless that Justin would be upset with me) all my hopes and dreams had died along with him. I became a hermit and a recluse. Seriously, I was getting pretty good at it! To quote Greta Garbo, *"I want to be alone,"* was my leading mantra. Thank goodness my editors and producers permitted me to conduct my interviews via Zoom and by phone. I was grateful for all the extended recovery time they allowed me to take.

Feeling disoriented, I dreaded leaving my house. Even to pick up necessities, for fear someone would know me and say the always inevitable nicety. *"I'm so sorry for your loss!"* To be blunt, I can't express how sick I was of repeatedly hearing that. "I'm sorry for your loss!" This statement is meaningless and did nothing whatsoever to comfort me or, most likely, anyone else who sadly ever lost a loved one! It effectively pissed me off, leaving me exasperated and increasingly bitter with each person who said it. It didn't help, nor console me that whoever stated it was, "So sorry for my loss!" This phrase is just irritating empty nonsense! I mean, seriously? Really? I'll show you…

"Well, OK then. *NOW*, I feel so much better because *YOU*, are so sorry for my loss!" Who came up with this bogus expression, anyway? I didn't lose him at the store like a cell phone. HE DIED! And, by the way, "He's with God now," or, "He's in a better place," is no better! A better place? Let's be clear here. He was in love with me, cherished his twins, and his life was perfect. He was a loved, successful doctor who lived in a mansion and helped so many people. There is no better place!

What happened to the old dependable standbys like, "What can I say?" "There's nothing I can say!" Or "Is there anything I can do to help?" What about no words at all and a nice, big, warm, and fuzzy hug? Even better, what about, "Hey, I left you a big box of chocolates, a Starbucks Latte, some homemade chocolate dipped peanut-butter cookies, and a bottle of wine on the kitchen counter." And then, quickly slip away! For sure, that's a really good idea! It works like a charm! Sorry, I'm bitchy. It's my grief talking!

Shamefully, I pushed my friends away too. I really wanted to be by myself, to bask in the exquisite solitude of my insatiable misery and grief. The only constant in those dark days was my work, endless tears, and far too many unhealthy carbs, even for a forlorn woman and her sad lost love to consume. I stooped as low as Dove Ice-cream bars and Little Debbie's Oatmeal Cream Pies. Aha yes, I did. And if I'm coming clean, I also ate her Nutty Bars and Swiss Rolls! On another caloric note, I'm willing to bet our Lil Deb was *not* so very little! Again, my rage talking. My worst fattening sin was devouring *packages* of Zebra Dark Chocolate and White Caramel Popcorn. A trillion calories there, but so very worth it!

I was a guilty mess! Resisting my return to the real world, I concluded I desperately needed a timeout to hide and to nest. No dinners, concerts, movies, parties, no long walks on the beach, no visits to the gym, and *no shopping. No shopping? Well, that pretty much explains where I was at!* I wanted my spectacular depression, my cozy jammies, and my lonely seclusion to wallow freely in.

At first, my posse let me be and frequently called to check up on me. They would occasionally stop by with food, wine, sugary sweets, magazines, and videos. Those necessities were appreciated immensely. Especially when they didn't knock and left it outside my front door with a text warning me to retrieve what they left.

I understood my friends were offering their love. Still, all I heard was a lot of, "Blah, Blah, Blah, girl. Snap out of it and move on. Blah, Blah!" I thought, "Please, just go away! Let me be! Stop trying to cheer me up! I'm happy being unhappy!" I didn't say any of this to my thoughtful, caring pals. Though, I really wanted to.

With unlimited caring support, my friends continued to push me gently back into life. They tried everything imaginable to help me through these dreadful days. After months of trying and getting nowhere, despite their failed, calculated, unsuccessful attempts, they agreed to form an intervention. A Garrison-type invasion.

They all met at Starbucks, caffeinated up, created a plan, and proceeded to my house. Boy oh boy, were they not playing around anymore. They came jam-packed with plenty of, "Get the fuck out of the house, ammo!" They progressed down and dirty and went at me with guns fully loaded with their "When all else fails" speech!

They also shot me repeatedly in the back with an *assault big-mouth rifle,* like an AR-15, and played the ruthless, *"Enough is Enough Card."* And *"Justin would hate seeing you like this!"*

I never imagined they'd stoop this low as to shuffle and deal me, that painful, harsh hand. I was upset they'd go all the way to the unsympathetic, brutally cruel Gestapo approach. It was almost unforgivable. Their insensitive, "tough-love plan" didn't work.

Their whack-o-mole strategy backfired! They hurt and upset me so much that I shut them and everyone else out of my life. With the exception for my work. My emotions were drowning in a gloomy sea of misery. I was alone, lost in the thick brush of limbo, right in the middle of a dense forest. I could not see a glimmer of light shining through the trees, only hopeless despair, pain, and anguish. Having fallen into a deep hole of emotional torpor, I didn't deem it possible, or even want to find the path of strength to get through this ordeal and return to the light of hope. Missing Justin brought a burning sting of endless, infectious tears.

THEN, A MIRACLE...

One morning, many months after Justin had passed away, miraculously, and out of nowhere, very well hidden in my panty drawer, I found a small Cartier gift bag. Inside the bag was a pretty, little wrapped box and an envelope from Justin. Marked on the outside, written in gold and pink letters, were the words, *"Just because!"* Inside the box was a stunning gold Cartier Bracelet with two gorgeous, dangling charms. One was a gold & diamond Cartier Key, and the other was a gold & diamond Cartier Heart Locket. Typical of Justin, how he romantically placed a beautiful photo of us inside the heart. Engraved on the back of the locket read, *"I will love you with all my heart till the end of time! Endlessly yours, Justin."* He also engraved the magical date we first met on the back.

Inside the card, Justin wrote tender words of his undying love and intimate feelings about what I, and our love, meant to him. He completed his note, writing, "With this bracelet, my precious, I give you the key to my heart, and all the love in my heart overflowing with my devotion and affection for you. Yours, for all eternity, and forevermore… Justin!"

His card was my lifeline back to the world of the living and one of my greatest treasures. Justin's sentiments through his life-saving words pulled me back into existence and changed everything. I marveled at his gallant, unimaginable selflessness!

Scary. it was almost as if he knew this could happen to him one day. It was his loving instinct to protect me and let me know he'd always be with me. Just in case something happened to him. And to remind me of his infinite love, hoping it would see me through all my pain. I cried and smiled back into reality and towards the future. I framed his card, and I will never take his bracelet off. I appreciated *how blessed I was to be the beneficiary of his love.*

It took a long while for me to come out from my comfy haze of self-pity and depression, which I had long been wallowing in. I also finally realized the constant pushing from my dear friends was their way of showing true kindness and trying to help me. Because of Justin's beautiful card, I ultimately arrived at the crossroads where

I could forgive them and fully grasp their immeasurable love. My besties were coming from the depths of genuine friendship and the most gentle, compassionate, caring place, with no personal agenda. I loved them all for never leaving my side or giving up on me. The only wish my devoted friends kept in their hearts was for me to move on and continue searching for happiness. I had protected myself in such a secluded, enclosed shell that it was virtually impossible for anyone to enter. But it was time to break open my hermetically sealed shell of protection, stop my grieving, return to the land of the living, and begin to live again.

Later that week, the Saturday night after finding Justin's card and bracelet, I dusted off my TV and turned on "Saturday Night Live." They were doing a funny political satire. I couldn't remember the last time I had laughed out loud, but it seemed it had been forever. For the first time in months, I giggled. Really giggled! It felt amazing. I felt happy. It was comparable to what an A+ might feel like to a failing student. My burst of laughter felt like Christmas morning to a 5-year-old. I accepted it was essential to reassess my behavior of living in the gloomy shadows of life.

And boy, did I ever! The next morning, like a happily ever after Hallmark movie, the sun rose, clouds blew away, birds sang, and I felt a heartbeat. I felt, 'My Solo Heartbeat,' for the first time in forever. On that amazing Sunday afternoon, I called each one of my friends to thank them and to apologize profoundly. And above all, to tell them how much I loved and appreciated them.

Shara responded in her standard, loving, Shara panache...

"Yeah! OK! Whatever! Who the fuck cares?! You want to go out and party?" Which translated, meant, "Wow, so thrilled you're back! I missed you so much! There's no need to apologize or thank me!

I love you too! Let's go to dinner and a movie! I desperately need some popcorn and M&M's!!!" (With peanuts, of course.)

Because of Justin's well-hidden gift of everlasting love and the support of devoted friendships, I took a baby step back into my life. I felt myself leaving behind my gloomy bed of darkness and walking toward hope and happiness, searching for the promise of heavenly grace, and a future filled with love. As I moved on, I could slowly see the pulsating bright lights of joy. Standing firmly back into my life, I remembered all the many blessings and incredible opportunities which my life presented.

I was reborn. I left my house, stopped Zooming my interviews, and went back to work in person. I rejoined the gym, started a diet (Lil Deb, we are finished! I'm breaking up with you and all your calorie-infested, hard-to-resist sugary pals!), and returned to the awaiting arms of my best friends and the many pleasures of life.

Oh, and yes. The dreaded, crazy, haunting
world of online dating!

Alas, I had again arrived at…

"Once Upon, A Here We Date Again!"

CHAPTER 13

The Russian

AKA, THE VERY LAST THING I NEEDED... NEED I SAY MORE? BUT, OH... I'M GONNA!

His name was Nikolai Abromskivitch. But of course it was! What else "woulda, coulda, shoulda," a full-blooded Russian man's name be? Perhaps Romanov, Vladimir, or Putin? I am not speaking about an American-born Russian, either. Nickolai was born and raised in St. Petersburg, Russia. He was an authentic, 100% pure-blooded Russian man. Russian, as in, beef stroganoff, borscht, caviar, Vodka, Matryoshkas Russian Dolls, the "Kalinka Malinka song and dance," the Bolshoi Ballet, and the "Doctor Zhivago Movie," degree of 100% pureblooded Russian. FYI, *in case you were always dying to know,* they filmed that classic movie in Finland and Spain as it was banned in the Soviet Union at the time. No surprise there.

Nik was breathtaking to glance at and a visual Chagall, Masterpiece of a man. He brought a stylish Russian exotic bar to the word "wowza" or, in Russian, "Bay." Totally eye-candy. His huge, deep-set, violet-colored eyes were uncomfortably piercing. Confidently flaunting his thick long lashes, I wanted to slap on some black mascara to highlight them for fun. It's a girl thing. Let it go! His hair was sophisticated and Vogue-chic. There wasn't a strand on his 38-year-old Russian head out of place, and without having to resort to expensive gels to accomplish this feat. His skin was tan, glowing, and unblemished. His body and the stylish way he pranced, strutted, flounced, swaggered, and romped about, was European classy. I was so impressed, as I watched him move like a dancer, with such elegance and grace. Oops, I forgot, he also paraded about. He was mysteriously equal to a lion. All 6 feet of Abromskivitch looked tasteful and aesthetically impeccable. There was no mistaking Nikolai was physically movie-celebrity fabulous, mesmerizing, and possessed just a little more than a touch of star quality. He was clearly a sight for this girl's sore online-dating eyes! For sure. Oh, and yes, he certainly was quite aware of it, too.

There's no way around the fact that Nik's appearance was excessively showy and overdone. While dripping with charisma, refinement, and radiating elegance, he was the swankiest man I've ever seen. Nik was entirely "trendoid fashionable." Sorry English 101, professors. It's essential to use a bevy of adjectives describing the Russian. My apologies, Professor Smith. I swear, I tried not to!

Like Bobble Drew, his wardrobe came from all the top designers. That includes this year's most sought-after styles, just walking off the latest European runways. Yet, unlike Drew, Nik's wardrobe sported his own unique style of flashy perfection. His fashion-forward sense of panache was tasteful, hip, and yet ultra-elegant. What put his flair over the edge was how he creatively pulled it all together, with outlandish colors, patterns, precision, and finesse. This theoretically qualified him as a fashion genius. I don't know many men over thirty, (*And straight!*) other than Nik, who could pull off this uniquely ornate look as well as he did. Moreover, even his unique accessories, such as necklaces, rings, shoes, cologne, sunglasses, and watches, were designer trendy. He had his own, out-of-the-box (Not to be confused with Drew-in-the-box, book 1!), visible gift for trends and up-to-the-second styles. Fortunately for Niki, his sexy hot buff body would've made anything he wore look impressive and attire perfect.

Yet, as enamored, and charmed as I evidently was with this Russian, from the moment we spoke on the phone, I was suspiciously wary of him. I grew exponentially disturbed, unable to determine why I sensed such an eerie mistrust of him. My instincts continued to alert me that something wasn't right. I couldn't exactly pinpoint what seemed so off about him. Nevertheless, I suspected something was up with Nik. And not a good up! Regardless, there was no substance or logic for my ominous thoughts of caution. Feeling uneasy, I couldn't shake my gut warnings of the deception he was concealing many things from me. Consequently, hiding much of the truth about himself. Everyone has his or her version of the truth, and Nikolai Abromskivitch was no different. My knee-jerk intuitions implied he was wearing and hiding behind a mask. Imprudently for me, the cloud of his good looks and élan camouflaged these critical warning signs. *BTW, I'm not very proud of this shallow flaw of mine.*

Nik was (allegedly) highly educated and earned several degrees in both Russia and America. We shared many ideas, intellectual beliefs, philosophies, and personal viewpoints about life in general. He flowered me with spectacular compliments and grand gestures of verbal affection. He was a master of the old-world, gentlemanly ways. At every turn, he displayed genteel manners so old-fashioned he could only have learned from old Hollywood films or past generations. Nik possessed the refinement of a prince, the worldliness of a pioneer, and flamboyantly paraded about like a peacock. (I told you he paraded!) Furthermore, He was soft-spoken and eloquent, always exaggerating his thick Russian accent, adding to his persuasive, super dangerous sex appeal.

He was indeed bright, clever, scintillating, (perhaps too much so), and loved speaking about everything, endlessly. His interpretations were esoteric in nature. The effortlessly suave Russian was debonair in an overly assured, aplomb demeanor. Regrettably for me, once he started on a topic, there was no stopping his ranting. I attempted to change the subject, but it never worked. Nik continuously and relentlessly jabbered on for hours, including every minute detail on basically any subject at all. His excessive babbling easily put me to sleep most nights without the aid of sleeping pills. Which optimistically was the silver lining.

With benevolent hopes of staying awake and acquiring something beneficial and humorous from all his rambling, I learned to copy his heavy accent. It was actually a golden opportunity to enhance my repertoire of international accents. (Remember, 60s Cameron?) You see, I would put the phone on mute as he spoke, which enabled me to practice, without the risk of him hearing me. Luckily, his nonstop gibberish provided me with plenty of practice. After perfecting his accent, I shared it with him. Nik protested, stating he found my actions highly offensive. Disappointingly, he didn't appreciate my mimicking him and speaking with his heavy Russian inflections. Evidently, he was not taking it in the jocular manner I meant it to be. No problem, I stopped performing my Russian twang for him. Still, I'm no fool. I continued to practice with my cell on mute the entire time!

After speaking with Nikolai for months (Probably about a billion hours, and always trying desperately to get him off the phone), I couldn't decide if he was the greatest guy ever. Frustrated, for I was unable to determine if he was the most intelligent, loving, caring, romantic, giving, adorable, sweet, decent, moral man on the planet. (Reader, take in a deep breath here.) Or, if on the contrary, he's a swindler, a liar, an immoral fraud, a bastard, a trickster, a dirty scoundrel, a sneaky shark, or an unethical gigolo scum! FYI, that was yet another strong example of a major run-on sentence, prizing you with a *solid "F,"* in your Jr. High, grammar class. (Regardless of the *befitting "F,"* I like it and will continue to do it.) Potentially, he was all the above combined.

As one could imagine, all this uncertainty was uncomfortably exacerbating. It placed a huge, unnerving, noticeable question mark about the Russian across my forehead. How could he be so entirely elusive and impossible to read? Moreover, I've never felt this bewildered about a man's character before. No matter how much I liked him, I didn't trust him and continuously had my doubts. In fact, this guy flew so low under the radar, even the most sensitive, foolproof, red flags couldn't detect or even spot him.

He boasted, without batting an eye, hard-to-fathom grandiose tales. And lots of them. Such extravagant legends included one where his family was equal to Russian Royalty. I so desperately wanted to fall for it, for as you very well know by now, I love wearing tiaras and crowns. Nikolai went on. (And on!) And on!

"I am a renowned, internationally recognized, highly in demand doctor." He continued to brag further. "Additionally, I am a celebrated expert in rare cancer surgeries. I have set the bar on the most advanced, cutting-edge cancer research. And as a child prodigy, I was able to accomplish so much at such a young age."

Bored and past my comfort zone of qualm, I decided to stop being so naïve, and 'Rush-In' to do some research on the all-inclusive truth of him. And nothing but the truth, so help *him,* God.

And just like that, I found out he genuinely **was** a doctor. The key word being '*was!*' Unfortunately, he lost his medical license 2 years prior to malpractice and gross negligence. When I confronted him, asking him to explain what he had done, he was overly composed, unruffled, and very calm. He defended himself from my accusations, affirming, "I did nothing wrong! All the negligence was the fault of the unethical clinic I worked for. You must believe me when I tell you this. Sadly, for me, I was unwisely roped into the whole rotten scam." He emphatically clarified. "I didn't have an inkling as to what was going on, right under my very nose. I assure you, my dear, lovely Mollie, it was the heads of the clinic who deceitfully exercised all the unethical tactics and malpractice. There is no way on earth I could ever do anything corrupt or immoral." He further simplified, "I never, in any way, became involved with those other docs. I strictly devoted all my efforts to my own patients and my highly respected medical standards of practice and protocol. I promise you! I am innocent."

Cooler than a cucumber, he justified. "When the malpractice suit began, completely unfair, and without any previous notice, I found out at the very last minute I had to appear in court that day. I was innocent, unprepared, and without any legal defense or counsel." He unequivocally went on to say, "The owners of the clinic threw me under the bus, simply to protect themselves. Underhandedly, like Oswald, I was their scapegoat, their patsy, and my being Russian made me an easy target as the fall guy. I became the stooge for this unethical group. And devastatingly, my medical license was taken from me. Correction. Stolen from me! The worst part of all, the clinic is in operation to this day. It makes me so sick!" I sensed he was forlorn and perhaps even justified. Perhaps!

"I was guiltless, traumatized, and completely distraught. I was painfully upset, not only for myself but for all my trusting patients.

They were sick, afraid, and desperately needed my medical expertise. It broke my heart abandoning my patients, right in the middle of their cancer treatments and surgical procedures. Not to mention their other medical and emotional needs. The corrupt clinic ruined me!"

Readers, I wish you could've heard that whole speech through his thick Russian accent. It made his defense so much more convincing, and besides, a whole lot of fun to hear. Stellar stuff! This dejected, allegedly innocent man was so sincere, his story almost broke my heart. He expressed to me warmly, "No worries, I currently have a team of attorneys working to get my license reinstated and clear my good name. For now, I fly to Europe where I can still practice, perform surgeries, and counsel other specialists on the innovative, advanced cancer procedures I have been working on.

Alrighty then, *psychology fans. Here's your test:*
"Was all of that mumbo-jumbo True or False?"
Stay tuned for the answers!

When we hung up the phone, I was uncertain what to make of all his nonsense or what to believe. Before I could break it down in my mind, Abromskivitch immediately flooded me with emails, including his board certifications, licenses, and letters of praise from his patients. I received over 50 emails from him that night. I thought it was an odd thing for him to do, and it made me feel like I was his guest on the "Slow-Motion Train Wreck Reality Show. "

This mysterious man puzzled me! Running through my mind were endless unanswered, "Buts!" After hearing his stories of sketchy excuses and dimly professing innocence, I was clueless and entirely unsure about trusting the handsome, provocative Russian stranger. "The Shadowy Stranger!" (A perfect movie title.)

Having been given assignments in New York the following week, I eagerly agreed to meet Niki. It sounded like an exciting plan. I mean, what could go wrong? Apparently, more than I imagined. I kept hearing in my mind the quote from the film, "Forrest Gump." *"Stupid is as stupid does!" "Run, Forrest Girl, Run!"* Was I stupid or just compassionate? After all, it was less than a year since losing Justin, and I was obviously rebounding. The question is, should I run from Dr. Zhivago, or give him the benefit of this major doubt? The air was bursting with flags and distrust.

Arriving in New York a week later, I was super busy the first day and had to get together and work with other journalists. On my second night in town, I was to meet Niki at the designated time and place. The place was a lovely, expensive, popular, 'it' *restaurant* in the city. I instantly found him charismatic and utterly sexually irresistible. Unable to ignore this fact, and despite all the warning alarms that were so loud, I nearly could've gone deaf; I ignored the cautionary sirens blasting away in my ears. You see, people, let that be a sobering reminder. Because I didn't heed my *own rules,* I can effectively warn & advise you from my experience!

The moment Nikolai and I met in person, his first words (with a strong Russian pronunciation) were, "Chuu sa B-U-tifol, Chuu sa B-U-tifol." Which translated, without the accent means, "You are so beautiful." He then gently placed my hand in his, and ever so softly kissed my wrist. Debonair, suave, undoubtedly most intriguing, and quite the pro, was how I summed him up. Moreover, Nik was unreasonably gorgeous. Throwing all caution to the wind, I chose to ignore his eyes that were filled with hidden, mysterious secrets.

Finding myself wickedly infatuated, I questioned. Would I have continued with the unnerving Russian, had he been average looking, with an American accent? I didn't know the answer. It was clear my judgment was severely impaired from recently coming out of such a dark place after Justin. Yet another reason I should have waited to meet him at another time, down the road!

Anyway, we dined and spoke while enjoying a delicious bottle of "Castello Banfi Poggio all' Oro Brunello di Montalcino Riserva 2004," the beguiling Russian selected. As it had been so long, I was aching for him to reach toward my face across the table and press his lips onto mine, with a not-so-tender kiss. Unfortunately for me, he was a perfect gentleman the entire evening. A total characteristic, "*Player Move*," the cynical me surmised. I really didn't want to be this suspicious. I truly desired to believe and *ho-ho-hope* for a happy ending. Ah, yes, the pure joys of stupidity.

Naturally, it stands to reason after all I had been through, my "*GPA Dating Score*" was at an all-time low. I needed to stay somewhat vigilant, since I recognized this guy was as smooth and easy to swallow as a bottle of fine Russian Vodka. It was visibly impossible not to notice how most of the women in the restaurant couldn't take their eyes off him, totally crumbling (like a crumb cake) by his presence. It made me giggle watching them melt, like Russian snow on a sunny winter day, as they were momentarily captured under his enigmatic spell. UGH! Anyway, I hope he didn't think I was one of them.

While Niki was politely chattering, munching away on his lamb chops, I quietly pondered. After meeting this elegant Russian, I was more puzzled than ever. All I kept thinking throughout this lovely dinner was how could this stunning, kind man sitting before me be a classic swindler, a con artist, a gigolo, a lying cad, an unethical, immoral bastard, and a trickster shark? (*That surely qualifies to be yet another deserved, educational, grammatical "F!"*)

Oh, no! In a bit of a panic, I suspected! Should I be concerned the

KGB and the Russian Mafia were watching us at this very moment? Suddenly, I felt like a damsel in distress, captured amid one of those old Tinseltown, star-filled, Russian Spy Flicks. Flaunting a timeless, horrified, theatrical gaze, I looked around the restaurant, seeking a white knight to save me. Man, as if I needed more drama in my life. KGB or otherwise!

Back to reality. There was no mistaking this convincing, smooth-talking Casanova could sell a dripping purple and cherry popsicle to a woman wearing white satin gloves. Work with me, people! I was starving for affection after my extended hermit solitude. It had been such a long time since I had experienced a romantic situation. And evidently, Nikolai Abromskivitch was visibly more than a magnetic, promising, amorous escapade. This *flimflam man* was certainly captivating, I mused, looking over my shoulder, continually scouting for the KGB. I was bewitched, wooed, and beguiled. Just for the record, I have never been any of those things in my entire life, let alone all 3 together. I don't even like the sound of them. What do they really imply? Bewitched, wooed, and beguiled? It sounds like what a sorceress would chant while brewing up an incantation for her evil spell: *"Bewitched, Wooed, and Beguiled! Bewitched, Wooed, and Beguiled!"* Those silly words most likely originated from the same guy who came up with, "I'm sorry for your loss" and "He is in a better place!"

While straining to resist the inevitable Abromskivitch pitfalls, I was entangling further into his Russian mob, KGB kissable lips, and his overpowering web. Despite each critical doubt and question mark popping up in my mind, I wanted this sexy, alluring man. This was extra humiliating because, "He very well knew that I knew that he knew that I knew that I wanted him!" Dammit to hell! I was now entirely convinced being a hermit was so much easier.

Niki effortlessly pushed every one of my hormonal, erogenous buttons. Not having had sex for such a long time, I was as horny as a college male freshman at a frat party, abundant with flirting, gorgeous babes. So horny that my appetite and lust for him would even impress a nymphomaniac! I was pitifully failing all the "tried-and-true advice" and "words-to-the-wise" from the Cosmopolitan Magazines, and all the other magazines and books on romance I had ever read. Shite, as Sienna would say, I wish I could stop the million kinky, carnal thoughts I was imagining. My inner voice screamed, "Walk away from the Russian, and no one gets *KGB-eed*!" Then my other inner voice argued with my inner voice and rationalized, "No. Have a blast. Enjoy having exciting sex with the Russian. You'll have a fun, Kalinka-Kalinka time in bed!" Next, my inner voice yelled back, "You are heading right for a dangerous cliff, my friend *and self*!" Then my other inner voice argued back, laughing. "Oh, girl, come on! Yo, self, don't be ridiculous! This is a perfect opportunity to experience Russian joy and let go of your silly fears!" But the question remained, which one of me should I listen to? The intelligent me, or "The Fool on The Hill," me? (Thanks Beatles!) Further worrisome, I was arguing with myself, my inner voice, and my other inner voice. That can't be healthy.

So that's it. We, *"all three of me,"* were amid a real-life "Doctor Zhivago" movie. Only without the popcorn, World War 1, the Russian Revolution, the Kremlin, Lenin, the Bolsheviks, blizzards, the Reds, the Czar, and outlandishly heavy costumes! However, I love the fur hats and coats. The Russian physician and poet, Yuri Zhivago (Omar Sharif) was now being played by the understudy, Nikolai Abromskivitch. And his love interest, Lara Antipova (Julie Christie) was now being played by the understudy, yours truly. Online dating, just kill me now! Gosh, *the KGB might get to me first!*

Nonetheless, being with him tonight was great fun, wining, and dining until we closed the restaurant at 3:00 in the morning. At the end of the evening, while we said goodbye outside the restaurant, I leaned in for the classic, highly anticipated, goodnight movie kiss. I was super embarrassed when Nik skirted away from my physical suggestion. He abruptly put me into a taxi, kissed my hand sweetly, and said with a heavy Russian accent, "*Ettt vus gret tu ffffinlly mit chhu,*" and sanctimoniously swaggered off.

What? Huh, I murmured, sitting alone in a NYC yellow cab. I was squirming all the way back to the Plaza Hotel, feeling awkward and frustrated. I mean, there I was, looking beautiful (except for the necessary reapplication of my red lipstick), with my silent, miffed attitude of, "What the fuck just happened here?" No kiss! Not a single kiss? "*Boy, is he good or what?*" I spoke aloud, shaking my head while reapplying fresh lipstick. The cabbie turned around and glanced at me with a kind, validating smile.

Arriving at my hotel with a smirk still displayed across my face, I walked with some major attitude into the Oak Bar for a nightcap to settle my erotic nerves. No matter how hard I tried to fend off the lingering uncomfortable negative feelings boiling up within me about this man, they persisted. Grinning and sipping a cosmopolitan with strawberry sugar around the edge, I found my situation ironic. All these adverse thoughts I sensed about the Russian only made me hornier and desperate for his touch, all-the-more. It appeared we were playing a real-life, "*Cat & Mouse*" game, and I was obviously *not the cat!* I detested being in this underdog ('undercat') situation. I was trapped in the middle of a spectacular Russian Ballet. Now dancing with the Russian, who was spinning, lifting, directing, and leading me around on the stage of his life. Like the Russian-born star of the Bolshoi Ballet, Mikhail Baryshnikov, he was in control.

I wasn't comfortable or familiar with this story. All the same, I couldn't resist the exquisite dance!

Abromskivitch and I met again the following night for dinner after wrapping up a rather stress-filled, controversial political interview on Wall Street. I needed to go down on a Russian Vodka, *in or out* of a glass. I anticipated the Russian suggesting we meet at the famous New York, Russian Tea Room for dinner, and ordering Beef Stroganoff. I was happily surprised Niki selected Eric Ripert's fine dining temple, Le Bernardin. Walking into Ripert's, still maintaining a sharp lookout for the KGB, I immediately noticed in this restaurant alone more cosmetic surgery than all of Beverly Hills combined. I saw more plastic here than in the whole LEGO toy factory. Sadly, all these plastic people reminded me of how much I loved and longed for my safe, wonderful Justin. No alcohol in the world could drown my sorrows about our interrupted tragic love story. I still missed him desperately and surely would for the rest of my life. I guess time won't ever change that. I smiled, looking down at the gorgeous diamond ring & bracelet he gave me.

I attempted (to no avail) to ward off Nikolai's efforts to keep me unbalanced. Thus, I faked an attitude of being in control, like the cat! The fact I could see it bothered him was troublesome. We remained in the restaurant until receiving the notorious dirty, annoying looks, making it clear as glass that management wanted to close. What a foodie's paradise this fine establishment was. The only thing that could have enhanced the delicious cuisine was long, sweet kisses, which never came. Once outside, before I knew it, Niki placed a soft, friendly kiss on my cheek, bid me a fond adieu, and again whisked me off in a yellow taxi. I didn't know if I was relieved or irritated. Whatever, I still want to be the *Cat.* Dammit!

I remained in the city for a few more days working with some reporter friends. When flying home, I was pretty much in a baffled state the entire flight concerning Niki and his romance dodging.

The following 6 weeks, we spoke nightly. I avoided answering the phone many nights to escape Nik's treacherous, non-stop talking about himself and his alter ego, "*Peter the Great!*" He spoke, rarely stopping to take a breath. I was starting to get annoyed with him, for I was falling behind on my work, spending this much time listening to him bragging and keeping me on the phone for so long.

Ultimately, to vacate the limbo of my uncertainty, I agreed to meet Nik in Ohio, where he resides. Although, after checking out his house on Google, I was reluctant to stay with him for many obvious reasons. Other than the apparent *"stranger-danger factor,"* I was hesitant and afraid of the 3-mile, desolate entrance to his home, without another house around for 17 acres. Not to mention the menacing photo of the shed in his backyard, which also came up in my search. That's essentially when I panicked and quickly recalled all those real-life criminal shows and "Dirty John" type movies. There always seemed to be that same suspicious shed in the murderer's backyard, where he stored all the chopped-up body parts. I really must stop watching the Investigation Discovery Network! Seriously, I could hear spooky music playing in my head along with Jenny shouting, "Run, Hurry! Run Forrest Girl, Run!" I could hear the breaking news story. "*Good Morning, America! A girl was found in a spooky shed, robbed, raped, murdered, and her body parts were chopped into little pieces in Ohio! Stay tuned for more!*"

I pulled myself together, realizing, "*Oh, please, no one is ever murdered in Ohio!*" It probably has something to do with the political phrase, "As Ohio goes, so goes the nation!" I resolved to visit

THE RUSSIAN | 247

Niki, but prudently made sure I went over the escape plans with my friends. Plus, I cautiously programed into my cell his local Ohio Police Department's number on Speed Dial.

Two days later, I was back with the handsome, surreptitious hunk of a Russian at his impressive, manly-man home. That night, we sat outside in front of a late autumn roaring fire. Nik played soft music and served a lovely array of food, wine, chocolates, and Bailey's coffee with whipped cream. We talked and cuddled until we were exhausted. Sadly, he was the consummate gentleman. But hooray, at last, Nik kissed and held me tenderly all evening. Jeez, the man could kiss! We fell asleep holding each other throughout the night, fully "pajamaed." Hey, listen, so what if *"pajamed"* is not a real word? I like it! I don't care if I get *another "F," Professor, sir!*

At 7:00 in the morning, as those annoying bluebirds of happiness were tweeting (And I'd like to add, I'm never happy with those damn birds waking me up so early!), the sunlight came shining through the window onto my brow. Unfortunately, I didn't wake from a restful night's sleep. And not because I had to stay up all night due to the Sleeping Beauty posing scenario. I slept maybe 2 winks for fear of being drugged, raped, slain, and massacred to death in his bed, and then having my body parts hacked up and placed in that ominous shed in his backyard. I was justifiably terrified, for no one could have possibly heard my blood-curdling screams, being that his house location was isolated and secluded. Ergo, I stayed awake listening to the rhythm of the toads and crickets all night. The good news was in the morning, I was alive, in one piece, far from the dreaded, ominous, mysterious shed.

I could hear Nik banging around downstairs, so I brazenly and curiously tiptoed into his ginormous clothes closet. I wanted to see if he had more colorful, outrageous designer clothes than he had previously worn with me. I searched through his wardrobe in amazement because of the insane amount of clothes he owned. Peculiar, I gasped, because I noticed price tags were still attached to most of the garments. If he lived to be a hundred, he couldn't conceivably wear all these clothes. Oopsie, he abruptly crept up behind me and frightened the couture fashion out of me, silently sneaking up at my side. With pure astonishment, I interrogated him. "Nik, why do you have so many clothes and why on earth are the tags still on them? I've never seen anything like this. What's the deal here, man?" He arrogantly laughed as my eyes bugged out in astonishment at the sight of his closet. It looked like a ritzy, overpriced designer department store. His clothes were crammed into his closet, even with all the outlandish space it offered.

"Mya luffff," (My love, without accent) they are so very last year, so I would never wear them!" That was all he said about the clothes with hanging tags! Mystified by him from the very beginning, I shushed and let it go. Though I didn't believe his story.

During my visit, the Russian arranged one romantic surprise after another. He hospitably prepared and served delectable breakfasts with a different rare colored, extra long-stemmed rose, 4 mornings in a row. Like a renowned 5-star chef, he proved he could pull off a gourmet meal, from leftovers in the refrigerator, in just minutes. Regardless that his behavior was sweet, carefree, and relaxed, he was altogether eccentric. He really ruffled my feathers.

Niki didn't miss a trick. One evening he took me into the city and awaiting our arrival was an all-white, Cinderella horse-drawn carriage. My personal, *"Peter the Great,"* previously arranged with the coachmen to take us for a ride through the entire downtown area. The event included champagne, flowers, and a fur blanket.

During my stay, we also enjoyed lovely lunches and dinners at his favorite hangouts. I would consider him a food, wine, and restaurant connoisseur. And, just like a player, he knew *too much*!

Nik's well-practiced coquettish glares, his flirtatious stares with his spectacular eyes, made it hard not to sink into his control, like quicksand. His powerful gazes could force a flower to bloom its petals, or an old, sullied diamond to reclaim its sparkle. His well-oiled moves, polished body language, and subdued patience kept me completely off my game. I was disturbed noticing his erotic facial suggestions and secretive looks of dark deeds. Everything about him kept me on the mysterious edge of the unknown. It was the perfect fusion of fear and excitement. This man was radically fetching, but by the same token, I was disconcertingly suspicious. Nik possessed more than his fair share of charm and seductive charisma. I could have fallen *"in like"* with him, if not for the ear-piercing, menacing, annoying hazardous bells that were ringing and haunting me at every turn.

I agreed to continue sleeping in his bed, as long as we both kept our clothes on. Although I did wonder why he stuck to my rules, ensuring there'd be no hanky-panky. Like none whatsoever. He never stepped over the line. What guy does that? Really!!! What guy? What man who likes a girl ever obeys the strict, *"no sex rules"* without a single complaint, attempt, or objection? It was too strange to under-stand. Unmistakably, in this case, *my rule was indeed meant to be broken!* Of course, we cuddled, hugged, kissed, and felt each other's bodies, totally pajamaed. But how could he resist the temptation of not just me, but of sex in general? Maybe he can't get it up? I was more than amused by this thought, for that would be such a waste of a gorgeous man. Sure, in fact, he did cheat one time and went under my shirt to feel my breasts. To be accurate, it was only one breast. I get that I said, *"No,"* but even so, how could he stop there with only one breast? Maybe he needed Viagra and ran out? Ah-ha, now there's a valid thought. Maybe he had an outbreak of herpes? Well, then good for him and me, for his abstaining! Maybe he knew the *KGB* had him and his house under surveillance. Maybe he was really a transgender man and didn't want to tell me yet that he still had a vagina and was waiting for his penis? Goodness, that wasn't at all true, because I did manage to get a glimpse of his Russki jewels while he slept. Unbeknownst to him, his pants kept sliding down all night. Hmm, "Kalinka-Malinka, Me!" If his (Stone) thing was man-made, his surgeon deserves a global award. Anyway, I was quite happy to notice he was circumcised for the prospect of future endeavors. A huge, *Nostrovia! (Cheers, in English!)* I did take as a consolation prize the awesome, back and foot massages, he gave me. Still, I didn't get his lack of sexual desire. Was he playing me? Didn't like sex? Or was he sincerely just a respectful gentleman? Either way, to tell the truth, I was somewhat relieved. Truthfully, I was hardly ready for sex so soon after Justin, to drive down that unknown open road.

Anyway, I couldn't stop worrying about that apocalyptic shed in the back. When I asked to see it, he became extremely agitated and overly panicky by my request. Also, that bizarre, rattled look in his eyes did not comfort me, nor promote a peaceful night's sleep. Luckily, being so knackered, that night I fell asleep despite my shedding, innate death fears.

It goes without saying, I was happy as hell when I awoke in one piece! After another spectacular breakfast adorned with a rose, we dressed for the day. Niki surprised me with a romantic chartered boat ride around a peaceful, picturesque lake. After a few hours of floating around, we were brought onto a grassy knoll for a gourmet picnic, with blankets, pillows, flowers, wine, and music. I couldn't help remembering JFK's legendary grassy knoll story.

He pulled every Playboy trick in the book. But if I remained in one piece, it was just fine with me. He was a joy to be with, and I welcomed the attention into my life. Above all, he surely was the consummate gentleman. Regardless, I was nervous when the man who guided our private tour left us all alone. I began to imagine horrific thoughts of Nik hacking up my body right there on the knoll, and later transporting me back to the shed in pieces. After all, that notorious knoll didn't end well for JFK, either! I attempted to erase the gruesome thoughts now racing through my mind.

Throughout my visit, he shrewdly planted extravagant gifts at every appropriate moment. Among the gifts were Chanel Sunglasses, a gold bracelet, a designer Dolce & Gabbana little black dress with shoes to match, expensive Gucci Perfume, designer jeans, and 2 stunning Valentino Sweaters. Eventually, I started to feel funny and became uncomfortable with the gifts. It was, in fact, way too much. Seriously, though, what's a girl to do? Say No to Couture???? Ridiculous! Unthinkable and absurd.

After a seemingly wholesome, sweet, and exciting 4-day interlude together, and pampered with extravagant food, wine, romance, gifts, kisses, and serene relaxing moments, I needed to get back to work. When I got home that night, I slept 12 long, peaceful, safe, *shed-free* hours with all my body parts attached. He surely made quite an unsettling impression on me.

We continued our relationship, speaking on the phone for about 4 weeks. When it suddenly dawned upon me that it was time to ask him to visit me at my house. It's only fair! So, I invited Nik to come for 3 days. However, I was confused and alarmed when he decided to change my invitation and stay for 10 days. I was not pleased with his rearrangements without checking with me first. But what could I do? He bought his ticket. I kept an open-mind and decided to wait and see what happens. I liked him, and who knows? Maybe it would turn out great! A big maybe, there!

As the days passed, his arrival was rapidly approaching. I began to juggle my work to prepare for his visit. There was a lot to do on my *"To Do List."*

Suddenly, and unexpectedly, I was struck down by an urgent, worrisome feeling in the pit of my soul. I could no longer ignore my intuition, distinctly yelling, alerting, and forewarning me. It became unavoidable and impossible to disregard the flailing flags, swinging signs, and pure instincts shrieking inside my head. As sexy and enchanting as Nikolai was, I certainly couldn't continue to be this clueless. Hence, I knew I had to take real action. I called upon my trustworthy private detective, Diane Hellmer. I filled her in on all my fears, concerns, doubts, and suspicions about Niki.

"The Ominous Shed and All!"

Without romance, passion, or skin in the game, it took her no time at all to uncover the truth about the Niki tales of mystery.

"Bingo," she voiced!

Huh? Did they play that in Russia, I speculated? The bevy of information Diane presented me with was unquestionably chilling. I discovered I was literally playing *Russian Roulette,* and with very bad odds at that. Thank heavens, I didn't go all in!!!

Diane continued to speak.

"In the case of Nikolai Abromskivitch, I have concluded he is nothing more than a colossal liar! Although disappointing for you, Mollie, no real surprise there." She went on with her findings. "He was found guilty in twenty-five enormous malpractice lawsuits against him, and him alone! He was indicted and lost all these suits for the most horrendous and despicable medical misconduct. They threw the book at him for negligence, unnecessary procedures, and wrongful and unethical botched surgeries. Understandably, he was fired from the 'vindicated and exonerated clinic' that he touted was to blame! Consequently, he had his license taken away forever, without the option of ever reinstating it. So, naturally, he lied as well about hiring a team of lawyers to work on reinstating his license! Furthermore, he also lied about being able to practice in Europe. Not at all a good or honorable guy, my sweet Mollie."

Diane picked up her momentum. "In addition, dear girl, all the clothes, jewelry, cars, and fancy possessions he bragged about had all fallen off a truck. Wink! Wink! Jobless, the Russian illegally purchased those goods with the hopes of selling them to make money to live off. Thus, how he got all the fancy gifts he gave to you, and his endless clothes with price tags still attached. Moreover, He is flat-out broke and in debt up to his fancy coiffured hair. Which, by the way, happens to be fake hair as well. While it's real hair, the very best money can buy, it wasn't his real hair!"

"Oh, for the love of God, Diane. No wonder he grabbed my hands when I tried to run my fingers through it, even though I informed him it was my thing. It would have come off in my fingers. Oh hell, I would've died laughing forever! Maybe longer."

"Hon, you'd have taken a knee laughing. Shall I go on, Mollie?"

"Are you kidding me? There's more? Please, go right ahead!"

"Mr. Russian owes funds up to his beautiful deep-set, long lashed, eyeballs you were telling me about. I mean, major debt, including a mammoth balance he owes to the IRS. It's not good!!!"

All the information Detective Hellmer relayed sickened me. Diane went on to tell me, the kicker. As if all that knowledge didn't kick me in the ass hard enough already. "Girlfriend, you're gonna want to sit down for this."

"Why? What? You're freaking me out, Di! *OMG*, I knew it! *You found naked, hacked-up body parts in the terrifying shed? I just knew it!*"

My dear friend responded laughing and went on. "No. No body parts. But his house is foreclosing on the same day he is to arrive at your home. No wonder he wanted to stay longer, and why he changed the dates you had invited him to come. How very convenient and manipulative. Mollie, he has no money, no credit cards, no job, and no place to live. The guy is basically destitute and penniless! He obviously had been scheming, plotting, and calculating to find an easy mark, even before he met you. And when he found you, he went full speed ahead with his plan as the lovely, perfect, successful gentleman. He must have spent his last dime wooing you. I'm assuming all this from my many years in the business. But confident I'm correct. Nevertheless, don't feel bad, Mollie. There are tons of these men out there scheming this game."

"Wow, Diane, in a word, Fuck! *Don't feel bad? LMFAO*, I feel like a fool! Thank you with all my heart for rescuing me from more hell! You've proven once again to be invaluable. As always, you're amazing! I fear where I'd be without you. Yeah, don't answer that!"

In retrospect, I instinctively knew in my gut from the very start that Nikolai was always obfuscating the truth and essentially unethical in every possible way. I was grateful, whatever his reason was, that we didn't make love. I would have regretted having sex with him for like, EVER! Now, thinking about almost giving myself to this cad makes me cringe. Again, readers, this is precisely why I caution you against rushing into sex until you truly know the person you are having sex with. Just because they tell you extraordinary and incredible things about themselves doesn't mean they're true. You'll soon learn that you, in fact, didn't know them at all. The key word being, Wait! You'll never regret waiting.

Nik knowing where I lived concerned me. And the million-dollar question remained. How would I finagle my way out of this paradox without making him feel anger and rage toward me? Also known as, *"Help! 911! Please, Get Me the Fuck Out of This Dilemma!"*

In keeping with my better judgment, (finally!) I couldn't run to my phone fast enough to cancel Nikolai from visiting, with my deepest apologies. I called, he answered, and I began to explain...

"Nik, you're a lovely, very special, good man. Sadly, though, after further thought, we are two different people, and it would never work out. I'm so sorry. I want you to know I genuinely like you! Still, I feel I must say goodbye and wish you all the very best."

Touché! I was profusely relieved. But alas, to my chagrin, my victory dance didn't last very long. Just when I thought he understood and was fine with my explanation, his response was intimidating, indifferent, cold, and stoic at best. In his true fashion (and I'm not talking about clothes), he portrayed a zealous sense of fake pertinacious calm. It was unnerving to the degree of chilling. His Avant-Garde superiority began to diminish and unravel as he responded in a hostile, threatening, furious voice.

"Don't you dare tell me I am a lovely, good man, wish me well, and tell me not to come. I'm not stupid and I am also not an idiot. I can't believe you are behaving this way and rejecting me! I know that you are not being honest with me, and I am sure you have other reasons for your actions. BYE!"

As he slammed the phone down, my heart was pounding out of my chest with fear. I was bursting with anxiety and terror about what he'd do to retaliate against my rejection. I doubt he easily accepted being denied anything by anyone. Then I remembered the daunting *shed* out back! Shit!!!! Although Diane *shed* some light on that, I was still petrified and braced for what was coming next.

I totally dropped the ball, for I knew I should've snuck into his backyard to look inside that fucking shed. God only knows how many women have been chopped up and secretly laid to rest there.

The situation put me on edge, giving me the creeps, the sweats, the shivers, the heebie-jeebies, and the willies. I don't ever recall getting all of them at the same time. I suggest you never try to combine them. It's quite unnatural. I was not digging it in the least. Just the sound of using all 5 in the same sentence, describes how crazy scary, and awful my situation was.

After that call and for the next month, Nikolai relentlessly sent me an infinite number of startling, hair-raising, frightening, terrifying, horrific, disturbing texts, emails, and phone messages. They included death threats and the murder of other people I knew. He didn't stop there. He went on to the, "You should have fallen for me, and now you're going to be sorry," threats.

He continued with shocking sentiments of fury and outrage, spoken in slow, sinister, ferocious tones. He left insane messages expressing things he wanted to do to me, harming me physically, forever. I purposely didn't block him, for fear he'd come and find me if he didn't have any other way to contact me.

Dealing with his threats, I justifiably became discombobulated.

By the way, that word was probably also penned by the same authors who wrote the words, Heebie-Jeebies, and the Willies.

This destitute, obsessive, narcissist man, with all his alarming guts & guile, didn't leave me alone. Dealing with him felt like being on an emotional rollercoaster, without the straps to hold you in. Eventually, it became necessary to obtain a restraining order and change my cell phone and home numbers, plus my email address.

Ultimately, as luck would have it, I thankfully never heard from this attractive Russian fraud again. He might have once been a doctor, but he was, No Doctor Zhivago!

Ironically, the Russian leader Putin once said, "It's better not to argue with women." Mr. Nikolai Abromskivitch, I wholeheartedly believe that's a good idea for you to follow in the future!

To this day, I remain in fear of the Russian. I continually look over my shoulder for the KGB, the Russian Mob, and the trepidation he will pop up again. *And his little shed too!*

I was fortunate to have discovered, with Diane's help, dating Nikolai Abromskivitch was like stepping on a dangerous land mine. He was an inexplicable grifter and a Hollywood thriller unto himself. Which would likely be directed by Wes Craven, Quentin Tarantino, Steven King, M. Night Shyamalan, and possibly all four.

Alrighty then, *psychology fans...*
"Now you know, all of that mumbo-
jumbo Niki declared was False!"
But I bet you guessed that already.

Shedding the notorious, sinister, diabolical Russian, online chapter of my life, I was grateful to have escaped unharmed. I had 'pre-gret' intuition about Nikolai from day one, but foolishly didn't listen!

Let my story be an example to you, girls and boys, online or offline. Always, listen to your gut. If it doesn't feel right, it isn't!

Hence, never judge a book by its cover or any handsome guy's cover as well! Please *trust* and know the signs and your feelings (which I have unpacked for you) are never wrong!

And Lastly, Don't Ever *"RUSSIAN"* Into a Relationship!

P.S. I will never have closure concerning that creepy, threatening, mysterious shed. I will always wonder what or whom Nikolai Abromskivitch might have been hiding inside there.

Because he was so very furious when I asked to see it, I'll forever be suspicious. I never could decide who was the bigger Boogeyman. Niki the Russian, or his secret shed?

That's when I overheard my inner-self say to my other inner-self, **"Ha-Ha! You Didn't Listen! And** again, *You Totally Got Maled!"*

And Go Figure...When you get right down to it,
I would have been much better off with the KGB or Putin, after all!

One Last Very Important Rule... *"Always, Be the Cat!"*

CHAPTER 14

God, Therapy, and Friendship

OR 911... PLEASE, HELP ME!

Dearest Lord, I cannot withstand any more of this dating lunacy. What's up with trying to find "*The One?*" Why is it so unbelievably difficult? I'm weary, traumatized, and fundamentally kaput.

Isn't it written somewhere, Lord, that you only give us what we can handle? And no more! I've been told this proverb all my life, and I've counted on it to be true. Ultimate ruler of the world, father, and King of the Universe, I'm exhausted. I humbly express my desperate needs and desires to you. Almighty one, I'm subserviently begging and meekly asking for your dating guidance and mercy! I've looked everywhere and tried everything. But I found my soulmate! And now he's gone. My Justin was "The One!"

Supreme Being of Creation, I feel hopeless. Is there someone else out there for me? I can't go on dating any more weirdos from the Twilight Zone. I don't understand why, but I am certain and trust you made so many of these odd fellows for a good reason.

Could you please have pity on me, and wave your magical godly wand, causing my next soulmate to appear right away at my doorstep? Like, POOF! "*Soulmate-Cadabra.*" Would you kindly, fairy-dust, POOF him into my life? I imagine you can *easily* manifest him. I'm certain you can. Like seriously, you made the universe in *six* days. *The Entire Universe, for God's sake! Oh, sorry, for your sake!* After that miraculous Godly feat, how hard could it be to send me one little soulmate? In all fairness, I'm only asking for one guy. One, out of the entire universe, that you created so beautifully. One! Just one! You're God, so it should be a piece of cake. Right? Where's the guy, already? *"My Guy!"* Like the song.

Dammit, I hate to admit it, but I have become a Serial Dater!

(Reader, insert now your favorite Crashing Mysterious Music.)

No! Please, no more endless dating, dear loving, compassionate, empathetic, benevolent Lord! Stop the insanity…

"UMMM… Are You Listening? Hello! Hell-A-Ooooh?

Hello? Lord? I'm Talking to You?

Can You Hear Me???? Wherefore Art Thou?

Oh, Heavenly Father, Hello Up There? Ah-hem???? Ahem!!!!

Chhaaaaaa? Chhaaaaaa, Chhaa! Chhaaaaaaaa… … … Chhaaaaa? Sorry, that was terribly rude. I'm just saying, I am not in the happiest place on earth, Dear God!"

Speaking of which, Walt Disney once said, and I quote… … … "It's kind of 'fun' to do the impossible."

"Hey Mr. Walt, let me tell you. Online dating is *impossible* and not all that *fun!* Still, you do deserve respect. After all, you are the celebrated creator and master of fairytales. You are the King of 'Dreams come true.' 'When you wish upon a star,' and 'If you can dream it, you can do it.' And let's not forget the Seven Dwarfs, Mickey, Minnie, and all the other charming Disney characters."

I fear I've become jaded, burned-out, and at best, I've entirely lost my mind. I am aware I should shake it off and not let it affect me this deeply. Wait, that's the ticket! I needed a spoonful of sugar.

With a Tinker Bell abruptness, what I needed, in fact, was therapy! Yes, that's it! I'm suffering from, *'MMCD.'* *"Multiple Mental Calamities Disorder,"* resulting from endless tragic dating. Fairly apparent that I was in dire need of an emergency therapy session. How did I not think of this earlier? Although I had never been to therapy, I accepted the fact I required it. At once! I was currently on *'Stress-Tilt,' overload.* You know, when you furiously bang the pinball machine, after unfairly losing the silver ball, because the flap was broken. Or pounding the candy or soda machine after losing your money. Yep, that kind of *tilt.* Only far worse!

The thing is, I'm usually skilled at bizarre, disappointing, and outlandish situations. So why was I having so much trouble coping? I imagine it's because this dating process had gone on far longer than expected. Not to mention, all the time and hours getting ready for each date. In addition, the expensive clothes, shampoo, conditioner, make-up, gas, and perfume were all wasted on these futile dates. *A lot ventured, but nothing gained!*

By the grace of God, I was still sane enough, (barely) to accept I needed help. Regardless of the financial expense, this course of action must be taken. My condition had progressed to a bona fide, imminent medical catastrophe. To set the record straight and in my defense after stewing over it for weeks, things had become too outrageous and disturbing to handle online dating. For anyone, let alone me, in my present disheartened condition.

I questioned. "Was I being delusional? Was finding love online nothing more than a cruel joke or a pathetic game?" Frantically, but with refined poise and elegance, I scheduled an emergency therapy session. I thank my lucky stars she had an opening.

That statement triggers the topic of *"lucky stars."* Do they even exist? Look, obviously, I know there are stars. There are an infinite number of stars, indeed. But how can we distinguish the authentic lucky stars from the normal, every night, run-of-the-mill stars? This then begs the question. "Are the normal, run-of-the-mill stars unlucky?" Even Disney encourages us to wish upon them and reassures us that our dreams will come true if we do. But did he mean for us to only wish upon the lucky ones or all of them? He never made it clear or differentiated the diverse stars in his philosophies. Great, perfect, I'm talking about stars now.

The prefrontal cortex part of my brain was fringing on the tiny threshold of a dangerous encounter. Incidentally, that would be considered way beyond a "Tilt!" I'd say it would be equal to kicking the whole damn pinball machine completely over, broken glass everywhere, and silver balls flying in the air.

Excuse me, that was a momentary neurotic thought from a woman who is a double-stuffed Twinkie, short of losing it.

Gosh, have some compassion. I just dated a lying Russian scoundrel, with a freaky-looking shed in the back of his house. It's still fresh in my mind and continues to haunt me. Might I remind you the KGB is also on my ass? Honestly, do I need to go on?

At noon on the dot, with my questions in hand, I arrived for my session. (BTW, is there an actual dot at noon, on a clock? Asking for a friend.) My therapist was there on time, exactly on that questionable dot, and precisely where we agreed to meet. There she was, as always, smiling at me with a whimsical look on her face while shaking her satirical head. Shara, my rock, my north, and my very Best Friend Forever! She stood patiently waiting, directly in front of the therapeutic, sympathetic, and comforting shoe department of Bloomingdale's. We met for the most proven, scientific *"heeling"* therapy of all. "Shoes and Clothes Shopping Therapy!" More commonly known as, "*SACST!*"

"Thank you for coming, my true-blue BFF!" I giggled while giving her a bear hug. I was in dire need of my friend and, yes, Bloomingdale's, of course. She was the only one who could feasibly make me laugh and bring on the happy, at this insufferable and bewildering time in my life.

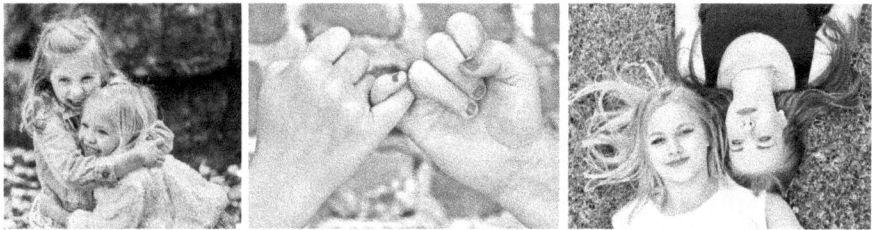

Shara is my caustically sarcastic, comedy touchstone, who always brings reality, wisdom, and understanding into my world. She makes it easier to cope with every situation by dressing it up and delivering it all through her outrageous humor and quick-witted sarcasm. She also sets the bar on what is right, what is wrong, and what is, *"Get the fuck outta here"* and *"over the top injustice!"* Moreover, she has a fierce set of therapeutic balls and has no problem using them with anyone, anywhere, and at any time. I respected this about her. She tells it like it is and makes me chuckle simultaneously. At first glance, Shara is sophisticated, refined, beautiful, and classy. That is until she speaks! She is a classic, contradicting, astonishing marvel.

My friend does not come off as your typical mushy-gushy, kind of girl. Yet inside, she so very much is exactly that. It's adorable how she believes she's hiding her warmth and fuzziness from the world. My girl is misleading no one with her foolish denial. Everyone who knows her sees through her facade and futile attempts to be diehard, tough, and callous. She is like looking through a sheet of cellophane. Shara is inherently the queen of compassion & kindness. But be aware, she's not known for saying loving, sweet sentiments, or dishing out flowery compliments.

My BFF loathes the OMG, screaming girly hellos, exaggerated displays of affection, public scenes of any kind, long bear hugs, and demonstrative drawn-out sensitive goodbyes. At the end of our time together, we seldom say goodbye. She mysteriously seems to vanish before my eyes, disappearing into thin air, like a true Fairy Godmother. Although she *never* says, *"I love you,"* more importantly, the divine Miss Shara feels this emotion very much within. Nevertheless, she shows her love, with her actions, not words. She has never let me down and is forever there with her implacable sarcasm, wide open heart, relentless bitchiness, and constant mocking support, via rolling her eyes and shaking her head. It's the enchanting way she displays her generosity, love, and devotion. Shara is my classic "BFF hero!"

Plus (and another perk), my friend is a mind-blowing, talented, intensely wicked fashionista. She wondrously pulls together every outfit with the finesse of a couture designer. I was comforted by the assurance and knowledge that she would protect me today from making the dreaded and tempting, *"I just went out with yet another frickin' asshole and had to drown my sorrows with a bad outfit purchase!"* She'd spare me the time, regret, and embarrassment of awkwardly returning everything the next day.

Mid-therapy, over lunch at Bloomie's, Shara randomly blurted out. "WTF, Mollie?! First Drew, then Cameron, Rocket-Man, Justin, and now the Russian? Does it ever end? Honey, you are a real-life Soap Opera. You really should think about ending your journalism career. I'm not kidding. You should have your own reality show instead. Seriously, though, the KGB part sounds super fun!"

Laughing miserably, agreeing, it never ends! "BTW, you forgot, Bam Bam! Hey, fuck you, Shara. Back off and be glad you're not me!" We laughed in unison, impolitely too loud. Which is another one of her pet peeves. Being watched and humiliated in public.

Replying in her cynical, nonchalant, blasé, little girl's voice, "About that topic... Why do people constantly say '*fuck you*' when they're angry with someone, or don't like someone? Why do we wish people, who we are pissed-off at, something that feels so fucking good? Why don't we just say, 'Audit *you*,' 'Get fired, *you*,' 'Jury Duty, you,' or 'I hope your medical and car insurance goes up, *you?*' At least that makes logical and rational sense to me!"

You gotta love her gumption! Sincerely, how could you not?

Then my dear friend boldly blurted out, holding up a suggestive pickle. "Cheer up, kid. I have an idea for you. Let's talk about '*the best things ever*,' to get you out of this insufferable, very unflattering funk you are wallowing in. Do you know what the best thing ever is?" She asked, not allowing me to answer, as usual. "Shopping for shoes, jewelry, and purses! They always fit, they never make you look fat, and they never talk back. Bonus, they continually bring pleasure, make you feel tall and cheerful, and perk you up after life beats you way the fuck down. You do agree, don't you? You can always find a cool pair of shoes, a piece of jewelry, or a bag you love, and simply must-have. It is the best cure for anything shitty that happens in your life. Come to think of it, in the immortal words of the great philosopher Marilyn Monroe." She goes on to quote, "Give a girl the right shoes, and she can fucking conquer the world."

While Shara can be ballsy and a touch loud at times, she has this adorable little girly voice, which makes everything she says even funnier. She interrupted me before I could reply.

"I couldn't agree with Marilyn more. Though I wonder, did she really say fucking in the 1950s?" Unable to ask, for she went on talking nonstop and throwing in a typical, Shara tag bomb…

"But of course, we all know great sex with a perfect stranger is always one of the best things ever! Hmm? Possibly even better."

We giggled, in harmony, "Practice safe sex. Wear a condom!"

She added, "Love Marilyn and her shoe quote. Truly, there has never been a more fascinating statement." She quickly inserted. "Unless, of course, you want to believe Bill Clinton's statement." She quoted Bill, "I did not have sexual relations with that woman!"

"And while we are on the Billy subject, here's an action-packed question for you, Mollie!" She pointed her perfectly polished, manicured finger at me, boasting a fabulous emerald ring, with her mouth full of chicken salad. "And be honest with me now!"

I responded like I was being interrogated. "About what, Shara?"

"About my next question. Oh, come on now. Relax. Don't look so worried. You're not on the record, like one of your live television feeds. It's a simple question and a simple answer."

Nervous and munching away, "OK! Go ahead, feel free to ask."

"Now, hear me out before you respond. If you were Monica Lewinsky, a very average-looking, 21-year-old, single girl, a White House Intern, who was naïve, aggressive, hoping, and aspiring for great sex… Whoops-a-daisies! Gee, I meant success? And the gorgeous, charming, dazzling, most powerful man in the world, the President of the United States of America, wanted you in the Oval Office! *Would you have said NO?* Come on, would you have? Cigar or no cigar, how many of us would not have lit up his tip with a blazing fire?" Laughing out of control with her childlike voice, "Sometimes it's so much damn fun playing with fire." We cracked up as the table of old biddies next to us sneered in utter disgust.

Hmm? I paused, contemplating her immoral and seemingly unethical question. Meanwhile, Shara wasn't done yet and went on to clarify further.

"Bill was smoking hot, even without the cigar. I know for certain that I absolutely would have done him. Hell, I'd still do him! I believe one should never confuse politics and sex. Just a passing, politically incorrect thought for the day!"

Still chuckling, I couldn't answer her questions. I was still stuck on what she had said previously.

"Whoops-a-daisies? Whoops-a-daisies, Shara? Are you for real?" She raged on with a fanciful tone.

"Oh, for Pete's sake, let it go. I just watched Julia Robert's old film, 'Notting Hill' last night!"

"No. I can't let whoops-a-daisies go! Impossible, no way. And even though you hate hearing it, I love you! You're the best!" And just like that... she 'Shara-ed' me!

"Yeah, yeah, like I give a shit! Tell someone who cares to hear that sort of crap. Love, shmove! And now, you're buying lunch!"

She swiftly turned around, calling out to the server.

"A slice of the chocolate, and the coconut cake, and two more glasses of wine, please. Don't worry, I was kidding before. Lunch is on me. God only knows you have more than enough to deal with."

After laughing our "whoops-a-daisies" off and fending off scornful dirty looks from the six elderly, ultra-conservative ladies at the next table, I realized she was right, as always. Shara might've had a valid point about Monica. Who would've said no? Trust me, I'm not defending Lewinsky. But who among us in the same situation, especially at that age, would have done otherwise?

Next, the princess of sarcasm and truth continued with her Monica rampage. Only much louder this time for the old biddies to hear. "You know what else? Being the President is a very stressful job. Also, it's a proven, irrefutable fact that sex reduces tension. I believe Monica did a great service to her country, giving Bill a lavish blow job. For this reason, I consider her a devoted, American patriot who selflessly went out of her way to relieve and de-stress the POTUS!" With that said, and her hand placed over her heart, she affirmed, "And may I proudly add, God Bless America!"

Visibly upset, 3 of the offended ancient ladies furiously stood up and walked out in a huff. They left angry and quite shaken up. We laughed uncontrollably as one of the 3 remaining women gave us horrifying, snarky stares. With apparent revulsion, the old red-headed lady threw down a $100 bill, which landed on the floor. She refused to accept my help and struggled bitterly to pick it up. If that wasn't enough to traumatize the rigid, conventional threesome, Shara scrutinized each of them and then spoke out righteously. "Trust me, ladies. Washington, Roosevelt, Lincoln, Eisenhower, Kennedy, and most of the others probably got lucky and had wild sex in the White House too! Don't kid yourselves!"

The gray-haired lady sporting a 'VVS1, 6 Carat, G-colored, huge diamond ring' gasped. "My word!" They fled as if the place were on fire. More accurately, they trudged away with canes and walkers.

Before they could take off, Shara boldly spoke out once again.

"Now, now, ladies, was it something I said? Have a cigar! No? Well, too bad! Audit you, and we hope your medical and car insurance goes up! '*Shoe-shoe*,' gals, and don't forget to vote." They hobbled out, fuming and enraged.

We were immature and giggled so hard I thought I'd die. 'Ruh-Roh!' I hope we didn't get into *Bloomingdale's* trouble for our atrocious behavior. As expected, the fuddy-duddy old women reported us. When the manager came over to our table, Shara said with the cute innocence of a 4-year-old, "Whoops-a-daisies!"

I fell on the floor laughing and so did the manager. He was adorable and surprisingly sent over more wine. Gratis! A great punishment. That was the laughter I needed to bring me back to sanity. A while later, when we got up to leave, Shara seemed preoccupied, searching all around the room.

I questioned her. "So, what are you looking for?"

"Hmm, scouting around for the KGB. Could be rather exciting!"

"Shara, you're such a bitch. I love you! Let's go find shoes!"

Spending the day shoe shopping is a very "heeling" process, for sure. It's essentially as basic as physics or biology. Ah, yes, how I just adore the exotic smell of new leather and its soft silky touch.

You see, men might have more power in the *"Man's world"* we live in. But for now, we girls, *we got the heels!* However, times and mindsets are finally changing, and we women are thrilled. It's magical (Bibbidi-Bobbidi-Boo) how the archaic adage, *"It's a Man's World"* is rapidly disappearing!

On that footnote, today's therapy was cheaper, helped far better, quicker, more fashionable, and extra beneficial than any analyst could have accomplished for me today. I asked myself, could a therapist have matched the joy, closure, and emotional cleansing this fabulous designer dress I just bought on sale brought me? Could

Freud's psychoanalytical theories have brought me as much happiness and contentment as the leather Chanel heels and purse I just purchased? Could Carl Jung's principles bring me the laughter and joy Shara lavishly brought me?

I don't even have to hear or justify the answers. Four deliciously drama-free hours with Shara, mocking little old ladies over lunch, (Gee, I hope they are, okay.) immense laughter, a new purse, two pairs of shoes designed by Jimmy Choo and Chanel, and a polka dot Dior dress later, made me as good as new. I was restored and exquisitely "heeled!" After shopping with my best friend forever, in Bloomie's, I was happy with a new perspective, new goals, and a fresh, brand-new outlook.

"Hey, Shara, look how great my thigh gap looks in these Jimmy Choo shoes! Yo, Shara? Where'd you go? Come on, where are you?"

"Hey, Shara? Girl, where did you go?"
"Hello? Hell-Ooooo? Where are you?"
"Shara? God? Disney? Yo, Shara?"

Whoops-a-daisies?!?!?"

CHAPTER 15

Two Quickies Without the Sex It's Gettin' Old!

AND MY HAIR WAS PURPLE!!!!!!

1. AND THEN CAME... THE JULIAN DEBACLE!

Unlucky for me, I chose wrong again! Although, in my defense, he sounded super nice on the phone. But then... Yeah... Not so much!

I was assigned to be in Dallas to write a feature story on the George W. Bush Presidential Library and Museum. As I was scheduled to be there anyway, I decided to meet "online Julian" after a few weeks of speaking on the phone. We met at his favorite restaurant, which he belligerently promised was award-winning, nouveau-chic, and served fabulous food. I came to discover, in a word, it sucked. However, entirely irrelevant to this story.

At first glance (and 2nd) I wasn't physically attracted to this 6'4"guy, with deep frown lines around his mouth, crow's feet at the corners of his eyes, and 2 Robert De Niro moles on his face. Still, I decided to give him a chance by revisiting the idea of, "You never know." Frankly, "*You Always Know!*" There were enough blazing red flags here to start a forest fire and alert Smokey the Bear into full action. And Yogi & Boo-Boo, too!

The dinner chat was essentially all about him. Predominately, most of the conversation was Julian, bragging about Julian, and how rich Julian is. He claimed (allegedly), "I was a general family doctor and owned six walk-in clinics. I retired early only because I had so much money, that it was pointless to continue working. This is what happens when you're the best!"

Let's be real here, for a Tick-Tock, shall we? No successful person, including Bill Gates himself, would make up such a dumb statement for retiring. He retired because he had so much money? Laughing flags, waving in my face!

I responded questioning. "Really Julian? Honestly? In my opinion, I don't think anyone would seriously retire so young for that reason."

He quickened. "It wasn't your decision. Now, was it, honey? It was mine, Cutie-Pie. It's not about you, nor did I ask your opinion!"

Fairly shocked and startled, I could only answer with a polite kiss-ass, "No! I get it! I was just joining in with my own opinions."

He swiftly attacked. "But It's Not About, Your Opinions, Honey! It's About ME, and MY, opinions!" Julian went on crowing regarding his inventions that supposedly earned him billions. Or was it trillions, I forget? Anyhow, he vehemently went on about his wealth. "Supposedly!" I wasn't impressed in the least by all his swanky gloating. At one point in the conversation, I tried to interject something about myself. Except he arrogantly grunted, "Again, It's Not All About You, Cutie-Pie. Wow, you are something!"

Having been silenced and stunned most of the night, I silently thought, what a jerk. Silly me for chiming into the discussion! Must be painful for him to involve another. Although I didn't respond to his rude remarks, I vividly remember my head tilted involuntarily, like a confused cocker spaniel. It's one of my better looks. But again, "It's Not About Me. Also, now known as… Honey-*Cutie-Pie!*"

Dinner ended at 10:00, and before I could stand up, Jules ran out instantaneously to smoke a cigarette, leaving me by myself. His smoking was an addiction he neglected to inform me of and lied about in his profile. When I met him outside after a quick pit stop to the ladies' room, he planted a yucky-smoker's-breath kiss on me. If Julian thought mints disguised the *Ewe-ness,* in smoker's breath, he should be advised they really don't! Being the fair-minded Cutie-Pie that I am, I let that go as well.

Wanting to end the evening quickly, "Ciao. Nice meeting you, Jules." I bid him a fond, Ewe-Filled, All About Him, Goodnight!

The following afternoon, knowing it was *"All about Me,"* I completed the Bush story assigned to me by the magazine rhyming with, "Booze Leak." Ahead of schedule, feeling accomplished, with a Café Latte in hand, I ran to catch an early flight back home.

Why, I wondered (And I truly don't understand it myself.), did I continue to speak with Julian? I suppose, though ridiculous, he kind of grew on me, like a fungus or a wart. Plus, my friends were encouraging me to move on. As the calls began to get monotonous, we discussed his coming out to visit me. However, I was beginning to have a change of heart, as Julian continued boasting incessantly about his billions. He basked in the total fabulosity of himself.

I grew increasingly suspicious and continued feeling apprehensive, with ginormous, bright red flags of doubt. I had to make sure who he really was before I opened myself up to him and allowed him to enter my home, my world, and my den of iniquity.

Logically, this was the perfect time to call in Diane, my private investigator. Boy, was I ever keeping her rolling in laughter.

Wham-Bam, and in no time at all, she delivered powerful information equal to a World-Class fighter's punch in the gut. She dug up records, disclosing the fake billionaire Julian had filed for Chapter 13 bankruptcy 2-years prior. Plus, he was going through a foreclosure on his house and was being evicted from the one he was renting, which he claimed to own. Tsk-Tsk, Sheesh, and yikes! It's a foregone, discouraging conclusion that a lot of online men are appalling liars. Although, I assumed women might be as well!

Diane also reported that Julian was married a 2nd time, which he artfully failed to inform me about as well. His first wife (according to him) was a compulsive liar, who was lazy, uncaring, miserable, and a negative bipolar woman who turned his kids against him. His 2nd wife, he alleged, was a real bitch and cheated on him. It's fascinating how all men who badmouth their exes say the same thing, and pretty much in that order.

I came to appreciate after just one date that no way in his right mind would he voluntarily disclose the kind of personal information Diane had uncovered. Especially to someone he just met. Meanwhile, I was still confused as to why he droned away nonstop about how rich he was in the first place. What made him lie this way when he knew he wasn't rich and went bankrupt, to boot? I decided to stay quiet about Diane's discoveries and let this intriguing intelligence stay in my pocket. It seemed more pressing to find out if I liked him before confronting him. It could all wind up being a moot point, so why bother embarrassing him now?

The following day, Julian explained, "After much reflection, I'm deathly afraid of flying. I'd be happy to buy your airline ticket if you'd be kind enough to fly back to see me." (Flag, flag, flag!) Foolishly (and again, I can't explain why), I didn't want to end the relationship yet. Besides, I was relieved to go there instead of revealing and sharing my world and domain with him.

The night before I was to fly to Dallas, Julian called and asserted candidly, "Cutie-Pie, we are gonna sleep together in the same bed. Right?"

I reflected with my puzzled Cocker Spaniel look plastered upon my face. "Is this a trick question?" Ignoring my look, he asked me again. "Gosh, I don't know, Jules. I haven't even thought about it! Regardless, I have a friend in Dallas I'll be staying with since you haven't mentioned anything about accommodations before now. Nonetheless, Julian, the one thing I can absolutely confirm is that we are not going to have sex! Not on this trip, anyway. I mean, geez, we just met. So please calm down. OK?"

"I'll calm down, Cutie-Pie, but it's not just all about you, ya know. Well, in that case, I'll be honest and tell you that there is no way I can sleep in the same bed with you all night without having sex. I'm a very sexual man who is attracted to you. Accordingly, sleeping in the same bed with you and not having sex will leave me suffering from a huge hard-on all night. And what am I supposed to do with that? Women are different. Hugging and kissing may be sweet and fun for you girls, but it will not cut it for me, Cutie-Pie! We're not in High School. Just so you know, I'm a great lover, and my joystick is humungous. I can Tit your Tat! How about that?"

Cute, a little rhyme. So gross! His comment would make a puppy growl. What the hell is with men and their schlong size? It seems to match their grandiose egos. After his childish revelation, I was incensed and thought of canceling the trip. (I should have!) I couldn't get over his insatiable ego and demanding "I want what I want when I want it" attitude. I answered his spoiled little child, boo-hoo, presumptuous desires with, "I understand Julian and respect your views. Regardless, come hither, there will be no sex!"

"Well, Cutie, it's *Not All About You, Honey!* Ya Know? And why are you being such a baby about this? Grow up, little girl!"

Ladies, when a man mocks you in this way for not giving in to him, this is when you know he's an ass and does not respect you, or your integrity. Here is where I should have told him without any pretense, "Jules, Go Fuck Yourself," and then hung up! Instead, I chose the high road. For the record, I hate that road! It's a bullshit road, with scary winding curves, not well-lit, gets you nowhere, and is too snooty a superior road to have any fun on!

Instead of what I wanted to say, I stated, "Au contraire, Julian. You are acting ignorant and pushy. While I am being cautious and mature. My mind, body, and heart must be in alignment to make love. For now, I have a plethora of good reasons to abstain. Including, I hardly know you!" I reflected, pleased that I knew more about this bankrupt narcissist than he thought I did. Thanks to Diane's report, revealing he was lying about most everything.

He completely ignored what I had said and lashed back with, "Gee, Cutie, it's only because I feel we need to... Oh, never mind!"

"No... Oh, never mind what, Julian?"

"I just feel we need to have sex, so we know for sure if we are compatible before deciding to move on."

Laughing at his nonsense, I contradicted him.

"Oh, I see. Well, I believe we need to get along and be compatible before rushing into sex. We should see how that goes first, so we don't make a mistake by having sex with someone who we don't even like! Do you understand this decision is not *All About Me,* but *All About Us!*" He hated my logic and morals. At times, I admit, I did too. But this wasn't one of those times. Instead, I added, "Please, stop calling me *Cutie-Pie.* It's quite degrading!"

We agreed I would stay at my friend's house the first night and in the guest bedroom at his house for the next three nights. Since his two teenage kids lived with him, I felt safe enough to agree to these terms. Well, as safe as one could be. He exasperated me further by opening his mouth again. "Remember, babe, I refuse to let you sleep with me if you are only willing to kiss and cuddle."

I swear to God, I never once begged him for kisses, or to sleep in his bed. Other than sheer stupidity, I have no idea on earth why I flew to Dallas to see him. This was rather troubling because I didn't even like the guy! Readers, in case you didn't spot the huge red warning flag, flashing like a Vegas Billboard, flying off to Dallas was a flag as big and bright as they glow. I imagine I went temporarily brain-dead, running off to Texas after that conversation. I was caught in a senseless *blonde cluster storm.*

To bring a splash of support to my crazy rationale, I missed the chance to go to NorthPark Center on my last trip there. It's a shopper's nirvana. Sure, I realize this sounds shallow. But come on! A shopping paradise will light up any girl with a happy, idyllic, colorful retail glow! Anyway, even with a chance to visit the renowned center, I really should have flown to Never-Neverland instead. But wait, it gets better.

A few hours after my plane landed, I settled into my friend Shannon's house. Later, I met Julian, as planned, at the movie theater for a movie and dinner at 4:30. I must point out, who the hell under the age of 75 or 10 years old goes to a movie at 4:30 on a Saturday night? Making the situation even worse, Julian greeted me with a smelly cigarette kiss and a very inappropriate, disgusting lick on my neck. Like, who does that? Gyrating weirdly, he squealed like a little child, yelling, "Ick! Oh, gross! Ewe!"

"Wait, what? Ick, oh gross, ewe, what, Jules? It's just perfume, and I wasn't expecting to be licked like a dog." I couldn't believe this creep made me feel bad about wearing a $1,000 an ounce perfume by Caron Poivre. Justin's favorite. Apart from his licking, spitting, and shameful manners, it's a huge fashion sin to waste perfume! Such gall and the craziest reaction I had ever seen or felt.

Walking towards movie theater number six, I couldn't help but notice Julian, Mr. Moneybags, wasn't any sort of gentleman. He didn't hold my hand, even to help me walk down the steep stairs in stiletto heels. Instead, as if he were royalty, he arrogantly walked way ahead of me. Do I look like a subservient Geisha Girl, with my long blonde hair and blue eyes, I wondered? I also learned Jules wasn't affectionate, helpful, or thoughtful. I desperately wanted to be back home in a T-shirt, with my wine, and Netflix shows.

During the film (which was a comedy, I might add), Julian glared at the screen, engrossed, and concentrating. Concentrating intensely, as if he were at a lecture on "Surviving the climb up to the top of Mount Everest" he would attempt in the morning. It was scary watching him. Hoping to be frisky and loosen him up, I leaned in to kiss his cheek. (I don't know why I did.) He grumbled back, angry with me. "Stop! Stop it! I am watching the movie!"

Mortified, I went on eating my complimentary tiny bag of popcorn and sipping a 4-ounce pour of cheap red wine. Jules ordered a Ginger Ale and four filet mignon sliders. It was disturbing because he didn't even offer me a bite. Not cool at all! Later, he was very put off when I ordered another glass of wine.

After the movie ended and before we even stood up, he looked at me and said, loud enough for the rest of the movie patrons to hear, "Oh, My God! Are you kidding? You ate the whole big bag of popcorn? I can't believe you ate the whole, entire bag by yourself! Geeze, aren't you a little piggy!"

OK! You see now, in my world, Mollie-Land, those are fighting words. I responded even louder. "No, I shared it with the pink giraffe & the big red armadillo sitting on the floor next to me!" The angry look on his face and the remaining people in the theater who were now pointing and giggling made it all worthwhile, no matter how hard he might swing back. Thank goodness he dropped it.

Julian informed me he wasn't hungry and that we should remain here and order 2 appetizers downstairs at Ranzy, the theater's restaurant. He ordered, without asking my preference, and ate 99% of it. I, the now "Legendary Popcorn Pig," having not eaten a meal all day, remained starving.

To set the record straight, it was just a *small bag with half a cup* of popcorn in it. I'm just throwing that out there *for the record!*

I excused myself to visit the ladies' room and called my friend. Famished, I asked her to meet me at Sushi Yama for dinner. All I heard on the other end of the phone was her laughing hysterically and validating, "Absolutely Mollie, I'll be there!"

When I returned, Julian was nowhere to be found. I searched for over 10 minutes. Hoping, could I possibly get this lucky? No, darn it. I found him outside, taking a smoke. He whined with his disgusting smoker's stench. "Cutie-Pie I'm tired. I'm going home. Unless, of course, you want to come over and have sex?"

"Julian, that would be a hard no!"

"Your loss! Fine, let's meet tomorrow night 6:00 at my house. Hey, listen, it would be a good idea for you to dress nice this time!"

To begin with, "This Time?" Secondly, "Cutie-Pie?" Replying with an annoyed attitude, "Julian, it's only 8:00! How tired can you be? You're retired. And I mean it, stop calling me Cutie-Pie!"

Fuming like a chimney, I must argue with his outrageous remark. I dressed adorably in a pink Stella McCartney skirt and a ruffled matching top. Outraged, I couldn't say goodbye fast enough.

I happily spent the rest of the evening eating dinner and hanging out with my amusing, dear friend Shannon. I filled her in on my ludicrous experiences with the fool. All of it. Down to him, licking my neck and spitting out my spectacular perfume.

"Mollie, I'm not sure who the bigger fool is in this drama?" She laughed so hard that the sushi and soy sauce were dripping down her chin. Trying her best to speak, as she was squealing and cracking up. "Shit girl, look what you did. You made me spill eel sauce all over my shirt. Such a pig, you can't take me anywhere!"

I quoted, *"Shan, honey, it's not always about YOU. Ya Know!* You can be *Sushi Pig,* but I reign supreme as the *Cutie-Pie-Popcorn-Pig!"*

"OMG, you are so funny, it hurts. Be honest, Mollie. Are you just exaggerating, or is he really that crazy and as bad as you say?"

"Not at all! He's great. In fact, I think you should go out with him! You'll love um. Dress nicely this time, and don't order wine.

Spilling more eel and spicy mayo sauce and avocado pieces all over her shirt, she choked, laughing. "No way, and waste expensive perfume? Oops, Mollie, I think I just farted from laughing!"

"Awkward! You sure it wasn't a shart? Girl, look at you. You have food stains all over you. You look like a messy 2-year-old."

We were crying and laughing out of control. I think we were probably disturbing the other patrons. I shrugged it off and sent them a little piece of Shara. "Oh, yeah, whatever, and Audit You!"

"What? Mollie, what the heck does that even mean?"

"Forget it, too long story! Pass the fried rice before you spill that all over you, too."

Back at Shannon's, neither of us got much sleep. We had so much fun reminiscing about our college days, drinking homemade margaritas, and eating whatever we found in her pantry.

The following evening, while dressed very nicely as ordered (As if I had to be told?), I rang his doorbell at 6:00 sharp. Julian slowly sauntered to the front door, making me wait five minutes before he finally greeted me with a cigarette-reeking kiss on the cheek. I was relieved he was a quick learner, and just kissed me on the cheek, without licking me this time. Damn, too bad. I deliberately added a few extra splashes of perfume everywhere. Just in case he tried. He nodded, "Hey, babe, I missed you! I want you to know I'm crazy about you. You really get me. I think this could be it. I believe you are the one that ends my search!"

Seriously? This was unequivocally one of my biggest online dating *"What the fuck, are you kidding me"* moments. I wanted to tell him he'd best keep searching. Flabbergasted, I contemplated. If this was how he treated me, believing that I am *"The One,"* I shudder to think how I'd be treated in five years. Silence is golden at times, and it appeared this was one of those 14 Karat gold times.

I would've happily traded his fake, baloney flattery for a hello greeting, handing me a glass of wine when he answered the door.

Further insulting, he said nothing about the way I was dressed, *"This Time!"* But I didn't care. No need for him to tell me I looked ravishing because I did! I wore my *"Do me, when I am ready for you to, do me"* sexy, low-cut, little black dress, ultra-trendy, extra-high rhinestone heels, and attached a *bunch* of purple extensions in my hair. Just for fun. I was dressed far nicer than this troll deserved.

Oh, Justin, my darling Justin. Look what you left me with...

Julian invited me into his *secretly rented, soon-to-be-evicted,* humble abode, not befitting a billionaire. (Or was it a Trillionaire? I forget.) He had Family Feud blasting on the TV. We sat there for over an hour and a half, watching it. Family Feud People, wearing Versace!!! He didn't even offer me a glass of wine, which made it impossible to endure this insanity. I asked, "When are we going to dinner? So, you know, I'm not big on television or game shows."

He offensively stated again. "For real, Honey? Honestly, it's Not Always About You!" At least he changed it up this go-around. I realized, on the contrary, it never would be about me with him. More to the point, I learned, I didn't want it to be.

We left for dinner (Which I'd been told to dress nicely for, "This time!") only to find him driving up to a hole-in-the-wall, nothing-special Chinese restaurant. It was in an old strip mall that appeared to be mostly takeout. Gee, he really did think I was a Geisha Girl. Halfway through the steamed dumplings, pork fried rice, and orange chicken, I looked at Julian and noticed he had fallen asleep at the table. Sitting up! Let me make this dynamic exponentially clear. He Fell Asleep. at 8:30 p.m. at a tacky Chinese restaurant, (where the table & menus were sticky) whilst I was wearing Boobs and *Purple Extensions* in my hair! What the FUCK?

I scared him abruptly with a loud and noisy tone. "Hey, Rip Van Winkle, wake up! Are you frickin' kidding me, falling asleep?"

He reacted defensively. "What? I'm tired!"

He belligerently got up and ran outside for a smoke, leaving me alone, overdressed in Versace?! Utterly speechless, I could only smirk, watching the people now glaring at me, wearing their tacky cut-off shorts and tattered, gross-looking tank tops. If Julian were looking for a feud, family, or other, I would surely help him with that. As if things weren't humiliating enough, I had orange sesame sauce on my now-stained designer dress. There I sat, looking like a high-class hooker, wearing a short dress, with trendy purple in my hair, and my breasts at attention, presented as if they were on stage. I was irritated and alone thinking, "Isn't dating grand?" He returned to the low-budget eatery, paid the bill, and firmly shouted at me, "Come on, let's go. I have a special treat for you!"

"What, you chartered a private jet to fly us to Dubai for brunch?" He didn't appreciate my reply. Ignoring me fervently, he drove to a frozen yogurt place to bring some back to his TV-Land.

"Julian," I asked inquisitively. "So, come on. Tell me. What's the special treat already?"

"What do you mean? Yogurt with toppings is a great treat."

"I guess? If you're 5!" Unable to stop myself, "Ooh-La-La fancy!"

Returning to his soon-to-be evicted rental (instead of Dubai), he plopped down on the sofa and resumed his lazy couch-potato stance. We watched Crime Show reruns for 2 hours. There should be legal consequences for forcing this upon a woman. Maybe four counts of TV harassment. Bored, and just for kicks, I tried to kiss him. I shamefully don't have a clue why I would do this. Really beginning to worry about myself. The man shocked me when he roared, "Stop, I'm watching television. I'm trying to concentrate."

I responded with my best "Oh, Hell No," expression. And with that, I flew into the kitchen, grabbed my yogurt, ignored him, and pretended to watch the crap he had on TV. In the middle of my *"Special Treat,"* he screamed out, panicking, as if I had stolen his remote. "You took my yogurt! You are eating mine! Man, it certainly is always about you, isn't it!"

Furious, I rebelled. "I'm done! I'm going to bed." Unable to sleep, I tried to figure out a nice way to get out of this predicament.

In the bedroom's bathroom, I discovered there was no soap or towels. A little too late for my own good, I further realized there was no toilet paper to, you know, wipe with. Thank heavens I had a ton of Starbucks napkins in my purse. This guy couldn't possibly have made me feel more unwelcome. What was I doing here lying in bed, showerless, with a man I don't even like? I felt so uncomfortable and foolish, I couldn't sleep a wink all night.

Shannon and I text back and forth for hours, trying to come up with an escape plan. She couldn't find it in her heart to let the story go. She mocked me. "Let's see now. Cheap Chinese food, he fell asleep at dinner, a yogurt surprise, TV reruns, game shows, stinky smokers' breath, and no toilet paper, soap, or towels? I bet you're glad you put purple extensions in your hair! Sorry, not to be mean, but I can't stop laughing. It's hilarious, Mollie, and you know it! And don't you dare even think about eating my yogurt! Now, go and put Bewitched or Bonanza on the antique television. Ha-Ha…"

What could I say to her other than, "Yeah, OK, Shannon, lick me, and go put Bewitched on yourself!" Gosh, that girl sure can laugh!

In the morning, exhausted from being up all night, I dressed rapidly and went downstairs. It was 6:14, just in time to witness the master of the house smoking and watching some game show on the couch. "Well, you're up late! Wow…"

"Julian, are you joking? You honestly believe 6:14 in the morning, all dressed and ready to go, exemplifies getting up late?" Which is the sophisticated code for, "Go fuck yourself, dick wad, and bring me coffee!" I sat there patiently, waiting for him to offer me anything at all. I finally asked, "Hey Jules, got coffee?" He came back with a small cup of instant. Instant coffee, people, with no sugar or milk. "Jules, do you have milk, sugar, food, whatever?" Fuming, I silently thought, "I mean, if you can't give me toilet paper, a towel, or soap, then you sure as shit better give me a great big cup of real coffee, non-fat milk, and sugar in the morning!"

I suppose he finally grasped I was his captive guest, and after a few minutes, sent his son out for bagels and spreads. We sat in front of the TV watching old medical shows. I think it was, "Marcus Welby." (Whoever that is?) When I uttered the correct diagnosis within seconds, he turned to me with his vulgar smoker's mouth and sarcastically stated, "Huh? So, you think you are a doctor now, too?" Ignoring him, I devoured my bagel and a second cup of black, shitty, instant coffee. Aghast, in a woman-hating tone, he barked, "My God, you ate the whole bagel? You were mighty hungry!"

Game over! Besides the fact I wasn't hungry at all, I marched into the kitchen and made myself another bagel with double cream cheese and smothered it with Nova. After finishing it and feeling painfully stuffed, I asked. "Jules, do you have any popcorn? I'm starving!" He looked at me, horrified, with indignant astonishment. Oblivious, I don't think he got the dig.

I remarked, perspiring. "Sorry to bother you. But could you please kindly turn down the air? It's super Dallas, humid, hot in here!" He looked at me as if the thermostat set at eighty-two degrees in the house was plenty comfortable.

"What? Are you going through *Menopause?* And My God, are you still eating? You are still hungry? Man, it surely is all about you, for real."

I refused to babysit this scoundrel any longer. I went ballistic and *wicked-witched* him.

"First of all, Julian, *Menopause?* I am 31 years old! In case you didn't notice, it's hot as shit in here. Second of all, *yes,* I get hungry, all 100 and 8 pounds of me. And third, to let you in on a secret... Since I met you, No Julian. It Has Never Once, Been All About Me!"

I couldn't stand being around this toxic man another second and I wasn't going to make up a lie to leave. I had to cut him out, like deleted scenes from a bad movie on the cutting room floor.

"Julian, I've done the math. You're a nice guy (a necessary white lie), but I feel we are just going through the motions. This is not going to work out. We aren't right for each other. *And This Is All About You....* You do need to go on searching! To be blunt, there is no chemistry between us, nor do we share any of the same interests. It happens. Let's just call it quits now, so neither of us needs to pretend for another 2 days. Trust me, that scenario won't end well." Unexpectedly, he tried to talk me out of my decision.

"What? I don't understand! I'm crazy about you. Please, let's try a little longer. You're wrong, we have amazing chemistry!"

"Julian, get real. You went on relentlessly about sex, yet you haven't even kissed me without spitting. You never held my hand, even when it would have been the gentlemanly thing to do. Nor have you shown me any warmth or kindness. It's ok. No worries. I'm going to leave now. I'm off to visit my friend for a few days. But it was lovely meeting you!"

"Please, just give it some more time, honey," he begged.

I also begged, musing silently. I'm not liable for any injuries that may occur here if I stay.

He placed his arm around me and put on another old TV show. I think it was the original Sherlock Holmes. He didn't break a smile when I asked if this show was from the early 1600s. Tough crowd!

Increasingly desperate to leave after a few murderous television moments, I noticed Jules scratching himself and itching more than what is considered normal. Even for him.

Yikes, now what? Holding my breath, "What's up, Jules?"

"Nothing, a little itch. I was gardening before you woke up."

"Please, just pull up your sleeve and let me look at it. Oh my gosh, holy shit, Julian! You have a poison ivy rash all over you!"

"Hmm, pathetic, you clearly do think you are a doctor."

"Julian, stop it! Cut the crap. I just know what you have."

He shouted at me with contemptuous rage. "Again, honey, It's Not About You, Cutie-Pie!! It's About Me. I will figure it out myself!"

My, my, this dude was ruthless! He jumped up quickly and was gone for about 20 minutes. I bolted upstairs to gather my things and quickly threw them into my rental car. When he returned, noticeably distressed, he shouted, "I have Poison Ivy All Over Me!"

Benevolently, I wanted to remain silent and rise above the fray. Which, of course, I always hate to do with the fray! Lol, so I didn't.

"No shit, Sherlock!" He didn't laugh. Whatever! I welcomed and appreciated his fortunate rash and laughable itchy condition as my lucky getaway gift from heaven above.

"Jules, as you already know, being a doctor, this condition is highly contagious. Go out and get yourself some extra-strength cortisone cream and Benadryl. STAT! Be careful not to touch your eyes. Doctor's orders! Or, on second thought, you could just make your own ointment from Scratch."

I chuckled! What, not funny yet? Too soon? Yeah, oops, probably too soon! Uh-Oh, by the look in his eyes, here it comes.

He bitterly opened his uncivilized mouth for the last time and yelled at me, "You Gave Me This Rash, Didn't You? Didn't you!"

"OK… Yep… Cool! Let's go with that! Yes, yes, I did! I guess I neglected to tell you that I am a *tree*, seeping with sticky, oily urushiol. Ba-Bye Jules!"

I walked to the door but turned around. "And, by the way, did you even notice the fun purple in my hair? Never mind, I just wondered. Fear not, Julian honey, it still is and will forever be, All About You, Cutie-Pie! Oh, one last thing. Girls don't like being called *Cutie-Pie!* That is, unless you say it lovingly, or if the girl is under 16 years old."

With liberating delight, I didn't wait another minute to leap to my exit. I professed my Declaration of Independence by leaving fresh skid marks on his driveway. (Eeks, that'll be hard to remove.)

The next two days were an absolute blast, hanging out with

my laughing hyena girlfriend, Shannon. She literally peed in her Victoria's Secret Panties when I told her the poison ivy story. She laughed till she turned blue and called me a liar.

"Girlfriend, I can only wish I was lying."

Shannon jumped up. "Hey, want some Chinese food or yogurt? It'll be my special treat? Ha-Ha-Ha-ha-ha-ha!"

She went on, jubilantly teasing and taunting me.

"Cutie-Pie, **YOU GOT MALED!** *Big Time and to the Max!"*

"Nice, Shannon! Would you like some more eel sauce or spicy mayo to spill all over your clothes?"

We giggled till we couldn't breathe, and our sides hurt. It was great staying with her for a few days, being lavished with toilet paper, tissues, soap, towels, no television, coffee, wine, and her sweet, fun-loving friendship. Guess what, she never licked my neck even once! The best part was, Shan and I shopped till we dropped at the highly anticipated, awesomazing, NorthPark Center.

The four morals of this story:

1. Jules, are best left in jewelry and set into gold!
2. *It's not always about me! I was* lucky to flee with only myself to blame!
3. Don't waste fabulous purple extensions on a nasty idiot! And remember to always, always, take a ton of Starbucks napkins on your way out!
4. **"All men are 'Not' created equal!"**

 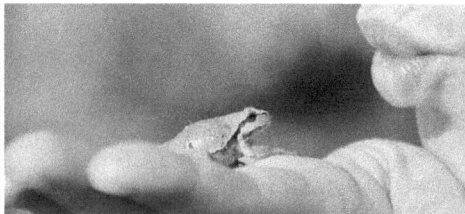 

2. THEN, THE IRS SWINDLER, LYING, CORRUPT GUY ROLLED IN AND OUT. INSISTING, "I AM INNOCENT! DAMMIT, I AM INNOCENT!"

Melvin Mickey Max, from Minneapolis, Minnesota, found me online. He was thirty-two years old and judging strictly by his profile photos (wearing a pin-striped suit and hat) he was in toto, exceptionally cute, unlike, and despite his name. We spoke several times and shared many conversations. He claimed he used to be a bodybuilder. Again, judging by his photos, he kept that up. But who knows? He explained, "I am a very successful (Aren't they all?) personal investment banker. I've accomplished all my financial goals and succeeded in making a fortune. Just to keep busy, I handle a few multibillion-dollar accounts. I'm fortunate, at such a young age, to be semi-retired and enjoy the freedom and time to do what I want. You know what I mean? *Fuck You, Money!*"

Melvin sounded great on paper. I'll give him that. Nevertheless, I inquisitively would've liked to see that paper up close. I first had my serious doubts about him when he kept mentioning things like:

"I'm involved with the mob." And bragging, "I'm one of the 'Good Fellas' you'll want to bring home to meet your family." (Yeah, sure, if my family name was Capone or Gambino!) I grew more concerned as he continually spoke about private family matters before we even met. Too much info, too soon in the game.

He would discuss things such as, "I take care of my elderly parents and raised my daughter completely by myself. Plus, I also took full financial responsibility for my Ex-girlfriend's daughter, including her private schooling." Since he professed, he only dated her for six months, I thought it was rather peculiar why he continued to be the daughter's benefactor. This made me believe he had something funny going on with the daughter, in addition to the mom.

Suspicious, I carefully tiptoed in with Lucky Luciano.

Mickey Mouse, oops, Max, spoke mostly about himself. "I am a respectable, decent, honorable, honest man!" I found this worrisome, as he said it repeatedly, time and time again.

We made plans for the (Bugsy Siegel) "honorable guy" to come to Vegas for three days. He would stay at Caesars Palace, and I would drive to the city to be with him. I enlightened him, (a critical thing I've learned to do) there'd be no sex until we knew each other much better and decided if we wanted to start a relationship.

Without any hesitation, he responded immediately with a respectful, "Of course, Mollie. No worries. I understand and feel precisely the same way!"

At midnight, unable to sleep listening to the tick-tick-tock of the clock, the evening before Melvin was supposed to come to Vegas, I was alarmed when the phone rang.

"Mollie, it's Melvin. Forgive me for calling you so late. I'm sorry, but I need to come clean with some things I thought you should know. Some information I probably should have told you before."

All righty, then! I thought to myself at 12:00 in the morning. *NOW*, he thinks to tell me something important! *NOW*, he needed to come clean with some things he thought I should know, and probably should have told me *before!* That is obviously a statement a girl living alone never wants to hear at midnight, or indeed, any other time. My heart raced as he spoke, fearing this wasn't going to end well.

"Honey, I have a bit of a problem. I hope it won't matter to you. It really shouldn't. Being upfront, I don't know why it would."

"OK, Melvin. What's up?"

"Not a big thing, honey. But…"

Thinking, Ah-Ha! *The Deadly But!* Here it comes, wait for it…

"I sort of, in a way, a little bit, got in some trouble with the IRS. I was working with some guys doing a bit of a, kind of a, in a way, somewhat of an illegal Ponzi scheme thing. But I swear I am clean. I didn't know what was going down at the time. I promise you. It's not at all my fault. I didn't know. I really didn't! I innocently got involved in a huge business that scammed and cheated the IRS big time. It turned out to be an enormous, scandalous, epic story. It was all over the national news. The top players (who just happened to be in the mob) went to jail for two consecutive life sentences. They cheated the IRS out of exorbitant amounts of money. I imagine some people were killed. Not sure. Fine, maybe a few died. OK, maybe more than a few are sleeping with the fishes.

It was a 2-year trial. There were about 50 other guys like me involved. We were all completely innocent. You do believe me, dear? Are you still there on the line, Doll?"

Mr. Clean grew exponentially more anxious. "Um, um, Ahhh?" He continued. "Hon, I'm telling you now because I kinda owe over $500 grand to the IRS. So, as you can understand, I had to go bankrupt. You do understand and believe me. Don't cha, kid?"

I calmy answered him. "Well? I mean?" (Which is code for, NO! And there go my weekend plans!)

"You can trust me, babe. I'm truly innocent. I am not guilty, I tell you! However, since I've been informed that the FBI and the IRS are still watching me and, staying on my back, I don't think it's such a good idea for me to come to Vegas right now. The trial ended only a month ago. But since I very much want to meet you, I was wondering. Do you think you could come visit me here in Minnesota instead? I'm excited to meet you, Sugar. You do believe me, don't you?"

It appeared the Donnie Brasco, Scarface story, that the unscru-pulous Mickey Mouse wrote, ended at *Chapter 11.* Maybe it was Chapter 13. Either way, I put an end to our story at *Chapter 1.*

"Mickey, I mean, I like, 'kinda, sorta,' in a way, can't come to Minnesota, because my Restless Legs Syndrome is acting up again! Dang-it!" From his claims of being a bodybuilder, I imagined that would be a legitimate excuse as to why I couldn't come.

"Doll, you believe me when I tell you I am innocent, don't you?"

"Well, you know what? Honestly, I don't. I believe the IRS and the FBI. Sorry, I don't trust your slick kabuki dance. Mr. 'Good Fella,' you got your necktie caught in the fan. You were busted, rightfully so. And please, tell me, what part of this crime, didn't you realize weeks ago that I should've known about?" (You kidding me?)

"Melvin Mickey Max, all I can say is, Fuhgeddaboudit! Take care of yourself. See 'Youse,' never again. Bye now!" **Click and Blocked**

I'm not stupid. I didn't believe or trust Melvin Mickey Max from Minneapolis, Minnesota. Not one word! (Besides, you should never trust a guy that needs five M's to explain himself!) But, on the off chance he was telling the truth, Mickey Mouse was old enough to know if you hang out with bad people, bad things will happen. It's like playing with matches at a gas station. It could and did blow up in his face. I suppose claiming total innocence and using such hyperbole can make a guilty man feel better about himself. In the end, he was nothing more than your basic phony con artist. He was a double-dealing liar, a deceitful criminal, a fakeoholic, a cheater, and a real mob rat. Ha, I really should put that on a bumper sticker.

Maybe because he came off so squeaky-clean and virtuous, recapping he was one of the "Good Fellas," I foolishly and stupidly didn't think to check him out. I let my guard down. You see, people, this is exactly what I'm saying, and why I'm warning you! Check them *all* out. Don't assume these guys are all sunshine and candy. Heed *all* the flags. I plead with all of you out there, once again, no matter what, neither here nor there, come hell or high water; you must carefully check every one of them out! In addition, don't fall for their "boo-hoo" stories!

Heaven knows this is when Jell-O-Shots, and M&M&M&M&M's work nicely for a gal. Clearly, there's never a dull online moment.

"All men are 'Not' created equal!"

It's official. I was living in a three-ring circus going out with these clowns. The only silver lining was I didn't have to pay for admission! Speaking of which, where were my circus peanuts, popcorn, candy apple, & cotton candy? I believe I've earned them.

Why is it that most men today don't know how to treat a lady? *Why* don't men understand what's important to us girls? *Why* are there so many clueless men out there? *Why* are men and women so vastly different? Why is this even possible?

These *"why"* thoughts are only a sampling of the most confusing questions I needed to examine. I'm astounded by most men's ignorance when it comes to the female species. Men and women who act like worms, do indeed, open up a *can of thoughts.*

After hanging up on another crazy one, I was disillusioned and left feeling deceived and disheartened. I plopped down on my bed and looked up toward the heavens, dumbfounded and dazed. *This prompted me to think of other problematic anomalies in life. I am sure, readers, that you've also contemplated these, "Why" questions.*

THE WHY'S... SUCH AS:

- What are the secrets, meanings, and purpose of life?

- Why are we here?
- God, do you really exist? And if you do, who put *you* there?
- What happens when we die? Is there life after death, or is that a myth too?
- Is reincarnation real? Why do we have to die in the first place?
- And on that topic... Why do the *good* die young?
- Why does pregnancy have to last for nine long months?
- And on that topic... Why does labor have to be painful?
- Why is it, when we finally get ahead financially, something expensive falls apart. Our cell, car, fridge, ceiling, or computer?
- Are we alone in the universe, or are there life forms on other planets?
- What frightening things are hiding under the oceans and seas? Is there a secret world or dimension we don't know of?
- Why is any form of prejudice or bigotry necessary? Moreover, why do we tolerate it?
- Why hasn't anyone cured cancer or the common cold already?
- Why do we ever have to break a nail or experience bad hair days?
- Why can't we all learn to get along? Seriously, it's time.
- How the hell did Noah get all the animals to not kill each other on the Ark? I'm serious. Really, how!
- Why can't we eat anything we want and never gain weight?
- Why are there calories in food, anyway? We shouldn't have to count them.
- Who really shot Kennedy?
- Why didn't my father own stock in the electric company, instead of yelling at me to turn off the lights?
- Why do people hurt other people? Does it make them happy?
- Why can't money grow on trees? I mean it. Why?
- Why do they use 21-year-old models for anti-aging cream ads? We're not idiots! Get with it, advertisers, use older people so we

believe the damn cream works! Infuriating.

- Why do we get zits and our periods at the worst possible times?
- Why does *"shit"* happen? Moreover, why does it have to?
- Why do we girls have that one gnarly, wiry hair that grows on our chin? Really, don't we have enough to do and look for?
- Why, when we call to find out some serious medical test results, does the person on the other end of the phone always say… *"Hold please?"*
- Why do we always fall in love with the wrong person? **WHY!**
- Why do people hurt their children? It can't ever be tolerated.
- Why do the airlines only lose the luggage we pack our favorite clothes in?
- Why do we resort to war instead of working things out peacefully? I'll never grasp war. Killing the most people, wins?
- Did Marilyn really kill herself as reported? Or did the mafia, the CIA, the FBI, Russia, the Kennedys, Melvin Mickey Max from Minneapolis, Minnesota, or someone else kill her? A cover-up!
- Why do we have to age, become sick, weak, saggy, bald, toothless, and wrinkly when getting older? Isn't coping with aging and dying bad enough? Why can't we get better looking when we age? Like a reward?
- Who murdered Princess Diana? We *know* it wasn't an accident!
- Who really murdered Jeffrey Epstein? We know it wasn't suicide!
- Why do makeup companies stop making our favorite products?
- If God didn't love gay people & other minorities (as some fools believe) why did God, make so many of these great people?

Ultimately, in the end, after all the drama and crazy insanity, I have learned there's a damn good reason why so many of the available men out there are divorced or still single!

Then, in the blink of an eye, lying in bed, hours after the Melvin fiasco, **It Hit Me!** The realization made my mouth drop like a stone.

It was time to give up!!!!

I had endured and experienced enough disappointment for a lifetime. I gave it my best shot. And now, I was finally done with all of it. Overwhelmingly, I hit my limit, my out-and-out online dating rock bottom, and the grand finale of my extensive journey to find "The One" is over. My long, storied dating history had, at last, come to an end. The gravity of this situation has proved to be too much.

Though my ego hated to quit, I was ready to concede and admit failure. I had become hopeless and cynical. The time has come for me to justifiably, and understandably pack it in. All of it!

So, there you have it...
I QUIT!

And Just Like That, I Surrender! I Give Up!

"AND I GOT MALED," For the Very Last Time!

Don't Let That Fool You. Snap out of it! Don't you remember I told you to never quit, surrender, or give up? Where's the faith? Keep Reading!

CHAPTER 16

"Done Finished Over!"

I QUIT!

Done! As in Bruce Jenner transitioning and leaving his manhood behind. Like, ex-football hero, O. J. Simpson falling from grace. **Done!** The 2 rats, Bernie Madoff, and Jeffrey Epstein, sinfully dishonored. **Done!** The decline of the disgusting, disgraceful Harvey Weinstein. **Done!** The fall of Rudy Giuliani, R. Kelly, Amber Heard, and Bill Cosby. All **Done!** And, finally, I was **done**, now too! "My *Happily Ever After*" *dreams* were smashed into pieces.

I lined up all my dominoes in a long and winding row. I examined each domino, which represented an online guy. One by one, the domino men fell, knocked over, and bumped off. Suffice it to say, enough was enough. I couldn't continue the absurdity or dress up the narrative! Even with fancy shoes, diamonds, or tiaras.

Reviewing all my epic dating fiascos, the charades, enduring wacky, outrageous, humiliating dramas, and infinite *"Are you kidding me"* situations, it simply had to stop! And OMG, the stories!

How could I ever forget the scary, menacing Russian and his awful *shed-ding* lies? The 60s Cameron, Broken vagina Bam-Bam, Aubry without an E, Like a BOOM Fabrizio, Tango Wwhannn, and all the other players in my world of online men. The mean, dumb, short, ugly, and evil ones, but now, I must throw in the towel.

Yet, there were unimaginable blissful times spent with Bobble Drew, my treasured Rocket-Man, & the infinite love in my heart for my beloved Justin. But they were the rare & cherished exceptions.

The thought of swimming another lap in this pool of travesties was a hard NO! You'd think one would get used to all the disappointments & lunacy. Dating nowadays never ceases to shock or amaze me. And now it's time for everything to come to an end.

Throughout my life, I religiously believed in never being a quitter. In retrospect, for no lack of trying or perseverance, I couldn't slay the overpowering online dragon. It was time to walk off the field. For you men, I was hanging up my jersey and throwing my playbook into the trash. Damn, it's such a shame. There were some original, great plays in that book!

BTW, to the open-minded men who are still reading, wow, and good for you! Physically and mentally exhausted from playing the game, I tossed in my well-worn, beaten-up, pathetic dating uniform. It was drenched with suffering tears, dowsed in the dirt, saturated in pain, experiences deep in undisputable, batshit crazy situations, and flooded with too many "What the fuck" sentiments.

In all fairness, who could blame me? I know none of you who have made it up to this chapter would. Yet, I swear, I gave it the old, strategic bona fide college try. Courageously, I jumped into the shark-infested, dangerous waters, and plotted, calculated, planned, schemed, and went with the flow. I even (and dear Lord forgive me) lowered my standards beyond what I dreamed was imaginable for any woman. I stooped to the very bottom, and the deepest depths of the oceans, going out with the Jerry Springer and Maury Povich uncivilized guys. Not proud, and I'm shaking my head with humility because it happened! You know the guys, I mean. The, "*You don't know me. You don't know me,*" guys! And the, "*I never slept with that bitch, Jerry. I only slept with her mamma and her stepsisters.!*" And the, "I *ain't* the baby daddy, hell no, I '*ain't*' no daddy," guys! Oh, BTW, don't forget to ask for your Jerry beads.

To those guys I say, dude, get real. Man up like Darth Vader. Just tell your kid, "Luke, I am Darth, your father." Although you might consider using your own name, and your kid's name, with this approach. Just a little idea there for you.

Anyway, I was defeated, trounced, beaten to a "Pulp Fiction," and crushed emotionally. I was crushed, like grapes in a wine distillery or breasts in a mammogram. Crushed, like nuts in a nutcracker, without the lovely ballerinas and sugar plum fairy tutus. Crushed, like 10 teenagers squeezing into a Volkswagen Beetle. As for me, I couldn't bear one more comedy or dramedy.

I was through with online dating, or any other form of dating. There should be words to express, *"through-ier than through,"* and *"done-ier than done." (Again, sorry Professor.)* I needed to recover and salvage the remaining pieces of my shredded heart. I'm talking shredded, like when a politician, a president, or a company CEO frantically shreds incriminating papers, secret documents, and damaging evidence before leaving the Congress, the Senate, the White House, or a corporate company. Indeed, shredded like that!

Catching the spirit of the truth, I discovered I was a stranger to luck. Sadly, I learned many of these men contrived sandcastles of lies, using dry sand that crumbled, with its foundations falling apart, unable to sustain the fabrications of their deceit and deception. (Wow, that was a mouthful!) And through it all, I kept my sense of limerence, burning brightly for "*The One.*" Yet, in the end, finding "*The One*" was all but a make-believe, unrealistic fantasy. At last, it was time to face the painful truth and admit it was all but a wish on a wing and a prayer. Looking back at what seemed to be a never-ending 2 or so years (more towards the, 'or so'), I was finished with love. My heart was broken, wounded, closed for business, disenchanted, and impervious to the prospect and risk of starting another hopeful, "All shiny and new romance!"

I don't mean to sound bitter or bratty in any way. Nevertheless, if my Romeo wants me, his Juliet, well then, he better come and find me himself! I was indeed "through-ier and done-ier!" Facing reality head-on, unlike the idealist storybooks, my *White Knight* wasn't in the stars. Not even in the lucky ones.

Later that evening, coming to terms with my decision, I went through my monthly bills and credit card charges. I noticed one of the online dating sites, *(that rhymes with* Catch, Carmony, K-Mate, Flenty of Dish, Crumble, or whatever the hell that 'dot com' site is called) charged and renewed my membership for another year, without my approval or my knowledge. "Well! Why I Oughta!"

"Wow, we shall see about that, won't we?" I resentfully *murmured and flushed!* Yep, those ridiculous words used 2,000 times in "Fifty Shades of Grey!" Believe me, *my* murmured and flushed, weren't the least bit sexual. I was so enraged by the dating site's nerve and moxie to charge my credit card, that it kept me up the whole night. Their renewal trickery without my authorization was absurd, and I was going to put a stop to it. My wrath kept building throughout the night. Rage, like when people drive slowly in the fast lane, junk mail, robocalls, credit card fraud, slow Wi-Fi, or those dumb, *I am not a robot,* tests. I terminated all the dating sites I was on, but luckily only one took advantage, auto-renewing (or as I call it, stealing) my membership for another bloody year.

Still diamond-less and single, the audacity of this charge made matters more infuriating. Truthfully, I should bill, "them," for all the drama I had suffered from the awful, amoral men on their site.

I called first thing in the morning, at the crack of dawn. Or more accurately, in my world of "up-all-night journalism," at noon. I raised my fire-blazing rage with the poor girl who answered the phone on the *dot-com* site. I persisted with my furious grievance in such a belligerent, rude tone that she immediately connected me with a supervisor without my asking.

"No, Stop, Nooo," I screamed! *"No, Dammit! Bloody hell. No! Just credit my account! Stop, I don't want a damn supervisor,"* I shouted vehemently. Urrr! *"Shit, shit, shit! Just take me off the frickin' site."*

And then...

"GOOOOOOD Morning! I'm Edmond, a senior supervisor. I was informed of your great dissatisfaction and wondered how I could be of assistance?"

I detected a fabulously whimsical, gay voice on the other end of the phone, which shut me right down. How could I quarrel with his splendid, gaylicious *"Zip-A-Dee-Doo-Dah"* influence before coffee?

But I did! I was proud of myself for not backing down. I argued, keeping my obnoxious manner. "Hello, Edmond, I didn't ask for a manager. But how are you this fine, cold, angry, and life isn't fair, summer day? I bet you wish that you called in sick today, huh?"

He gracefully responded, giggling. "I'm fabulous. However, I did notice in your tone a slight unhappy sarcasm. So please, if you would be so kind to explain to me precisely what it is I can do for you to make you happy, Miss... hmm, I don't see your name here!"

Hells-bells he had me at Miss, instead of saying the dreaded Ma'am. He was so frickin' pleasant, I almost forgot I had an axe to grind. He effortlessly removed the bloody axe right out of my hand.

Over an hour later, with a homemade Starbucks cup of coffee, and a credit to my American Express Card, Edmond and I instantly became *Best Friends Forever.* Moreover, we discovered he lived not too far from me in, "Whoo Hoo, It's Vegas Baby!"

Go figure. Ironically, *in the end, I finally found a guy online. Even if he was gay!* I've always said... there's nothing more wonderful in life than adding a new gay best friend to your inner circle of friends. He easily transformed my "Why-I-oughta mood."

Edmond and I planned to meet later that week at Kahuna Grill, my favorite finger food, pig-out casual restaurant. Interesting, after spending time on the phone with the dating supervisor, I felt as though I had known him all my life. I couldn't wait to meet.

The moment I laid eyes on him, I knew it was Edmond. He looked as impeccable in person as he sounded on the phone. Edmond is a 29-year-old, magnificent, stunning, trendy-looking specimen of a man. He stands over 6 feet tall and sports an old-world stylish refinement, far beyond his years! He was refreshingly genuine, friendly, immeasurably candid, and easy-going. I'll never forget the first words Edmond said to me with his luminous smile. "Girl, you are so damn gorgeous I could slap you!"

To which I responded, amused. "Ditto, so I will slap you right back!" Our first words to each other and the laughter that proceeded instantaneously bonded our friendship forever. Smiling intuitively, we were both delighted. While thinking those very thoughts, the spectacular Edmond declared the ever-so-famous quote from the classic film Casablanca.

"Louis, I think this is the beginning of a beautiful friendship!"

I replied warmly, "It's crazy. I feel precisely the same way. And stop calling me Louis!" Our laughter was very familiar. I knew in my heart our friendship was meant to be and exquisitely, kismet.

A piquant-tasting flatbread pizza, two fried avocado egg rolls, several sushi selections, and many chicken tenders later, we got to know each other pretty well. We laughed uncontrollably till our sides ached, stuffing ourselves silly, enjoying way too many mouth-watering, unhealthy greasy carbs. Plus, an overabundance of strong Sangria. It became noticeable that our discourteous levels of noise and laughter did not please the rest of the customers, who were now staring at us rather harshly. I mean, like who cares? We certainly didn't. What were they going to do, call the 'Laughter Police' on us? I once again took the Shara approach and very quietly yelled out to the people, judging, and gawking at us. "I hope your medical and car insurance goes up! And audit you!" Eddie looked at me as if I had completely lost my mind.

"What in heaven's name was that? What did you just say?"

"Never mind. It's a long story. Remind me to tell you one day!" It was astonishing and unbelievably rare that I adored Edmond by the end of my first glass of Sangria. And I told him as much.

"OMG, I know! Me too! Honeybunch, I adore you entirely. Now, have another tender. He grinned, stuffing one into my mouth."

"Honeybunch? Really? Damn, I'd rather you call me Louis!" He giggled so hard that he choked out a piece of his chicken tender.

During lunch, we discussed music, movies, Broadway shows, hunky Hollywood men and their fabulous bodies. We certainly had men in common, and the same type too, which all looked like him.

"Eddie, I knew you were gorgeous just by your voice on the phone. You are hotter than a sizzling August day in Death Valley."

"Mollie, really, and I'm the gay one? I only wish I was that hot!" Jabbing back, "Oh please, Mr. Humble! And you so know it, too." He said gushing. "Oh, girl, stop. On second thought, carry on."

The annoyed patrons stared as we continued to chuckle away.

We spoke about important, deep, and meaningful things happening in the world today! Vital things such as this season's hottest divine Louis Vuitton bags, Prada shoes, Gucci's latest, and the newest billboard hits. Every second with Eddie was a joy.

Don't judge us! "It's better than discussing boring topics such as politics, war, Russia, Syria, QAnon Conspiracy, Pandemics, North Korea, Global Warming, ISIS, Iraq, or weapons of mass destruction. Fine! Yes, we also spoke about those trivial topics for about half a second. World events or breaking news aren't as entertaining as fashion and gossip. Come on, everyone knows that.

Edmond is a fashion god, with his own original, polished flair. When I praised him, he educated me. "One of my secrets is adding a piece of vintage. Such as a bright colorful vest, a quirky jacket, a 40s hat, or a whimsical shirt to any couture ensemble. It creates a distinctly inventive look. Remember, *never* chiffon or 100% cotton. It wrinkles too easily. Lose the chiffon outfit and keep the shoes!"

The way his eyes glistened excitedly while speaking of style and fashion made me beam with respect and admiration for him.

He raised his glass for another toast. "Beautiful Mollie, here's to

Broadway, fun, fashion, Hollywood, and single men everywhere!"

"Perfect. I'll totally drink to that! May they all look like you!"

Edmond clicked my glass, spilling a splash of wine. He added a tremendous giggle and a huge hand gesture to his comment.

"Hardy, Har, Har, and a Big Sha-rar!"

"Wait! What? Ed, would you mind terribly if I let that ditty go?"

"Yes, please unhear that, and could you do it, YesterGay."

"Stop a second," I asked with trepidation. "What does it even mean, and why would you ever have any reason to mean that?"

"Sweetie, I'll tell you when you tell me what 'I hope your medical and car insurance goes up. And what 'audit you' means!"

"Fair enough. Still, you seriously might need to hand over your gay card for that '*Hardy, Har, Har, and a Big Sha-rar*' humiliation."

In a fit of laughter, he was only able to counter with, "Sure honey, that's Hunky-Dory with me!"

"Hunky-Dory? OMG, Edmond, stop it, you're 29! Don't get me started!" Our bellies were full of giggles. Spending time with my new friend was hilariously entertaining and the best time I had enjoyed in over a year with a man. He was so easy and delightful to be with that the hours flew by. The supremely immense bonus part of the evening occurred when we said good night. I didn't have to fend off or come up with any excuses for why I wouldn't, couldn't, or shouldn't, sleep with him after only a first date. Being candid, gay or not, I totally would have! And I told him as much.

Over the next few weeks, Edmond and I grew to be such close friends. I was his new, "Sweetie-Dahling." That's "darling" with an added "H" and a silent "R." We were having such great fun, that we started an "Eddie & Me night." Every Tuesday, we met with his *gay entourage* at a sports bar for trivia night. I hope not to sound as though I'm typecasting. But as a rule, gay guys are classically amazing at trivia, amongst everything else they achieve to perfection. I was thrilled and honored to be a part of his *clique*. Tuesday nights, I gladly used my *"Get-Out-of-Meeting-Crazy-Men-Free"* card. Or more commonly called, "My night out with the boys, and thankfully escaping men's inappropriate advances," card. Tuesdays with Edmond were always an event, my happy place, and a guaranteed party. Trivia night was assuredly rich with amusement and copious amounts of free-flowing, pain-numbing drinks, paired with sinfully delectable, fattening nibbles and shareables. This quickly became my favorite night out these days, which I counted on and looked forward to.

I shared everything with Eddie. All my dating war stories, heartbreaks, and disappointments. He innately knew what to say, when to say it, when not to say it, and how to say the sweetest, most tender words of love and praise toward me. And basically, to everyone else who was around. I loved our mutual adoration club for two and the deep respect we felt toward one another. For now, he was the ideal man for me and warmed the cockles of my heart.

WOW, scary. I've never said that before. What the heck does it mean? And what in the world is a cockle? Is it a penis endearment? Having an inquiring mind (but never having read the "National

Enquirer") I was compelled to look up its origin. One theory is, that the cockles of my heart are derived from the Latin description for the heart's chambers, "cochleae cordis." The medical opinion is that the ventricles of the human heart resemble the concentric shells of small mollusks or snails. So, basically, it means to warm and gratify one's deepest feelings. Like the lovely saying, when someone or something gives you a *"warm and fuzzy feeling."* In other words, Eddie does all of that for me and more.

I was extremely grateful he came into my life when he did. I desperately needed the peace, hilarity, and joy he brought to my world. It was evident we both treasured our newfound gift of friendship. Although, I was quite surprised at the speed with which we became so close. He quickly plugged his thumb drive right into my heart. We understood and *got* one another without any words at all. The connection we shared was amazingly rare. Oddly enough, we owed the good fortune of meeting one another to online dating. Go figure! At least I found lasting love with one fantastical, perfect man, regardless of the many horrendous online dramas I had to endure. Essentially, meeting Edmond was entirely worth it all. Well? Well?? Umm, Well??? No, well! Of course, it was!

Whenever we got together, he forced me to tell him countless tales of my weird and disastrous dating stories. They never failed to amuse him, as he roared and fell to his knees with laughter. I couldn't begin to recall how many times he called me a liar. Good God, I only wish I were lying!

1. In summation: If you took, every great guy you had ever met.
2. Plus, all the warmhearted, worldly, classy, intelligent, and funny men you had ever come across.
3. And, also, every gorgeous-looking man you had ever seen,

including movie stars, the rich, and the famous. And then, threw them all into a paper bag and shook them up. Out would come Edmond.

He was the man of my dreams. Gay and all. With a passing thought, I wondered. Did this spectacular man want children? What? I can dream, can't I?

At last, in the best way possible, and as happy as one could be, I realized. "**Mollie, You Got Maled, Great!!!!!!!!!!!!**"

With that in mind, and as much as I could die and literally gag saying this in a whisper, and for sure, this will make you lean in…

"**Thank You, Online Dating!?!??**"
"Ick, gross. I think I just threw up in my mouth. Oh, My God, Ick!"

CHAPTER 17

Getting Ready for The Ball

NO GLASS SLIPPER...
SO STUART WEITZMAN WILL JUST HAVE TO DO!

Inevitably, after only four months of friendship, Edmond and I became inseparable. By this time, he had met my besties, and they all mutually fell in love with him. Though we quickly became very close, it still came as a surprise when he invited me to his parents' legendary gala. To be exact, a formal high society, prestigious annual Ball. I grasped by the excitement in his voice that this was a huge deal and a privileged invite. He flamboyantly explained.

"Mollie, this is an ostentatious, posh, unforgettable New Year's Eve gala with family, friends, and *A-list* celebrities. Just so you understand my dahling, this is lavishly more than an extravagant, outrageous celebration. Throughout the evening there will be excessive partying and a night of fun you'll never forget. It is the greatest soirée like none you have ever attended, and the number one, *primo eleganza* party of the year! More to the point, it is a totally authentic, *'Putting on the Ritz & Glitz' celebration to the 10th power!* Sweetie, I guarantee you the most *Faaaaaa-Bulous*, amazing, and 'the stuff dreams are made of,' night of your life."

Readers, note the word "*fabulous*" is spoken slowly, especially the

"*Faaaaaa*" part. It must be pronounced in a singing, high-pitched voice. Then, hold the "*Bulous*" for a few seconds. There, you got it.

He went on to clarify playfully. "You simply must attend, my angel. I will not accept any form of *NO*, as your answer. Honestly, though, if you did, it would indeed call for a complete mental health evaluation. And girl, I know you don't want any part of that. Besides, whatever would I do without my Bobbsey Twin? Honey-Hon, it will be the most memorable night ever, ever, ever."

He went on. "With that said, you have 2 months to get ready. And you will need every bit of it. That's why I'm inviting you now.

Here is my strong advice. Listen carefully. You cannot possibly dress fancy enough for this occasion! Helpful words? Wildly over-the-top, Met Gala worthy, excessive, concert costume decadent, extreme, beyond stunning, glittery, and Defcon-5, fashion crazy!

Dahling, hurry up and accept my spectacular, life-changing invitation. I asked you a whole 2 minutes ago, so say yes already! *Who knows Mollie, you might even have a **serendipitous experience!**"*

I pondered, "Who wouldn't want a serendipitous night never to forget?" And seeing as this year had brought far too many nights I anxiously wanted to forget, I accepted his sweet, exceedingly enthusiastic invitation. Still, I couldn't help my innate curiosity about what my dear friend had up his sleeve. Indeed, there was something up in there, for he was acting way too giddy and secretive. Come to think of it, he is always giddy and secretive.

"Ok love, I am excitedly down with it! I'm all in! I'm there."

"Awesomazing, of course, you are! After all, I trained you well." We giggled enthusiastically until he blurted out exasperated...

"Oh, Damn!"

"Oh, Damn what, Eddie?"

"Sweetie Dahling, I am great friends with *the leading* buyer for Stuart Weitzman and Manolo Blahnik shoes. He could get you whatever gorgeous, amazing heels your little heart desires for next to nothing. But…"

"No, no, no. NO! There are 'NO BUTS' imaginable here! There can never be a *But,* following the names, Weitzman or Blahnik!"

He continued with a disheartening sigh. "Unfortunately, I can't reach Liam. He's on a buying trip, traveling throughout Europe for the next 4 months."

"OK, now you're just being cruel. Like, crossing-the-line, cruel."

With a giant bear hug of comfort and compassion, he smiled.

"No worries, beautiful. I promise I will positively make it up to you! I swear."

"Impossible! I don't think that's at all likely, my friend! I am downright crestfallen! For real, what a way to crush a 'Shoe-Girl's' hopes and dreams. This could be the end of our friendship, you understand!" We were both amused and roared with *laughter.*

"Now remember dahling, when shopping for the Ball, here is your mantra." He continued in all his magnificent fashionista glory.

"It's Prada or Nada! Louis or Phooey! Dior or it's a Bore! And, Chanel, because you can tell!!!!"

"Gotcha, it's cool, for I'm no fool," I replied with a couture slam-dunk. "By the way, Mr. Sterling, I absolutely love you. Except, when it comes to shoes, you seriously have a lot of making-up to do!"

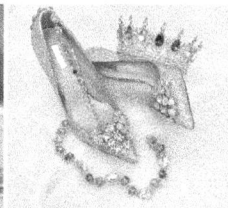

While December 31st was rapidly approaching, I felt much like Cinderella going to the Ball without anything new, or ritzy-glitzy enough to wear. I needed an extravagant, all-gussied-up, Oscar-worthy, Met Gala-glamorous, over-the-top, dazzling gown for the Ball. I felt anxious and worried since my fairy godmother was MIA, and I wasn't on speaking terms with her singing birds and mice to whip me up a Cinderella gown. To solve this overwhelming fashion situation, there was no other recourse but to gather my posse.

Four weeks later, a month before the Ball, the grand gala, I met my *"Sex and the Witty"* best friends. AKA, my "Fidus Achates Clique" for a New Year's Eve Outfit Shopping Spree. It was a major coup, clearing our schedules to find a day and time for all of us to get together to spree.

We met up at Starbucks, of course, on the designated morning for lemon loaves, pumpkin scones, and lattes. I also like their cranberry scones. BTW, Starbucks bigwigs, I miss your crumb cake that had an extra thick layer of crumbs on top. And the salted caramel squares with pecans you used to sell. Yum. I wonder why you stopped. "Big mistake, big, huge!" Bring um back.

At the chosen time we agreed to meet, I walked in ten minutes late, laughing, and affirming out loud, "Hail, hail, the gang's all here!" There we were, packed in like sardines at a corner table. We gathered to plan and strategize which stores to visit in search of uniquely extravagant, elaborate selections on our fancy shopping spree lists. We must have looked like a noisy herd of wolves. The people at the surrounding tables merely glanced and smiled. While others weren't fazed in the least, as they typed away on their Apple Laptops. Anonymity is one of the reasons I love Starbucks. Everyone does their own thing and happily minding their own darn business.

Watching my girls all together, I couldn't help but smile and reflect. Being with them was my purest form of joy and happiness. No matter what, at the end of the day, it is always our friends who help us through everything in life. They embrace the good times and the bad, laughter and tears, the shitty and the shittier times, and without a doubt, the normal, abnormal, and all the *WTF*, astonishing occasions. There they huddled, my loveable crew, Shara, Elizabeth, Debbie, Joyce, Corrine, Geri, and Melinda. My *inner circle of besties*. It was infinite joy, catching up and reminiscing with my "Schmoozerati!" When we are fortunate enough for all of us to get together, hilarity prevails, and stories fly.

My besties are a beautiful, perfect medley of every type of woman imaginable. These remarkable ladies are wise, successful, fun, loving, entertaining, intelligent, and each one astonishing. This begs the question. (And you know how much I hate begging.) "Why were we all single? How is it possible that eight terrific, attractive, unique, up-and-coming, prominent women are still single?"

My darling friends have saved and rescued me many times over. They have loved me back to health. My dear friends have held my hand, wiped my tears, laughed with me, laughed at me, poked fun at and mocked me, fed me, listened, pretended to listen, advised, encouraged, left me alone, and refused to leave me alone. They cried and suffered with me through these challenging years of dating and the unending epic disasters that occurred. Each one of my friends deserved an Olympic Gold Medal of Friendship.

Nevertheless, I found it interesting how they all shrewdly stayed back on shore, letting me go first to test out the online dating, danger-infested waters all by myself. No disasters or scratchy grains of sand stuck between their cleavage or butt cracks. They were evidently the smart ones.

As we all got up to leave Starbucks, I screamed out. "Wait! Wait! Don't forget to take a bunch of napkins."

They broke into laughter remembering the Julian story.

As always, we had the "bestest time ever" that day. Although we each went our separate ways, we reconvened intermittently to share, question, judge, and boast about our newfound treasures. Joyce never left my side all day. She emailed photos back and forth to *Shara, the maven,* for her criticism or approval, and to ensure I'd find the most perfect, glamorous outfit money could buy.

Elizabeth, in true fashion, kept texting outfits with oodles of bling she thought I would like. Debbie and Geri were mainly concerned about accessories. Corrine was obsessed with the shoes. Melinda was focused on hair and makeup products. Between them, I had all bases covered. I was blessed to have these cherished friends who always have my back. And front! With their endless affection and support, they knew, (as part of my *love recovery) I required* an "*Oh My God, spectacular, glitzy Cinderella gown for the Ball."* Their love protected me from any further wicked characters and prayed for my prince to magically appear.

After finalizing her purchases, Shara met up with Joyce and me. Proud as a peacock, parading and swaggering about, she held up her designer outfits. Shara flaunted her couture as if they were first prize trophies, singing in her little girly voice.

"OSCAR DE LA RENTA And ARMANI - DOLCE & GABBANA And DIOR—VALENTINO, VERSACE, GUCCI, & MORE! Shazam! Behold!"

Smiling ear to ear, "I Love You so, Shara!"

"Yeah, yeah, who gives a shit!" Our gang roared with laughter.

By the end of the day, we were successfully victorious. Each with a new fantabulous outfit, shoes, purse, make-up, and faux jewels to attend our separate New Year's Eve galas. We triumphed with fashion today. I was ecstatic about my Dolce & Gabbana little red dress and thrilled with my sparkling (Full-priced) Stuart Weitzman strappy rhinestone silver sandals and a glitzy Dior clutch that topped it all off. The whole ensemble was entirely decadent. I must admit. I would never have coughed up the preposterous amount of money for those shoes if it weren't for the insistent, mighty pushiness of Joyce. "You are buying them," she demanded! The girl blew like a raging tornado! "And that's that!"

"But Joyce, it's obscene how much they cost and totally against the *status quo of realistic* shoe shopping." Boy, did I ever ask for a designer shoe whooping lecture. She forcefully retorted back at me with the conviction, worthy of a 5-Star General, in the middle of an epic war, cracking her knuckles.

"First of all, (she pointed her finger sporting her blue gel manicure) who is frickin' being realistic? Second, I say defy and reject the status quo! Third, obscene is always a great thing! Lastly, I am telling you, *They Are Going to Bring You Luck!!!!I Feel It. I promise! You will soon see that!* Besides, just look at all the credit card, double air miles you will earn from this purchase alone."

Commanding and screaming, like a drill sergeant in a shopping spree, basic-training exercise, "Woman, zip it up, go to the cashier, pull out your American Express, let er rip, and march!" Then…

"Left! Left! Left! Right! Left," she roared, giggling."

Like a good private first-class, I saluted her firmly. "Sir, Yes Sir, General!" I do believe I was just chastised and stepped into a major black hole of shellacking! When Joyce and I first became friends, I learned that you never argue with *"The Joyce!" Still,* I can't rightly justify spending this eccentric amount of money for one night.

Maybe it was my reward for surviving this nightmare of a year? I couldn't help but think of what Justin and Rocket-Man might have said had they seen me dressed up in this new, unaffordable, designer princess getup. How I missed them both dearly. I often dreamt of being back where my heart belonged. With them. Painful, whew, sometimes love had sharp edges. Two great loves, two great losses, and two great examples of why I should have faith and hope in my future.

At the end of this wonderful day, all shopped out and ecstatic with our spending-spree selections, this little gang of mine and I went out to dinner for a triumphant outfit victory party. We drank far too many cocktails and then wined and dined rejoicing. Lastly, we all dolce & cappuccinoed merrily for hours. Although, for tonight only. We clearly understood, all too well, for the next few weeks we'd have to watch every single calorie and carb to fit perfectly into our new designer outfits.

I realized this fact more than the rest. For I had been food reckless, out of control, throwing calorie caution to the wind. I spent too many fattening nights with Edmond and his friends, having fun dining at all the gourmet hot spots. It makes me wonder. How come these guys could eat everything they wanted and never gain weight? Not a pound!

As for me, it was now time to face the "Shit, I gained weight, music!" I had to focus immediately my attention on returning my body to gala shape. I must exercise, diet, and work on my New Year's Eve, *belle-of-the-Ball,* flawlessly toned, star-worthy figure. My new little red dress was only one carb away from not zipping up. I was determined, excited, and writhed with enthusiasm.

Gosh. All this fancy gala talk almost feels like high school again, remembering I was the homecoming queen. I chuckled, imagining Edmond would seriously love to know all about that little fact. He would be so thrilled, proud, and amused.

As for the present... Pass the carrots and celery sticks, please!

CHAPTER 18

"Look at Me, I Can Fly!"

DREAMS REALLY DO COME TRUE...

It was 4:30 p.m. on December 31st, and I couldn't comprehend why I sensed such powerful feelings of astonishing exhilaration. I felt as though electricity was running wild through my veins. This extraordinary energy and excitement were pulsating within my entire body. Perhaps it was the anticipation and promise of Ed's statement that fed my fantasies…

"A FABULOUS, SERENDIPITOUS EXPERIENCE, AND NIGHT TO REMEMBER."

So as not to become overly nervous or stressed getting ready for the big night (wanting to look perfect), I left plenty of time to glamorize. I accomplished breaking my record for the "longest amount of time to gussy up!" In plain English, that means to dress 'really fancy.' It took me over 2 hours to prepare for the Ball. "The Ball?" How adorably cute and dated it all sounds. Nevertheless, that's what it was called. I was a little surprised that Edmond, the adorable prince of romance, didn't command 2 footmen and a horse-drawn pumpkin carriage to come fetch and transport me to the Grand Ball of the season. I was tickled pink by the mere thought of it.

Triumphant at 105 pounds, I easily slipped into my Dolce & Gabbana little red dress and my full retail-priced, good-luck, rhinestone, strappy, sparkling silver, Stuart Weitzman sandals. A monumental victory! Looking in the mirror, I was delighted with my reflection and loved my new shade of confidence. After three weeks on the HCG diet, I successfully lost those 8 ½ "crisis pounds" I had gained. Reaching my happy weight, the once snug, size-2, little red dress, was now flawlessly accentuating my waist, curves, and voluptuous breasts. I dare say, of course, I realize that statement sounds abundantly arrogant and super conceited. Whatever! I believe it to be deservedly justified. Healthy, even. It had been a long time since I felt this positive and euphoric. I was proud of myself for "I made it through the rain!" Yes, Barry Manilow, I did! But, perhaps, it was more like a hurricane. And I am now joyfully basking in my newfound inner peace.

At last, New Year's Eve had arrived. The gift of a new year was my invitation to erase and let go of the bad, the sad, and the endless disappointments that had occurred over the past year. Now, fortunately, a new year with dazzling prospects, jubilant optimistic hopes, and gleaming heights of opportunities were going to begin at the stroke of midnight. Bursting with excitement and elation, I cheerfully embraced my pure, childlike eagerness.

I stood regal, self-assured, and dressed way beyond the 'nines.' I do allege that on this night, I was every bit a princess in my spectacular, unaffordable couture ensemble. Plus, the bonus and the holy grail. This was the perfect, appropriate occasion to wear the befitting and essential, exquisite, faux-diamond tiara adorning the top of my head. Whilst my shoes weren't glass slippers, they were classically princess-esque, Stuart Weitzman. And that would have to do! There I was grinning proudly, all dressed up with professionally placed hair extensions and eyelashes, my nails, and toes beautifully manicured, and the brand new sparkling KIKO makeup from Milan, meticulously applied, thanks to Melinda.

I may not be royalty, but on this eve of a new year, I looked and felt as if I were. For the first time in months, I no longer suffered from any emotional sorrow. Eddie, my hero, made sure of it. With my sexy, jovial, poised attitude, I approached the driveway of Edmond's family home. And since I had never met his family before, I was thrilled. Standing in front of his parent's home, I gasped, seeing it was more like a compound or a mansion. Who knew, or would have ever suspected, that my darling Eddie, "The online dating supervisor," came from such enormous wealth?

As the clock struck 8:00 P.M. (it literally struck 8 times), Eddie grinned affectionately, greeting me in front of the magnificent, custom Stained-Glass, Tiffany doors. With 2 blue cocktails in hand, he announced with his gaylicious, exotic self...

"Sloan, I'm so delighted you are on time. Gorgeous, we can't waste a single celebratory minute. And Wow-Za! My GOD, you look dreamy! Just look at you, sweetie-dahling!" He lovingly twirled me about with his delicate yet masculine fingertips. "Now, aren't you just the most totally glorious, fetching, awesomazing, glamorous HRH in the entire universe! Goodness gracious, great balls of gussied up fabulous! You're a paragon of beauty and a breathtaking vision of loveliness and seduction. Not to mention, ultra-couture-ized, my exquisite, ravaging princess! I say, sweet Bella, you listened to me wisely and nailed the fashion perfectly."

"Aw, shucks, thank you. You're making me blush," I managed to snap back, coyly. "By the way, Eddie, did you mean ravishing?"

"No Dahling, I meant what I said. You are a dangerously *ravaging* beauty. Every straight man here will want to ravage and capture you in his tangled web of desire! Truly, you are the most pulchritudi-nous woman I have ever seen. My celestial princess, to be straight (pun intended) this is the first time I have ever felt total remorse and raw, painful regret that I'm a gay man! The first and only time, mind you, but I will never admit to saying it. I will simply have to dwell in my deeply conflicted gay sorrow. Now there's a serious oxymoron. *'Gay sorrow?'* Meanwhile, even though it has nothing to do with discounted shoes, I am now crestfallen!"

As usual, we both cracked up while I fell into his arms for an endearing embrace. "I adore you, my precious Edmond, but we both know all that fancy rhetoric was just a total crock of crapola!"

"Not so eloquently expressed being dressed so fancy, my luv."

"What? I was being couth. I could have said crock of shit!"

We burst into our typical synchronized, harmonious laughter.

"Sure, dahling. Regardless, you are radiant and pulchritudinous!"

"Wow-Za, yourself, my stunning Edmond. Aren't you just a puffy white marshmallow of pure divine perfection! And come on. Look who's talking! You gorgeous, dazzling man all dressed up like a runway prince! Good God, you are too spectacular for words."

"Oh, honey-girl, this old thing? I've had it for hours!"

"Hilarious, and don't be so humble. You are fiercely, elegant and chic. Mr. Armani, and Gucci, and Prada, My-My! Truthfully, all those designers would be greatly honored and privileged if they could see you wearing their latest creations. Let me tell you something. No one could ever look as dapper as you with such classy charm and ease. You're undeniably spectacular man-candy!"

"Now now there, princess, you're wickedly embarrassing me. But please do continue!" We laughed a bit too loud for the noise level of the room. He probed demurely, "But dahling, the big question remains. Am I pulchritudinous, too?"

"Indeed, you're ultimately pulchritudinous and ravaging!"

Snickering coyly, "I'm delighted. Lovely Mollie, seeing you look so regal, I believe you should always wear a tiara. I mean, always!"

"I Know! Right?!?! I should never take it off." Chuckling away, I continued with his very own embarrassing words. The words I had promised I would never bring up again. "Edmond, here's to us, to tiaras, and to a fabulous, *Hardy Har Har, and a Big Sha-rar!*"

He swung back hard. "Princess girl, really? Honestly, you're going there? Don't do it. Okay, fine then. In that case, I so hope your medical and car insurance goes up. And audit you!" We burst out laughing in our famous duo laugh and yelled out in unison.

"What does that even mean? Jinx!" My gosh, how he giggles

like only a sweet little girl or Anderson Cooper can do! I loved that about him, among a million other things.

The ever-so-suave Edmond had a stylish way of walking. It was as if he strolled and glided. I imagine it was more like a strut. Which is how he gracefully floated us across the gigantic, excessively plush, dreamy, yet warm and masculine stylish decor.

He formally introduced me proudly to everyone who crossed our path. There seemed to be over 1000 guests gliding about the palace. He made me feel like a genuine princess who came to the Ball, as the belle of the Ball. Translation, "Like a movie starlet on any given day."

Though I've been around the block more than a few times and exposed to mass riches, by no means was this my 1st *Rodeo-Ball*. Still, I was awestruck with everything I saw, and all the red-carpet-worthy *women in gowns* & men in tuxedos. *Being a girly, bling girl, I noticed they were all adorned with huge, genuine, priceless jewels.*

All the "Glamourotti" celebs and Hollywood superstars looked magnificently bedazzled and bejeweled to-the-max. Anyone who's anyone was present. Even though I had met and interviewed most of the invited celebrities, I was unusually captivated and virtually dizzy from all I was hearing and witnessing. Yet, I was extremely humbled and flattered by how many of the famous guests recognized or remembered me from having interviewed them. It felt surreal and lovely as they came up to greet me with their warm, respectful sentiments. "Hello. How have you been?"

I also recognized a few legendary guests, fortunate enough to exhibit and enjoy the "Hands of Justin's rejuvenation" upon their ageless faces. I smiled reassuringly, giving them no cause for concern about letting their secret plastic cat out of the bag.

I so desperately missed my love. You can bet they did too! Sigh.

My mind wandered briefly, appreciating at this moment just how grateful I was to Joyce. Thankfully, I obeyed her when she brutally talked me into this outrageously unaffordable, impressive couture ensemble. Good ole Joyce, she's always right, that one. I felt secure and confident, for my designer outfit put me right up there with the rest of the best, making me appreciate that I too, belonged. I was back! It felt whimsically fairytale-esque, dressed in this enchanting Kate Middleton opulent fashion. I became a real-life Cinderella, as she appeared at the *end* of the story, floating about Edmond's family Ball. As ho-hum and trite as all that sounds, it was true. So much so, I momentarily thought of leaving one of my Weitzman glittery slippers behind, as the clock struck twelve. (Literally, 12 gongs.) Then, I regained my senses, remembering they cost mega bucks. So that wasn't happening!

When my attention flashed back to the present, I looked around the room. It warmed my heart to observe how sincerely loved and adored Edmond was by everyone who knew him. Although I had only known him for the lesser part of six months, it was as if I had known him my whole life. For he, no doubt, was my soulmate-brother. And this is precisely and logically why I found it odd, why he never once divulged even a hint as to his astronomical wealth. Or anything else about his family, for that matter. I imagine it was his modest, private, non-braggadocious character, that caused him to keep his family and personal life secret and clandestine. For me, it wasn't Edmond's enormous family wealth, which, naturally, I found wildly impressive. It was his huge, generous heart, his pure kindness, goodness, and relentless humor that made me fall so deeply into friendship-love with him. Nonetheless, it didn't stop me for a second from scolding him!

"Edmond," I criticized. "Why have you not told me of your

fabulously rich & famous family and their extraordinary lifestyle?"

"I know, that's the billion-dollar question, Ms. Robin Leach. To be frank, I guess it's truly not all that important to me. My family's success isn't what we focus on. We strive to give back and be the best we can be! I suppose it's an embarrassment of riches, isn't it?"

"I'll say, Frank!" We giggled. "Still, my beloved BFF, for the life of me, I don't get it. Why, and I do mean *why*, are you working at an online dating site when you don't need to? Actually, for that matter, it appears you don't even need to work at all."

He didn't waste a second before joking. "Oh, sweetie dahling, do come on. Earth calling Mollie. Honey, you know how I totally adore the *'drama-drama-drama'* of it all. And don't call me Frank!"

Our contagious merriment filled the air. I grasped he was being entirely honest about his love for the absurd, romance drama. We simultaneously clicked our martini glasses, filled with icy cold cosmopolitans, dipped around the rim with blueberry sugar while formulating yet another New Year's toast.

"Do tell, Eddie my love. What are your New Year's resolutions?"

"Girl, puh-leeze. I don't believe in them. My princess, I never start anything I know for certain I won't finish. Even though we promise to begin or end something, those resolutions are only meant to make us feel better when we fail and continue our bad behaviors. All because we gave it a try. Essentially, it's what those silly resolutions are all about. Personally, I believe they're intended to be broken. Don't you agree, gorgeous?"

"Frank, you are a funny man. Fair enough and a valid point. OK, I won't make any resolutions either. Gee, that's a big relief!"

"And stop calling me Frank! Wait a sec, princess. We could create a bunch of them for the glorious fun of breaking them together. What do ya think? And who the heck is this Frank guy?"

I laughed so hard that I snorted. (Awkward, so unladylike!)

"I do so completely love you, Eddie. You're everything I'm looking for in a man. Come on. Marry me. Please, just marry me already!"

"Mwa-ha-ha-ha, and give up the fabulous gay business? Wait, Mollie, on second thought, yes! Yes, I will marry you, and this will be the very first resolution we shall break together on our almost wedding night.

"Stop, don't make me laugh! I'm holding a huge red martini. For goodness' sake, that could ruin a girl's Dolce & Gabbana dress!"

With sweet angelic delight, he countered. "Ouch, I am enormously sorry. *Nothing,* and I do mean *nothing* on earth, could be more tragic. Okay, Dolce, let's go. Andiamo! Andiamo!" Grasping my hand, he pulled me onward.

While dragging me gently across the enormous ballroom, with its hand-knotted, colorful antique Oriental carpet and exquisite marble floor, he bellowed in a bogus British accent, still clinging onto my hand.

"Sweetie Dahling, allow me to introduce you to *mumsy,* Anastasia, and my *faaatha,* William." For the sole purpose of annoying his dad, he spoke enthusiastically, with an extra bouncy, animated, colorful touch of gay splendor. "Mum and Dad, this is my lovely Mollie. Mollie Sloan."

Putting it mildly, I was caught off-guard and mentally unprepared for meeting them so abruptly. Still, I was delighted and comforted by how they wholeheartedly welcomed me with their friendly, delightful affection.

Anastasia expressed warmly, "Mollie, it is such a great joy to make your acquaintance. My dear, aren't you just so very lovely! Like an angel."

William responded. "Mollie, dear, we've heard so much about

you. Edmond illuminated what an extraordinary, intelligent, gorgeous woman you are. I can see now he understated that vastly. It's marvelous to meet you, finally. Your friendship means the world to our Edmond, you know."

I was pleased and flattered Eddie had told them so much about me. "Mr. Sterling, I feel the same way about Edmond, sir. And I want to thank you both greatly for inviting me to your incredible Ball. It is such an honor and a privilege!"

Anastasia beamed, "Sweet Mollie, don't be silly. No need to thank us. It's our pleasure. In fact, we are thrilled and tickled you could attend. I hope this won't embarrass you, but we enjoy watching you on TV all the time. You are such a brilliant reporter."

"Awfully kind and thoughtful of you to say, Mrs. Sterling."

"Please, call me Ana. No need to be so formal. Besides, it's New Year's Eve. It's a night to celebrate, to be free, merry, and joyous."

Eddie chimed in with a wink. "Yes, tonight we must all be *Gay!*" William grunted disapprovingly, while Ana simply chuckled.

Attempting to change that still delicate subject for William…

"Your home is remarkable, Ana. With its warm, stylish panache and décor, everything is elegant and stunningly chic. Artistically, you also managed to keep it feeling enormously comfy."

William responded with great humility and moral decency, which is his character. "Thank you, and yes, we are very grateful, indeed. Moreover, I believe I speak for our entire family when I say how important it is for us to help, give back, and do kind things for others less fortunate. Wealth is wonderful. But it's imperative to understand that 'Health is Wealth.' We hope to spread this type of wealth around, to promote health and well-being. Mollie, dear, I hope not to sound too exceedingly preachy, but to quote Franklin D. Roosevelt, who so eloquently stated." He paused and continued.

"The test of our progress is not whether we add more to the abundance of those who have much. It is whether we provide enough for those who have too little."

At that philanthropic moment, I was never more grateful, in my entire life that Shara, (my incredible, sometimes unfiltered, best friend) was not standing there, about to respond with one of her brutal, off-color, but hysterical (to most) remarks. For instance...

"Seriously, are you fucking kidding me? Keeping with your quote, you're aware that Roosevelt apparently got too little himself at home. Ergo, he got it on too much in the White House, right? Mr. Sterling, is that what you meant? Oh, and let me tell you all about Bill and Monica. Talk about an altruistic, patriotic, American gal!"

Edmonds *faaatha*, went on. "It's one of my favorite quotes. Forgive me, I believe that certainly was exceedingly preachy. Regardless, Molly, your praise is deeply appreciated."

Seeing my *"seriously, for real"* dazed look still on my face, Ana came to our rescue. "Eddie, Mollie, stop wasting the last night of the year with us boring folk. Run off you two. Go on and have fun."

Eddie smiled affectionately at his mumsy. "What are you talking about? We love hanging out with you. You guys are the coolest people here, by far!" As he continued, I drifted away.

Reflecting introspectively, meeting these astonishing people was a true privilege. Anastasia and William were the portrayals of grace, goodness, and humanitarianism. I felt as though I were meeting the Queen and King of England. Only they were far more dazzling looking, sincere, intelligent, unpretentious, and had earned their position, rather than inherit it. Profoundly awestruck, I didn't know if I should salute them, bow down, or curtsy. Realizing if I had, I would've fallen right down onto the Calacatta Marble palace floor, wearing such a tight hugging dress and tall high heels. The

Royal Family (The House of Windsor) had nothing over Edmond's majestic Royal American family. These divine, incredibly gorgeous people portrayed a modern prototype through their elegant refinement. I was further impressed, for they were modest, humble, down-to-earth, and I dare say… godlike.

Funny, I said those exact words describing my Romeo. Wherever the *Hell the bastard is!* Chillax, that was my inside voice.

Edmond and I didn't run off just yet. Listening to the three of them excited and enthusiastic about supporting some new foundation for the homeless, I was overwhelmed and self-effacing. Taken aback by their generous humanity, I wondered. Do people genuinely behave this benevolently and graciously? In my experience, it's typically a person who wants something that displays this type of charitable behavior. Like a politician!!!!

In a flash, Eddie beamed, saying to his parents, "Later!" I could hardly respond quickly enough before Eddie whisked me away.

I respectfully called back. "Wonderful to meet you both! We'll see you later. Have a happy, joyous, and healthy, New Year!"

Exquisite Ana replied, flaunting her dynamic, contagious smile. "Lovely wishes, dear. The same to you and more, beautiful Mollie!"

Edmond escorted me to where everyone was dancing. He swiftly cuddled me up into his arms like a big, huggable teddy bear for a dance. The DJ was playing the Michael Bublé version of the song, "Wonderful Tonight." As he held me snugly in his muscular arms (a result of endless hours in the gym), I looked up at his gorgeous, chiseled face and moaned miserably…

"Seriously, why? Why do you have to be gay, Eddie? Are you entirely certain you're gay? You could be wrong, you know! You could be mistaken. Isn't it possible you might have jumped to the wrong conclusion?"

He laughed. "Geesh. Scary! Now you sound like my *faaatha!*"

I grinned. "You very well know I don't mean it that way. It's just that we do love each other. Correct? We are MFEO, and so perfect together. So why do you have to be gay? *Is there any possibility you could be straight?* Curses, and off with your head!"

With perfect timing, he replied. "Ouch, which head? And dahling, not only am I not straight, girl, I can't even *think Straight!*"

I chuckled, with an embarrassing smirk, and reiterated. "You, see, that is exactly why I adore you so! Come on. Do it. Marry Me!"

With a crooked grin, "My dahling, you can't have it all, right? You surely must know, princess, if I were straight, you'd be my forever love! But you are my love, anyway. Huh, come to think of it, you'd be my very first sexual experience with a girl."

"How cool is that," I spoke disappointed with a straight sexual preference sigh. "You'd probably hate it anyway." I giggled. "My beloved precious Eddie, you know that I love you completely!"

With a devilish look on his impeccable face, he gushed. "Do go on, my lady, and feel free to embellish."

Suddenly, Eddie looked shocked by what he just noticed. "My God, Mollie, would you just look at the poor girl over there? She looks like she fell on a Target sale rack and said, I'll take it! And beauty insider Sephora, what's with the Marilyn Manson makeup?"

"You are so bad." We chuckled too boisterously, judging by the looks of the beautiful guests near us. Edmond noticed, then pranced us away ceremoniously towards another outlandish, much-needed, colorful drink.

"Must keep up, exquisite girl. Crown it," he demanded playfully. The guy could talk me into anything. Which is, by itself, uniquely rare. He led, and I gladly followed. So unusual for me, yet I was happily willing.

Just as I had hoped to sneak away to add a touch of lipstick, blush, a spritz of perfume, and check myself out in the impressive, 24-karat gold leaf-adorned powder room, I heard Edmond yell out.

"Stop everything!" He impishly put his arms around my waist.

"Sweetie, I'd like to introduce you to my remarkable sister, Sophie, and my incredible baby sister, Juliana. Ladies, this is Mollie."

I gasped, silently. Oh, come on! These young women were drop-dead beautiful and entirely "Vogue Magazine Fashion Model" candidates! Even before all the standard airbrushing. His family was unreasonably exquisite. Their images should be the photo inside a picture frame when you first buy it.

The gorgeous siblings replied in unison. "Charmed, I'm sure!"

In my inside voice, with a tilted head, I imitated them. *"Charmed, I'm sure? Stop it! Are they kidding me? Get outta town."* Their high-society words transported me right into a sappy 40s film. I never imagined people spoke that way in real life.

It appeared I could've used Shara's help, after all. These are the times I missed my *Nigel. Nige, I need you!* Honestly, how can one possibly respond (nowadays) to the "Charmed, I'm sure" greeting?

"It's a pleasure to charm you? Are you sure you are charmed? Bitchin? Cool? Ditto? Charmed back atcha? Are those implants?" Those were a few of the politically incorrect, inappropriate responses that immediately came to mind. Luckily, his spectacular sisters gave me no time to respond with a classic, idiotic blunder.

Sophie expressed, sweetly. "A lovely welcome, Mollie, Ed's best friend forever. And a very splendid Happy New Year to you." Before I had a chance to answer, Juliana immediately chimed in.

"It really is great to meet you. You do realize our Ed loves you like crazy! Just so you know, he never stops talking about you."

Struggling for something to say (which never happens as a journalist). I replied with, "Awe, thank you. It's fantastic meeting you both. I've heard so much about you. I also absolutely feel the same way about Eddie. And the happiest ever, New Year to you!"

Awesome! I felt that my response was simple and emphatically well done, putting me in the safe zone. *Phew! Covfefe and Bigly.*

Sophie smiled at me with her impossibly spectacular smile. "Mollie, you look magnificent. I adore everything you're wearing. I'm totally jealous. And naturally, Ed, you look fabulous as always!"

"Jealous? Hardly! You and Juliana look radically breathtaking."

Eddie quipped, "Thanks honey-bunnies. Breaking News Flash, (He winked at me), all three of you ladies are gorge. And Mollie, don't cha just love all the jewels, glitter, and sparkle in the room?"

"How could I not? I'm having so much fun, it feels like the front row at fashion week. This Ball is a couture fashion and bling fest."

It was hard not to notice Edmond's sisters are an annoying, rare breed of perfection. Not only were they spectacularly dope and magnificent looking, but they were also brilliant and highly educated scholars. Luminous Sophie was getting her doctorate at Yale in science. The radiant Juliana was studying to be a gynecologist at Princeton. Sure, of course, they were!

I hope no one noticed the green smirk, visibly portraying my momentary mean-girl, meow, catty emotions. Eeks, that was radically a non-Zen expression of emotion. Not like me at all, I thought, giggling to myself. I'm only kidding. The sisters are great! Although, I get it. My body, mind, and soul must be completely out of alignment. I must search for a Buddhist chiropractor and stat!

Anyway, Edmond's remarkable sisters were brilliant, rich, fun, and kind. Not to mention, these perfect girls were unbelievably *nice*, on top of everything else. If you can believe that.

Relieved to be interrupted by my inner bratty, childish sarcasm. Juliana enthusiastically asked me the inevitable question.

"So, Mollie, where did you go to college? Tell us about your alma mater. The school must be proud of your success and fame."

Doomed. Suddenly I was humiliated and disgraced, having to say I had graduated from the now-appearing inferior and ordinary UCLA. I can imagine Joe Bruin, our beloved mascot, frowning at my uncalled-for, unwarranted humiliation. Yet, I didn't want to let Joe down, because UCLA is a great university. I'll thank you very much. I decided to speak out loud and proud. I took a deep breath and confidently responded in a higher-than-normal, peppy, Rah-Rah-Rah, College Cheerleader Voice.

"I attended, *1 2 3 4 5 6 7 8, UCLA, fight, fight, fight!!!!!*"

The uncomfortable expression on Edmond's face said it all. Whatever! I continued. "It was a great educational experience and a wonderfully memorable collegiate environment!" I did all but yell out, "Go Bruins, Go!" Even with a few blunders, I imagined I was doing well. Confidently, I thought, until Sophie questioned me about what sorority I was in.

Crash, bang, boom, thump, sinking ship, wipe out, and checkmate! Who did they think I was, Elle Woods, in "Legally Blonde?" Oh, my God, I suddenly felt like a scandalous, super Ivy-less, undesirable, inferior, scholastically bankrupt, collegiate criminal. I feared

I was trapped in a college catch-22, and in for major sorority hazing. Defensively, I clung to reverse snobbery.

"Honestly, I wasn't a sorority kind of girl back in those days!?!"

And game over! I believe I would've been far better off making up a big lie, judging by the frightfully lost expressions on their magnificently spectacular faces screaming, What? Wa-ha-what?

It was quite evident they couldn't comprehend, in the least, my lack of sorority appreciation and membership. Their faces turning white, and their discussion going speechless, verified that for me.

Regardless, I liked them both so much. Despite all their "Gama, Delta, Gamma, Phi, Alpha, Kappa, Delta Sigma Theta, Welta, Kelta, Shmelta, Chelta," or any other Greek letters, sorority type lingo, or philosophies they so cherished. In addition, I could only assume they were unquestionably the presidents of their sororities. Still, I didn't have the heart, nerve, or gumption to ask. I was just happy the shame of it all was over. But, no, they couldn't seem to let it go.

"Wait," Sophie asked, as if I were deprived or cheated. "Mollie, you missed out on so much fun! Are you telling us that you never were a pledge, never had a big, a little, proms, social weekends, slutty-heels kind of nights, frat parties, I'm never drinking again experiences, being fined, recruitment, the rush, the bid day, sisters, or the infamous secret initiation ritual ceremony?"

"No? Not really?" I thought they'd explode at the notion of my not being in a sorority. I confess I was laughing wildly within. What non-sorority girl wouldn't? I was relieved to be supported by the inconspicuous nudges and swallowed laughter from Eddie. He bent down, having my back as always, and whispered in my ear.

"Princess, the university Greek-life, and all its rituals are pretentiously rubbish." Hidden under our breath, we silently groaned so as not to offend the girls. "Moreover, there are no words to tell you,

Mollie, how much I despise it when they call me *Ed!*" Thankfully, he felt my uneasiness and swiftly expressed an animated, "Ta-Ta sistas. See you in a tick-tock on the clock!"

In unison, the lovely sorority queens replied, "Love you, Ed! See you later, Mollie. It was tremendous finally meeting you!"

Still sensing their pity, "Yes, same here, and Happy New Year!"

Dashing away, Edmond turned to me, laughing hysterically. "Mollie, I really thought you were going to bitch slap them, silly!"

"Golly, Ed. I'd never do such a thing. Well, in public, anyway."

Teasing playfully, "Don't *Ed* me. You, Judas, sorority trader!"

"Hilarious! All joking aside, *Ed,* your sisters are remarkable!"

"They are. But call me *Ed* again and I'll *take you right back to them.*" Our laughter was so rampant, I thought my dress split open.

My hero sprinted me off towards another elaborate cocktail. With fresh drinks in hand, we headed to his gaylicious pals for a reality check and a safe respite. I don't know if it was all the alcohol or the bombshell surprise of Edmond's regal world that kept me floating on air. So be it. For I was having the promised time of my life. A new beginning and a clean slate, with expectations of hope and promise, were on the immediate horizon.

After 20 minutes, Eddie leaned in and murmured. "Sweetie, I'll be back in a few. Don't worry, you are safe here with my group!"

"Sure, no worries. I was going to the powder room, anyway."

A short while later, nearing 11:30, I returned to his friends. It was fun chatting with the guys, but I was worried about Eddie and wondered where he was. My concern was interrupted, as the DJ played my absolute favorite song, "I knew I loved you before I met you," by Savage Garden.

At that very instant, as the ballad I love so much began to play, Edmond ecstatically and breathlessly returned to the ballroom. I couldn't help but notice he walked in, arm in arm, holding onto another exquisite man's hand. He obviously had a huge, man-crush bromance going on there. They were unmistakably bursting with elation, clearly displayed on their faces. I naturally assumed, by their glowing smiles, that this stunning secret man and "knight in shining Armani," was Edmond's new "Love-AAAhhh!"

In a matter of seconds, I was going to be overjoyed, eagerly delighted, and charmed, I'm sure, to make his new Love-Ahhh's, acquaintance. Yes, this would be the perfect time to use both these phrases for the first time in my life. Ever!

Although excited, I confess, I was a little more than hurt and miffed by him. You see, I assumed Eddie and I were besties. And yet, he never once talked about his new, breathtakingly gorgeous "Love-Ahh." I wondered why since we shared a mutual trust. It must be serious, I imagined, if Eddie kept him so hidden away and private, even from me. I was disappointed and upset, for I didn't think we had any secrets from each other. Alas, live and learn.

Interrupting my miffed, chagrinned thoughts of feeling left out, Edmond vivaciously made yet another introduction this evening.

"Sweetie-Dahling, this is..." (A very, very long pause ensued!) His pause seemed forever. I waited baffled, thinking yes, who is it?

"Mollie, this is my beloved, older brother...
Madison Daniel Sterling!"

And with that, the music grew louder, and the lyrics sang out…

"I knew I loved you before I met you,
I think I dreamed you into life,
I knew I loved you before I met you,
I have been waiting all my life…"

I knew without a single doubt or reservation,

I had finally met him... *"The One." "The One!"*

Completely confident, blissful, and safe, I cracked open my chest, and all the feelings in my entire soul poured out...

Just like in a timeless, sentimental, old-fashioned, Hollywood picture, the moment our eyes met, I felt my heart stop beating.

Edit: My heart grew stronger and developed an extra heartbeat!

Time stood still. No! That's not at all correct.

Amendment: *Time sped backward and forwards simultaneously!*

My knees went numb. And yet, *I stood strong!*

My eyes closed demurely with childlike innocence. Yet widened with the conviction & sophistication of a self-assured, proud woman!

I grew weak and vulnerable. Yet, at the same time I grew secure, confident, powerful, and protected!

I felt faint. However, it was quickly overshadowed *by a powerful strength, which sent me soaring bravely up to the heavens!*

I sensed caution and restraint. Nevertheless, *it was overpowered with a bold and daring reassurance!*

I felt deliciously sinful and wicked. However, *it was paired with angelic purity and a chaste spirit.*

Understandably, my mind was spinning out of control, with an abundance of data being fed far too rapidly into my mind's USB port. I was

sensing brain and heart overload with so much to assimilate, compre-
hend, digest, grasp, take in, and understand all at once.

With every nanosecond that passed, I was inundated with an inor-
dinate desire for this winsome stranger. He was seducing me with
his heart. I girlishly hoped to disguise the mesmeric effect he effortlessly shined upon me. I don't believe I managed to conceal any of
my amorous emotions and insatiable passion for him.

With my heart exposed, the gracious, urbane Sir Madison
stepped forward and gently took my hand with all the masterful
suavity he knew so well. Gazing into my eyes, he formally said the
very first words I ever heard him say to me. His gentle voice, laced
with velvety tones, crooned as he smiled at me warmly.

"Mollie, it is such a delight to meet you!" His touch was mysti-
fying and beguiling. Yet oddly familiar.

Breathless, I muttered my silly first words to him. Embarrassed,
nevertheless confident, for I knew it was *him!*

"Are You, The One?"

He responded to my ridiculous question. *"Am I, The One, what?*
But I hope so! I think so! Yes. Yes, I trust I understand what you
mean. To answer your question, I do believe I Am, The One! And
I trust, you are also, The One!"

Madison rescued me from looking like a silly little fool.

With that, Sir Edmond smiled and felt comfortable enough to
leave us alone. He walked away with a lively jaunt in his step and a
sprightly effervescent personal satisfaction. Shining like the sun on
his perfect face was a grin, boasting a gleeful, vivacious, zealous,

"I did it" expression.

Surprisingly, Madison noticeably appeared spellbound and
intrigued by me. I was greatly comforted, for I felt the same way.

From that moment, that very second, we froze, captured in time. It was as though our hearts merged, then mysteriously condensed into a *"love-encasing, that was marked forever."* We appeared to have been mystifyingly pierced with Cupid's intoxicating arrows of love and now encapsulated eternally. Ridiculous? Obviously! Even so, believe me, I distinctly knew the difference after everything and everyone I had gone through. (Remember, this is a true story.)

There was an indescribable magnetic pull between us from the instant our eyes met. Feeling drunk with affection and romantic emotions, I fell instantaneously in love with his very presence. As stereotypical as a Bruno Mars mixtape, ours was a magnetic pull more forceful than the former star SGR 0418+5729. The biggest magnetic field ever documented. You can't fight science, people!

It was unmistakable that my world would never be the same. I wished upon a star among the billions of stars in the galaxy, and I caught my star as it fell from the sky. Indeed, a very lucky one! (You were right, Mr. Walt Disney!) I knew I found him. "The One." It was surreal, for I could see and feel the warmth of imaginary gold sprinkles raining down from heaven.

Madison, in every way, from his looks and intelligence to his heart, compassion, and humor, was the *'straight'* version of Edmond. Talk about global warming? These two men were so hot, they could heat up and melt the entire universe. And my heart.

Defenseless, I fell completely under his spell. It was uncanny how I explicitly understood I belonged to him, and him to me. Feeling 100% whole in his presence, my search had ended.

As romantical and gushy-sentimental as a Nicholas Sparks film, I knew this was my man. I recognized his heart. For Madison's heart, I had known and had been with before. I felt angelic stomach butterflies dancing within me from his presence. My soul remembered him at once. He was, is, and will always be, *"The One!"*

I jumped into his beautiful eyes, which transported me directly into the innermost depths of his being. The essence of *"us"* was *one soul*, infused with extraordinary spiritual certainty, and divine transcendent harmony. We were inevitable. We were meant to be. We were destined. He is my other half, and I was finally *home!* Home, where I'd forever be loved, cherished, and safe from love's pain, evermore. I had waited and searched for Madison my entire life. But *'HE found ME,'* at last, and I was no longer afraid.

I was grateful to have gotten to this stage in my life where I had learned the ultimate lesson. "I must stand on my own two feet *first before anyone could stand by my side." This knowledge* created the porthole opening, making it possible for Madison to find me.

Whether by chance, fate, or destiny, it was the miracle of meeting Eddie that brought into my world the love of my life. He surreptitiously presented me to the man who would join my heart, my existence, my life, and fulfill our future happiness evermore. Everything I had done and experienced in my life, prepared, and led me to Madison, on this blissful night of New Year's Eve.

I am enormously grateful to the astonishing men I loved before him. Yes, I loved Justin, I loved Rocket-Man, and I loved Drew. We have many loves in our lives, and all of them have purpose and meaning. There are no accidents. Only, they were not my "*forever.*" Each of them lovingly molded, guided, shaped, and primed me for Madison. Each, in their own fashion, helped me to grow, to love, to acknowledge, and to recognize my destiny, when he would arrive.

How profound and ironic my Romeo turned out to be Madison, the brother of my BFF Edmond, "*The Online Dating Supervisor!*"

Returning from my private dreamy thoughts, I stood before Madison, mystified like a wondrous incantation had been placed upon me. A tear came rolling down my cheek. I must have been shaking from ecstasy because Madison threw his jacket over my exposed shoulders and gently wiped a teardrop from my cheek. He looked adoringly at me and asked. "Why the tears, beautiful?" There wasn't enough time, words, or Kleenex to explain.

Knowing him only but a few moments (love at first sight), Madison turned towards me, as if he were reading my mind.

"Angel, as long as I live, I never want to see another tear falling down your gorgeous face again!"

When I looked up, I saw Ed with his halo beaming and glowing. Across the ballroom, his self-satisfaction proudly boasted a loving, all-knowing smile barely contained on his face. With a euphoric smile, I mouthed to my dear best friend. "Thank you. Thank you!"

Eddie, unbeknownst to me, shrewdly planned and delivered me like a stork delivering a baby, right into Madison's awaiting, loving, open arms. Unbeknownst to us, his prearranged, romantic strategy was impeccable. Edmond, in his irresistible, glorified, fabulous self, pranced up to us and whispered into my ear.

"*You* see, my love, I am, *after all*, your **real-life**, '*Fairy*' **Godmother!** *A true, serendipitous evening to remember! Wouldn't you say, Princess????*"

Watching him gloat, I smiled, for there couldn't be a statement more accurate. Edmond literally, *"God-mothered"* me! He secretly plotted, making all this happen. Even without a magic wand, he brought me the fairytale. And suddenly, as the three of us were standing together, the palace clock struck 12:00.

And then it happened. At the precise stroke of midnight, of a brand-new year, *'Our very first kiss!'* Our embrace was magnified, lasting the entire 12 loud gongs of the clock. It was heavenly how our energy danced in the air.

Eddie was ecstatic, knowing true love had just been born. He leaned in, kissed and hugged Madison and me, then magically, without a puff of smoke, disappeared, vanishing into the crowd.

And just like that, Madison and I were inseparable for the rest of the Ball. We spoke very little, as words seemed too trivial. I am powerless to describe the phenomenon which transpired between us on that evening. What we experienced was textbook chemistry and light-years more than infatuation. I had never known such intense blissful feelings and loving emotions as I immediately felt for this man. I knew with all my heart that I wanted to spend the rest of my life feeling all of them and being with him, side by side.

Madison had that certain something, rather indefinable. It seemed mysterious, yet natural and easy the way he overpowered me. We danced the night away, mostly for the perfect excuse to be close to each other. We never stopped holding hands. It was as though we were afraid of letting go, for fear the other would somehow fade away. Madison and I, at long last, found each other. Justifiably, there was no way imaginable we'd ever let go now. It was dreamlike, sensing such overwhelming, electrifying emotions which now raced through me, merely by touching someone.

Meeting Madison at the Gala was truly unexpected. It was so out of the blue that I was certain I must've been dreaming. Now, fully convinced it was all but a silly fantasy. Soon I would wake up having only imagined this extraordinary joy. I feared it was purely an illusion, and sadly I'd be back online searching for love again. I had to pinch myself to ensure he was real, and to prove I was not a silly victim of my imagination. However, this story was happening.

And for the first time, I knew undeniably, I had found my true love.

At that very instant, I felt my beloved Justin smiling down at me with his immeasurable love. He was confirming and declaring on this night, miraculously, two had become one. I felt him reassuring and comforting me that I was safe now. Asking me to trust and realize with Madison, I will be loved now and evermore. Be happy, my angel.

Unlike before, no flags were flapping. No red flags or any other color. And you can be sure, I looked for them. There were no dark clouds of fate hovering above. No doubts, fears, or uncertainties. No Bobble Drew mysteries, KGB scary sheds in the backyard, no concerts to perform, and no crazy. Only Madison, myself, and love.

Like in any enchanting fairytale, I was the princess who had just met her Prince Charming. And as promised by *"The Joyce,"* my rhinestone, strappy, sparkling silver, *full retail,* Stuart Weitzman, high-heeled sandals, indeed brought me the luck of my dreams!

By the warm stares from everyone in attendance, especially Edmond, William, Anastasia, Sophie, and Juliana, it was unmistakably visible, love's magic was in motion. It was evident by all, in the wee hours of a New Year, *"Love at first sight"* truly exists. Gee, I even felt Shara's cynical, but loving wishes for my happiness.

Signs were flashing all night, but entirely different from the negative signs I had known in the past. For these signs were all marvelous and comforting. Madison and I were aware and sensed deep in our souls, without any words, that together we had found the apex of love and the zenith of life's genuine, eternal fulfillment.

Around 3:30 a.m. the glitzeratti, savoir-faire invitees began to leave the Ball, one by one. Anastasia and William presented (as a parting gift) to each of their guests, an impressive set of posh, expensive Baccarat Crystal Wine Glasses, with this year's date, elegantly engraved on them. This miraculous bewitching New Year's Eve, I also received the extraordinary glasses of love and celebration. It was more than *Baccarat Crystal clear* I was given something far more precious. On this grand evening, I received my forever love, and his heart was instantly engraved into mine.

It's astonishing how life can drudge on monotonously, or it can quickly and remarkably change to spectacular in an instant. Irrational as it sounds, when Madison and I first touched, we realized we were stricken by the power of love.

It was as swift and strong as an electric current. Still, it wasn't all that strange when I paused to think. For the reality is, every day of my life, I had been secretly falling in love with Madison. Surprised and overjoyed, on the first day of a brand-new year, the divine union of our hearts came to be, and our love was born!

Before I left the Ball, on that wondrous serendipitous evening (And *not* leaving my storybook, crystal, lucky Cinderella slippers behind) Madison confessed to me, singing…

"My love, *I knew I loved you before I met you!*"

He was singing to me, all my dreams! (As predicted.) And I sang back with a smile in my voice, *"I think I dreamed you into my life!"*

On the spot, just like in the movie Twilight, *"We imprinted!"*

By the way, even though this is a book, I can hear your powerful, endearing, warm, and fuzzy Ahhhhhh's, right through the pages. And I thank you! You understand. You get it!

As for the rest of you, pessimistic, not-so-much romantic, gag-me-with-anything-you-have-handy, types. I, of course, fathom all this syrupy, mush, and gush, is making you sick, and you are screeching for the toilet. I get it. And you know who you are!

To you nonbelievers and skeptics, I say a simple… Whatever!

And Yeah… That Means You Too, SHARA!!!!

CHAPTER 19

About Madison

As you have probably assessed by now, Madison and I are hopelessly and passionately in love. My happiness, good fortune, and fate proved to be way beyond my hopes and dreams. I thank my very lucky stars every day! Incidentally, it really was true. Like the song says, *"I dreamed him into my life."* It took all I had gone through (And *that's a lot of **all***) to bring us together.

I imagine you are probably wondering and would also like to know more about Madison. I'd be remiss if I didn't divulge some important details after all the drama and tribulations you have read about. Perhaps my *"disastrous to miraculous"* tale could bring optimistic hope and comfort to the dating world and those of you searching for love. And if you are lucky, you might also discover, as did I, that "You Got Maled" in the most extraordinary way.

Maddy and I started on a peak and skyrocketed to the moon from there! Silly as it may sound, our love gives me wings to fly. My Romeo, a gorgeous descendant of Roman gods, is 34 years old. He is a very successful entrepreneur, a prominently celebrated engineer, and a highly in demand international architect.

Madison has blue-green eyes, which are both the same color. (I psychically forecast that one wrong.) He is 6 feet, 2 and 3/4 inches tall, exceedingly handsome, and sports an exquisite head of thick brown straight hair. As I predicted, he has that one strand of hair that constantly falls down his forehead. I laugh, finding it incredibly adorable and sexy, even though it annoys him so.

My love is (Take in a deep breath!) loving, kind, sensitive, caring, sweet, tender, affectionate, nurturing, well-endowed, understanding, funny, (take another breath) patient, brilliant, easy-going, emotionally sound, pro-active, hilarious, classy, creative, even-tempered, well-endowed, (Hmm, I think I said that one already, but worthy of repeating.) a renowned philanthropic donor, and much more.

I warned you back in volume 1 that it would take an exorbitant number of adjectives to explain my spectacular Maddy. *Again, sorry Professor Stein. Nevertheless, this is where Stein would've written a large bold 'F,' in red, at the top of my paper, demanding I write it over! To describe my Madison, I would gladly take the F!*

Keeping in mind his generous nature, Madison loves spoiling me with jewelry, cars, clothes, and other fancy gifts. I realize it's astonishing and I'm lucky as hell, but don't hate me! Also, as I predicted, he lovingly gave me 3 quarters of the closet and drawer space. I imagine it's fair to say he admires my shoe collection so much that he designed a large, spacious diamond tiara of a closet for me. My God, even Carrie Bradshaw would be jealous.

I adore his sophisticated refinement and class. Nevertheless, he is also adorably mischievous, playfully silly, delightfully amusing, witty, and wonderful fun to be around. We laugh continually and have become each other's best friend. (In addition to my besties, of course!) I'm not one of those girls who'd ever abandon their friends for a man. My friends and I continue to hang out as usual. People don't ever forsake your friends. It's not right and entirely unacceptable. Your friendships are your lifeline to happiness.

Madison and I behave like two high school kids together. We are cuddly, affectionate, spontaneous, and always joking around. His laughter is highly contagious. In fact, sometimes we act in such an adolescent manner, I feel like I need to go to my locker before homeroom. He's a titan of fun, entertainment, and romance. Our playtime begins around 7:00 p.m. to 3:00 a.m. or so, depending on our next day's agenda. We share infinite conversations, focusing and ranting on foolish as well as intellectual topics. I enjoy how we tit-for-tat. It's lovely the way we respectfully parry back and forth during our discussions. It's even more fun when Shara and Edmond join in. We share many inside secrets and jokes, which drive those around us crazy, not understanding our private codes.

As projected, we've indulged in sex at very inappropriate public establishments. Regrettably, we've never been caught, despite our foolish, naughty hopes that we would. Madison and I routinely indulge in gentle, passionate, sweet love. On other occasions, we also enjoy our nasty, wild, hot sex, which gets rather torrid. Sure, we've tried bondage sex. However, it's not our thing. We are too much in love and sexually attracted to one another to justify playing those games. Love, respect, intimacy, and passion remain our focus, which easily creates our carnal excitement.

We are not one of those couples who need the TV on at night. We prefer to light a fire, pour a nice bottle of wine, share intriguing conversations, and listen to music with candles flickering. While cuddling, huggling, and kissing. I do realize this is all extremely nauseating for most people. Can you only imagine how Shara feels!

FYI, huggling is the same language as romantical, fantastical, pajamaed, sexgasm, and awesomazing. *Apologies Professor Stein! And Sir, I state with attitude, it's not going away. So, deal with it!*

In other breaking news, I can finally, honestly say to that *famous A-List American actress* from the elevator scene in Napoli with Bam-Bam... *"Girl, eat your heart out!"* If she saw Maddy, she surely would. BTW, I have interviewed her many times since then. I even divulged the whole Bam-Bam story. Yep, she laughed till she cried.

ABOUT THE PROPOSAL...
Romance To Infinity and Beyond!

I'm guessing you'd like to know how Madison proposed to me in Paris. Including all the romantic, quixotic details. Unfortunately, I'm unable to share most of it, as it's too personal. But I will share a few things with you. Anyway, if I told you everything, you would unquestionably hate me forever. And who could blame you?

The ring he proposed to me with was even larger than the one I had sadly (and rightfully so) given back to Rocket-Man. By the way, that ethical and moral decision still burns! I'm only kidding!?

Maddy arranged (An impossible task to accomplish unless one has major clout) a *private Parisian Champagne & Sunset event at the Louvre.* Just the 2 of us alone, observing the *Mona Lisa* after hours. I will never forget when he softly whispered in my ear.

"My angel, my treasure, my love, you are far more lovely and extraordinary than the renowned Mona Lisa or the Venus de Milo!"

My dear readers, I can't begin to explain Shara's sarcastic reaction to Madison's remark. I won't even try, but you can imagine.

We continued the evening, floating on an exclusive, private candlelight dinner cruise along the Seine River. After dinner, we enjoyed loving, mind-blowing sex. Discreetly. Or so we thought!

Maddy and I also shared another memorable romantic experience. We put a lock with our names written on it and attached it to the very famous Pont des Arts, "Love Locks Bridge." As legend instructs and promises, we threw the key into the river, which guarantees our love will live on forever, locked in eternity.

Next came our ultra-private, VIP access to the summit of the Eiffel Tower at midnight. A truly amazing, awe-inspiring vision as the tower of love and her city lights twinkled, danced, & flickered.

If all of that didn't seal the best evening of my life, the best of the best romantic gestures of all time began. While we were all alone at the tower's summit, Madison (old-world style) got down on one knee. And with the most perfect, sparkling, spectacular princess-cut diamond (with a trillion-cut diamond on each side) and his heart overflowing with love, he so poetically spoke to me.

"My angel, my princess, 'The One,' and the love of my life… I cannot go on another day without us being committed to one another. We waited long enough to be united, and I don't want to wait any longer to begin our lives. It's not too soon to know how much I love you beyond love, with all my soul and my entire being! I have loved you long before we ever met. You are my world. I Burn for You! *My darling Mollie, will you please, my angel, bestow upon me the unbelievable honor. Will you Marry Me?"*

Like a typical girly-girl American, I screamed at the top of the tower for all of Paris to hear. "Yes, my precious! Yes, in every way, yes! I'll marry you in this life and all the ones to follow!" I fell into his arms, weeping with joy. My heart still smiles, thinking about it.

Overlooking Paris atop the Eiffel Tower, Madison promised me, all bundled up in his heart, his everlasting love. That night, by his marriage proposal, Madison presented to me all my fairytale hopes and dreams come true! *Honestly, so much more. And for the first time, I finally heard my Ding-Dong wedding bells ringing loudly!*

Moreover, knowing the Eiffel Tower was my vision and symbol for love and romance, my love performed the most romantic and compassionate gesture of all time. Because of Madison's unselfish, generous heart, he didn't want me to miss out on Justin's dreamy Eiffel Tower proposal. Which tragically never came to be. This is why (and being a staunch romantic) he brought me to Paris to ask for my hand in marriage. My beloved also insisted that I continue to wear Justin's diamond. The diamond, I swore, (on that heartbreaking day he passed) I would never take off for the rest of my life. To make this possible, Madison lovingly designed a stunning necklace. He had the jeweler place a cubic zirconium stone where Justin's diamond stone would later take its place. After placing his dazzling diamond ring on my finger, he put the necklace around my neck for memory's sake, above the city's glimmering lights. His extraordinary gesture was the epitome of unconditional love. I hadn't cried that much since Justin died. I worshiped Madison for everything he is, and all he does for me.

"Please don't cry, my precious fiancée. You've made me the happiest man on earth. Mollie, there is no place for tears anymore. Only our love and happiness!" He smiled and kissed me tenderly.

Later, I discovered Maddy had planned yet another surprise. He had arranged for the entire proposal to be videotaped. He did so, knowing I'm a sentimental mush, and to be able to share the moment with friends and family. *They* say," the true definition of love is how a person makes you feel about yourself. How right "they" are. Maddy makes me feel loved, blessed, and categorically the most important person in his life. By his side, I feel that I can achieve anything. His love makes me strive to be a better person. He fills my heart beyond my wildest imagination with peace, security, and total fulfillment. He has given my life real meaning.

As it turned out, Madison was my real-life Prince Charming. He mended the pieces of my many times shattered, broken heart, and gifted back to me all my unrealistic childhood dreams come true.

Indeed, dreams do come true! Although, you must prepare for endless nightmares, night sweats, night terrors, and bad dreams before your little-girl fantasies and dreams transpire. You might have to go through the blazing fires of hell to reach the fairytale. Hey, I'm only the messenger. But if I got through it, you will too!

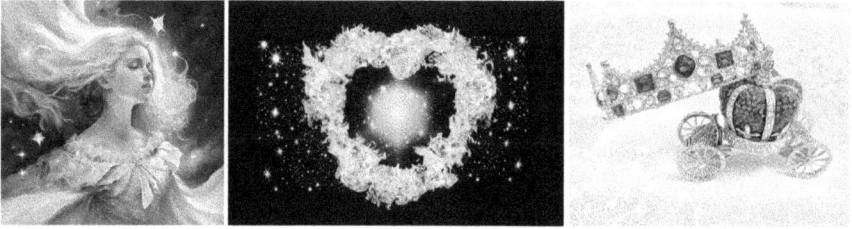

Ironically, due to my personal philosophies, along with the truths and realities of life, I realized there are certain steps you must accomplish before you can find and appreciate love and happiness. I learned that I must complete *myself*, be happy with *myself*, and love *myself first. No one completes you or can make you happy, but you!* We all must complete ourselves *by ourselves.* Once that was accomplished, only then was it possible for Madison to enter my life, making it possible for 'two to become one.' I came to appreciate how all my endless tears and love for Justin grew into strength and success for Madison and me. If you are mindful, there is much wisdom and pain behind the many lessons of love.

Hence, my loyal readers, I am living proof that "The One" is out there! Sure, it might take you much longer to find than you hoped. It might even come to fruition differently than you expected or imagined. Surprisingly, it might be the very last person you'd ever think of who ultimately turns out to be "The One."

The big lesson and takeaway? Hang in there! For we all have a soulmate, and we all need, want, and deserve love. Heavens to Betsy, I shudder to think, that all those weirdos, creeps, and bat-shit-crazy freaks roaming around freely, merit love, as well.

I'm so sorry, Betsy, for dragging you into this foolishness again.

Talking and discussing my beloved Madison's romantically French marriage proposal is private, top-secret, strictly confidential, and *Entre nous!* Ergo, I will not divulge another single thing.

Forget what you know!

FINI! AMÉNAGE! FAITE! LA FIN! JE SUIS FINI'!

CHAPTER 20

Happiness

ALSO KNOWN AS HAPPILY FOREVER AND AFTER! THE TOTAL FAIRYTALE...

And, as I innocently predicted, since I was a little girl, all the things my one true love and I would do together had come to fruition. Things like walking to Krispy Kreme at 4:00 in the morning for fresh hot doughnuts. Or running to the bakery around the corner for just-out-of-the-oven warm bread. Oh, incidentally, he does give me the better doughnut! The one that is bigger, perfectly shaped, and has more glazed sugar on it. He also gives me the larger bagel, with extra seeds and nicely browned. Our late-night rendezvous has become a ritual we've kept to this day. Furthermore, we often stay up late at night, solving the many problems in the world. Which includes talking about aliens, spirituality, family, friends, travel, politics, movies and just about everything imaginable.

Because of all my adverse past dating experiences (such a charming way of saying disastrous failures), I was expecting the other shoe to drop at any second. Or, in this case, my Cinderella slipper plopping off, ricocheting off the wall, and hitting me on the head, causing a severe concussion. Happily, that never happened, because Madison was the perfect fit. And you know what they say. "If the shoe fits!"

I philosophically discovered my search for Maddy was my own personal "Armageddon." More accurately, put, "MenAgeddon!" With all the men-drama I had suffered through over the years, Madison was indeed my "Last Romantic Battle between Good and Evil, before the Day of Judgment." On this judgment day, it was the universe and Edmond that brought Madison and me together! The day my soulmate, my Romeo, my champion, and the mythical, *'The One,'* and I united.

FIRST CAME LOVE.
THEN, CAME MARRIAGE!

Madison and I were married less than six months later, on a picturesque June afternoon in the bay of Naples, Italy. Our wedding ceremony was in the Gardens of Augustus, overlooking the breathtaking panoramic vistas of Capri and the majestically renowned Faraglioni's rock formations. This heavenly setting was beyond romantic movie enchanting and phantasmagoric.

There were close to a thousand people in attendance. Both of our families, business associates, and, of course, all our friends were present. Each person brought with them immeasurable wishes of love and happiness. They were filled with joie de vivre for us. I was glowing with inner peace, looking around and seeing the loving, encouraging faces of my friends. Like an overly excited child, I was peeking out from the tent to see all the amazing people I dearly love from behind the white satin curtain. The curtain I was going to walk out from, to marry my beloved. I could see the warm, shimmering smiles of my besties waiting for the ceremony to begin. There they sat, (Big breath!) Shara, Elizabeth, Geri, Angela, Joyce, Debbie, Barbara, Melinda, Corrine, Dara, Janet, Beth, Estella, Freddy, Frances, Josh, Rachel, Dan, Shaina, Richie, Aubrey, Shino, Alejandro, Adonis, Roberto, Linda, (Take another big breath!) Fred, Roberto, Giuliana, Lucrezia, Guiditta, David, Merrill, Monica, Dave, Jill, Sandy, Glynnis, Jeff, Adriana, Stephanie, Robin, Chloe, Jennifer, and countless celebrities. (Are you OK? Relax for a moment and take a sip of water!) Many others came to Capri as well. Such as Angie, my boss, Sidney, Justin's only wife, and, of course, my forever love, Rocket-Man.

Oh, My God! I caught a glimpse of Jedediah Jones, and I could not believe my eyes. He was sitting with a magnificent man. Holy, Mollie! Were they holding hands? Whaaat???? My mouth dropped open. When Jed spotted me, my mouth was still hanging wide open. With a smarty-pants smug expression, using air quotes.

"Damn, Jedediah! *You, Are, Gay! BOOM!!!*"

He smiled, miming back. "Yeah, I finally came to terms with it and appreciated I am gay!" Jedediah Jones sealed it with a wink!

I winked back with an approving, warm grin that screamed, *"I knew it. I just knew it!"* My savvy gaydar had never even once let me down. I felt exonerated and mouthed back giggling, *"I'm happy for you, Jones!"* He blew me a kiss and his very handsome partner presented a 2-thumbs up, and a very excited, giggling wink!

All these beloved people flew over 6,000 miles to Italy to help us celebrate. They came to share in our, "happily forever after, and our new, storybook beginning." I could feel the invisible male ghosts of my online dating past floating above. Like "Bobble, *Who* in the Box?" **Who?** Bobble Who! Today at last, came the fantastic, victorious *closure* I've waited for.

At the stroke of 3:00 in the afternoon, I Heard Wedding Bells!!! I was ecstatic hearing those euphoric *Ding-Dong* Wedding Bells I longed to hear, ever since I was a little girl playing Bride & Groom!

After the (Oh, thank God, my Ding-Dong bells finally happened!) blissful wedding bells finished ringing, "I Knew I Loved You Before I Met You" marked the start of our wedding ceremony. As our song ended, the music segued into Mendelssohn's traditional wedding march, performed by four violinists, a harpist, and two flutists.

I awaited my cue, holding onto my loving daddy's hand. My dad, gazing at me with his Sinatra blue eyes, was overjoyed with happiness, and tears of immense warmth and affection. He has supported me every day of my entire life with boundless love, and today was no different. Before my dad, my hero, walked me down the aisle to join my beloved, he turned to me, shaking his head with immeasurable pride, and adoringly poured his heart out.

"My extraordinary daughter, Madison, is 'The One!' He is the one you have dreamed of ever since you were a little girl. 'The One' you imagined and visualized the hundreds of times you played 'Wedding Day,' all dressed up in your room with your little friends. Sweetheart, you will have your happily ever after with Madison! I feel it! I'm sure of it! Mollie, my sweet little girl, you deserve this happiness and more! My wish for you both is the love and respect you feel for each other today will remain all the days of your life!"

Then my adoring father bent down and hugged me with every ounce of love in his heart. How could that not make a girl weep?

As we floated down the extra-long aisle, decorated with white Italian lace and satin, adorned with fresh white roses and gardenias, I couldn't feel my feet touch the ground. Shaking with intense ecstasy, thank goodness for my dad, *Leon*, who was virtually holding me up.

When Madison witnessed me approaching, I could see him melting with eternal affection as tears streamed down his exquisite face. He was aglow with delight, openly flaunting his love and adoration for me with his every expression for all to see. Dressed in unparalleled elegance and class, MY GOD, the man is so handsome he took my breath away. Balancing smiles and tears, Maddy (*"TPIEWG"*) managed to mouth the words across the room. *"I will love you forever and beyond."* Those were the exact words he chose the first time he told me he loved me. I tried with all my might not to cry, mostly because my makeup was so fantabulous. Plus, even more so, Edmond was giving me evil looks that shouted, *"Girl, stop crying! Photos, Photos, Video, Photos! Don't even think about it! Makeup and mascara all over your face? Not your best look! You know you're an ugly crier!"* I held my tears back as best I could as Eddie ferociously mimed, *"Girl, forever wedding photos!"*

When we reached the wedding canopy adorned with infinite gardenias, violets, and roses, my dear father, my protector, and my very first love lifted my veil. He affectionately gave me my last single-girl kiss. He then gently placed my veil back down. This moment froze forever in my mind. I couldn't help but think about the billions of kisses he had given me and the never-ending unconditional love he showed me every single day as I grew up. He continues to shower me with his love, even now as a grown woman. A girl could not possibly love her father more than I loved this king, this champion of a man. He always said to me, "You're so incredible, amazing, intelligent and gorgeous!" He smiled back at me with tears cascading down from his eyes. My daddy gave me away with immense confidence and trust in Maddy, and profound pleasure, which appeared noticeably across his loving face.

Dorothy, my darling mother, whom I treasured, could not contain her waterworks of absolute jubilation. She was adorable with all her profuse weeping. My mom is the most loving, sweetest lady who ever lived. Her *out loud* cries of joy brought warm, endearing chuckles to all the wedding guests. So that's where the phrase "Crying out loud" came from? Growing up, the only thing my devoted mom wanted and dreamed of was to see me happy. How lucky was I to be raised by two such outstanding individuals?

By now, there wasn't a dry eye in the house. "Sorry, Eddie," I mouthed, tilting my head, and smiling as tears rained down my face. I noticed tears trickling from his twinkling eyes as well. I only wished this was a movie set. Because here was the moment when the director would've said, *"Cut, Makeup, and Take Five Everyone!"* *Honestly, we all needed a Take Five.*

Oh, Em Gee! How could I have neglected to describe my magnificent, super-star princess wedding gown? Don't even try to imagine how heavenly and astonishing this bridal dress of perfection was. I wore a dazzling one-of-a-kind, Vera Wang Bridal Gown. It was from Wang's exclusive private collection my mumsy-in-law, Anastasia, helped me acquire through her vast connections. Of course, obviously, it had to be entirely approved by Edmond. It was breathtaking with the perfect amount of sparkling, bridal bling, sophistication, and divine elegance. Not even Cinderella, Snow White, Sleeping Beauty, or the real-life princesses, Diana and Kate wore a more spectacular fairytale wedding gown than I wore! It was entirely regal, with a sweetheart neckline, Venetian lace, and a fitted bodice cinching in my 24-inch waist, which provided almost enough room to breathe. It was a classically romantic, over-the-top ball gown, bursting with beading, pearls, and endless Swarovski crystal rhinestones. Vera Wang personally customized it for me (well, for Anastasia) and designed an extra-long train like Diana, Queen of Hearts wore. For the wow factor and an abundance of romance, Madison's name was embroidered in white satin, dramatically decorating the train. I get chills just thinking about it.

The best part ever? Like ever? I mean, EVER, and to die for? I got to wear Anastasia's Royal-esque, *Real Diamond Tiara! TA-DA!* The ultimate opportunity to wear an extraordinary, bejeweled tiara out of the house, and it wasn't Halloween! Wheeeeee! Another blissful, crazy, amazing, and dreams do come true, event.

And yeah, let me tell you another thing. For sure (And I mean it!), there is absolutely no way, no way in any scenario imaginable that Ana is ever getting her tiara back. It's never going to happen!

I also walked down the aisle with my good luck: Stuart Weitzman, silver, rhinestone, strappy sandals, which I wore the night Madison and I first met. For sentimental reasons, my Cinderella lucky slippers had to be part of this fantasy wedding. Without sounding too braggadocious, I was the perfect, enchanting vision of a fairytale princess bride. After all I had survived, I believe I deserved a little brag or two. (Or ten!) So, consider my lovely vision of gorgeousness a justifiable bit of arrogance, and a well-deserved occasion to brag. I imagine on this one magical day, my wedding day, I was, without a doubt, "The Fairest of Them All!" And I didn't even need the "mirror, mirror, on the wall" to see that!

My chic, Prince Madison, wore a one-of-a-kind, original design by Valentino. He looked astonishingly regal. He'd majestically even make Valentino proud! My Love would outshine and make the most famous, handsome movie star pale in comparison. Honestly, I literally expected paparazzi stalkers, or a Joan Rivers want-to-be, running up to him in the middle of the wedding to inquire. "Who are you wearing? Or I smell an Oscar!" Maddy and I matched inside and out on our wedding day. We could've walked right off the pages of any romance novel. Speaking of Danielle Steel, sovereign of romantic stories. She'd love for him to be one of her leading characters. Even Madison Daniel Sterling, is such a 'Steel' name for one of her male heroes. No Steel, you can't have him. He's *MY* hero!

Naturally, Anastasia, my mom Dorothy, Sophie, Juliana, and Shara all wore Vera, as well. William, my dad Leon, and Edmond wore Armani. No joke. We looked like we were doing a photo shoot for the latest cover of Couture Bride Monthly. Ana single-handedly created a fashion-elite dream wedding. Although not at all true, it appeared she made it happen with ease by waving her magic wand with a snap of her bejeweled finger.

Only two other people were involved in the wedding ceremony, Shara and Edmond. It was as it should be. Our dearest friends surely would have been included in the ceremony. But we didn't want to put them through the infamous wedding party ordeal, drama, or torment. We wanted everyone to come to Italy and have the most memorable, fun, magical time imaginable.

As our guests expected, Madison and I wrote and shared our own personal wedding vows. We expressed promises of undying love and devotion in our own heartfelt words. Our sentimental feelings of respect, adoration, and commitment were so intimate and personal, that they made our vows even more touching and romantic. My voice quivered, my tears overflowed with bliss, and my heart was pounding out of control as I recited my words of love for Madison. It surprised no one to see our public outpouring of affection and emotions. All eyes were filled with tears. Frightening, even Shara was crying! It was disturbing, she wasn't even rolling her eyes from all the mush and gush. It must've been a cold day in hell or a hot day in heaven for this phenomenon to occur. Shara? Shara, my best friend, was crying? This was clearly a newsworthy headline and an unsettling breaking news story.

After reciting our vows and exchanging rings, we were pronounced, "Man & Wife." Madison stepped on the glass, smashing it into pieces like a superhero. Ana retrieved the shards to make into a gift. It was so unbelievably *divine, as my "Ding-Dong Wedding Bells" boldly rang and rang and rang. Goosebumps all over.*

And just like that, We Were Married!

Madison and I, along with my "Oh, for crying out loud," doting mom and everyone in attendance, cried tears of elation. Thank goodness for Anastasia's attention to every detail in planning this last-minute, huge wedding. She was intuitively wise in hiring makeup and hair artists for the duration of the wedding celebrations for everyone invited. Who does that? Ana does! Moreover, all her perfectly designed preparations were spot-on!

This wasn't, by any means, a modest wedding. However, our love, the warm affection of our guests, and the magnificent beauty and seclusion of this glorious location delivered a cozy, intimate aura. The unimaginable ambiance of romance floated in the air throughout the day and evening. I don't believe anyone, including myself, has ever felt this level of euphoria, or such warm affection and splendor at a wedding. Ana, manifesting the infinite arrangements for this epic celebration was a huge coup. She gifted us her creative talents of elegance and grace with every bit of her love. I was so lucky to be the daughter-in-law of "Ana, The Great!"

The speeches and toasts, wishing us happiness through humorous and emotional stories of friendship and family love, continued nonstop during the evening. However, the tear-wrenching testimonials at dinner given by my parents, Leon and Dorothy, Madison's parents, Anastasia and William, Edmond, and his sisters (the Kappa Kappa Gammers) did me in. My flawless bridal perfection visibly began to crumble. Helpless, looking at their adoring faces, I wept with infinite love and appreciation. I owed the world to these amazing people. The final demise of my flawless, picture-perfect makeup arose with the father-daughter dance to the Tim McGraw song, "My Little Girl." That did it. I was such a hot mess that even Ana's "Take Five elves" couldn't help me.

Nowhere to hide, I caught Edmond's stern, pointy edge disapproving eyes on me as my mascara melted, dripping down my face. At that tearful moment, Eddie ran up to scold me. "Girrrrrl! You know this is going to ruin your photos. Stop it, cease with this weeping nonsense! Hell's bells, you've probably ruined 73 shots already. Sweetie, you are a supermodel today. There is *no crying in fashion!*" He gently blotted my tears with a mischievous wink and yelled out, commanding, and clapping his hands. "Makeup artists, come tend to the bride's face at once! Rapido."

"Ed, I love you from Uranus to Pluto and back down to Earth!"

"Ga-irl, my name is Edmond, not Ed, and please leave my Uranus out of this! And don't you dare make me cry! I can't do makeup. Well, here at least! It's my fashion obligation and duty to look flawless in every photo. Seriously, my job is never done!"

I giggled, "Edmond, you always turn my tears into laughter."

"As you very well know, princess, there's nothing I hate more than looking messy, un-coiffured, and all red and teary-eyed in professional photos. It's sinful. Besides, this is one of the most famous photographers in the world. The universe, in fact. He shoots for Vogue! He's Vogue's lead photographer, Mollie! So, don't blow it." We laughed boisterously as he kissed away my tears.

During the wedding festivities, Edmond found several private moments for us to be alone, signaling me with his boyish grin and nodding his head. During one of our moments alone, I hugged my brother-in-law with pure gratitude. "Eddie, you are more than my *'Fairy'* Godmother. You are my Superman and soul brother. I hope you know I wish you all the love and ecstasy you are solely responsible for bringing into my life. You, alone, have changed my entire universe. How can I ever repay you?"

"Sweetie Dahling, stop this foolishness immediately! *'Dang It,'* you're making me cry again. Just so you know, I did nothing that wasn't already predestined to happen. Regardless, always remember and never forget *that it was me* who loved you first. Even if I do prefer men! Mollie, you do realize you would have been my sole choice had I been born straight. Let's be honest here. We both know you totally would've married me first! Though fear not, I will never divulge to Madison the knowledge that he came in a far second.

That shall remain our *hush-hush* little secret. Shhh! **But** if I couldn't marry you, I'm thrilled my brother did. At least one of us kept the New Year's resolution we made to break for fun."

"You're indeed correct. I remember begging you many times to marry me. But wait. Back up a sec, Eddie. *'Dang It?'* Did you literally just say, *'DANG IT?'* Is that the same as Hardy-Har-Har and a Big Sharrar?" We chuckled and sobbed, toasting to our devotion.

He whispered emphatically. "To set the record straight, I'll never in this lifetime admit to saying, 'Dang It!' So, let it go! Moreover, and let it be known, I hate doing anything 'Straight!' Including setting the record!"

Laughing wildly, almost tearing my gown, "I adore you, Eddie!"

"Ditto! Now, let's stop our tear-ruining-demolishing-photo-op madness. Dang it, it's time for another exotic cocktail! Shall we?"

"What a novel idea. And yes, we shall. Dang It!"

Edmond and I arrived back at the ballroom just in time to see my sarcastic, cold-tongued, but wonderful BFF Shara standing up to make her Maid of Honor Speech. To put it mildly, I freaked.

"Oh, shit, shit, shit. Eddie, Shara is about to speak!"

"Honey, freaking out is not a ladylike thing to do. Especially when wearing an original Vera Wedding Gown, a humongous diamond ring, and a bedazzling real diamond tiara," he cautioned me. Still, I was as petrified as if I were about to watch a horror film or a rerun episode of 'Keeping Up with The Kardashians!' Panicked and gliding back to my husband's side, I dug my nails into his leg. "It'll be OK, baby. Come on, Shara loves you. She knows just how far she can go and still behave with dignity. Relax, my angel."

"Yes, she loves us. But behaving with dignity? Shara? Her sarcasm and humor have no boundaries or limits. She strives to behave without dignity," I said, fidgeting. As we listened, I didn't know if I was stunned, surprised, or disappointed. The divinely cynical Miss Shara gave the most loveable, endearing, sentimental speech of the whole evening. Chilling! Talk about "shock and awe." Her sweet kindness felt uncomfortable, making me squirm more.

Following her speech, in true Shara style, she didn't allow for any sappy displays of affection, fuss, or warm hugs. Later in the evening, when Madison and I went up to thank her, I gushed. *"Ah, Ah, Shara.* Thank you, my dearest, best friend forever, for your uncharacteristically sensitive speech. It was truly unforgettable."

Maddy jumped in. "We loved and appreciate your toast, Shara."

She adorably and caustically replied. "Don't Ah, Ah, Shara me!"

"Seriously, Shara, your words were super mushy, tender, and fuzzy. You surprised everyone. As for all the sugary sweet things you said, I can only say thank you, and you've touched our hearts!"

"Yeah, yeah, yeah... What-the-Fucking-Ever! With so many people and such a fancy-schmancy wedding, I had no choice but to make up a lot of icky-gooey gibberish. And, just so you know, it was all totally exaggerated. I didn't mean a word of it. And one more thing. You guys better make this marriage last forever. Because I'm telling you now, I will never do that again for either of you!" She grunted like the Grinch when we both tried to hug her. With that, the 3 of us roared, laughing.

Shara's impossible to resist. You had to love her. No way not to.

Everything about my husband and our luminous, glorious wedding was impeccable. It was my forever-dream-come-true beginning. The little girl inside me was smart. She never stopped hopelessly believing in love and the happily ever after. But this wasn't a childish, make-believe fairytale. It was surreal and my new reality. This was far better than all my 'little girl, dress-up imaginary weddings.' Greater than the extravagant, wedding day prophecies, I played a trillion times in my silly romantic girly head.

Late in the evening, around 2:00 a.m., when we all assumed it was getting close to the conclusion of the all-day wedding, Eddie caught the garter. Of course, he didn't have the slightest clue what in the world to do with it. I hollered out to him with enthusiasm.

"Dang It Eddie! That surely is a Hardy Har Har & a Big Sha-rar!"

Simultaneously, Shara, smirking in disgust, unwillingly caught the bouquet as it hit her in the head. She swiftly handed it to a little old lady standing next to her. "Here! Enjoy, it's all yours!" I believe I heard that she was the 90-year-old Great Aunt of William, the Prince of England, on Maddy's "Faaatha's" side of the family. Anyway, the royal old lady was delighted with the bouquet.

As only Shara would dare, she marched over to Edmond, who was now struggling with the garter. She put it on top of his head while shaking hers. Eddie replied in the gayest voice he could. (He so loved upsetting his dad for fun!) *"Thanks, Maid Shara! It looks smashing on me, I dare say. Don't you agree?"* I heard Shara and Eddie, who were now buds, laughing across the enormous glitzy party tent. So grateful their priceless scene was captured on video.

Throughout the wedding and the celebration party, I was concerned with Rocket-Man's feelings. I worried how he was dealing with his emotions and coping with me marrying another. But in true rocker fashion, he reassured me. "Luv, it's all good! Nothing in the world could make me cheerier than seeing you this happy. What we shared and continue to share is amazing. Our love will live on forever. You surely know that *I will always love you!*"

I smiled, for those words, that song, "I will always love you" is how we ended our love affair. "Rocket-Man, I'll love you forever!"

The wedding festivities went on from 3:00 in the afternoon to 4:00 in the morning. We ate, danced, sang, and partied for thirteen hours of blissful celebrations, and sentiments of enormous congratu-lations! Remarkably, no one became upset or complained about how long the wedding went on, which went way into overtime. No one protested, not the band, the DJs, the people running the grounds, the photographers, the make-up artists, or the caterers. They cheer-fully performed their jobs for the entire wedding with unwavering friendliness and thoughtful, generous attention. I love that about Italy and pretty much everything else!

As each guest departed, Anastasia presented them with a lovely wedding parting-gift. Nestled in the blue satin box were Swarovski Crystal mementos of our wedding. Inside was a sparkling, gorgeous Cinderella slipper, a top hat, and a heart. These lovely keepsakes were extraordinarily apropos, ridiculously lavish, and extravagant to present to 1000 or so guests. Yet these gifts were typical of Ana's generosity and panache. The more I learned about Anastasia, the more I understood why her 4 children were such remarkable individ-uals. I grew to love her and the entire family. Despite that Madison and his siblings were raised wealthy and privileged, (Having it all.) it was remarkable how they didn't turn out to be like those spoiled, 'affluenza' kids! They were unpretentious, genuine, and taught to appreciate, give back, and to earn everything for them-selves. Although the Sterling kids enjoyed a wonderful, steadfast upbringing, they were mindful and very appreciative for the good fortune they were given.

While it was a weekend wedding, brunch was to start in 8 hours, so the party began winding down. Somewhere around 3:45 a.m. I noticed Joyce leaving, trying to slip out quietly to return to the hotel. Sprinting to catch up, I unintentionally frightened her.

She gasped. "Mollie, you scared the Capri Italy out of me!"

"I'm so sorry, honey. I didn't mean to sneak up on you!"

"Hey, did you notice the hunkiest guys in the world live here?"

"Joycie, if I weren't so madly in love with Maddy, I might have. But you go all in, honey! Listen, I had to talk to you before you left." With friendship and adoration in my heart, I presented to Joyce my Stuart Weitzman Cinderella Slippers and whispered, "They belong to you, now! I'm telling you they're going to bring you luck!" I used the exact words she spoke when she forced me to buy them to wear at the New Year's Eve Ball. When she cried, I giggled. "Hey, I expected more from you. Stop crying, or I'll take them back!"

Knowing how much those sentimental shoes meant to me, and what it meant to give them to her, Joycie replied emotionally.

"I'm so happy for you, and I'm more than blessed to call you my dearest friend! And Mollie-Pollie, with all the stunning, hot men running around here, I imagine I'll need to put them on right away! Girlfriend, have the sexiest honeymoon ever. I love you so much."

We giggled our happiest giggles. I whispered ditto, and we embraced. Thank God Shara wasn't anywhere in sight. Because all that emotional mush would have clearly made her sick.

There I stood, alone and barefoot in Capri, Italy, wearing my one-of-a-kind, stunning Vera Wedding Gown, now completely soiled on the bottom. With a warm breeze blowing through my *borrowed* tiara, I smiled with overwhelming happiness, more than I thought humanly possible. In denial about the *borrowed part,* "I don't care what the repercussions are for my actions. There's no way in hell Ana is ever getting her tiara back! Good grief, that was a skosh nasty even for me. Yeah (giggling) whatever, I still mean it!

I turned to look for Shara now that the coast was clear. I had a wonderful surprise gift for her, too. Shara! Shara? But, in true Shara style, she had disappeared. Luckily, she showed up at the brunch the following day to receive it. Sorry, readers. The gift was too personal to share with you! But I can reveal it was a present filled with years of sentimental memories, far too emotional for Shara to deal with. She must've utterly hated it. I alleged, giggling.

Making love for the first time as Mrs. Madison Daniel Sterling

Well, seeing as most of you have been with me, reading through my dating calamities and disastrous events (the good, bad, sad, and ugly), allow me to share my wedding night with you loyal readers. Not that I usually kiss and tell, but seriously, you totally deserve it!

By the time we were alone at last, the sun was rising over the majestic Island of Capri. I draped my magnificent wedding gown across the pink silk settee atop Maddy's elegant couture tuxedo. It was so 'us,' that I had to snap a photo. The celebratory sounds of our wedding and the joyous conversations of our beloved friends had faded into sweet silence. The sliding doors of our honeymoon suite were wide open, displaying the miraculous view, as the sea breeze gently blew in. We lay together, serene, idyllic, and cradled in each other's arms. With candlelight, our favorite music, and bottles of champagne, we beamed *rejoicing*, "WE'RE MARRIED!"

Sharing pillow talk, he boasted. "My precious wife, you are the most exquisite, breathtaking, angelic bride who ever lived! My heart stopped beating the moment I saw you walking down the aisle toward me. I couldn't contain the sea of my euphoric tears."

"My darling, no groom has ever looked more elegant and stunning! The moment I saw you waiting for me under the canopy, I felt so much love for you, I almost ran down the aisle and jumped into your arms. Thankfully, I regained my senses and bridal protocol, fearing your mom would be permanently horrified.

"Good thinking!" He laughed his splendid laugh I so adore.

"Mollie, I've never known such immeasurable feelings of joy in my life. I believe my greatest achievement was becoming your husband. I'm so proud of you, hopelessly in love with you, and humbled you agreed to marry me. I want to bring you happiness every minute for the rest of our lives! That's my promise to you!"

Cooing bashfully, "My husband, (I love saying husband) you've already made me feel more loved, brought me more security and happiness than I've ever known, or had the audacity, to hope for. And Maddy, I am greatly honored and blessed to be your wife. From the moment we met, you have made me truly happy. You are my everything. Gee, I can't stop the flood of my happy tears."

He leaned towards me, brushing away the hair from my eyes. His mere touch sent shivers up and down my body, pushing me over the edge of ecstasy, even before we made love. The heavens opened as he kissed me in earnest. I could hear the crashing sounds of the Italian waves breaking against the rocks below.

I loved this man with every part of my being. I'd eagerly cater to his every whim. When I'm close to him, all sense of reason deserts me. He is like a drug. Only a healthy one! My wide-eyed dreams & innocence of youth were satisfied and complete. He was more than everything I had fantasized, dreamed of, or hoped for.

Interrupting my sublime thoughts, while never taking his eyes off me, he questioned. "Baby, are you ever taking off the tiara?"

Retaliating, I implored strongly. "Nope. Not now. Not ever!"

He chuckled with appreciation. "I completely love that about you and everything else, my precious, beautiful bride, my wife!"

Madison ran his fingers along the nape of my neck, down my bare back, and across my ribs, feeling the two dimples above my buttocks. My yearning for his touch was insatiable. He began stroking my hair around the esteemed tiara. I held my breath as he moved down my chin, caressing me with endless, tender kisses. His hand slid across my naked chest. Feeling my breasts, he pulled me closer to him, pressing his exquisite face against mine, while gently playing with my nipples. He awakened every pore in my body. He was masterful and sure of himself. How I loved this man.

Every sound, touch, and feeling brought endless enchantment as the new Mrs. Madison Sterling. I loved the smell of his silky hair as we kissed. His smell, his lovely smell, always makes me horny.

Slowly and discreetly, I slid my hand down to feel his pulsating, hard cock rising. I felt his heartbeat and heard his hungry moans of desire. As he reached down to touch me, I stayed perfectly still, for fear he might stop. Slowly and gradually, he slid down, putting his mouth between my legs. Filling me with excitement, I drifted out of my body with lustful passion. So completely turned on, I couldn't stop the ravenous throbbing of my wet vagina from its incredible, deep-seated pleasure. Glancing down, I was ever so delighted to see the thick perfection of his impressive erect penis.

Suddenly and unexpectedly, he picked me up in his toned, masculine arms and gently brought me onto the veranda. Holding me close, we danced to *our* wedding song. "I knew I loved you before I met you," blasted from the Italian Sonus Faber speakers. The cool gentle breeze blowing through our hair, and our naked bodies pressed against each other, overlooking the Mediterranean Sea, was a most memorable moment of my life. I felt safe. I belonged, and I was home in Madison's arms. With flutes of Champagne, he professed his love with a toast.

"My gorgeous Mollie, I appreciate all you went through and everything it took for us to find each other. Darling, I promise, our lives will be unlike anyone else's. We will forever be as we are at this moment. I give you my assurance and vow my eternal love."

I returned my husband's toast right back. "My darling, Madison, everything in my life, every venture, and every moment, has guided me here to be with you today. I would not change a thing, for it all led me to you, to us, and to our love!"

We danced for a few more songs, naked in each other's arms. I could feel his firm penis pushing against my pussy. Oh, how sexy!

With Maddy's weight on top of me (which I craved), I could feel him growing harder and bigger, pushing against my awaiting horny body. I was desperate to feel him inside me. But instead, he teased me further, moving his body in slow motion, rubbing his penis against my clitoris. He brought me to the edge of mind-blowing arousal before he plunged his bulging stiff, hard-on into my embarrassingly wet and warm pussy. Grinding slowly, he fell deeper inside me. Tightly wrapping my legs around his neck, I rocked and swayed to the pace of his erogenous rhythm.

I never wanted this to end. And boy, oh boy, did he ever know exactly what he was doing! I urgently needed to release the moans of my untamed, excruciating pleasure. I was so desperate to orgasm, but I wished to hold back, wanting to build this into a grand climax. Clearly knowing what I was up to, he abruptly stopped moving, kissed me, and smiled, with eyes filled with erotic lust. I could barely breathe. Holding me to his chest, he roared, "I love you!" He hugged me tightly, jostling me about with frantic greed. With one last throbbing push, I gave in to the force greater than myself. *AHHHH!* There it was. The extraordinary grand finale.

We felt the blurry warmth of cumming together as our muscles collapsed. We sealed our first orgasm as *man and wife,* consummating our marriage. With a kiss and the harmonious lingering tenderness of our passionate love, we lie with our bodies intertwined. Merely by the way my husband looks at me is all the love I need to know and feel, now and forever.

Madison swiftly seized me, pulling me up into his arms, and twirled me about our honeymoon suite. "My princess, with *my mother's* justifiably befitting tiara, "I will love you for all eternity and forever after!" Tossing me forcefully back onto the bed, he frantically entered me. I moaned out sounds I didn't know were humanly possible or natural.

After sharing marital sexual bliss, we lay together content and serene. After a few minutes, looking over at the clock, we realized we had to dress for the "After-Wedding Brunch."

"Hey Maddy, let's skip it and call in sick. What do you think?"

"I'd love to. I want to stay in the warmth of our love forever. But we'd probably regret not thanking and saying goodbye to our guests. Let's get dressed so we can hurry back inside each other."

"You are always so thoughtful Your parents did a splendid job raising you. Okay, fine, I'll get dressed… But I'm wearing the tiara.

"Baby, you are a queen, and you don't need a tiara to prove it. But wear and enjoy it for as long as you desire. My mother loaned it to you, and she'd love to know you wore it dancing, stark-naked on the balcony over Capri, for all to see."

Giggling, "Knowing Ana, she probably would!"

"She absolutely would be thrilled to know how much fun her tiara had at sunrise. She'd be so delighted she loaned it to you."

"Of course, she would. Wait a minute. Loaned?"

We laughed till tears slid down our cheeks.

After the luncheon (we were obligated to attend), before I knew it, I was once again transported back onto the bed of our hungry wedding night passions. Madison stayed inside me for the next 10 days. *There was lots of honey* on that moon!

Oh, one more very important thing...

I must correct Madison's statement!

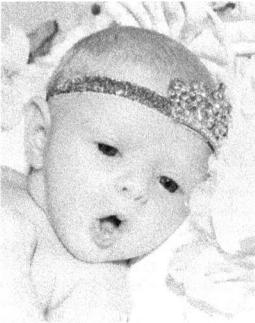

"MY Tiara!"
And THAT IS THAT!

LOL!

CHAPTER 21

Then Came Mollie with the Baby Carriages

YES! I SAID CARRIAGES!!!!!!!!

Nine months after our storybook wedding, Madison and I were incredibly blessed. We became the proud parents of identical twin girls, beautiful Jennifer & Chloe! My dream of being a mommy, and being a family came true. As I said, lots of honey was on that moon.

As you'd expect, the Sterling clan was beside themselves with unimaginable excitement. They loved and adored the babies. Naturally, Madison and I asked Edmond to be the girl's Godfather.

Can you imagine how shocked and embarrassed we were when he vehemently refused the honor? Worse yet, right in front of the entire family. We didn't see that coming. Truthfully, we were hurt.

However, Eddie didn't wait very long before changing things around and making his demands known.

"All right, you two, now listen up! If you really love me that much, if you genuinely want to honor me, and sincerely want me to be that involved in the twins' lives, then fine. I will."

Naturally, Maddy and I breathed a huge sigh of relief.

*"Here is my non-negotiable, demand. I shall **only** accept the title of Fairy Godmother!"* Everyone roared. Goodness, even William, with his predictable, disapproving grin, appeared amused.

"Of course, my dear brother. It is befitting and so granted. Thus, Mollie and I Knight You, Sir Edmond. Hereafter and forevermore, the girls shall call you *Fairy Godmother!* And so, it is written." Eddie turned blushing red, beaming ecstatically.

"I now formally accept, and so it shall be! Hey, what are we waiting for? Let us drink to it, Dang It! I Edmond, hereby make a toast with these sentimental crystal glasses, To ME! The best Fairy Godmother who ever lived. And here's to my precious, adorable, beautiful Goddaughters, who are completely loved. To Jennifer and Chloe, who are soon-to-be, the best-dressed, fashionista twins, this planet has ever known! Watch out world, and you spoiled Hollywood brats. The influential Sterling babies are coming to rule the elite baby fashion scene. Now, go on family. Drink up and be gay!"

"Eddie, wait! Hold on there. As I am the mom, I boldly enhance your toast." Everyone cheered happily. "To Jennifer and Chloe. Here is to you, twins. With a Hardy Har Har and a Big Sha-rar!"

Juliana and Sophie blurted out. "And you bet those girls better be in a sorority! No way they are going to miss out on all that joy!"

While the whole family chuckled, I gazed about the room, thinking with my heart overflowing. How lucky can a girl be? My God, I couldn't love Madison and his entire family more! Fate smiled upon me. I pinch myself every day with gratitude for the overwhelming blessings I've received in my life.

And as promised, Jennifer and Chloe now and forever call Edmond, their Fairy Godmother. He coos and lights up every time they call him by his well-deserved royal fairytale title.

FYI, I kept my job reporting right up until my water broke. After the twins were born, I gladly decided to stop traveling as a journalist until they grew up. Or perhaps, get sick of me. Whichever comes first. Most likely the latter. I didn't want to travel anymore. I just didn't have the heart to leave my family for work. It wasn't worth it anymore, for my entire world had changed.

Madison and the babies have become the most important thing in my life. It's funny? What used to be so important to me seems feckless now. Being married with children, I have learned what is truly important. As my priorities have shifted, I have discovered my new family has brought my life true purpose and real meaning. Now wait a sec. Don't misconstrue that statement. Come on now, I still love my bling, tiaras, and shoes! Funny & true.

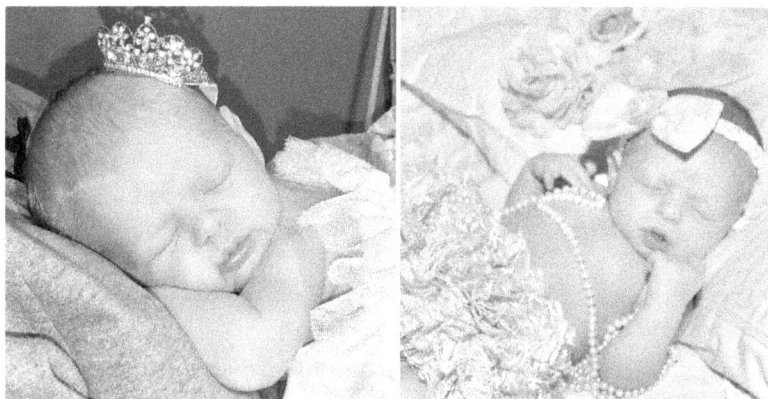

Ultimately, while searching my whole life, I have finally achieved fulfillment, love, and harmony as a stay-at-home wife and mommy. I'm perfectly content moving on, sitting with my laptop, and writing books. Like the one you are reading now! Don't forget to also read, "Heart to Bump Conversations!" It's all about being pregnant, concerning all the funny and true things that happen!"

To my faithful readers, I have learned this important lesson:

Life is filled with waves of happiness, sorrow, hope, despair, tears from the darkness of the clouds, and bliss, joy, and laughter from the ecstasy of sunshine. Ultimately, if you believe and have faith, it will all turn out well in the end. All my positive energy and fortitude kept my boat afloat during the many storms and rough seas of online dating. And it will be for you, too. If you stick with it.

And as a result, I now have…

"A loving husband, TWO gorgeous baby girls, and a fabulous tiara!"

From the New Year's Eve Ball where my soulmate and I first met, throughout our wedding, the blessed birth of our twin babies, and every celebration since (and future), Madison and I sentimentally toast every occasion, lovingly, happily, joyously, gratefully, appreciating and knowing how fortunate and how blessed we are, each time we celebrate and toast with Ana's nostalgic, Sterling family's treasured New Year's Eve cherished Baccarat Crystal, wine glasses, with the year we met engraved on them.

Amazing. I did it!

That's the best example of a perfect run-on sentence, ever!

Dear Professor Smith... What do you think of that!!! HA!

OH! My! GOD! I almost forgot the best part of all. It is classically hilarious. Ready? Ok? Guess who Jennifer and Chloe's fairy godmother, Edmond, is engaged to marry? Wait for it. Wait for it...

Jedediah Jones! Yes, that happened!

My almost lover and friend who didn't know he was gay. I'm serious. They met at our wedding and fell head over designer heels in love. Poetic! Still, I did feel bad for the cute guy Jones brought to Capri. But let's be real. No one on earth is more fabulous than Edmond. Except for Madison, that is! And I made darn sure Jones knows it, too! It was awesome that I was able to return the favor, being a matchmaker for Eddie.

My goodness, Ana is having the time of her life planning their wedding! She is in all her glory, being permitted to go as over-the-top as she wants. No one does it better than Ana. Why not? After all, it's a gay wedding. And so goes, another storybook beginning...

I am delighted to dwell in Madison's orbit, living together in the center of our cosmos. And we live "Online-Dating-Free" and blissful evermore! My hopes and dreams for the future now beat in the hearts of Madison, Jennifer, and Chloe. They are my entire world. The vibrations of their presence consume my being.

And so, In the most beautiful, perfect way imaginable…
"I GOT MALED!!!!!"

The Beginning…
When Two Became One.
And One Became Four!
AND THEY LIVED,
HAPPILY, EVER AFTER!

"OK, seriously? Stop laughing, SHARA!"

"Now, Back to You in The Studio, Bob…."
"Standby… … And… … … We're Out!
Good Job, Mollie Sloan Sterling…

"You Maled It!"

CHAPTER 22

Yes, I Believed and So Should You!

ALSO KNOWN AS, CHILDHOOD DREAMS AND DELUSIONS: THE BEST, AND MOST WONDERFUL PART OF BEING A CHILD!

Yes, I believe in true love! I always have! What's more, I believe in the *holy grail of love*. In the de facto of truth, I've imagined and daydreamed about it ever since I was a little girl, with my hair up in pigtails and bows.

IN OTHER BREAKING NEWS... ON THE TOPIC OF "BARBIE AND KEN?"

Seriously, don't pay any attention to what Barbie said to Ken in the "Barbie Movie!" That was just a Hollywood line. The truth is, the two Pisces are still together, in love, and living happily ever after!

And yes, of course, they both now wear eyeglasses and have lots of wrinkles, sagging skin, and thinning gray hair. Sure, they wear false teeth, have big brown age spots, and suffer from painful arthritis. Barb has diabetes, Ken has high blood pressure and needs a hip replacement, and they both have very high cholesterol.

It's irrelevant, and it doesn't matter that Ken has sleep apnea and must wear a cumbersome, unattractive mask apparatus to bed. Barbie couldn't care less. Meanwhile, she doesn't go to bed looking much better. She's immersed and drenched from head to toe in anti-aging, anti-wrinkle, and all the other age-defying, desperate anti-everything creams and ointments. Luckily for Barbie, she'll never know what Ken really thinks about her anti-aging daily and nightly rituals. That's because Ken doesn't have the balls to tell her they really aren't working. And heaven help us, let's not get into the topic of Ken's balls. Let me just say, that they don't hang like they used to when he first came out of the Mattel cardboard box over 62 years ago!

My point is that Ken loves her just as she is! Unbeknownst to Ken, Beautiful Barbie with all her vanity, did try extremely hard and made several attempts to get plastic surgery. Sadly, she was advised that she wasn't a candidate for such surgeries because she was already made of plastic. It was simply too dangerous, and no one would touch her. Man, doesn't life just suck sometimes? Barbie professed, "Who cares anyway? Surgery-Smurgery. Aging-Smaging! Besides, Ken's opinion is the only one I've ever cared about. He thinks I'm the perfect vision of beauty. But thank goodness he has terrible blurry vision, glaucoma, and cataracts."

But, in the end, so what? The legendary magical couple is still madly in love! Naturally, because Barb and Ken are getting up there in years, they do frequently forget who the other one is. But their love quickly reminds them. Yes, certainly, they can't hear all that well and miss most of what the other one is saying. Ken may even prefer it that way! I love the guy, but I don't believe he constantly (On purpose) forgets to put in his costly, Beltone Hearing Aids. Give him a break, Barbie. After all, my God, you've been together since 1961! Plus, at their golden age, they obviously need the assistance of walkers and depend on Depends. Poor dears, their little plastic bodies are no longer hard and toned as they once were. So, what! They still adore each other despite it all and love prevails.

For fun, they watch TV, play a lot of cards, make puzzles, sit in rockers on the front porch, and play 45-RPM records and albums on a 60-year-old record player. It goes without saying, they still don't understand how to use a computer or a cell phone. To them, Facebook is basically photos in their high school yearbook. They think "backing up" is getting the car out of the garage. They believe a firewall is a barrier around the house to prevent fires. They imagine a hard drive is how their old, classic, baby blue, 1965 Mustang drives. They consider a memory stick is Barb nagging, reminding, and sticking it to Ken. "Hon, remember to take your pills, your keys, cane, jacket, and umbrella." If Barb tells Ken, "Honey, you got mail," he clops all the way down to the mailbox with his walker. They allege that 'social media' is a party for news reporters. Barb & Ken also prefer to stick to an Olivetti Lettera 32 typewriter, a princess rotary dial phone, and write real letters through the mail, stamps, and all. So what? Who are you to judge the most famous doll-duo who ever lived? In Toyland, anyway.

More importantly, Barbie nor Ken are ashamed that Ken needs the assistance of Viagra. Eeks, sometimes he needs a double dose. Shushhh! But if Barbie doesn't care, why the hell should you have a problem with it? Whatever. To be fair to Ken, Barbie herself now needs the assistance of Astroglide Gel to have sex with Ken. You know, being a woman, Barbie, of course, went through *"dollopause!"* *Don't be critical.* Give them a break. They still, *"**Do it!**"*

In case you didn't know, little Barbara Millicent Roberts from

Willows, Wisconsin, was originally a 17-year-old teenage fashion model. Barbie had seven siblings: Skipper, Stacie, Chelsea, Krissy, Kelly, Tutti, and Todd. From the get-go, they all accepted and loved Ken. Speaking of Ken Carlson, he is 2 years and 2 days younger than Barbie. Our much beloved, sexy little doll turns out to be a Cougar. "You totally rock, Barbie girl!"

Truthfully, they were way ahead of their time. For Ken, never "*put a ring on it,*" as the song goes! Even though she had many wedding gowns (Which cost a small fortune for us girls to dress her up. It took lots of babysitting!), they were never really married. In those days, Barbie would have been considered somewhat of a slut and a bad girl. "You Go, Cougar-Slut, Barbie!" I bet they even smoked some toy-weed. It's a damn good thing our moms never found out about those two, or they would've been banned off the shelves. Gee, holidays and birthdays really would have sucked.

Yes, it's true, the beloved celebrated couple tragically did break up for a while in 2004. Our cougar-slut, Barbie, had a rebound relationship with Blaine, an Australian surfer. Oh, grow up, people. I totally get it! Have you seen Blaine? The dude was extremely hot, super-cute, and come on! That accent! So what? Barb needed a break! Haven't we all been there, done that, or at least wanted to? Except true love triumphed. Barbie & Ken finally reunited a few years later, on Valentine's Day. Once again, proving love conquers all. Let's face it, they're forever plastic sole mates.

You know, come to think of it, I've always wondered why they never had any little plastic kids? Perhaps Barbie didn't want to risk ruining her **5′ 9″**, 110 pounds, 36-18-33 perfect figure. Maybe they never wanted to get married because they wanted to stay happy. "Ba-dum-Dum, tsshhhh." Just kidding, back off!

Over the many years, they've been through everything together, shared a lifelong, unrivaled love, and are still rockin' it together, happily, ever, and after. Even if they are mostly doing it in rocking chairs! Granted, the way Barbie and Ken first met in their clear plastic, built-in window, Mattel cardboard boxes for $3.00, wasn't all that romantic. Regardless, their relationship stood the test of time. Even though they have grown old, well-worn, and not at all flawless looking anymore, (as when they first met), you know what 'they' say, "Love is blind." Nevertheless, our girl Barb, still and forever, continues to get all dolled up!

As I predicted from the beginning and stated in chapter one, Madison's family loves, worships, and adores me. Well, anyway, they love me. You should know, that when you marry, your mate's family is part of the deal. Luckily for me, I inherited a great one.

Another Oooohs & Ahhhs, thrilling, Breaking News Flash. My wonderful mother-in-law, Anastasia, gave me with her love, the gift of all gifts. Her bejeweled tiara! Miraculously, on that blessed day, after giving birth to Jennifer and Chloe, Ana officially gifted me the spectacular diamond tiara that evening. *Joy to the world and me!* Well, being honest, I still had possession of it. I 'kinda-sorta' kept forgetting to give it back to her after the wedding. However,

Ana gave the tiara to me with the outright *stipulation* I would give up the twins for her to raise. I so made that deal!

Oh, Stop! I'm just kidding! I only gave her one of the girls! Good lord, chillax. Don't you people know me better than that by now? Shame on you. What really happened was, Sophie and Juliana didn't want it?! If you can believe that! So, Ana gave me the royal gift, with the promise that I would pass it on to the twins to wear at their weddings. Afterward, they would share it, and later pass it on to their girls one day. And so forth.

What I personally could never understand was, where the heck did Ana fail so miserably and go so very wrong with her girls? How in the world could they not want a Real Diamond Tiara? My mind could not wrap my head around it. Such a tragic, unimaginable jewelry failure! Hah, and they call themselves sorority girls!?! They'd be dishonored and shamed right out of the Sorority Alumni Association immediately, for that alone.

Regardless, I promised Ana faithfully the twins would inherit the tiara upon their wedding. But do let me add to the equation, beautiful Chloe & Jennifer, "Are Never Getting Married!" Still, until then, I wear it to sleep every night. I'm joking. I only wear it on the nights that Madison and I go to Krispy Kreme at 4:00 a.m. Well, and birthdays, anniversaries, holidays, and yeah, weekends too. To be candid, I also wear it when working out, bathing, writing, and watching the girls. "Don't judge me! You haven't seen the tiara!"

Speaking of the twins, I am overwhelmingly proud of them. At only seven months old, they are already reaching to grab the stunning tiara off my head. Further proud, they also grasp for my necklace, rings, and bracelets. Although Chloe is much quicker and seems more relentless in her approach than Jennifer. Yet, I have absolute faith in baby Jen. She'll catch up! Even at such a young and tender age, I've already instilled in them true values and real priorities! Gosh, isn't motherhood grand!!!!

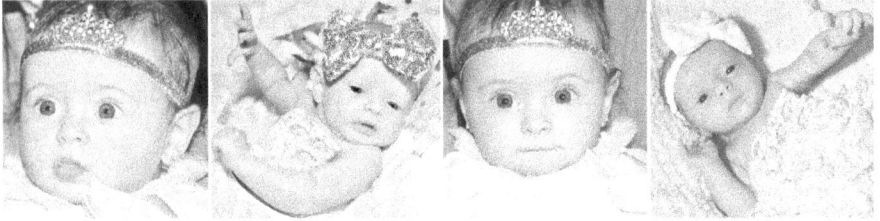

"Now Back to You in The Studio, Again, Bob!"

"Standby… And… … … We're Out! Good job, Mollie!"

That's a wrap!

CHAPTER 23

What I Know, for Sure???

ALSO KNOWN AS... WHAT I KNOW FOR SURE, FOR SURE!!!

Some people find *"The One"* quickly or serendipitously. Others find their true love easily. As for me, and most probably for you, that was not the case, or you would clearly not be reading this book.

Through blind faith, trust, luck, and my determination to believe, I met the love of my life. We were brought together, most surprisingly, and indirectly, through online dating. It's downright shocking, and yet it happened! It appears I am now the poster child and main advocate for online dating. Hence, in a roundabout way (which still counts), after all the drama and theatrics, it worked. Proving, you never know what life has in store for you.

Essentially, dating is equivalent to gambling. For example, betting on a roulette wheel, red or black, has a 50/50 chance of winning. Not ideal, and even fewer odds than that for successful love matches. At least you won't have to fly to "Whoo-Hoo, it's Vegas Baby" to place that bet.

So then, What Is the Moral to this very long story?

What are the underlying meanings? What are the messages? What lessons do we take away from these many tales? What wisdom and teachings have been brought into the light of day? What were the educational moments that brought forth the many 'Ah-Ha' moments for you? The 'easy-breezy, I get it,' flashes! What knowledge or insight have you gained from my book?

People, what have we learned here?
Perhaps to always call the dating site, very angry, when they renewed your membership and charged your credit card without your consent? Probably not so much...

What did you discover? What helped you to grow?
Yeah, most likely "Not A Damn Thing!"

No real morals, no ethics, no Mahatma Gandhi wisdom, no Deepak Chopra spirituality, or any Dalai Lama type philosophies. And certainly no Shakespearean poetry. No tangible important lessons except, of course, fashion, what shoes, diamonds, labels, tiaras, purses, and luggage to buy. Don't trivialize the importance of shopping knowledge. Surprisingly, it just might come in handy one day, and you'll smugly come off looking like a genius.

Truthfully, there are certain things in life you can't control. And dating in any fashion is one of them. Dating is difficult, tedious, and a huge pain in the butt. (Even with butt implants.) Trying on dating prospects for size can be as painful as trying on bikinis in the dead of winter. Dating can be a never-ending, disappointing, full-time job. Like, as if we don't have enough to do already? Dating exposes you to an entire circus of crazy and bizarre wacky parades. Although, if you stay with it, your patience and perversity of mind will keep you sane, heading toward a chance at love and success.

But I will tell you this...

I've learned many things along life's bumpy, potholed during my search for Madison. Things I now know "For Sure," that might even sound cliché. But they're true and bursting with my brand of *"wis-dumb."*

Warning! This wisdom will cause you many moments to pause and ponder. So, go on. Uncork a bottle of wine and pour a glass. Make a bucket of popcorn, light a candle or two, and put on some pondering music.

What I For Sure Know, For Sure...

1. I know for sure to believe relentlessly and strive to achieve whatever it is you want in life. Don't worry that others may think your visions and ideas are merely silly fantasies. Most people thought Steve Jobs was foolish and crazy with all his far-fetched, ridiculous ideas! Well, gee. We're all enjoying his crazy, ridiculous, foolish ideas today! So, there you go. Believe!

2. Never lose faith, reaching for your dreams. Whether it is an orgasm or a college degree. Know with certainty, *"There's Always a Way!"*

3. I know to never let doubt creep into your goals, dreams, creativity, and aspirations. Doubts will destroy your most creative thoughts and ideas. Successful people, inventors, visionaries, scientists, doctors, creators, and artists never permit doubt to enter their doors. They'd never open their doors to death. Your aspirations are your sails. These sails balance and push you through the rough seas of life and drift you toward the exciting tides of success. Surely, you'll have moments of hesitation and indecision. These moments will help you tweak and perfect your ideas. *Don't doubt!*

4. I know for sure when conflicts arise in life (And no doubt they

will. Murphy's Law and all.), keep your certainty. Don't be afraid. Instead, tell yourself, *"You're excited!"* This simple shift changes everything. Even the chemicals & endorphins in your body, as well as your outcome. Being afraid brings failure. Saying, "I'm Excited!" brings success. This is my favorite advice.

5. *Don't give in to insecurity or fears!* In its place, tell yourself to have some major **Attitude**. Follow that word to the depths of your soul. If you cannot find a way to cop that *attitude*, then fake it till you feel it! You know, like an orgasm! Say aloud… Attitude. Attitude! Attitude! It works, and I totally love this one!

6. **Never** say, *"I Can't!"* Saying you can't, only guarantees that you won't. Can't, is a negative word. "I Can, They Can, and So Can You, dammit!"

7. I know for sure never to judge anyone until you walk in his or her Jimmy Choo, or Manolo Blahnik shoes. Period! Nuff said.

8. When things pile up, stressing you out with life's daily problems, like most of us, you freak out. So, at that moment, stop. Ask yourself, "Will I even remember this situation in 5 years?" I know that 99.9% of the time you won't. So, in my best Gandhi or "Frozen" advice, *"Let it go. Just let it go!"*

9. When your caboose of life falls off its track, don't bitch and complain. Put your darn car back on the track and ring the train's whistle with moxie and pizzazz. Fix the problem, don't look back, and proceed with vigor. To Monday morning quarterback, is only positive if you're a football coach. Fix it!

10. I know when you are between relationships, *"**DO NOT**"* go back to an old flame more than once. We all do this when we feel insecure or lonely. It won't work. Nor did it work all the other times you went back, either!

11. I know real growth comes from change. "Change and grow!"

Quoting Star Trek, "Fear of death is illogical. Fear of death is what keeps us alive."

12. I know all the "What if," "Maybe I should've," and "If I only," types of doubts have an ugly way of haunting us. Don't permit them to linger. It only brings sadness or regret. "What if" and "Maybe" you just don't go there.

13. Disappointment, failure, and loss are the roads back to eternal success. I know you hate to hear that, but it's true. Go with it.

14. I know you must trust in yourself, even if you don't! Jump into the deep end of life. It's where all the magical, phenomenal things happen. Embrace the unknown, not your fears. Remember, *"Be Excited with Attitude!" (They both totally work!)*

15. I know gravity will 100% win the fight over your now perky breasts. It will also leave you with sagging skin, wrinkles, and a turkey neck. It sucks! I will repeat that. It's unfair, and it sucks!

16. Original ideas lead to innovations. Don't say, "One day, I'll do it!" Or "When I have more time, I'll do it!" I'll do it never comes. Life always gets in the way. Understand that "**NOW**" is the time!

17. Sure, it's OK to fake an orgasm every now and again. (God only knows you'll have to!) But don't fake the relationship. Life's too precious to share yours with the wrong person.

18. I know for sure, *"When someone shows you who they are, believe them the first time!"* This is my favorite quote, by Maya Angelou, and indeed one to live by.

19. I know for sure my soulmate wants my life overflowing with infinite happiness. He doesn't want to dominate, control, frighten, hurt, intimidate, boss, or overshadow me.

20. If you don't truly *like* someone, then **love** is worthless. Remember this.

21. Failure doesn't mean you're broken. Failure is a chance to start

over. Another one you possibly hate to hear. But also, very true.

22. Men make the weirdest faces when dancing! FYI, they make the same creepy faces during sex, too. Check it out. But don't laugh at them. They hate it! Make fun of them later with your friends.

23. If you've learned anything from this book, heed three things. One: Popcorn and Milk Duds make everything better. Two: Realize Karma is the biggest bitch of all. Three: *"The Left Lane is the Passing Lane, People!!!! Do you hear me? The PASSING LANE!"*

24. I know for sure, for sure, you'll never find love if your heart is closed.

25. I know it's better to make the best out of the worst situations than to complain about it! Sometimes the worst situation turns out to be the best thing ever. Recognize we are being guided. *"You don't live life. Life lives you!"* *"Man plans and God laughs!"*

26. I know for sure and have discovered that Love isn't blind. Trust is!

27. I know that determining the success of a person's life is measured by the love and beautiful memories of the people they have left behind.

28. Love doesn't hurt! Causing pain or suffering is not love! Walk away. And boy, do I mean quickly. This abuse won't change.

29. Jerry Maguire was so wrong. No one can complete you. Only You can complete You! Appreciate that it is you, and you alone, who creates the symphony of your life. You're the architect of your world. Orchestrate your opus well and with great care.

30. It is impossible to love someone who you can't laugh or cry with.

31. *"Nothing Worthwhile in Life Comes Easy!"* Post this as a daily reminder. It is why the reward of accomplishment is so great.

32. Surely, the biggest love-hate relationship in a woman's life is her scale!

33. Disappointments arise with our failures. Other times, victory

results from our failures. Look at all the scientific and medical discoveries developed through failed efforts. Amazingly, many turned out to be the breakthrough links for other cures and theories. Embrace failure's advice. Instead, profit from failure.

34. Move forward. There is *no* potential in the past or you'd still be there! We all cling to the familiar, but it's a dead end. Move on.

35. I know for sure that saying to a man, "I trust you," is sometimes a greater compliment and means more than, "I love you."

36. I know beyond a shadow of a doubt that "Doing the Hokey Pokey and Turning Yourself Around," is NOT, in any way, what it's all about. Like, not at all!

37. I know when you pick your nose in your car, someone always sees you and says, "Gross!" You're not invisible like you thought when you were five. Men, it also applies to your balls.

38. I know a lot of people who always look happy and appear to have it all together. Truthfully, they're not as happy or together as they seem. Don't be envious. Pay attention to yourself. Like in school, "Keep your eyes on your own paper & your own *life!*"

39. Single men are called bachelors. It sounds so very sexy and cool. Then why are single women referred to as spinsters? Like we're ugly old hags or losers? Another issue with women.

40. I know that being kind and nice to someone you really like is far easier than being kind or compassionate to someone who has really done you wrong.

41. Stop your homophobic ignorant behavior! Gay people are the best of both sexes and pretty much balance the "Yin and Yang" of the universe. They can Feng-Shui anything. Blindfolded! I bet in ancient cultures they were considered mini gods. Stop being judgmental. This goes for hate, prejudice, and bigotry, as well. If you believe what you preach, God loves us all! Right?

42. When you get stuck for answers, don't worry about doing the wrong thing. The only wrong thing is not doing anything. "If you don't try in life, then you haven't lived your life!" Einstein said, "A person who never made a mistake never tried anything new!" So true. Don't be that person! Get out and try new things.

43. If someone is unkind, abusive, or cruel, opt for door number 3. "See Jane, run!" Run fast no matter how smoking hot they are!

44. Don't poo-poo infatuation, puppy love, being enchanted, love-struck, smitten, or a crush. It's a great start, even if it isn't forever! If nothing else, it's a wonderful sensation that'll make you feel alive while it lasts.

45. Don't scrunch up your forehead. It creates wrinkles and lines. Don't frown either. You can just look at older people and always tell who the miserable bitches were by those frown lines. My God, I am teaching you important life lessons here, people! I can see you scrunching now. Stop it! LOL!

46. I know for sure that it gets damn cold up there on the moral high ground. Bend a little. Needing to be right all the time, can sometimes be quite wrong.

47. Don't just look at a rainbow. My goodness, climb it all the way up to the other side and grab it with both hands!

48. When you meet someone you really like, good God, don't pretend to be something you are not. Be "You," from hello! You are special simply by being you. So then go on, and be the *"You-e-est,* You," you can be!

49. Don't harp on your past mistakes. Honestly, nobody really cares or wants to hear it. You must appreciate that it's all your screw-ups that make you successful and interesting and provide fascinating tales to tell at parties. Embrace them.

50. Too much good or bad, is not good. Balance is the key to life.

51. If you love someone, then love completely with all your heart and soul. Don't hold back for fear of being hurt. Besides, holding back won't protect you. If you hate someone, forgive them "**for yourself**!" Hate will hurt and destroy you! *Not them.*

    I once asked a Holocaust survivor, "Why aren't you bitter and bursting with unimaginable hatred? How could you forgive and move on after all the horrible abuse and injustice you have suffered, endured, and lived through?" She answered...

    *"My dear, if I didn't forgive, then **they** would have won. Hate and anger would have destroyed what was left of me, robbing me of any future happiness, joy, success, and accomplishments! I survived, so I chose mercy and forgiveness. Without hatred in my heart, there was room for me to blossom, triumphing with victory, love, & bliss. So, you see, my dear, I won! Understand,* if you feel people have been unfair or treated you badly in your life, don't seek revenge. Living well is the best revenge of all."

52. Change is the only constant in life. So, get used to it!

53. I have learned, interviewing world figures, that there is more smut in Washington than in Hollywood. At least the Hollywood smut can't hurt us! Washington, I surely know, can hurt us all!

54. Don't rush, it only slows you down!

55. Human birth control pills work on gorillas. "Just in case any-one out there needed to know because they're having sex with a gorilla?"

56. I know for sure that you should live your life completely while you are young. And live life even more grand when you are old! I pledge I will Never Grow Old Gracefully!!! That is what old people do! It's far more interesting and fun staying young at heart! Then, like a rebellious teen with gusto, I will go down kicking & screaming in a tiara and fabulous heels! For sure,

that's happening for me, and it should be for you, too.

57. Fact: A pig's orgasm lasts around twenty (more or less), minutes. Good heavens, "No wonder they are called pigs! I'm just saying, this needs to be studied a whole lot more!"

58. Another thing I surely know. I would love to be a man for just one orgasm. I want to know what it feels like for them because it appears men are so addicted to sex. OK, maybe even two orgasms. No… ten. Yeah, twenty-five orgasms!

59. I know for sure that behind every great man is an even greater woman, who is exhausted from having to step in front of him to take care of everything he does, or he forgets to do.

MORE THINGS I KNOW FOR SURE!

Our inner child is wise, knows all the answers, and is never wrong. The fun, carefree, foolish kid who lives within us is the best part of us. Trust, protect, and never lose your child. Your inner child is the shining star that guides you in all the best things that you do.

Protect and indulge your fun, zany, silly side. Naturally, there are moments for tears and sorrow. Regardless, trust that you must make room and create more moments that are filled with pleasure, fun, and laughter. This will keep you healthy, thriving, and joyful.

Dare to be daring. Explore diverse things life has to offer. I don't care if it's disco dancing, running up to people and saying, "You're it," painting upside down, sleeping in haunted houses, time travel, prank calls, fake gossip, nude-skydiving, or ordering weird stuff anonymously on Amazon for a friend like a big penis vibrator.

Stop predictable patterns. Experience fun, exciting new ventures. Continue to learn and grow. Even if you can't afford it or have the time, you'll be amazed by how much happier your life will be, engaging in and trying new endeavors. There's always a way.

I also know that it's critical to take great care of your heart, mind, body, soul, skin, teeth, nails, and hair. Hmmm, maybe hair should come first? Nails? I'm thinking!!! Anyway, nurture your body in the same loving way you'd take care of a newborn baby.

Furthermore, it's essential to spoil, pamper, and take care of yourself, or for sure, you will burn out. Indulging is important too. Depriving yourself of everything from food to fun will backfire and prove counterproductive. And stop being so tough on yourself. Let your hair down and be happy-go-lucky. Chill out more!

THE FINAL 3 THINGS I KNOW FOR SURE.

1. *Working out* is vital to your health and well-being. Do it!
2. *Get enough sleep* and eat well. Hard to do. But try your best.
3. *Take your makeup off every night before bed and moisturize!*

No matter how challenging your journey in life is, don't be so eclipsed by anxiety and stress that you become incapable of being amazed by the splendor and miracles of life! If you tap into this mindset, you'll have faith instead of fear, and you'll be excited, believing in a better tomorrow. Success doesn't have a steadfast roadmap. Life is fraught with disappointments. So, create a positive, fun, navigational path to guide you through your journey!

Above all, cherish your friendships and family. Love, appreciate, treasure, and tell these special people you love them and how much they mean to you. There are no guarantees of forever. Time is not promised. Believe me, you don't want to live with nightmares of regret, especially with people you care about. Tomorrow is not a given. There are no second chances or do-overs in mortality. Sadly, *"We grow old too soon, and too late wise!"*

Ultimately, we all need to be loved. Without love from our family, friends, and relationships, life would feel empty and have no meaning. But appreciate that you must love yourself before you can love or be loved. Also, we must learn to love our fellow man beyond what we're doing. At the end of the *'rainbow of harmony'* is brotherhood. Yeah. Fine. I hear your violins mocking me in the background. Maybe deservedly so. But love anyway. Being in love or hurt by love, feeling happy or sad, being stressed or calm, intrigued or bored, are real emotions, and all a part of being alive.

Embrace it all and have fun trying something new you've never dreamed of doing. Travel, travel, travel, and travel some more! I promise it will be the best thing you'll ever do for yourself. When you travel, you will discover so much about life and learn things about yourself you never knew. It's my very best advice.

Lastly, I state with authority and attitude. Online dating can be a tough road to travel. It's like being caught in the Bermuda Triangle, looking for love. So, be careful not to disappear within it. Nevertheless, it's a good way to meet people to date, be friends with, and hopefully fall in love. So, open your heart and then proceed back into the Bermuda Triangle of Online Dating! Get out there and *search for 'The One' who is singing your dreams...*

I appreciate all this corny stuff sounds much like a greeting card from a Taiwanese Dollar Store. Nevertheless, it is all true!

And that's what I know for sure, for sure!!!

Epilogue

P.S. IT'S COMEDY PEOPLE!

In Summation...

If I offended any race, creed, color, sexual preference, religion, or anyone else by my usage of bad or sexual language, music or film preference, political views, opinions on people, men, handicapped situations, illness, or any other position which I might have upset or insulted any of you...

"It's Comedy, People!?!!?!"

All joking aside and to be perfectly honest, please understand... Everything said in this book that might have appeared to be mean or politically incorrect, was only meant to be humorous, amusing, comforting, and basically intended for the purpose of entertainment and fun. So please, don't be put off or offended.

Laughter is better than crying.

P.S.S. Those of you who went online and found your love quickly and easily, appreciate you were blessed, and your stars were very lucky ones!

About the Author

Robin Roth is an accomplished professional singer, comedian, and entertainer. This consummate performer has been described as "The Singer Extraordinaire with a Comedic Flair." She has performed her versatile one-woman show, "The Ultimate Entertainer" to sold-out crowds around the world. Robin can also be seen in her many acting performances and roles on commercials, television, stage, and in movies.

Ms. Roth has also enjoyed an illustrious, successful career in journalism. As a distinguished reporter, photographer, and writer, she has interviewed and photographed just about everybody who is anybody. Furthermore, she is a notable photographer for some of the biggest photo agencies.

Robin writes and shoots for prominent magazines and major Cable News Networks. She has photographed and interviewed six presidents as well as other prominent political figures, and famous A-list stars. These include… Actors, singing artists, bands, all-star athletes & teams, business figures, and well-known personalities and celebrities of the world.

Robin Roth is also a very proud and loving mother of two girls.

Look For Robin's Other Books...
"You Got Maled!" VOLUME 1
and
"Heart to Bump Conversations"
They Are NOW in stores everywhere!

You can also, CHECK OUT ROBIN'S TWO WEBSITES:

Robinrothreporter.com
Robinrothentertainer.net

www.ingramcontent.com/pod-product-compliance
Lightning Source LLC
Chambersburg PA
CBHW052107030426

42335CB00025B/2872